Denver Landmarks & Historic Districts

Timberline Books

Stephen J. Leonard and Thomas J. Noel, editors

The Beast
BENJAMIN BARR LINDSEY WITH HARVEY J. O'HIGGINS

Colorado's Japanese Americans
BILL HOSOKAWA

Colorado Women: A History
GAIL M. BEATON

Denver: An Archaeological History
SARAH M. NELSON, K. LYNN BERRY, RICHARD F. CARRILLO,
BONNIE L. CLARK, LORI E. RHODES, AND DEAN SAITTA

*Denver's Lakeside Amusement Park: From the White City Beautiful to a
Century of Fun*
DAVID FORSYTH

Denver Landmarks and Historic Districts, Second Edition
THOMAS J. NOEL AND NICHOLAS J. WHARTON

*Dr. Charles David Spivak: A Jewish Immigrant and the American
Tuberculosis Movement*
JEANNE E. ABRAMS

Enduring Legacies: Ethnic Histories and Cultures of Colorado
EDITED BY ARTURO J. ALDAMA, ELISA FACIO, DARYL MAEDA,
AND REILAND RABAKA

*The Gospel of Progressivism: Moral Reform and Labor War in Colorado,
1900–1930*
R. TODD LAUGEN

Helen Ring Robinson: Colorado Senator and Suffragist
PAT PASCOE

Ores to Metals: The Rocky Mountain Smelting Industry
JAMES E. FELL, JR.

Season of Terror: The Espinosas in Central Colorado, March–October 1863
CHARLES F. PRICE

A Tenderfoot in Colorado
R. B. TOWNSHEND

The Trail of Gold and Silver: Mining in Colorado, 1859–2009
DUANE A. SMITH

Denver Landmarks & Historic Districts

Second Edition

THOMAS J. NOEL AND NICHOLAS J. WHARTON

*With a foreword by former Denver mayor
and Colorado governor John Hickenlooper*

UNIVERSITY PRESS OF COLORADO
Boulder

© 2016 by University Press of Colorado

Published by University Press of Colorado
5589 Arapahoe Avenue, Suite 206C
Boulder, Colorado 80303

 The University Press of Colorado is a proud member of
the Association of American University Presses.

The University Press of Colorado is a cooperative publishing enterprise sup-
ported, in part, by Adams State University, Colorado State University, Fort
Lewis College, Metropolitan State University of Denver, Regis University,
University of Colorado, University of Northern Colorado, Utah State
University, and Western State Colorado University.

∞ This paper meets the requirements of the ANSI/NISO Z39.48-1992
(Permanence of Paper).

ISBN: 978-1-60732-421-8 (paperback)
ISBN: 978-1-60732-422-5 (ebook)
DOI: 10.5876/9781607324225

Library of Congress Cataloging-in-Publication Data
Names: Noel, Thomas J. (Thomas Jacob)
Title: Denver landmarks and historic districts / Thomas J. Noel and
    Nicholas J. Wharton ; with a foreword by former Denver Mayor &
    Colorado Governor John Hickenlooper.
Description: Boulder, Colorado : University Press of Colorado, 2016. |
    Series: Timberline books | Includes bibliographical references and index.
Identifiers: LCCN 2015024780 | ISBN 9781607324218 (pbk.) | ISBN
    9781607324225 (ebook)
Subjects: LCSH: Denver (Colo.)—Guidebooks. | Historic
    sites—Colorado—Denver—Guidebooks.
Classification: LCC F784.D43 N64 2016 | DDC 978.8/83—dc23
LC record available at http://lccn.loc.gov/2015024780

FRONT COVER. Photograph of the Civic Center's Voorhies Memorial,
courtesy, History Colorado.
BACK COVER. Top row, left to right: Paramount Theater, photo by Roger
Whitacre; Sanctuary Lofts, photo by Tom Noel; El Jebel Temple, Tom
Noel Collection; Bryant Webster Elementary School, photo by Tom Noel;
Denver Municipal Auditorium, Tom Noel Collection. Bottom row, left to
right: Equitable Building interior, photo by Roger Whitacre; Red Rocks
Outdoor Amphitheatre, photo by Tom Noel; Frederick W. Neef House,
Tom Noel Collection; Montclair Civic Building, photo by Tom Noel;
Brown Palace Hotel atrium, courtesy, Denver Public Library.

Contents

List of Figures   vii

List of Maps   xi

Foreword
  FORMER DENVER MAYOR AND COLORADO
  GOVERNOR JOHN HICKENLOOPER   xiii

Acknowledgments   xv

Introduction   3

1 Central Denver   13

  Civic Center Area   17
  Central Business District   22
  Larimer Square Historic District   36
  Lower Downtown Historic District   40
  Auraria Area   45

2 Capitol Hill   51

  Capitol Hill Area   53
  Cheesman Park Area   80
  City Park Area   89
  Country Club Area   94

3 Northeast Denver   97

  Curtis Park Historic Districts   99
  Ballpark Historic District   102
  Five Points Historic Cultural District   103
  Clements Addition Historic District   104
  Lafayette Street Historic District   108
  East Park Place Historic District   110
  Clayton College Historic District   110

4 Northwest Denver   111

  Highlands Area   113
  West Colfax Area   133
  Globeville Area   134

5   **South Denver**   135

Baker Area   137
Washington Park Area   142
Belcaro Area   144
Platt Park Area   146
University Park Area   148

6   **East Denver**   151

Hilltop Area   153
Montclair Area   155
Park Hill Area   159
Lowry Area   163

7   **Denver Mountain Parks**   165

Daniels Park   167
Dedisse Park   167
Red Rocks Park   168

Appendix A: Denver Landmarks by
      Designation Number   169
Appendix B: Denver Historic Districts by
      Designation Number   174
Appendix C: Denver Landmark Preservation
      Commissioners   175
Appendix D: Lost and Undesignated Denver
      Landmarks   176

Bibliography   179
About the Authors   183
Index   184

Figures

0.1. 1536 Welton Street demolition 4

0.2. Mayor Robert W. Speer 5

0.3. Kessler's parkway plan for Denver 6

0.4. Frank E. Edbrooke 7

0.5. Burnham Hoyt 8

0.6. Foursquare house plan 10

0.7 Interstate Trust Building, 1130 Sixteenth Street, implosion 10

0.8. Landmark Plaque 11

1.1. Civic Center plan 17

1.2. Voorhies Memorial 17

1.3a/b. Woman statue atop capital 18

1.4. Byers-Evans House Museum 21

1.5. US Mint 22

1.6. Brown Palace Hotel atrium 23

1.7. Navarre 24

1.8. Fire Station No. 1 24

1.9. Denver Athletic Club 25

1.10a/b. Paramount Theater 26

1.11. Masonic Temple 27

1.12. Hayden, Dickinson, and Feldhauser Building–Colorado Building 27

1.13. Denver Dry Goods 28

1.14a/b. Equitable Building, exterior and interior 29

1.15a/b. Byron White Federal Courthouse, exterior and interior 30

1.16a/b. Boston Building ca. 1900 and 1990 31

1.17. Odd Fellows Hall 32

1.18. Denver Gas and Electric Building 32

1.19. Denver Municipal Auditorium 33

1.20a/b. Daniels and Fisher Tower and Oliphant cartoon 34

1.21. Denver Tramway and Daniels and Fisher Tower under construction 35

1.22. Dana Crawford and Mayor Tom Currigan 36

1.23. Apollo Hall 36

1.24. Granite Hotel 37

1.25a/b. Gallup-Stanbury Building, 1875 and 1995 38

1.26. Crawford Building 39

1.27. Wells Fargo Building, 1860s 40

1.28. Market Center buildings 40

1.29. Oxford Hotel 42

1.30. Union Station 43

1.31. John Hickenlooper at Wynkoop Brewing Company 44

1.32. Golda Meir House being moved 46

1.33. St. Cajetan's Catholic Church 47

1.34. Tivoli Brewery 47

1.35. Buckhorn Exchange Restaurant 48

2.1. Trinity United Methodist Church 53

2.2. Crawford Hill Mansion 54

2.3. Dennis Sheedy Mansion 55

2.4. First Baptist Church and Rev. Malmborg   56

2.5. El Jebel Temple   57

2.6. Immaculate Conception Cathedral interior, 1911   58

2.7. Cuthbert-Dines House   59

2.8. Sayre's Alhambra, exterior and interior   61

2.9. Governor's Mansion, north facade and west elevation   62

2.10a/b. Grant-Humphreys Mansion, exterior and window detail   63

2.11. Adolph Zang Mansion   65

2.12. Croke-Patterson-Campbell Mansion   67

2.13. Dunning-Benedict House   68

2.14. Molly Brown House   69

2.15. Temple Emanuel Event Center   70

2.16a/b. St. John's Episcopal Cathedral, exterior and Ronnebeck frieze   71

2.17. German House–Denver Turnverein   73

2.18. Zang Townhouse   74

2.19. Aldine-Grafton Apartments   75

2.20. Ogden Theatre   75

2.21. Emerson School   76

2.22. Corona/Dora Moore School   77

2.23. Governor Ralph Carr bicycling to work at the Colorado State Capitol   77

2.24a/b. The Mullen Building's original Art Deco shine   79

2.25. Aerial of Cheesman Park Memorial Pavilion, ca. 1920   80

2.26. Stoiberhof restoration   81

2.27. Denver Botanic Gardens Conservatory   82

2.28. Denver Botanic Gardens House   83

2.29. Sykes-Nicholson-Moore House   85

2.30. Milheim House   86

2.31. Raymond House-Castle Marne, ca. 1892   87

2.32. Pearce–McAllister Cottage, with a cast iron cat prowling the roof   88

2.33. Graham-Bible House   88

2.34a/b. The date of completion of the Frank Smith Mansion, hidden in second-story ornamentation   89

2.35. The pavilion and Floating Bandstand, west end of City Park's Ferril Lake   89

2.36. Park Hill Fire Station 18   90

2.37. East High School   90

2.38. Gates House   91

2.39. Bonfils Memorial Theater   92

2.40. Fire House 15   93

2.41. Bluebird Theater   93

2.42. Mrs. Verner Z. (Mary Dean) Reed, her dog, and her mansion   96

3.1. Huddart/Lydon House   100

3.2. Anfenger House   101

3.3a/b. Margery Reed Mayo Day Care Center, where the Sisters of Charity of Cincinnati cared for Curtis Park–area kids   101

3.4. Sacred Heart Catholic Church   102

3.5. Douglass Undertaking Building   103

3.6. Clements Addition Streetscape   104

3.7. St. Andrews Memorial Episcopal Chapel   104

3.8. Scott Methodist Church–Sanctuary Lofts   106

3.9. Zion Baptist Church, with Rev. Wendell T. Liggins cutting an anniversary cake   106

3.10. Gebhard/Smith House   107

3.11. McBird-Whiteman House on the move, 1993   107

3.12a/b. Archbishop James V. Casey celebrating Annunciation Catholic Church's restoration   109

3.13. Wyatt Elementary School   109

3.14. Clayton College   110

4.1. Conine-Horan House   114

4.2. Wheeler Block   115

4.3. Tallmadge and Boyer Terrace   115

4.4. Romeo Block   115

4.5. Asbury Methodist Church   116

4.6. Fager Residence   116

4.7. All Saints Episcopal Church–Chapel of our Merciful Savior   117

4.8. Crowds gathered at the home of Francis Schlatter   118

4.9. St. Patrick's twin domes   119

4.10. Our Lady of Guadalupe Catholic Church   119

4.11. Our Lady of Mount Carmel Catholic Church   120

4.12. Native American motifs in the tower of Bryant-Webster Elementary School   121

4.13a/b. Architect Temple Hoyne Buell's name in the facade of Horace Mann Middle School   121

4.14. Smedley Elementary School   122

4.15. Fire Station No. 7   122

4.16. Stonemason Hugh Mackay's craftsmanship extends from the retaining wall to the chimney   123

4.17. St. Elizabeth's Retreat Chapel   125

4.18. House with the Round Window   125

4.19. Woodbury Branch Library   125

4.20. Skinner Middle School   126

4.21. Smiley Branch Library   127

4.22. Elitch Theater   128

4.23. Cox "Gargoyle" House   129

4.24. Herman Heiser House   130

4.25. Frederick W. Neef House   131

4.26. Half-Moon House   132

4.27. Sloan's Lake, the setting and name for Lake Middle School   132

4.28. Spangler House   133

4.29. Frank Smith Mansion   133

5.1. Mary Coyle Chase   138

5.2. Mayan Theater   139

5.3. South Broadway Christian Church   139

5.4. Byers Junior High School   140

5.5. Country Club Gardens   141

5.6. Steele Elementary School   141

5.7. Washington Park boathouse and pavilion   143

5.8. South High School   144

5.9. Cory Elementary School   144

5.10. Belcaro   145

5.11. Sarah Platt Decker Branch Library   146

5.12. James Fleming House   147

5.13. Chamberlain Observatory   149

5.14. Fitzroy Place–Warren-Iliff Mansion   149

5.15. Fort Logan Field Officers Quarters   150

6.1. Four Mile House   153

6.2. George Cranmer House   154

6.3a/b. Stanley School   156

6.4. St. Luke's Episcopal Church   157

6.5. Baron Walter von Richthofen   157

6.6. Richthofen Castle   158

6.7a/b. The Molkery, now the Montclair Civic Building   159

6.8. Treat Hall–Centennial Hall   159

6.9. An old hangar converted into a new church   160

6.10a/b. The 1901 original Park Hill Elementary School and its 1912 addition and the school's baseball team   161

6.11. St. Thomas Episcopal Church   162

6.12. Park Hill Branch Library   162

6.13. Dr. Margaret Long leaving her house   162

6.14. Fairmount Cemetery Gate Lodge   163

6.15. Fairmount Cemetery Ivy Chapel   164

7.1. Red Rocks Outdoor Amphitheatre   168

7.2. The Red Rocks Trading Post, concession house, and museum   168

Maps

1.1. Denver Neighborhoods   14

1.2. Denver Historic Districts   15

1.3. Central Denver Landmarks   16

2.1. Capitol Hill–Area Landmarks   52

3.1. Northeast Denver Landmarks   98

4.1. Northwest Denver Landmarks   112

5.1. South Denver Landmarks   136

6.1. East Denver Landmarks   152

Foreword

Historic preservation has been a key to Denver emerging as one of America's healthiest, most flourishing cities. When partners and I opened Colorado's first brew pub in 1989, we chose to do it in a landmark building in the Lower Downtown Historic District. Since then, we and others have often used historic old buildings to launch innovative new enterprises. Landmarking and restoring seemingly doomed antiquated properties has rejuvenated communities all across Colorado and especially in Denver.

I am delighted to introduce you to this look at Denver's 51 historic districts and 333 individual landmarks.

When I first ran for Mayor of Denver in 2003, I toured the city's 74 neighborhoods to meet the residents and visit their special landmarked places—schools, stores, libraries, restaurants, churches, and above all the residences Denverites are proud to call home. Since becoming governor of Colorado in 2011, it has been my pleasure and privilege to annually bestow the Governor's Award on Colorado's most outstanding preservation project.

Author Tom Noel is known as "Dr. Colorado" for his teaching, writing, and tours acquainting one and all with Colorado's colorful history. After helping with some of Tom's tours and books, I can recommend this guide. Tom was a longtime National Register reviewer for Colorado and former chair of the Denver Landmark Preservation Commission; he also teaches Colorado history and historic preservation at CU-Denver. He will steer you to a great variety of special landmarked places in these pages. These include our just completed Colorado State Capitol, whose history and gold dome shine anew after a fresh dose of historic preservation. Our city and our state are much richer for these treasured landmarks.

COLORADO GOVERNOR JOHN HICKENLOOPER

Acknowledgments

Nicholas Wharton drew the maps and did updating and legwork in putting this book into your hands. Another star CU-Denver graduate student, Beth Glandon, edited, formatted, and fixed many errors in the manuscript. Savannah Jameson of the Denver Landmark Preservation Commission staff provided maps, data, and tours and resolved conflicting information. Landmark commissioner Amy Zimmer and former landmark commissioner Stephen J. Leonard, the preeminent Denver historian, helped ground-check many sites, comparing office and on-line information with curbside reality. All errors in my work, of course, are someone else's fault. Nevertheless, if you find mistakes herein, please contact tom.noel@ucdenver.edu.

The long out-of-print first edition of this book appeared in 1996. The National Park Service and the Colorado Historical Society (rebranded History Colorado in 2009) helped fund that project in a grant overseen by Tom and Laurie Simmons of Front Range Research Associates. Tom also provided many fine photos, including some used herein. Former Denver Landmark Preservation commissioners Jim Bershof, Phil E. Flores, the aforementioned Steve Leonard, the dear departed Barbara S. Norgren, and the wonderful Edward D. White reviewed the 1996 manuscript and made many helpful suggestions. That book celebrated 28 historic districts and 250 designated individual landmarks. This work covers 51 historic districts and 333 individual landmarks, an achievement that makes Denver a national pacesetter.

As always, I am heavily indebted to the crackerjack staff of the Western History and Genealogy Department of the Denver Public Library, especially Bruce Hanson who knows more about Denver buildings than anyone. The department's very helpful manager, Jim Kroll, photo specialist Coi Gehrig, and other experts on DPL's fifth floor were indispensable. At History Colorado my fellow former board and National Register Review Board members educated me further, as did the History Colorado library staff.

I suspect that my wonderful students at CU-Denver have taught me more over the past four decades than I have taught them. For this book and its predecessor I benefited from the work of students Jacqui Ainlay-Conley, Jasmine Armstrong, Kathleen Barlow, Mark Barnhouse, Gail Beaton, Owen Chariton, Bill Convery, Dan Corson, Jolie Diepenhorst, Dana EchoHawk, Peg Ekstrand, Sharon Elfenbein, Rosemary Fetter, Barbara Gibson, Alice Gilbertson, Beth Glandon, Marcia Goldstein, Leigh A. Grinstead, Eric Hammersmark, Ashleigh Hampf, Savannah Jameson, Jim Kroll, Leslie Mohr Krupa, Craig W. Leavitt, Patti Lundt, Dino Maniatis, Jim McNally, Kara Miyagishima, Marcie Morin, Judy Morley, Cathleen Norman, John O'Dell, Katy Ordway, Heather King Peterson, David Richardson, Vicki Rubin, Kevin Rucker, Rich SaBell, Darcy Cooper Schlicting, Julie Schlossser, Ron Sherman, John Stewart, Jonathan Tesky, Harry Thomas, Lisa Werdel Thompson, Heather Thorwald, Eric Twitty, Cheryl Waite, Evelyn Waldron, Don Walker, Ross Webster, Nick Wharton, Christine Whitacre, Nancy Widmann, Chuck Woodward, and Amy Zimmer. Craig Leavitt, our Center for Colorado and the West fellow at the Auraria Library, helped wrap this up for the drop box.

Over the last forty years I have learned much from architects Mark Applebaum, Jim Bershof, Temple H. Buell, Rodney S. Davis, Peter H. Dominick Jr., Curt Fentress, Paul Foster, Ken Fuller, Michael Graves, James Hartman, Dan Havekost, Kathy

Hoeft, Victor Hornbein, Dennis Humphries, Brian Klipp, Gary Long, Joe Marlow, Gary Petri, Stanley Pouw, John M. Prosser, Candy Roberts, Bob Root, Eugene Sternberg, David Owen Tryba, and Edward D. White Jr. They humored me when I made inquiries and helped me understand their work. At Fairmount Cemetery, Tom Morton took me through his wonderful tour of the mausoleums and tombstones of deceased architects, including Temple Buell's lavish last home and the Greek temple of Frank Edbrooke.

Fellow historians Chuck Albi, Mark Barnhouse, Gail Beaton, Richard Brettell, Richard Carrillo, Mary Voelz Chandler, Bill Convery, Dan Corson, Sandra Dallas, Lyle Dorsett, Dana EchoHawk, Peg Ekstrand, Don Etter, Jay Fell, Kim Field, Kenton Forrest, Mark Foster, Dennis Gallagher, Mark Gelernter, William J. Hanson, Rebecca Hunt, Dick Kreck, Dick Lamm, Steve Leonard, Dianna Litvak, Frances Melrose, Michael Paglia, Michelle Pearson, Kevin Pharris, Bill Philpott, Carl Sandberg, Clark Secrest, Shawn Snow, Paul Stewart, Annette Student, Bill West, David Wetzel, Rodd Wheaton, Sally White (the Denver Mountain Parks historian), Jim Whiteside, Diane Wilk, Diane Wray, and Amy Zimmer have inspired me personally and through their publications. Jack A. Murphy, former curator of geology at the Denver Museum of Nature and Science, generously guided me regarding building stones and their origins. Photographers Glenn Cuerden, Michael Gamer, Tom Simmons, and Roger Whitacre have graciously allowed use of their art herein.

Thanks to Sister Mary Aloys, SCL, and Monsignor John Anderson, as well as Silvia Atencio and Jesse Jespersen—the couple that has restored the Richthofen Castle and Gate House to glory; also to Chips Barry, Bart Berger, Bill Bessesen, Hugh Bingham, Charles Brantigan (who fathered the Lafayette Street Historic District), Cal Cleworth, Dana Crawford, Alan and Marcy Culpin, Eric Dyce, Elizabeth Casell Dyer (who shared her love of the Equitable Building, which she tends), Ruth Falkenberg and Larry Nelson (who have turned endangered buildings into showcase landmarks), Jill and Henry Fieger, John Fielder, Mike Fries, Barbara Froula, the indomitable Dennis Gallagher, Magdalena Gallegos (historian of Ninth Street Historic Park), David Gebhart, Rich Grant, Breck and Mary Lynn Grover, Jim Havey, Frank Hegner, John Hickenlooper Jr., Marjorie Hornbein, Jim Karagas of My Brother's Bar, Holly Kylberg (queen of the Daniels and Fisher Tower), Jim Lindberg, John Litvak, Jan and Frederick Mayer, Earl McCoy, Jay Mead, Lyle Miller, RTD guide extraordinaire Ryan Mulligan, Quigg Newton, Jim Noel, my indispensable partner Vi Noel, Mary Rozinski O'Neil, Dr. Bruce Paton, Jim Peiker (who championed the Wyman Historic District), Bonnie Reps, Jeannie Ritter, Barry Rose (whose tile work enlivens many buildings), Ron Ruhoff, Beth and Bill Sagstetter, Don Seawell, Frank Shafroth, Shawn Snow, Bob Sweeney, Henry Toll, Steve Turner, Marne Tutt, Mark Upshaw (who oversaw the Molkery's restoration), David Walstrom (savior of East Colfax), Judy and Tom Ward, Wellington Webb, Steve and Wendy Weil, Bill West (who fathered the Curtis Park Historic District), Nicholas' supportive spouse Christina Lee Wharton, and Luther Wilson.

Special thanks to Historic Denver, Inc., which has done so much to identify and designate landmarks ever since its 1970 founding to save the Molly Brown House. Executive Director Annie Robb Levinsky, Tour Program and Outreach Director Sophie Bieluczyk, and Preservation Program Director John Olson have been especially helpful. Historic Denver's publications include more than twenty books on Denver and its neighborhoods, which serve as wonderful introductions to the special charms of many of the city's seventy-four neighborhoods.

The Department of History at CU-Denver has been wonderful to me for nearly fifty years. I am blessed to have supportive chairwomen in Myra Rich, Pam Laird, and Kariann Yokota, collegial colleagues, and terrific support from administrative assistant Tabitha Fitzpatrick, who has bailed me out of many pickles.

At the University Press of Colorado, thanks once again to a wonderful crew who did the first edition and have this time turned a drop box of odds and ends into a book: Director Darrin Pratt, former director Luther Wilson, designer Dan Pratt, managing editor Laura Furney, marketing guru Beth Svinarich, and acquisitions angel Jessica d'Arbonne.

Finally, thanks to those of you we have inadvertently left out. So many of you have shared information, walking tours, and inspections of landmark buildings, as well as helped in other ways. Next time we see you, we're buying.

Denver Landmarks & Historic Districts

Introduction

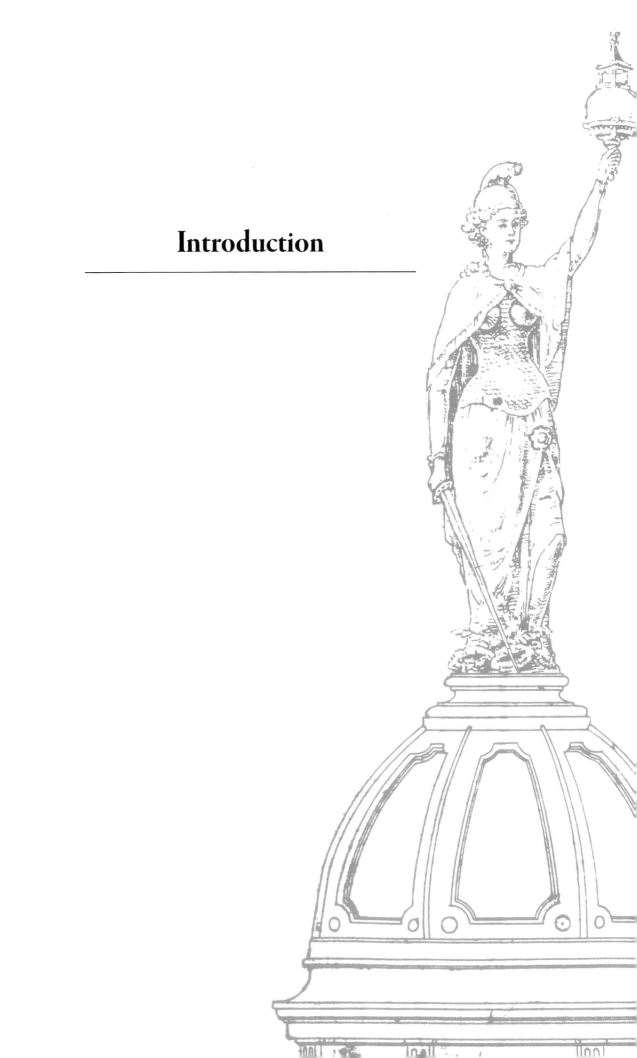

FIGURE O.I. Like the barbarians who sacked ancient Rome, developers have obliterated much of Denver's Neoclassical heritage, including this would-be Greek temple at 1536 Welton Street, demolished in 1982 (photo by Roger Whitacre).

Denver is unusually fortunate in having retained much of its structural architectural heritage. After much had been lost to urban renewal and other public and private agencies, concerned citizens rebelled. The Denver Landmark Preservation Commission (1967), Historic Denver, Inc. (1970), Colorado Preservation, Inc. (1984) and History Colorado (1879) have all worked to identify and preserve Denver places notable for architectural, geographical, and historical significance. Since the 1970s, Denver has designated 51 historic districts and 333 individual landmarks, more than any other city nationwide of comparable size.

Historic districts such as Lower Downtown have transformed once decaying core city neighborhoods, becoming a major factor in Denver's growth in population and prosperity. Whereas most core cities are losing population, the City and County of Denver has been growing since 1990. Before

that, Denver, like many US cities, was losing population in the familiar pattern of urban blight and suburban flight. Between 1990 and 2010, however, the city's US Census population grew from 467,610 to 600,158. Historic districts have played a major role in stabilizing both commercial and residential areas and in sparking restoration efforts that have increased property values and attracted many newcomers to the city.

These districts in particular have made Denver one of the most livable, prosperous, and steadily growing cities in the country. The aforementioned Lower Downtown Historic District reincarnation has sparked rejuvenation of many adjacent, once struggling inner-city neighborhoods, most notably Capitol Hill, Curtis Park, Highlands, and the South Platte River Valley. Two historic districts at the former Lowry Air Force Base have helped shape one of America's most successful conversions of a former military base to mixed residential, retail, and office use.

Preservation efforts have saved some of Denver's nineteenth-century masonry buildings, which reflect its gold rush origins. The discovery of a few specks of gold in the South Platte River near its junction with Cherry Creek led to the creation of Denver City on November 22, 1858. Founder William H. Larimer Jr. named the town for Kansas territorial governor James Denver, hoping to ensure its selection as the seat of what was then Arapahoe County, Kansas Territory. Larimer platted Denver City with streets parallel and perpendicular to Cherry Creek. Only after Denver began to blossom in the 1870s were outlying areas platted to conform to federal land grids based on cardinal compass points.

Aggressive town promoters, led by *Rocky Mountain News* founding editor William Newton Byers and territorial governor John Evans, enticed railroads to this isolated town 700 miles from the Missouri River frontier communities. After railroads steamed into Denver in 1870, this crossroads in the middle of nowhere grew into the second-largest city in the Far West. By 1890 Denver had a population of 106,713, smaller than San Francisco but larger than Los Angeles, Seattle, Phoenix, and any town in Texas.

Like other inland cities without navigable rivers, Denver's hub was the railroad station. The landmarked Union Station was reincarnated in 2014 as a luxury hotel and transit hub for buses and rail traffic. Railroads hauled gold and silver ores from mountain mining towns into Denver's smelters, producing fortunes that built a grand opera house, elegant churches, majestic hotels, imposing office blocks, and masonry mansions.

Flush times ended with the silver crash of 1893. After federal repeal of the Sherman Silver Purchase Act, a federal subsidy for silver, that year, the price of silver dropped from more than a dollar to less than sixty cents per ounce, devastating Colorado's most lucrative industry. Responding to the economic slump and population loss in the mid-1890s, Denver's power elite set about diversifying the city's economy. While still serving a vast, if faltering, mountain mining hinterland, the city also focused on becoming the supply and food processing center for farmers and ranchers. Architecturally, Denver shifted from mansions to more modest post-1893 classic cottages, bungalows, and foursquares.

Not content to be the regional metropolis only for Colorado, Denverites used railroads to extend their economic orbit to neighboring states. Agriculture and food processing, stockyards and meatpacking, brewing and banking, and manufacturing and service industries became mainstays of Denver's economic base. During and after World War II, federal jobs—civilian and military—stabilized the boom-and-bust city. Tourism has also emerged as one of the city's most reliable industries. Surging heritage tourism has capitalized on the Mile High City's preservation of many landmarks and historic districts.

The City Beautiful

Denver's City Beautiful movement encouraged orderly, planned growth. Robert W. Speer introduced this urban vision of the Progressive Era after his election as mayor in 1904. Speer had toured the 1893 World's Columbian Exposition in Chicago and, along with 30 million others, had marveled at the transformation of a swamp on Lake Michigan into an urbane, Neoclassical paradise. He brought the dream home and, as Denver's mayor, set out to turn a dusty, drab, unplanned city into "Paris on the Platte."

Speer first engaged Charles Mulford Robinson, a New York City planner and author of *Modern Civic Art, or the City Made Beautiful* (1903), to prepare a master plan. The 1906 Robinson plan, augmented by George E. Kessler's 1907 park and parkway plan, was further revised and extended over the years by Frederick Law Olmsted Jr., Frederick MacMonnies, Edward H. Bennett, Saco R. DeBoer, and others. Unlike many plans that remain on the shelf, the City Beautiful

FIGURE 0.2. Denver mayor Robert W. Speer, in office during the years 1904–12 and 1916–18, transformed an ordinary, dusty, drab western town into a City Beautiful (Denver Public Library).

agenda was vigorously implemented by "Boss" Speer, who operated both over and under the table. Denver became one of the better examples of City Beautiful planning. These schemes were later expanded with the help of New Deal programs and, more recently, were revived by Denver's first Hispanic mayor, Federico Peña (1983–91), and first African American mayor, Wellington Webb (1991–2001), as well as subsequent mayors John Wright Hickenlooper Jr. (2001–10) and Michael Hancock (2010–present).

Denver's City Beautiful landscape centers on Civic Center Park, surrounded by city, state, and federal office buildings. A network of parkways stretches out from Civic Center by way of Speer Boulevard throughout the city to many neighborhood parks. These neighborhood parks serve as mini–civic centers surrounded by schools, libraries, churches, and other public buildings.

The Denver Mountain Parks network consists of Winter Park Ski Area, Red Rocks Park with its Greek style outdoor amphitheater, Mt. Evans, and forty-five other parks covering about 14,000 acres in Arapahoe, Clear Creek, Douglas, Grand, and Jefferson Counties.

George E. Kessler, who created the Denver park and parkway plan, was a German-born, European-trained professional landscape architect who became this country's foremost parkway planner. Kessler worked on New York's Central Park, helped lay out the 1904 Louisiana Purchase Exposition grounds in St. Louis, Missouri, and gave Kansas City, Missouri, its park and parkway system. In Denver, Kessler abandoned the Parisian model of spoke-and-wheel diagonal avenues and connecting outer rings of boulevards. Too many buildings obstructed that ideal scheme, so Kessler superimposed parkways upon the existing street grid. He placed parks at the highest points to permit mountain views, as exemplified by Cheesman, Cranmer, Inspiration Point, and Ruby Hill Parks. These spacious parks set high landscaping standards for adjacent private properties. Parkways connected many parks to facilitate driving, bicycling, or walking the parkway system on a carpet of green.

To preserve this legacy—an amenity unmatched by even the richest suburbs—the Denver Landmark Preservation Commission has championed landmarking much of Denver's park and parkway network.

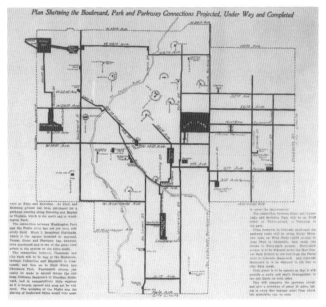

FIGURE 0.3. George E. Kessler created this 1907 plan for Denver proposing that parks be linked by parkways (Denver Public Library).

The public-minded Progressive-Era reformers of the early twentieth century created grand parks, parkways, and public buildings. These amenities still distinguish the city, giving it traditional Neoclassical moorings and generous landscaping. Denver fancied itself the capital of the Rocky Mountain Empire and favored Neoclassical buildings harking back to the Roman and Greek Empires.

The Architects

Robert S. Roeschlaub, Colorado's first licensed architect, came to Denver from Illinois in 1873. The Denver School District appointed Roeschlaub its architect, and his fine schools taught lessons in improved architectural standards in the hastily built boomtown. A half dozen Roeschlaub schools survive as designated landmarks.

Frank E. Edbrooke, Denver's most prominent nineteenth-century architect, was brought to Denver from Chicago in 1879 by silver-mining tycoon Horace Tabor. Tabor, a former stonecutter, explained, "Denver was not building as good buildings as it ought, and I thought I would do something towards setting [it] a good example." He did that with the now gone Tabor Grand Opera House, the city's finest structure, designed by Edbrooke and his older brother, Willoughby. Although Willoughby moved on, Frank remained in Denver. He introduced mainstream design influenced by Henry H. Richardson, the East Coast pacesetter whose use of Romanesque (round) arches and rough-cut stone in massive blocks characterized the popular Richardsonian Romanesque style. Edbrooke also introduced Denverites to technical achievements such as the steel skeleton of his best-known landmark, the Brown Palace Hotel.

Following Tabor's example, other capitalists commissioned out-of-state architects instead of locals. The flush times of the 1870s and 1880s attracted such notable Illinois architects as William A. Lang, who designed numerous stone and shingle homes in his own version of the Richardsonian Romanesque style. The Illinois influence can also be seen in Denver's early skyscrapers, which tended toward the flat-topped Chicago school rather than New York City's stepped towers and dramatic spires.

A notable attempt to professionalize building design and raise architectural consciousness was Jesse B. Dorman's *Western Architect and Building News*. This illustrated monthly magazine extolled architecture as the most

FIGURE 0.4. Colorado's premier nineteenth-century architect, Frank E. Edbrooke, designed many of the city's landmarks (Tom Noel Collection).

democratic and important art form. Dorman's magazine, as architectural historian Richard Brettell put it, was "a rudder guiding the course of the building boom." Although the Denver journal lasted only three years, from 1889 to 1891, it successfully promoted the Colorado Association of Architects, which in 1892 became the Colorado chapter of the American Institute of Architects (AIA). In 1909 the AIA persuaded the Colorado Legislature to begin licensing architects.

Nineteenth-century Denver architects such as the Baerresen Brothers, David W. Dryden, Frederick C. Eberley, Frank E. Edrooke, Aaron M. Gove, John J. Huddart, William A. Lang, Willis A. Marean, Albert J. Norton, Robert S. Roeschlaub, and Frederick J. Sterner used local

brick and stone to build in the Second Empire, Italianate, Queen Anne, and Richardsonian styles as each mode became successively popular in the eastern United States.

Neoclassical architecture, which became stylish after 1900, came to include Beaux-Arts revivals of Greek, Roman, and Italian styles. Jules Jacques Benoit Benedict, the first Denver architect to train at the École des Beaux-Arts in Paris, left many outstanding landmarks in that style. Sadly, his only known commercial building, Central Bank, was demolished in 1990 despite its landmark designation. The Neoclassical tendencies of the early 1900s resulted in two very common Denver residential types: the foursquare and the modest, one-story classical cottage with its central attic dormer and Tuscan porch columns.

Brothers William E. and Arthur A. Fisher dominated both residential and commercial building in Denver between 1910 and 1930. They favored the red tile roofs and thick masonry walls of Mediterranean design. The Fishers and their most prominent employee, Burnham Hoyt, produced many notable interpretations of Spanish and Italian styles.

The Fishers also used other revival styles trendy during the 1920s through the 1940s—French and, most notably, English, including Colonial, Georgian, and Tudor. The Fishers and other leading twentieth-century architects such as Maurice Biscoe, Theodore Boal and Frederick L. Harnois, Aaron M. Gove and Thomas F. Walsh, Harry James Manning, and Ernest P. Varian and Lester E. Varian gave Denver notable landmarked examples of various revival types.

Denver's most creative twentieth-century architect, Burnham Hoyt, designed the municipal outdoor amphitheatre at Red Rocks Park. The national AIA, for its centennial celebration in 1955, picked the best building in each state and selected Red Rocks as Colorado's finest design. The AIA praised Hoyt's minimalist construction, beautifully integrated with the natural environment. Few other architects have achieved such sensitive use of natural terrain and vegetation in their work.

Twentieth-century styles such as Prairie, Art Deco, Streamline Moderne, and Postmodern caught on slowly in Denver. As early as the 1930s, modern concepts, shapes, and materials were introduced by such architects as Robert K. Fuller, Eugene G. Groves, Victor Hornbein, Burnham Hoyt, Merrill Hoyt, Glen W. Huntington, G. Charles Jaka, and Eugene Sternberg. Before the 1950s, few architects could make a living by specializing in modern architecture.

FIGURE 0.5. Burnham Hoyt, a Denver native, mastered many styles to become Colorado's foremost twentieth-century architect. He designed what the AIA called the state's masterpiece, Red Rocks Outdoor Amphitheatre (which uses the British spelling) (Denver Public Library).

Temple Hoyne Buell, the state's most successful developer-architect, told the author in 1986, with a wink, "We don't fight over architectural styles. The client is always right." Denver architects, like their tradition-minded clients, usually opted for the imitative rather than the original, giving Denver handsome, solid, but generally conventional buildings.

Denver's Distinctive Architectural Characteristics

Denver buildings, although generally imitative of those in other cities, are often distinctive in three ways: spacious settings, masonry construction, and mountain views. Generous settings characterize a metropolis largely unconstrained by natural impediments. Denver developed with a western emphasis on elbowroom, producing single-family detached homes. Such residences, with side yards as well as front yards and backyards, predominate even in the poorest inner-city districts.

Unconstrained by large bodies of water or by the mountains 15 miles away, Denverites were free to build in every direction, and they did. Streetcars, and later automobile roads, shaped a metropolis that now sprawls through six suburban counties and over 2,500 square miles, from the Front Range of the Rockies on the west to the most spacious airport in the United States on the east.

Many landmarks in this book were constructed during Denver's greatest boom era, 1880–93. These monuments in brick and stone commemorate an optimism that has characterized the city since its gold rush origins. The native stones of the Rocky Mountains—rhyolite (volcanic lava rock), Colorado Yule marble, sandstone, travertine, and granite—were used to trim and face brick structures built during flush times.

Denver is a brick city. Because the nearest forest lies fifty miles away and clay beds underlie many areas of the city, brick was often easier and cheaper to use than local timber, which was generally soft wood. Bricks were also more fire resistant than frame and were encouraged by city ordinances after the Great Fire of 1863, Denver's only major blaze. Brick, reddish local sandstone, and, in recent years, tinted concrete give Denver its ruddy complexion.

Denver's setting is special because of its backdrop—the snow-capped Rocky Mountains. Mayor Speer realized that this mountain view was one of the city's greatest assets and limited building heights to twelve stories. Not until the 1950s did a growth-hungry city abandon the height ordinance to court high-rise developers. With few exceptions, developers have had their way to this day. They have built heavenward and demolished any old buildings in their path—witness the demolition of Benedict's Central Bank Building for the Four Seasons Hotel and condo tower and the 1996 demolition of I. M. Pei's Hyperbolic Paraboloid for a St. Louis hotel chain's aggressive expansion plans. To make matters worse for those wanting overviews of the city and the mountains, none of the forty- and fifty-story towers erected since 1980 have roof-level viewing areas open to the public. Recent ordinances have been only partially successful in preserving Denver's mountain views, a sight that can cheer up even the poorest and most depressed resident or visitor.

Ethnic Legacies

Greek, Roman, Spanish, English, French, and Italian influences are prominent in early-twentieth-century revival style architecture used for both residential and commercial structures in Denver. Denver's early "brick" ordinances, which mandated the use of fire-retardant materials in building construction, excluded adobe bricks, discouraging a functional, handsome Hispanic building tradition. Denver lacked the solid German, Irish, Slavic, Scandinavian, and other ethnic neighborhoods of many cities, although heavily African, Asian, Jewish, Italian, and Hispanic American areas did emerge.

Little Israel, the old Jewish neighborhood along West Colfax Avenue, is largely gone. Landmarked remnants are Golda Meir's relocated girlhood home and the Emmanuel Sherith Chapel on the Auraria campus. On Capitol Hill, the former Temple Emanuel Synagogue is now a public events center, whose Middle Eastern influences provide a contrast to the Gothic and Romanesque elements of Christian churches.

Little Italy in Highlands is represented by that area's heartbeat, Our Lady of Mount Carmel Catholic Church. Several other nearby North Denver landmarks—the Frank Damascio House, Cerrone's Grocery, and the Hannigan-Canino Terrace—are reminders of this now dispersed Italian enclave.

Germans, Denver's largest foreign-born immigrant population in the nineteenth century, have left notable landmarks, such as St. Elizabeth's Catholic Church, the Tivoli Brewery, and the Buckhorn Exchange Restaurant. The oldest ethnic clubs in Colorado are the landmarked Denver Turnverein on Capitol Hill and the Turnhalle Opera Hall within the Tivoli Brewery complex. Such institutions not only provided the food and drink but perpetuated the song, dance, music, and language of the homeland.

Anglo-Americans gave the city some of its finest landmark churches (Asbury Methodist and Trinity United Methodist), hotels (the Oxford and Brown Palace), and office blocks (the Boston, Equitable, Kittredge, and Masonic Buildings). Episcopal churches with notable English Gothic architecture include several landmarks—St. John's Episcopal Cathedral, St. Luke's Church, St. Mark's, and the Chapel of Our Merciful Savior. St. Patrick's Catholic Church, the city's first Irish parish, was a source of Hibernian pride and fostered one of Denver's most popular civic festivals, the St. Patrick's Day Parade.

The French Gothic style is celebrated in the Immaculate Conception Cathedral and the Ivy Chapel at Fairmount Cemetery, both designated landmarks. The Chateau style is best seen in the Croke-Patterson-Campbell Mansion, while later French Revival influences are showcased in the Frank Smith and Crawford Hill Mansions.

Of the black community's institutions, Shorter A.M.E., Zion Baptist, and Scott Methodist Churches are landmarked, as is the Douglass Undertaking Building. The restaurant of Barney Ford, the pioneer black leader, and the residence of Dr. Clarence Holmes, a major twentieth-century spokesperson, are designated landmarks, although Dr. Justina Ford's house, now the Black American West Museum, is not.

Hispanics, the first European group to settle in Colorado, have landmarks in Our Lady of Guadalupe and St. Cajetan's Catholic Churches and the Byers Branch Library, with its Spanish architecture and Spanish language programs. Denver has a Mexican-oriented commercial district on Santa Fe Drive between Seventh and Twelfth Avenues. Denver lacks a Hispanic-flavored historic district such as Olvera Street in Los Angeles.

Denver Styles

No distinctive Denver style has emerged, although brick foursquares became so common that they are locally known as "Denver Squares."

Coloradans generally borrowed traditional styles from the eastern United States and Europe, whose cities they hoped to emulate. As Richard Brettell explained in his 1973 book *Historic Denver: The Architects and the Architecture, 1858–1893,* "Denverites gave their commercial buildings gravity by the use of the Renaissance rounded arch; they gave their churches a 'churchy' quality by the use of the Gothic arch; and they gave their homes a 'homey' quality by the addition of a balustraded front porch."

Denver's earliest landmarks, especially those in Curtis Park, reflect the Italianate style popular in the 1880s. Denver has only a few examples of the earlier Second Empire style, notably the Crawford Building in Larimer Square and the Knight House in the Ninth Street Historic Park. More common in Denver are Queen Anne and Romanesque styles. Neoclassical types such as the foursquare and classic cottage also abound. Denverites, who used their buildings to convey a sense of tradition and permanence in a raw young city, favored historicist revivals like the Colonial, Georgian, and Tudor. Most Denver buildings are not stylistically pure;

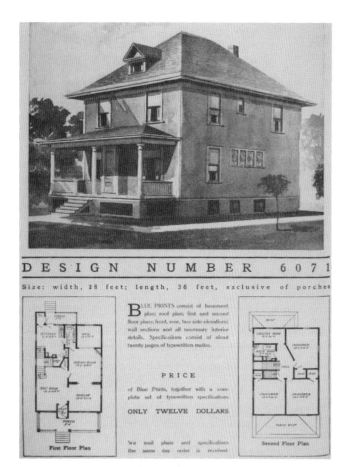

FIGURE 0.6. Foursquare house plan.

rather, they are vernacular versions, often an eclectic mix of elements from two or more styles.

The only exceptions to Denver's copy-catting of styles originating elsewhere are the tuberculosis houses found in the Montclair Historic District and a few other places. These single-story bungalow-like houses had long street-facing facades with screened porches on either end. A very open floor plan allowed air and sunshine to circulate around the house. Built especially for lung disease patients around 1905–10, most have been heavily altered.

Some architects experimented with the Spanish Colonial and Mission Revival modes. Arthur A. Fisher and William E. Fisher, the principals of Denver's most prolific early-twentieth-century architectural firm, argued that Spanish styles were ideal for a southwestern state with a Hispanic heritage. Furthermore, Colorado has a bright, sunny, dry climate, like the American Southwest and Spain, with temperature extremes that make stout masonry walls sensible because they keep buildings cooler in summer and warmer in winter. A derivative of the Spanish hacienda is the ubiquitous post–World War II ranch house, of which there is not yet an individually landmarked Denver specimen. Another common style, the bungalow popular from 1900 to the 1920s, is well represented in the city's largest historic district—East Seventh Avenue Parkway. Art Deco shaped only a few Denver residences, apartment houses, and commercial buildings. The Paramount Theater and the Cruise Room of the landmarked Oxford Hotel are examples. Denver has demolished or altered many of its few examples of Streamline Moderne commercial buildings, but residential examples can be found in Park Hill, the Country Club, and, most notably, the Bonnie Brae area. Twentieth-century styles remain underrepresented among designated landmarks.

Denver Landmark Preservation Commission

Urban renewal projects, speculation, and rapid and reckless growth spurts have eliminated many notable structures, especially in the Central Business District and Capitol Hill.

Wholesale demolitions led the mayor and city council to establish the Denver Landmark Preservation Commission (DLPC) in 1967. Since then, more than 9,000 structures, including individual landmarks and those in districts, have

FIGURE 0.7. When the wrecking ball proved too slow, explosives were used, as in this 1970 implosion of the Interstate Trust Building, 1130 Sixteenth Street, an 1891 design by Frank Edbrooke (History Colorado).

FIGURE 0.8. The bronze Denver Landmark Plaque protects buildings from inappropriate alteration and demolition. This one is in the hands of pioneer Denver Landmark Preservation commissioner Thomas Hornsby Ferril, Colorado's poet laureate, who argued for preservation in his poetry (photo by Glenn Cuerden).

been designated for preservation by the city council on the recommendation of concerned citizens with approval of the DLPC. Designations are made on the basis of architectural, geographical, and historical significance. After a structure is landmarked, the DLPC reviews any exterior alterations that require a building or zoning permit. The commission has ordinance authority to deny demolition in historic districts or of individual landmarks.

The state of Colorado has promoted preservation in several ways. A 1991 state statute provides state income tax credits up to $50,000 for authorized maintenance of designated residential landmarks and contributing structures in historic districts. In 2014 the state of Colorado greatly expanded its tax credits for historic preservation, leaving $50,000 as the maximum credit for approved improvements to a residential landmark but allowing commercial projects to be eligible for transferable credits capped at $1 million per project.

In 1990 Coloradans approved an amendment to the state constitution allowing gambling in the fading gold-mining towns Black Hawk, Central City, and Cripple Creek, with the provision that gaming taxes go to historic preservation. These funds are distributed through History Colorado's State Historical Fund (SHF), which has issued over $300 million to restore designated landmarks in all sixty-four counties. This incentive led many local government land-

marking agencies, recognized as Certified Local Governments (CLG) by History Colorado, to add sites to their lists. Those certified local landmarks and districts are eligible to apply for state historic funds. Denver, which obtained the first CLG, has received many millions in SHF funds to restore its designated landmarks.

How to Use This Guide

This is a guide to the Denver buildings and districts proposed by citizens and sanctioned by the Denver Landmark Preservation Commission and designated as landmarks by the city council and the mayor. Structures are listed by their original names, with prominent later names also provided. Notable buildings that are not individually designated landmarks but fall within historic districts are discussed in the text but are not numbered or mapped. If a building is also on the National Register of Historic Places, it has been identified as NR (or, in the case of a district, NRD for National Register Historic District). The highest federal designation, a National Historic Landmark, has been bestowed on Civic Center, with a second Denver NHL designation approved in 2015 for Red Rocks Amphitheatre. The National Register program, established in 1966, is similar to the DLPC program in that it identifies, designates, and attempts to preserve significant buildings and districts. Since 1990, Colorado has also identified locally significant landmarks by listing them on the State Register (SR). Many buildings and districts are listed on the National Register of Historic Places and are designated Denver landmarks. The National Register program is administered for the federal government by the Office of Archaeology and Historic Preservation (OAHP) of History Colorado and the National Park Service. National Register administrators, unlike the DLPC, have little control over alterations and demolitions of listed structures.

As with all architectural guidebooks, readers should be aware of some problems. Dates of building permits, building design, ground breaking, cornerstone laying, completion, and occupation usually stretch over several years. Here, I have listed the date of completion.

As to sometimes confusing architectural and stylistic terms, I have relied on the comprehensive glossary the Society of Architectural Historians developed for its Buildings of the United States series, as exemplified by the glossary in *Buildings of Colorado* (Oxford University Press, 1997).

The name after the date of construction is that of the architect. Individual landmarks and districts are arranged in what I hope will be a convenient order for walking, biking, and driving tours. For the most part, individual landmarks within a historic district are covered with the district, but sometimes the tour order suggested another placement. Four landmarks could not be squeezed onto the maps, so they remain unmapped here:

Bethesda Chapel and Gateway, 4400 East Iliff Avenue (#301)

Fire Station No. 18, 2205 Colorado Boulevard (#167)

Globeville School, 5110 Lincoln Street (#267)

Field Officers Quarters, Fort Logan, 3742 West Princeton Circle (#302)

For the latest updated list of individual landmarks and historic districts, check the City of Denver website (denvergov. org/landmarks) for maps, lists, and other information. New landmarks and districts are continually being designated. While this book was in press, the City designated three new landmarks in the National Western Stock Show Complex: The Stadium Arena, The Denver Union Stockyards Exchange Building, and The Armour Office Building. In south central Denver, The South Lincoln Street Historic District, in the 200 South Block, featuring smaller residential designs by William Lang, the city's foremost ninetenth-century residential architect, was also designated in 2016.

Over the years, Denverites have built many special places. Although the ones in this book are the officially designated buildings and areas of note, the great fun in rubbernecking around Denver is discovering other special places on your own.

I

Central Denver

Originally, a tiny business district and residences occupied today's urban core. As the city grew, much of the pioneer residential area was transformed into commercial or government buildings.

CIVIC CENTER AREA

CENTRAL BUSINESS DISTRICT

LARIMER SQUARE HISTORIC DISTRICT

LOWER DOWNTOWN HISTORIC DISTRICT

AURARIA AREA

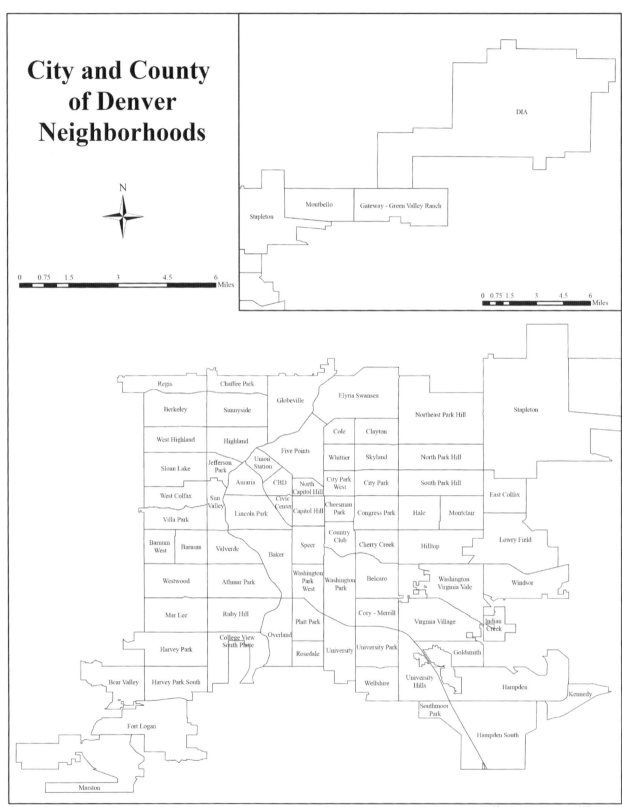

**City and County
of Denver
Neighborhoods**

N

0   0.75   1.5   3   4.5   6
Miles

DIA

Stapleton   Montbello   Gateway - Green Valley Ranch

0 0.75 1.5   3   4.5   6
Miles

Regis   Chaffee Park
                              Globeville   Elyria Swansea
Berkeley   Sunnyside   Northeast Park Hill   Stapleton

West Highland   Highland   Cole   Clayton
                          Five Points
Sloan Lake   Jefferson Union   Whittier   Skyland   North Park Hill
              Park   Station
                 Auraria   CBD   North   City Park   South Park Hill
West Colfax   Sun   Capitol Hill West   City Park   East Colfax
              Valley   Lincoln Park Civic
Villa Park   Center Capitol Hill Cheesman Congress Park   Hale   Montclair
                                              Park
Barnum   Country   Lowry Field
West   Barnum   Valverde   Speer   Club   Cherry Creek   Hilltop
                          Baker
Westwood   Athmar Park   Washington Washington Belcaro   Washington   Windsor
                            Park   Park   Virginia Vale
                            West
Mar Lee   Ruby Hill   Cory - Merrill   Virginia Village   Indian
                          Platt Park   Creek
              College View Overland   Goldsmith
Harvey Park   South Platte   Rosedale University University Park
                                                                  University
Bear Valley Harvey Park South   Wellshire   Hills   Hampden   Kennedy
                                                        Southmoor
Fort Logan   Park
                                                              Hampden South
Marston

Created by Nicholas J. Wharton

MAP I.I. Denver neighborhoods

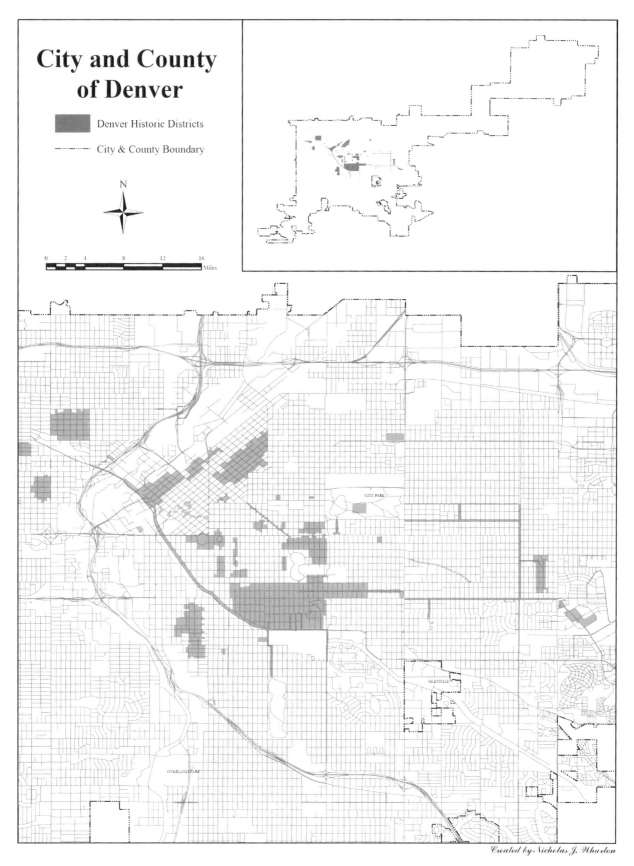

City and County of Denver

■ Denver Historic Districts

----- City & County Boundary

N

0   2   4   8   12   16
Miles

CITY PARK

GLENDALE

OVERLAND PARK

Created by Nicholas J. Wharton

MAP 1.2. Denver Historic Districts

MAP 1.3. Central Denver Landmarks

Civic Center Area

Roughly Grant to Elati Streets between Colfax and Tenth Avenues

HD-6 CIVIC CENTER HISTORIC DISTRICT

Roughly Grant to Delaware Streets between Colfax and Thirteenth Avenues, NHL

Mayor Robert W. Speer enlisted Charles Mulford Robinson, a New York planner and author of *Modern Civic Art, or, the City Made Beautiful* (1903), to do the initial 1906 plan for a government office park. Robinson used the state capitol as the eastern anchor of a civic mall for city, state, and federal buildings wrapped around a central park. Sculptor Frederick MacMonnies refined the Civic Center

FIGURE 1.2. Civic Center's Voorhies Memorial (History Colorado).

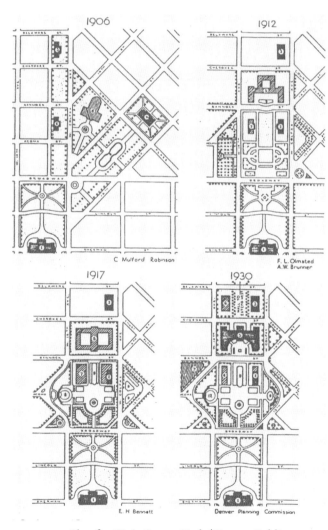

FIGURE 1.1. Plan for Civic Center Park (Denver Public Library).

plan while working on his Pioneer Fountain (1911), at the northwest corner of West Colfax Avenue and Broadway. He introduced the semicircles formed by curving West Colfax and West Fourteenth Avenues between Broadway and Bannock and placed the City and County Building on Bannock opposite the capitol, anchoring the western end of the civic mall. Frederick Law Olmsted Jr. also contributed a plan (1912), as did Chicago city planner Edward H. Bennett (1917) and Denver landscape architect Saco R. DeBoer. Today's Civic Center incorporates ideas from all of these planners.

Civic Center's north-south axis terminates in two classical structures inspired by the 1893 World's Columbian Exposition. At the north end, the Voorhies Memorial (1919, William E. Fisher and Arthur A. Fisher), 100 West Colfax Avenue, is a copy of the exposition's Water Gateway. An arcade of Turkey Creek sandstone curves around a pool with twin fountains of cherubs riding sea lions, designed by Denver sculptor Robert Garrison. In the lunettes of the arcade are murals by Allen Tupper True depicting bison and elk in Neoclassical style. Banker and mining entrepreneur John H.P. Voorhies, who lived across the street, funded the memorial.

The Greek Theater and Colonnade of Civic Benefactors (1919, Willis A. Marean and Albert J. Norton), West Fourteenth Avenue and Acoma Street, echoes and balances the Voorhies Memorial at the opposite end of the north-south axis. Edward H. Bennett, the protégé and successor of Chicago's famed master architect of the 1893 Exposition, Daniel Burnham, proposed this arrangement despite local critics who complained, "Why the hell does Denver need a Greek theater? We ain't got that many Greeks here!" The theater's arc responds to the curving wings of the Voorhies Memorial and is constructed of the same Turkey Creek sandstone. Two Allen Tupper True murals, *Trapper* and *Prospector*, depict pioneer types in forest settings. The theater's north side is terraced down into an open semicircular arena.

Plans for a sunken sculpture garden at the center of Civic Center Park solidified around two bronze statues by Denverite Alexander Phimister Proctor, *Broncho Buster* (1920) and *On the War Trail* (1922). Civic Center Park was restored and enhanced in 1991 by Long Hoeft Architects and again in the early 2000s by landscape architect Tina Bishop, who oversaw a $2 million facelift. The Civic Center Conservancy, a private nonprofit support group whose aim is to maintain and enhance Civic Center, has funded major improvements since its creation in 2004. Civic Center is the heart of Denver's park system and a relic of the standard Progressive-Era prescription for improving crowded, ugly urban cores. In pronouncing Civic Center a National Historic Landmark in 2012, US secretary of the interior Ken Salazar called it the best-preserved US example of City Beautiful planning for an urban core.

Colorado State Capitol

1886–1908, Elijah E. Myers, Frank E. Edbrooke. East Colfax to East Fourteenth Avenues between Lincoln and Grant Streets, HD-6

At the eastern edge of Civic Center, this cruciform four-story building culminates in a gold dome. The brick building is faced with Colorado gray granite from the Aberdeen Quarry in Gunnison County. Similar symmetrical bays characterize all four sides, with a west entrance portico overlooking Civic Center. Triangular pediments with bas-relief sculptures top triple-arched central entrances

on each side. Lighter, cheaper cast iron that matches the granite color is used for the three cylindrical stages of the dome. Colorado mining magnates donated twenty-four-carat gold leaf for the 272-foot-high dome, and the Cripple Creek and Victor Gold Mining Company donated a 2013 replacement.

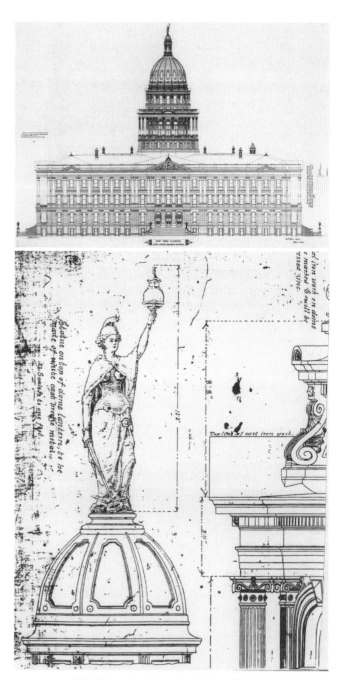

FIGURE 1.3. Elijah E. Myers's original plans for the Colorado State Capitol [3a] included this woman [3b] atop the gold dome (Colorado State Archives).

Elijah Myers also designed state capitols for Idaho, Michigan, Texas, and Utah. As with his other statehouses, Myers gave Colorado's a Neoclassical design of Renaissance origins. The Board of Capitol Managers dismissed Myers in 1889 to save money. Denver architect Frank E. Edbrooke, who had placed second in the original architectural competition, completed the structure, basically following Myers's 1886 design. Edbrooke substituted gold for copper on the dome and dropped the allegorical female figure with which Myers had crowned it. Apparently the legislature, after considerable study of models in various states of dress, could not agree on which was the shapeliest. A major restoration of the dome and relaying of its gold skin, completed in 2014, did not include the forgotten lady.

The interior features Beulah red marble and Colorado Yule marble wainscoting and brass fixtures. Of 160 rooms, the most noteworthy are the Old Supreme Court chambers, the senate and house chambers, and the central rotunda, whose first-floor walls display murals (1938) by Colorado's premier muralist, Allen Tupper True, with captions from Colorado poet laureate Thomas Hornsby Ferril. Fire safety improvements evolved into a major restoration in the early 2000s, in which a new attic museum was installed, showcasing the building's history. On the east side of the capitol is the *Closing Era*, a bronze Indian and buffalo crafted for the 1893 World's Columbian Exposition by Preston Powers, who once taught in Denver. The grounds were designed by Colorado's pioneer landscape architect, Reinhard Schuetze. A $17 million restoration of the dome by Quinn Evans Architects with Humphries Poli Architects, completed in 2014, included the new gold coat.

Colorado State Museum

1913, Frank E. Edbrooke. 1987 restoration and renovation, Pahl-Pahl-Pahl Architects. Fourteenth Avenue, southeast corner of Sherman Street, HD-6

For the stately museum on the south side of the capitol, Edbrooke used Colorado Yule marble on a Gunnison granite base in a Neoclassical style, echoing the capitol. As this building shows, Edbrooke had made the leap from nineteenth-century romantic styles to early-twentieth-century Neoclassicism. Richard Brettell, in his book *Historic Denver: The Architects and the Architecture, 1858–1893* (1973), wrote of Edbrooke's final major edifice: "The building is architecturally pure and its imagery exudes a hardened pomp and grandeur. Its memorial, almost funereal appearance is

appropriate both because it is a museum—a historical society—and because it was Edbrooke's self-consciously last building." Pahl-Pahl-Pahl Architects of Denver restored the edifice for use by the Colorado State Legislature in 1987. The Colorado Historical Society, re-branded History Colorado in 2009, is now located at 1200 Broadway in an office, library, and museum known as the History Colorado Center (2012, Tryba Architects).

State Office Building

1921, William N. Bowman. 1985 restoration, Urban Design Group. 201 East Colfax Avenue, northeast corner of Sherman Street, HD-6

Of a half dozen twentieth-century state office buildings clustered around the capitol, this is one of the finest. A Renaissance Revival palace guarded by twin bronze lions sculpted by Robert Garrison, it has an exterior of Cotopaxi granite and Colorado Yule marble. The exquisite interior features a black-and-white marble checker-floored central court, ivory-colored marble walls, and bronze fixtures under a stained glass skylight. After a narrow escape from the wrecking ball, a $4 million restoration preserved this classic as offices for the Colorado Department of Education and the State Library.

Denver Public Library

1955, Burnham Hoyt, William E. Fisher, and Arthur A. Fisher. 1995 addition, Michael Graves and Klipp Colussy Jenks DuBois. 10 West Fourteenth Avenue Parkway, northwest corner of Broadway, HD-6

On the north side of this full-block complex, the 1955 four-story Burnham Hoyt Library subtly plays on classical composition, using two-story window bands to represent a glazed colonnade and third-story fenestration arranged like a frieze. Its semicircular two-story bay overlooks Civic Center.

Such refinements deferring to the Neoclassicism of Civic Center were lost on Michael Graves, the famous Princeton, New Jersey, postmodernist who, with the Denver firm of Brian Klipp, produced the seven-story addition attached to the south side of the original building. This addition tripled the size of the library, creating a depository for over 1 million books, 2 million government documents, and a cornucopia of special collections. The addition's massive size is made visually smaller by breaking it into a variety of rectangles, colors, cylinders, and towers. Copper sheaths the domed entry pavilion of the children's library and serves as accent trim elsewhere on the exterior.

Graves used clearly articulated masses that express their functions. His drum-like rotunda houses the first-floor reference room, the third-floor periodicals room, and the fifth-floor Western History and Genealogy Department. The latter has a superb collection of Denver, Colorado, and Rocky Mountain region books, manuscripts, photos, art, maps, architectural renderings, and multiple other resources. This distinctive drum, Graves's signature shape, is centered in the set-back rectangular massing of the south elevation. Here Graves comes closest to Neoclassical harmony with a parade of columns along West Thirteenth Avenue. German limestone from the fossil-rich Solnhofen quarries covers the south facade in a creamy color that matches the Indiana limestone skin of Hoyt's 1955 library on the north side. Other elevations are clad in red and green cast stone that emphasizes the geometrical shapes of a structure local supervising architect Brian Klipp called "classically contemporary."

Graves excelled as an interior designer, using warm, golden maple for interior paneling, shelves, and furnishings as well as for his custom chairs, desks, and lamps in this eye-catching edifice that many find to be library heaven.

City and County Building

1932, Allied Architects, Robert K. Fuller. 1437 Bannock Street, southwest corner of West Colfax Avenue, HD-6

Balancing the Colorado State Capitol to complete a dominant east-west axis for Civic Center Park, this monument to Mayor Speer's City Beautiful was part of the initial 1906 Robinson plan but materialized slowly on its full-block site. The design was refined and implemented by a coalition of thirty-nine leading locals organized as Allied Architects, led by Roland L. Linder and Robert K. Fuller. The Neoclassical facade centers on three-story Corinthian travertine columns atop a grand entry staircase. Curving wings resemble outstretched arms reaching toward the capitol or, some say, toward taxpaying citizens.

Although Cotopaxi Colorado granite forms the base and Colorado travertine is used for the columns and interior, the upper walls are Stone Mountain, Georgia, granite, with fleur de pêche marble inserts. Mayor Speer's widow, Kate, donated the gold eagle and carillon clock tower that cap this handsome city hall in his memory. The slender bell

tower and the building's low profile preserve mountain views, Denver's signature attraction.

Tremendous bronze doors in the entry portico open to an interior featuring eleven varieties of marble, with Colorado travertine paneling the main corridors. A $10 million 1991–92 refurbishing brightened the interior and restored some features, including the grand lobby, Allen Tupper True's mural *The Miners' Court*, and Gladys Caldwell Fisher's bas-relief, *Montezuma and the Animals*. The most impressive interior spaces are the fourth-floor City Council chambers and the main entry hall, with a 1993 collage by Denver artist Susan Cooper depicting Denver landmarks. Busts of Mayor Robert W. Speer and landscape architect/city planner Saco R. DeBoer honor two key players in the building's history.

Carnegie Main Library–McNichols Building

1910, Albert Randolph Ross. 2010 renovation, Humphries Poli Architects. 144 West Colfax Avenue, HD-6

Denver's first freestanding library is a Neoclassical extension of the north wing of the City and County Building. It was to be paired with an extension of the art museum's south wing, but the art museum was eventually built on the other side of West Fourteenth Avenue. Fourteen Corinthian columns front this Greek temple in gray Turkey Creek sandstone on a base of Pikes Peak granite. This library pioneered an open stacks system later adopted by many other institutions and also first housed the Denver Public Library's superb Western History and Genealogy Department.

After the central library moved across Civic Center to its 1955 Burnham Hoyt building, conversion of the old library to other city offices led to many unfortunate "upgrades." Renamed for Mayor William H. McNichols Jr. and his brother, Governor Stephen McNichols, this Greek temple is being restored for arts and special events.

1. Byers-Evans House Museum

1883. 1898 addition. 1989 restoration, Long Hoeft Architects. 1310 Bannock Street, northeast corner of West Thirteenth Avenue, NR, HD-6

A rare remnant of the residential district that once flourished in what is now Civic Center, this two-story Italianate style brick residence shares the block with the north half of the Denver Art Museum. William Newton

FIGURE 1.4. The Byers-Evans House Museum celebrates William Newton Byers, Denver's ubiquitous pioneer promoter, and the family of John Evans, the territorial governor who brought railroads, the University of Denver, and churches to Denver (History Colorado).

Byers, founding editor of the *Rocky Mountain News*, built the house and lived here until 1889 when it became the family home of William Gray Evans, son of Colorado territorial governor John Evans. Evans doubled the size with an 1898 two-story south addition, with an entry hall, a library, two bathrooms and two bedrooms, a maid's room, and a sitting room. Inside, rich, dark interior colors complement the glossy woodwork. In 1981 the Evans family bequeathed the house to the Colorado Historical Society (now History Colorado). Restored in 1989 as a house museum containing Evans family furnishings, its exhibits focus on Denver history in general as well as on the Byers and Evans clans.

2. Evans School

1904, David W. Dryden. 1115 Acoma Street, northwest corner of West Eleventh Avenue, NR, HD-6

Designed by a prominent Denver school architect, this three-story red brick school exemplifies the Classical Revival style with its pilasters, Ionic columns, and pedimented portico with neocolonial accents, such as the large central copper-clad cupola school bell. All four elevations present detailed Neoclassical facades that might be mistaken for a main entrance. Back in 1904, the *Rocky Mountain News* reported, "The building cost $130,000 and is said to be the most modern and best equipped school building in the West and one of the finest in the United States." Named for territorial governor John Evans, it served the public

for sixty-nine years as an elementary school, a junior high school, and one of Denver's first schools for the deaf, blind, and physically handicapped. As enrollment diminished in the early 1970s, the school district closed the building and sold it to a private party. Since its closing, the Evans School has remained vacant awaiting a new fate. Recent exterior restoration has kindled hopes for a new chapter for the old school.

3. Ten-Winkle Apartments and Carpenter Gothic Houses

ca. 1893 apartments, Herman Ten-Winkle. 2005 restoration, Humphries Poli Architects. 404–10 West Twelfth Avenue, ca. 1885 houses, Herman Ten-Winkle. 2001 restoration, Blue Sky Studio. 1173–79 Delaware Street, HD-6

These rare surviving examples of early modest, middle-class cottages were built by a Dutch immigrant. The tiny Carpenter Gothic cottages initially housed the Ten-Winkle family and a family of renters. Ten-Winkle built the two-story brick fourplex at 404–10 West Twelfth Avenue a few years later.

4. Denver US Mint

1906, James Knox Taylor, with Gordon, Tracy, and Swarthout. 1987 addition, Rogers-Nagel-Langhart. 320 West Colfax Avenue, NR, HD-6

One of the three federal mints is located in Denver, reflecting the city's gold rush origins. It evolved from the private mint of Clark, Gruber, and Company. The present-day two-story gray stone fortress was supposedly inspired architecturally by the Palazzo Medici-Riccardi in Florence, Italy. The north entry porch, stairs, and base for the perimeter fence are made of pinkish, black-flecked Pikes Peak granite that contrasts with the Cotopaxi gray granite ashlar above. Marble lunettes with bas-relief eagles crown high rectangular windows on the first level. The granite cornice is bracketed above a decorated frieze. Wrought iron is used for the entry lanterns, window grilles, and fencing above a low granite retaining wall. Murals by Vincent Aderente in the main hall portray mining, manufacturing, and commerce. Although James Knox Taylor was the supervising architect in Washington, DC, the New York City firm of Gordon, Tracy, and Swarthout designed the mint. Additions have aspired, with debatable results, to enhance this monument to Colorado's golden beginnings.

3203 United States Mint, Denver, Colo.

FIGURE 1.5. US Mint (Tom Noel Collection).

The mint is one of the city's most popular free attractions, but the three subterranean floors where gold bars are stored are not open to the public.

Central Business District

Broadway to Larimer Street, Twentieth Street west to Colfax Avenue

Today's Central Business District (CBD) began life in the 1870s as a residential area on the southeast edge of the original commercial district between Blake and Larimer Streets. The 1880s boom led to furious commercial construction that quickly transformed the area. Of the initial residential area, the only remaining single-family residence is the Curry-Chucovich-Gerash House. Many demolitions, intensified by the Skyline Urban Renewal Project, erased twenty-six blocks of the CBD. These losses helped inspire the city to create the Denver Landmark Preservation Commission in 1967. The commission and city council have subsequently landmarked many of the surviving historic

structures. Major remaining landmarks were included in the Downtown Denver Historic District, created in 2000.

HD-38 DOWNTOWN DENVER HISTORIC DISTRICT

Thirteenth to Eighteenth Streets between Court Place and Lawrence Street

This non-contiguous district protects forty-three contributing historic buildings. Sometimes called the Chocolate Chip Cookie District, it selected the "chocolate chips" out of the downtown cookie. Generous incentives and city tax rebates inspired even reluctant owners to join this district. Among the downtown chocolate chips not in the district is the Colorado National Bank (1915, William E. Fisher and Arthur A. Fisher. 1924, Merrill H. and Burnham Hoyt. 1965 addition, Rogers-Nagel. 1975 tower, Minoru Yamasaki. 2014 hotel conversion, Klipp. Seventeenth and Champa Streets). The original Greek temple of Colorado Yule marble received a contemporary 1965 take on Neoclassicism, followed by

Yamasaki's masterful timeless tower. The 2014 conversion of the 1924 bank to a Marriott Renaissance Hotel included preservation of the grand atrium lobby, with Allen Tupper True's masterpiece mural series *Indian Memories*.

5. Brown Palace Hotel

1892, Frank E. Edbrooke. 321 Seventeenth Street, NR, HD-38

The finest work of Colorado's foremost nineteenth-century architect is named for Henry Cordes Brown, who homesteaded Capitol Hill and commissioned this $2 million palace of red Arizona sandstone on a base of Pikes Peak granite. Responding to the triangular site, Edbrooke gave the nine-story hotel three gracefully curved corners. The steel and iron frame, clad in terracotta and concrete as well as reddish sandstone, made this an exemplary fire-proof structure, according to a May 21, 1892, cover story in *Scientific American* magazine.

Repetition of arcaded window patterns; cornices above the first, second, seventh, and ninth stories; and banding around corner curves added horizontal emphasis to what was then the tallest building in town. Twenty-six stone medallions of native Colorado animals carved by James Whitehouse survive on the seventh floor. The now-closed former main entrance on Broadway retains some original stone trim, including a bas-relief bust of Brown.

At the base of the spectacular, sky-lighted, nine-story atrium, caramel and cream swirls flow through 12,000 square feet of onyx paneling in the lobby. The especially well-preserved Onyx Room has a ceiling mural of cherubs hovering in a heavenly blue sky. Two later murals by Allen Tupper True, depicting the stagecoach and airplane ages, adorn the Tremont Place entrance elevator lobby. Architect Alan B. Fisher, the son of William E. Fisher, designed the Ship Tavern, a nautically themed celebration of the repeal of Prohibition. The tavern sports marine artifacts, ranging from a crow's nest wrapped around the room's central pillar to a collection of ships in bottles. In addition to this splendid saloon, the hotel is famous for its two artesian water wells and its high teas. The Palace Arms Dining Room is a museum of Napoleonic War–era banners and trophies. Restorations have undone 1950s modernizations, returning Denver's grand hotel to its original Richardsonian Romanesque splendor. This grand dame of Denver hotels has been open every day since its 1892 arrival and has long been one of the city's favorite public spaces.

FIGURE 1.6. Brown Palace Hotel atrium (Denver Public Library).

6. The Navarre–American Museum of Western Art

1880, Frank E. Edbrooke. 1983 restoration, Fentress and Associates. 1725–27 Tremont Place, NR, HD-38

The Brinker Collegiate Institute was erected for $20,000 in 1880 as a private school to teach young ladies the liberal arts and Christian virtue. These aspirations ended in 1901 when the school became the Richelieu Hotel and then the Navarre—a café, gambling hall, brothel, and Denver's most notorious department store of vice. Restoration in 1983 as a museum of Western art removed a century of additions and revisions and resurrected the double-bracketed cornice and distinctive copper-colored cupola. With three stories plus a basement, this Italianate structure of red brick is enhanced by full-height bays with pedimented gables. A basement tunnel under Tremont Place to the Brown Palace Hotel is a utility tunnel, doubtfully large enough to have allowed the legendary patronage by hotel guests of the Navarre's *nymphes du pavé*. Billionaire Denver tycoon Philip Anschutz has converted the oldest building in the Central

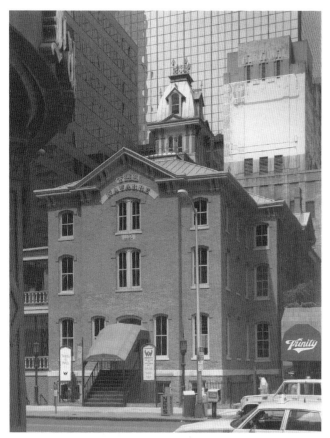

FIGURE 1.7. Named for the high-living King Henry of Navarre of France, since 1880 the Navarre has hosted fine schooling, fine female commercial companionship, fine food, and fine art (photo by Roger Whitacre).

Business District into a home for the Anschutz Collection, one of the most celebrated collections of US Western art in private hands.

7. Curry-Chucovich-Gerash House

1888, Fred A. Hale. 1982 restoration, Edward D. White Jr. 1439 Court Place, NR, HD-38

The solitary remnant of a vanished residential neighborhood, this two-story stone townhouse now stands alone amid asphalt parking lots on one of the city's original 25-by-125-foot lots. Hale, who started his Denver career with Frank Edbrooke, used rosy sandstone with carved stone trim for the facade of this red brick dwelling. James H. Curry selected rhyolite from his Castle Rock quarry for the foundation, coping, and front steps of his home. Denver's *Western Architect and Building News* hailed the dwelling as "a genuine two-story brownstone," with a "chaste and

happy" interior "of fresco and Lincrusta-Walton relief work" and a staircase arch "of intricate arabesque fretwork in oak." Vaso Chucovich, a Yugoslavian immigrant, later bought the house and lived there until his death. Chucovich, who owned and operated various saloons and gambling houses, became Denver's underworld czar. He died in 1933 a real estate magnate and millionaire who left $100,000 to build the children's wing of Denver General Hospital. Chucovich intended that wing to be a memorial to Mayor Robert W. Speer, whose powerful political machine had protected his unsavory businesses. In 1982 noted Denver defense attorney Walter Gerash restored the house inside and out for his law firm's offices. Gerash reported, "We even re-did the interior stenciling and added the Ten Commandments in Hebrew so none of my clients would be embarrassed."

8. Fire Station No. 1–Denver Firefighters Museum

1909, Glen W. Huntington and Company. 1326 Tremont Place, NR, HD-38

Behind the ornate gray brick and light sandstone facade topped by an elaborate dentiled cornice, the original firehouse interior is starkly functional, almost modern. This Neoclassical station with recessed second-story balcony became the Denver Firefighters Museum in 1980. Visitors can inspect vintage fire trucks and other equipment as well as the dormitories and fire pole.

FIGURE 1.8. The Neoclassical propensities of the City Beautiful era extended to even the most basic municipal buildings, as exemplified by Fire Station No. 1 (photo by Roger Whitacre).

FIGURE 1.9. The 1889 Denver Athletic Club is a reminder that the Mile High City's fascination with sports and physical fitness is nothing new (History Colorado).

9. Denver Press Club

1925, Merrill H. Hoyt and Burnham Hoyt. 1330 Glenarm Place, HD-38

This modest red brick clubhouse with a stuccoed facade trimmed in white terracotta quoins and window surrounds is more notable for its history than for its architecture. The first-floor bar and dining room, basement pool hall, and second-story meeting hall are haunted by the ghosts of prominent journalists such as Gene Amole, William Barrett, Paul Conrad, Red Fenwick, Thomas Hornsby Ferril, Jack Foster, Gene Fowler, Pat Oliphant, Damon Runyan, Lee Casey Taylor, and—after women were admitted in 1970—Sandra Dallas, Frances Melrose, and Marjorie Barrett. Herndon Davis decorated some of the walls with portraits

of a number of the more celebrated writers. Although founded in 1884, the Press Club lacked its own home until the completion of this cozy clubhouse.

10. Denver Athletic Club

1889 and 1892 matching addition, Ernest P. Varian and Frederick J. Sterner. 1951 addition, Lindner, Hodgson, and Wright. 1973 addition, Rodney S. Davis. 1984 addition, James Sudler Associates. 1996, Pouw and Associates. 1325 Glenarm Place between Thirteenth and Fourteenth Streets, NR, HD-38

The original six-story clubhouse sports a pink sandstone and red brick facade atop a sandstone base. It started out as an 1889 building, with an identical 1892 north addition.

Recessed spandrels between the third and fourth floors add horizontal emphasis to the paired round-arch windows. The Thirteenth Street addition (1973) and the Fourteenth Street addition (1984) offer modern minimalist reinterpretations of the Romanesque Revival style original. Inside, the bar and the billiard room, once a men's haven now open to ladies, are especially venerable spaces. Copycatting athletic clubs in big eastern cities, the Denver Athletic Club served as further evidence that Denver rapidly became urbane and fitness- and sports-minded.

11. Denver Public Schools (DPS) Administration Building–Denver Art Museum Administration Building

1923, William N. Bowman. 1937 and 1950 additions. 414 Fourteenth Street, southwest corner of Tremont Place, HD-38

Bowman, who designed many of Denver's public schools, also created this DPS administration building. The three-story brick sculpture is enlivened by terracotta trim, including the exclamation marks on the second-story level of the brick piers. In 1937 and 1950, additions were made to this building, which was converted to the administrative offices of the nearby Denver Art Museum in 1994.

12. Paramount Theater

1930, Temple Hoyne Buell and C. W. and George L. Rapp. 1621 Glenarm Place, NR, HD-38

A member of the firm headed by C. W. Rapp and George L. Rapp that designed many movie theaters across the United States, Temple Hoyne Buell created this 2,100-seat Art Deco picture palace. The pre-cast concrete block building is sheathed in glazed terracotta manufactured by the Denver Terra Cotta Company. The three-story Glenarm facade is divided into twelve bays of paired windows, with recurrent rosettes, feathers, and fiddlehead ferns, which also blossom on the elaborate Art Deco interior with its twin twenty-rank Wurlitzer pipe organs. Interior pilasters are capped by fan-shaped frosted glass figures, while the sunburst ceiling and the chandelier create a starry effect. Paramount patrons now enter and exit through the original exit doors on Glenarm Place. Historic Denver, Inc., helped save this last of Denver's picture palaces, which is now owned and operated by Kroenke Sports. The original now-gone Sixteenth Street grand entrance was through the adjacent Kittredge Building (1891, A. Morris Stuckert. 1992

FIGURE 1.10a (exterior) and 1.10b (interior). Of seventeen theaters once found downtown, the Paramount is the sole survivor (photos by Roger Whitacre).

renovation, Fentress Architects. 511 Sixteenth Street, northwest corner of Glenarm Place, NR). This seven-story steel skeleton, rhyolite-clad Richardsonian Romanesque beauty was named for its developer, Charles M. Kittredge.

FIGURE 1.11. Masonic Temple (photo by Tom Noel).

13. Masonic Temple

1890, Frank E. Edbrooke. 1985 renovation, C. W. Fentress and Associates. 1614 Welton Street, northeast corner of Sixteenth Street, NR, HD-38

Edbrooke, a Thirty-three Degree Mason, clad this temple with a base of Pikes Peak granite and upper levels of red-orange sandstone culminating in gable-like parapets. A central fifth-floor arcade echoing the ground-floor entry arches connects corner bays. The Welton Street entry is through a fifteen-foot-wide Romanesque arch with engaged columns supporting an extraordinary carved panel. After a 1984 arson fire, a new steel frame was constructed within the buckled walls, and new sandstone from the original Lyons quarry was sculpted to resemble and replace the granite removed from the first two floors in 1955. With the addition of a hipped glass penthouse and interior rearrangements, the temple has been enlarged from seven to nine stories. In front of the recessed Sixteenth Street entry, restoration architects added a sandstone arch that underscores the round-arch openings and arcades of this otherwise chunky, vernacular version of Romanesque Revival.

14. Hayden, Dickinson, and Feldhauser Building–Colorado Building

1891, John W. Roberts. 1909 addition, Frank E. Edbrooke. 1935 renovation, Jules Jacques Benoit Benedict. 1615–23 California Street, northwest corner of Sixteenth Street, HD-38

A 1935 Art Deco facelift transformed this red brick Chicago style commercial building into a beige terracotta

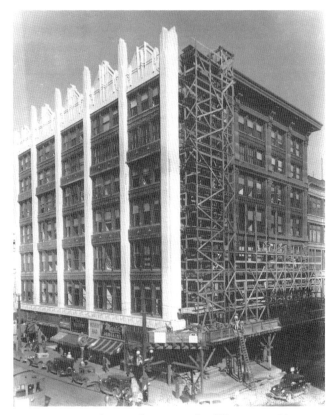

FIGURE 1.12. Hayden, Dickinson, and Feldhauser Building–Colorado Building facelift (Denver Public Library).

structure with an ornate parapet of alternating pinnacles and pediments. The terracotta overlay sparkles with geometric and naturalistic designs, including mountains and pine trees. Between the 1935 piers, the original spandrels and cast iron storefronts with acanthus leaf capitals are still visible. The remodeled building was given a new name, the Colorado Building. The five-story original structure had earlier received an additional two stories designed by Frank E. Edbrooke.

15. Denver Dry Goods Building

1889, Frank E. Edbrooke. 1898 and 1907 additions, Frank E. Edbrooke. 1994 restoration and renovation, John Carney and the Urban Design Group. 700 Sixteenth Street, southwest corner of California Street, NR, HD-38

Edbrooke was almost single-handedly responsible for downtown Denver's architectural maturity in the late 1800s. He created and then expanded structures such as this. The original three-story red brick structure at Sixteenth and California Streets for the McNamara Dry Goods Company

Home of the Denver Dry Goods Co.   The Largest Store in the Central West; 400 Feet Long; Seven Acres Floor Area; 1,200 Employes; A $2,500,000 Stock.   15th to 16th on California Street, Denver, Colorado.

FIGURE 1.13. Denver Dry Goods Building, ca. 1920 (Tom Noel Collection).

had limestone trim and plate-glass storefronts. His 1898 addition introduced a fourth story with round-arched windows, a wide festooned frieze, and bracketed cornice suggestive of the Renaissance Revival mode. In 1907, Edbrooke's third addition extended the building along California to Fifteenth Street. The Fifteenth Street addition has six stories and wider windows but similar broad bracketed eaves and classical details. In 1924 two stories were added to the original Sixteenth Street structure and stepped back to create a balustrade roof terrace for Denver's most famous tea room.

The Denver Dry Goods Building originated in 1886 as Michael J. McNamara's Dry Goods Company in the Clayton Building at Fifteenth and Larimer Streets. McNamara moved to 700 Sixteenth Street at California Street shortly before the Crash of 1893, when the Colorado National Bank foreclosed and reorganized his business as the Denver Dry Goods Company. Between the 1950s and the 1980s, this thriving store opened eleven branches in shopping centers from Fort Collins to Pueblo. The Denver Dry Goods Company's longtime rival, May D&F, bought the store in 1987 and closed it. After being restored outside

and remodeled inside with the help of the Denver Urban Renewal Authority, the building reopened in 1994 with various new uses.

16. Equitable Building

1893, Andrews, Jacques, and Rantoul. 730 Seventeenth Street, southeast corner of Stout Street, NR, HD-38

The Equitable Life Assurance Society of New York erected Denver's premier office building, using the design of prominent Boston architects who also planned the neighboring Boston Building. This nine-story edifice does not have a steel frame skeleton: the huge Pikes Peak granite blocks of the first two stories support the gray brick walls of the upper seven stories. This Italian Renaissance Revival edifice is invigorated with stone carvings, such as the "amorini" cherubs adorning the stone balcony on the fifth floor facing Seventeenth Street. The building's back-to-back double-E footprint not only displays the Equitable's initial logo but also allows light and air into the interior offices where the lower-ranking employees are often stuck windowless.

FIGURE 1.14. (a) Equitable Building exterior, (b) interior (photos by Roger Whitacre).

17. First National Bank–American National Bank–Magnolia Hotel

1911, Harry W.J. Edbrooke. 1962 remodel, James Sudler Associates. 1995 remodel and restoration, Guy Thornton. 818 Seventeenth Street, southwest corner of Stout Street, NR, HD-38

The First National Bank of Denver moved from the Equitable Building into this thirteen-story brick high-rise in 1911. Frank Edbrooke's nephew and employee, Harry W.J. Edbrooke, was the lead architect. Notwithstanding the Chicago style steel frame construction, the bank reflected the classical division of a building into a base, shaft, and capital (the structure of a classical column). The two-story base is clad in brownish pre-cast concrete, textured and colored to resemble granite, around enormous display windows. The base is separated by a prominent double cornice from the shaft—floors three through nine—which is clad in light brick. The capital, formed by the top three floors, has extensive terracotta trim and is topped by a bracketed metal cornice. Erected as the tallest and largest bank in Colorado, the First National Bank helped confirm Seventeenth Street's status as the "Wall Street of the Rockies."

When First National had Raymond Harry Ervin design a new twenty-eight-story home at 621 Seventeenth in 1958, it sold this building to the American National Bank. That bank had architect James Sudler add a then-stylish pre-cast concrete sunscreen, which hid the old building. In 1995 the sunscreen was stripped off and much of the original Edbrooke exterior was restored, as was the original interior light well, bringing natural light to a new drive-through entry court. Brothers Eric and Steve Holtze completed the $21 million remodel, assisted by the Denver Urban Renewal Authority and the State Historical Fund, converting the bank to the 250-room Magnolia Hotel. As a final reincarnation delight, the Holtzes reinstalled a large street-corner clock, the traditional symbol with which bankers advertised interest payments and reminded passersby by that "time is money."

18. Guaranty Bank Building

1921, William E. Fisher and Arthur A. Fisher. 1997 renovation, Fentress Bradburn. 815 Seventeenth Street, northwest corner of Stout Street, NR, HD-38

Denver entrepreneur John A. Ferguson replaced his three-story Century Building with this Chicago style commercial structure. Its sparse Neoclassical elements include paired Ionic pilasters and quoins cut into the smooth limestone skin. The US National Bank initially occupied the ground floor, with the upper eight stories leased for offices. The US National Bank merged with Denver National to become United Banks and moved to Seventeenth and Broadway (United later became Norwest, then Wells Fargo). In 1956 this building became the home of the Guaranty Bank and Trust Company. Landmark designation helped rescue this stately, if understated, edifice from the wrecking ball. The onetime haven for bankers was renovated for $10.9 million in 1997 as a residential 117-apartment loft complex.

19. Neusteter Building

ca. 1890. 1924 addition, William E. Fisher and Arthur A. Fisher. 1988 restoration and remodeling, Gensler and Associates. 720 Sixteenth Street, southeast corner of Stout Street, NR, HD-38

Max and Meyer Neusteter incorporated the three-story Hughes Block (ca. 1890) into this sleek 1924 expansion of their fashionable women's apparel store. This stone-sheathed, five-story brick building is given a horizontal emphasis by the wide bracketed eaves, clearly defined banding, and wide Chicago style windows. In 1941 Neusteter's expanded into the neighboring Coronado Building, 1540–44 Stout Street. In time, this popular and fashionable store acquired the rest of the Stout Street frontage to build a multi-story parking garage at Fifteenth and Stout Streets. The Neusteter family closed the store in 1985, but after an exterior restoration by Gensler and Associates and interior remodeling by John Carney and Associates, the building reopened in 1991 as condominiums above storefront retail shops.

20. US Post Office and Federal Building– Byron White Federal Courthouse

1916, Tracy, Swartwout, and Litchfield; Maurice Biscoe. 1963 renovation and restoration, Victor Hornbein and Edward D. White Jr. 1994 restoration, Michael Barber Associates. 1823 Stout Street, NR, HD-38

In the Neoclassical style favored by the federal government as befitting a vigorous young republic, this four-story Greek temple faced in Colorado Yule marble fills an entire block. On the building's Stout Street facade, sixteen three-story fluted Ionic columns form a heroic portico atop a

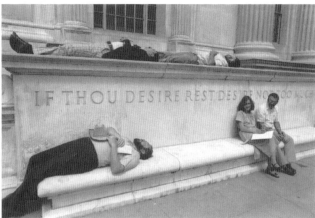

FIGURE 1.15. (a) US Post Office and Federal Building–Byron White Federal Courthouse (Photo by Glenn Cuerden). (b) This Colorado yule marble edifice discourages lounging with this inscription on its bench. (photo by Roger Whitacre).

cascading marble staircase. Gladys Caldwell Fisher, wife of Denver architect Alan Fisher, sculpted the granite bighorn sheep that flank the Eighteenth Street entrance. Indigents sometimes nap on the Eighteenth Street side's marble bench despite its carved admonition "If Thou Desire Rest, Desire Not Too Much." The US Postal Service surrendered this masterpiece to the federal judiciary, which lavished $28 million on the 1994 exterior and interior restoration while carving out four palatial federal courtrooms and renaming the edifice. President John F. Kennedy appointed Byron "Whizzer" White, a football star for the University of Colorado and a Rhodes Scholar, to the US Supreme Court in 1962. White, a native of Fort Collins, served on the highest court until his retirement in 1993. The building, now off-limits to the public, is arguably Colorado's finest rendition of a Greek temple.

21. Ideal Building–Denver National Bank–Colorado Business Bank

1907, Montana Fallis and John J. Stein. 1927, William E. Fisher and Arthur A. Fisher. 821 Seventeenth Street, northeast corner of Champa Street, NR, HD-38

For its headquarters, the Ideal Cement Company used the region's first major reinforced concrete structure. During construction, builder Charles Boettcher set the wooden frame forms on fire as a dramatic demonstration of the fact that his Ideal cement was fireproof. Subsequently, reinforced concrete became a popular way to build large buildings. In 1927 the first two floors were faced with Colorado travertine and the upper brick floors were stuccoed. Giant double bronze doors are adorned with bas-relief panels depicting Pueblo Indian ceremonies. A central two-story arch with an eagle keystone frames the entry, also guarded by buffalo busts. The Denver National Bank moved in and, along with the 1927 rear addition, redecorated the two-story lobby, whose ceiling is supported by steel columns simulating marble. An Arnold Ronnebeck frieze around the mezzanine illustrates the theme of money in history. Colorado Federal Bank remodeled the building as its home in the 1970s, and the Colorado Business Bank did a thorough restoration of the lobby after it moved in. The bank's huge basement safe has been converted to a private dining room within what is now a subterranean restaurant.

22. Boston Building–Boston Lofts

1890, Andrews, Jacques, and Rantoul. 1998 renovation. 822–30 Seventeenth Street, southeast corner of Champa Street, NR, HD-38

The Boston firm that designed the Equitable Building also produced this Richardsonian Romanesque nine-story red sandstone office building. Round-arched bays are repeated in smaller versions on the top two stories in pairs divided by colonnettes. Weathering of the red sandstone, quarried near Manitou Springs, forced removal of the original cornices, carved stringcourses, and other trim. The huge rusticated blocks of the base have been likewise shaved smooth to limit spalling. These huge building blocks are a reminder that this was one of the last tall masonry buildings constructed downtown. In 1998 the Boston Building was connected to the historic Kistler Building, and both were renovated to create the Boston Lofts, a $23.4 million renovation that created a 158-unit apartment building.

FIGURE 1.16. The Boston Building, ca. 1900 (a) and ca. 1990 (b) (photos by William Henry Jackson, History Colorado, and Roger Whitacre).

FIGURE 1.17. Odd Fellows Hall (photo by Tom Noel).

FIGURE 1.18. Denver Gas and Electric Building (photo by Louis C. McClure, Denver Public Library).

23. Odd Fellows Hall

1889, Emmett Anthony. 1983 renovation, Curt Fentress and Associates. 1543–45 Champa Street, HD-38

Colorado Union Lodge No. 1 of the International Order of Odd Fellows erected one of downtown's finest stone facades, rendered here with Eastlake trim. A pressed metal roof with cannonball finials, a scrolled cornice, and a corner tower crown the hall. A $3.4 million 1983 restoration provided new stone columns and encased in protective Lexan the grand third-story meeting-hall stained glass window incorporating the lodge's motto—the three links of "Friendship, Love, and Truth." Behind a dutiful facade restoration, architects rearranged the interior around a new sky-lighted atrium with a glass elevator and a set-back fourth floor. On the north elevation a ghost sign for the Dutch Mill commemorates the hall's longtime popular restaurant.

24. Denver Gas and Electric Building– Insurance Exchange Building

1910, Harry W.J. Edbrooke. 1990 restoration. 910 Fifteenth Street, corner of Champa Street, NR, HD-38

With 13,000 outlets for lightbulbs in the polished white terracotta skin, this is the brightest survivor of the "City of Lights" era, when Denver prided itself on the decorative illumination of its downtown. In this case the illumination attempted to brighten the dark public image of a monopoly that rigged elections to maintain its exclusive franchise. Harry W.J. Edbrooke, the son of Willoughby, began his architectural career in the Denver office of his uncle Frank. A 1990 restoration of what had been remodeled and renamed the Insurance Exchange Building uncovered the original ceiling and relit the dazzling geometric exterior light display. The arched tenth-story windows form an arcade beneath the flared cornice.

1855.   Wm. J. Bryan

Denver Auditorium——Where
Democratic Candidates were
Nominated, July 9-10, 1908

Jno. W. Kern

FIGURE 1.19. Denver Municipal Auditorium (Tom Noel Collection).

25. Denver Municipal Auditorium– Ellie Caulkins Opera House

1908, Robert Willison. 1941, G. Meredith Musick and Frederick E. Mountjoy. 1991 restoration, Semple Brown Roberts. 920 Fourteenth Street (between Champa and Curtis Streets), NR, HD-38

This Neoclassical marvel opened on July 4, 1908, to host the Democratic National Convention, the first national presidential election convention held west of the Mississippi. Second in size only to Madison Square Garden at the time, the auditorium of beige brick with terracotta trim borrowed much from a prototype auditorium in St. Paul, Minnesota. Seven thousand lightbulbs outlined the Denver edifice's pediments, domes, dentiled cornice, and quoins. The 12,000-seat hall could be converted to a 3,300-seat theater with a movable proscenium arch and walls lowered from the ceiling. Along with conventions and concerts, the auditorium has hosted everything from opera to auto shows, from basketball to wrestling, from high school graduations to Mayor Speer's funeral. The auditorium was expanded in 1941 to fill the entire block and received a facelift in the early 1990s, when part of it reopened as the Temple Hoyne Buell Theater. Buell, who reveled in architectural escapism, would probably enjoy the theater's neon accents and theatrical postmodern facade. The remodel included facade restoration and relighting of the exterior lightbulbs of what was renamed the Quigg Newton Denver Municipal Auditorium. The interior, after a radical modernization, became the Ellie Caulkins Opera House (2005). A vaulted clear plastic roof connects the auditorium to the multi-story parking garage, making a galleria (1978) of what was once the 1300 block of Curtis Street.

26. Baur's Confectionery Company

1881, Leonard Shaw. 1512–14 Curtis Street, NR, HD-38

Denver's most notable and longest-lasting maker of candies, cakes, and other sweet treats, Baur's Confectionery Company operated in this three-story red brick, Italianate style building from 1891 until 1951. German immigrant Otto Paul Baur founded this family business in 1871 as a confectionery, which later expanded into a soda shop, restaurant, and catering operation. Baur's became "famous for good things to eat," as its motto declared. Baur's became celebrated for its ice cream and cakes, to which it treated the city's children at a party each year. Baur's claimed to have invented the ice cream soda, supposedly as a cure for hangovers. Baur's ice cream was shipped throughout the United States as a delicacy treat. After Baur's death in 1904, his nephew John Joseph Jacobs took over the business. Jacobs added the restaurant in 1918 and made it famous for its deviled crab entrée and chocolate Mija pie. By the 1950s this popular place had branches downtown and in the Cherry Creek Shopping Center. After Baur's closed around 1970, various restaurants operated out of its generous first-floor space, with offices in the upper two stories. Baur's large restored neon sign is the sole survivor of many such signs and marquis dating to Curtis Street's heyday as Denver's theater row, when it was the brightest-lit street in the Rocky Mountain West.

27. Twentieth Street Bathhouse/Gym

1908, Robert Willison. 1011 Twentieth Street, northwest corner of Curtis Street, HD-38

To scrub away some of Denver's pungent frontier heritage, Mayor Robert W. Speer built the first municipal bathhouse, which also contains a gym, poolroom, and recreational center. The brick building with sparse Neoclassical frosting is still open to the public for a variety of recreational programs. This structure commemorates the Progressive-Era commitment to improve the lives of all citizens, including the unwashed poor, who bathed for free.

28. Daniels and Fisher Tower

1911, Frederick J. Sterner and George H. Williamson. 1981 restoration, Gensler and Associates. 1995 and 2003 restoration, David Tryba Architects. 1101 Sixteenth Street, NR, HD-38

This 325-foot tower is loosely modeled on the campanile of St. Mark's Cathedral in Venice. It typifies the efforts of American cities to imitate and update European monuments. The *Denver Times* gloated that, thanks to the flagpole, this tower was 6 feet taller than its Italian prototype. The tower was once the corner beacon for Daniels and Fishers, the city's finest department store. It narrowly escaped the Skyline Urban Renewal Project demolition that erased the rest of the structure and much of old downtown

FIGURE 1.20. Daniels and Fisher Tower and Pat Oliphant's August 20, 1965, cartoon helped awaken citizens to the threatened demolition of downtown's premier landmark (*Denver Post* photos).

Denver. Mismatched brick indicates where the demolished wings were attached. This first major victory for Denver preservationists represented a turnaround toward restoring buildings rather than demolishing them. Blond brick and creamy terracotta cover a steel skeleton set on a 24-foot-deep concrete foundation for the 40-foot square tower. Protruding cornices set off an arcaded observation deck topped by Seth Thomas clocks with 6-foot hands. A two-and-a-half ton bell occupies the two uppermost stories.

Restoration workers found an urn containing the ashes of the dreamer behind this Renaissance Revival apparition, William Cooke Daniels, the dilettante son of the company's co-founder. From conception to completion, the tower was his project—and his tombstone. David Owen Tryba, an architect whose offices were in the tower during the 1990s, restored the top in 1995, re-gilding the gold domed bell tower. Additional restoration completed in 2003 has made this one of Denver's showcase preservation projects with a reincarnation of the gilded entry, entry lamps, and trim as well as the Della Robbia style medallions. Ornate exterior lighting makes the tower a nocturnal spectacle, especially at Christmastime. A basement cabaret, various offices, and a top-story special events space have brought the tower back to life night and day.

29. Denver Tramway Company–Hotel Teatro

1912, William E. Fisher and Arthur A. Fisher. 1999 restoration, David Tyrba Architects. 1100 Fourteenth Street, corner of Arapahoe Street, NR, HD-38

The family of territorial governor John Evans demolished its pioneer home to use the site to build the corporate offices of the streetcar monopoly headed by his son, William Gray Evans. Renaissance Revival–inspired trim in white terracotta climbs the eight-story red brick tower, from the street-front arches to a top-floor frieze with the tramway's T logo. The brass entry lamps hint at the interior opulence of a lobby, with pink Tennessee marble floors, green Vermont marble trim where the walls join the floor, and wainscoting of white Arizona marble. Marble trim, handsome hardwoods, and bronze fixtures survive throughout the tower. In 1957 the tower and the three-story attached streetcar barns were converted to the University of Colorado's Denver campus. After CU-Denver moved out, the interior was remodeled and the exterior restored for a renaissance as the Hotel Teatro. A new set-back ninth story perfectly echoes the trim below. The car barn attached to the tower/hotel is now occupied by the Denver Center Theater Company.

30. Hover-Bromley Building

1901, Robert S. Roeschlaub. 1348 Lawrence Street, southeast corner of Fourteenth Street, HD-38

William A. Hover, a prominent wholesale druggist, erected this commercial Renaissance Revival style building, the last intact commercial design by Roeschlaub in Denver. In the 1960s the building was converted to the library for the University of Colorado's Denver campus, and a connection to the Tramway Building was added. At that time the building was renamed for CU regent Jim Bromley.

31. Denver City Cable Railway Building

1889. 1974 renovation, E. James Judd. 1215 Eighteenth Street, corner of Lawrence Street, HD-38

Denver's once extensive cable car network had its corporate offices, car barns, and power plant in this two-story brick building. The Romanesque Revival edifice wears a variety of brick patterns, courses, corbelling, and trim in a brick mason's tour-de-force. Pairs of round-arched windows occupy round corbelled insets and echo the two-story arched, recessed grand entry. Ornate brickwork also distinguishes the 110-foot smokestack, which was shorted 10 feet by a lightning strike. Denver engineer Judd saved the structure from demolition and restored what had been converted to a garage to second-story offices and a first-floor restaurant with a magnificent Neoclassical back bar and what claims to be Denver's longest-front bar. Vintage cable car no. 54 serves as an intimate dining room.

FIGURE 1.21. The Denver Tramway Company and the Daniels and Fisher Tower are racing to completion in this 1911 construction shot (Tom Noel Collection).

Larimer Square Historic District

HD-1 LARIMER SQUARE HISTORIC DISTRICT

1870s and 1880s. 1965, Langdon Morris. 1990s, Semple Brown Roberts. 1400 block of Larimer Street, NRD

Larimer Square, like Larimer Street, is named for William H. Larimer Jr., who founded Denver on November 22, 1858. The 1400 block of Larimer Street features a creative adaptation and reuse of antique brick buildings with cast iron storefronts, metal cornices, and ornamental stonework. The eighteen commercial structures have been opened with cut-throughs, recessed facades, interior courts, and open basements. This effort to spare this face block from Denver Urban Renewal Authority bulldozers proved successful enough to inspire the rejuvenation of the rest of Lower Downtown. It also preserves some of Denver's earliest commercial buildings, with the oldest structures dating to the 1870s. Landgon Morris, the original preservation architect, was a member of the Denver Landmark Preservation Commission. Dana Crawford organized Larimer Square Associates to restore and renovate the block. "Back in its skid row days," Crawford's son Jack reminisced in 2009, "Mother used to drive me and my little brothers through the Larimer Square alleys. We were terrified when bums would surround the car but she just sped up and told us: 'You boys will have to get used to them for the time being.'"

32. Apollo Hall–Congdon Building

1870s. 1960s restoration. 1421–25 Larimer Street, HD-1

Libeus Barney, a shrewd and literarily inclined Vermonter, built a two-story frame structure on this site. He kept a saloon downstairs and a hall upstairs that hosted early theater performances and the initial meetings of Denver's first vigilante city government. Barney, in his posthumously published *Letters of the Pike's Peak Gold Rush*, claimed he found a small fortune in gold dust by sweeping up his tavern floor. For much of the twentieth century, the two-story 1870s brick structure that replaced Apollo Hall housed the Schaefer Tent and Awning Company. After the 1960s restoration, the building was named for Tom and Noel Congdon, early principals in the Larimer Square project. Since the 1970s, a food market and coffee bar have occupied the street floor.

FIGURE 1.22. Dana Crawford initiated Larimer Square to rescue one face block of old Denver from the Denver Urban Renewal Authority's wrecking ball. Here she leads Mayor Tom Currigan and a delegation of city councilmen on a tour of the 1400 block of Larimer Street, 1965 (photo by Jim Milmoe).

FIGURE 1.23. In this 1861 William G. Chamberlain photo of what today is Larimer Square, Apollo Hall is the frame building with a balcony where Denver's first city government was conceived, born, and raised. The Congdon Building is now on that site (Denver Public Library).

FIGURE 1.24. Granite Hotel, 1978 (photo by Jim Milmoe).

33. Clayton Building–Granite Hotel

1882. 1456–60 Larimer Street, corner of East Fifteenth Street, HD-1

George Washington Clayton acquired city founder William Larimer's 1858 log cabin in 1859, put a frame false front on it, and opened a general store. In 1882 Clayton replaced his shop with this handsome five-story corner edi-

fice, which he built with his brother, William M. Clayton, the mayor of Denver from 1868 to 1869. The Claytons are memorialized by the inscribed stone atop the angled entry of this colorful cornerstone of Larimer Square, with its red-orange sandstone, lighter rhyolite blocks, and gray granite pillars. Converted to the Granite Hotel and then to shops and offices, it retains its original skylight, several stained glass windows, and cast iron columns.

34. Gahan's Saloon–Miller Building– Ted's Montana Grill

1889. 1401–7 Larimer Street, northwest corner of Fourteenth Street, HD-1

City councilman John Gahan Sr. welcomed constituents and politicians alike to his groggery. Both groups flocked there from City Hall, which once stood across the street on a site commemorated by the bell from the old tower. Gahan's switched to soft drinks during Prohibition and was reopened by John Jr. as a saloon and restaurant after the Prohibition Amendment was repealed in 1933. Numerous saloons and restaurants have followed Gahan's. This three-story red brick building boasts red sandstone trim, brick corbelling, and cast iron columns framing plate-glass storefronts.

35. Gallup-Stanbury Building

1873. 1445–51 Larimer Street, HD-1

In the Tambien Saloon, opened on this site by Avery Gallup and Andrew Stanbury, western artist Charles Stewart Stobie raffled several of his landscapes and portraits of Ute Indians to help pay his bar tab. The false-front saloon was replaced by this three-story brick Italianate building decorated with stone and cast iron pilasters that blossom into metal flowers. The makeshift frame parapet is a duplicate of the original, a Gilded Age gimmick to embellish the facade.

36. Hotel Hope

ca. 1888. 1993 addition, Semple Brown Roberts. 1404 Larimer Street, northeast corner of Fourteenth Street, HD-1

A metal frieze atop the third story of this building has a distinctive off-center pediment surmounted by a peculiar curved parapet with a central finial. Numerous storefront businesses and hotels have occupied the brick structure over the years, with the Hotel Hope the most memorable long-term occupant. In 1993 a one-story addition was made to the southwest side of the building, erasing a parking lot and carrying the structure to Fourteenth Street. The addition's red brick and cast red stone match masonry construction typical of Larimer Square. The 1993 addition is topped by an outdoor deck along the old brick sidewall of the Hotel Hope, giving customers sunshine, fresh air, and views of Larimer Square, the Auraria campus, and the Rocky Mountains beyond.

FIGURE 1.25. The Gallup-Stanbury Building crowns this 1875 photo by George Chamberlain. The 1995 photo shows less exuberant finials (photos by George Chamberlain [1875] and Tom Noel [1995]).

37. McKibben Building

ca. 1890. 1411 Larimer Street, HD-1

Constructed in the commercial Victorian style, this two-story stuccoed brick building sports keystoned arched windows on Denver's original 25- by 125-foot standard lots. Over the years it has housed a millinery shop, physicians, a cigar and tobacco emporium, the Board of Trade, a grocery, and a sheet metal works. With the opening of Larimer Square the building has housed upscale boutique shops and restaurants.

38. Barnum Building

1889. 1412 Larimer Street, HD-1

This handsome three-story brick building replaced the undertaking business of John J. Whalley, a cabinetmaker drafted to make Denver's first coffins for victims of lead poisoning and rope burn. Numerous businesses and upper-floor hotels conducted business here over the decades. With the creation of Larimer Square, the building became second- and third-floor offices and the first-floor Gusterman's Silversmiths.

39. Lincoln Hall

Early 1880s. 1887 and 1891 remodels. 1413–19 Larimer Street, HD-1

This two-story Second Empire brick building gained a stylish mansard third story in 1887, along with a dance floor suspended from cables for more bounce. Lincoln Hall became a rowdy, notorious dance hall. To the relief of Denver police, in 1891 the building was converted to the Fred Mueller Harness Shop, which remained there until the 1960s with the slogan "Stick to a Mueller Saddle."

40. Kettle Building

1873. 1990 remodel, Semple Brown Roberts. 1422–26 Larimer Street, HD-1

George Kettle's butcher shop, the oldest building in Larimer Square, is only twenty feet wide, with a cut stone facade and a fancy molded cornice. The tiny shop's first floor was gutted in 1990 to create an arcade leading to a rear courtyard. Above the native sandstone walls, a vaulted stucco ceiling features a mural (1988, Evans and Brown) depicting early Denver characters. The San Francisco artists fancifully portrayed General Larimer prospecting with a Greek urn.

41. Sussex Building

1880. 1430 Larimer Street, HD-1

This four-story brick structure, trimmed in both smooth and rough-cut red-orange sandstone, has a cast iron storefront that has housed various businesses over the years. This Chicago commercial style structure is capped with a large cornice. Larimer Square Associates enhanced access in the mid-1960s by constructing rear access and a rear arcade.

42. Crawford Building

1875. 1437–41 Larimer Street, HD-1

This rare Denver specimen of the Second Empire style was renamed to honor Dana Crawford, who spearheaded Larimer Square's rehabilitation. "I used to go antiquing in the old pawnshops down on Larimer," she explained. "Then one day I noticed that these buildings themselves were fabulous antiques." Opulent detailing includes the ornate cast iron columns (made by the Union Foundry in Chicago), second-story lintels with scalloped and broken pediments, and a grandiose pressed metal frieze, large bracketed cornice, and scalloped parapet.

FIGURE 1.26. Crawford Building (photo by Tom Noel).

Lower Downtown Historic District

HD-15 LOWER DOWNTOWN HISTORIC DISTRICT

Cherry Creek to Twentieth Street between Market and Wynkoop Streets

Before the city designated this historic district in 1988, demolitions were reducing Lower Downtown to little more than parking lots for the Central Business District. Market Street, its southeastern boundary, was Denver's red-light district between the 1870s and 1912. Today, many of the old taverns, bordellos, and warehouses have been rehabilitated, and the Lower Downtown Historic District has become Denver's drinking, dining, and partying hub. Many warehouses have been converted to lofts in what has also become a trendy residential area. An outstanding example of sympathetic infill is the Cactus Club (1990, Peter H. Dominick Jr.), 1621 Blake Street, a private club that borrows inspiration from the two-story Oxford Hotel addition on Wazee Street.

43. Wells Fargo Building

ca. 1874. 1338 Fifteenth Street, HD-15

This pioneer stagecoach office is a reminder that Denver became the territory's transportation hub even before the arrival of the railroads. Well-armed guards rode shotgun on the stages leaving with gold. This much-altered one-story

FIGURE 1.27. Wells Fargo Building (Denver Public Library).

red brick building on a rusticated rhyolite foundation has unusual Gothic arch portals. Parts of the 1866 stagecoach depot may survive in a structure that received a second-story addition (since removed) during the 1870s. Ben Holladay, for whom Market Street was once named, opened this as his stage depot but sold out to Wells Fargo in 1866.

Colorado Bakery and Saloon

ca. 1863, Frederick C. Eberley. 1989 restoration, Larry Nelson. 1440–44 Market Street, HD-15

This is a particularly fine revival of what may be Denver's oldest store. Tall, arched, second-story Italianate windows, cast iron fronts, generous glass storefronts, and a bracketed metal cornice typify the first generation of Denver's brick business buildings.

FIGURE 1.28. The Columbia Hotel (*far left*) and the Hitchings Block (*far right*) bookend the six landmark buildings in Market Center. These representatives of the original mining boom are dwarfed by oil boom high-rises behind them (photo by Roger Whitacre).

44. Hitchings Block

1893. 1620 Market Street, HD-15

The Reverend Horace B. Hitchings, a wealthy New Yorker who became rector (1862–68) of Denver's St. John's in the Wilderness Episcopal Church, built this four-story brick investment property, with a pediment inscribed with his name and the date of construction. In recent decades, restaurants and nightclubs have occupied the basement and ground floor, with offices upstairs. This is a cornerstone of a row of six buildings restored in the 1980s as Market Center, a rejuvenated retail and office complex that provides a striking brick and stone foreground for downtown's newer glass, metal, and concrete towers.

45. Liebhardt-Lindner Building

1881. 1624 Market Street, HD-15

Gustavus C. Liebhardt built this headquarters for the Liebhardt Brothers Commission Company, which supplied Denver with California fresh fruit, as well as flowers from the Liebhardts' thirty-six-acre Rose Acres Farms at 6320 West Twenty-Sixth Avenue. In 1937 the Lindner Packing and Provision Company, a meatpacking and wholesale meat market, moved into the Liebhardt Building. Lindner's later became Mapelli's Meats, then Sigman Meats, and then part of Greeley's huge Monfort/Swift Meat Company. Handsomely remodeled inside for restaurant use, the building retains some of the meatpacking apparatus as interior decor. On the imposing facade, an intricate cornice overshadows a corbelled frieze.

46. McCrary Building

1889. 1634–38 Market Street, HD-15

Napoleon Bonaparte McCrary built this structure for his wholesale grocery firm. The third story, with its round-arch windows, gives the facade an arcade feeling. Recessed spandrels separating the second-story windows further the illusion. Roundels above the pilaster add to the rhythmic elegance of this restored gem.

47. Waters Building

1888. 1642 Market Street, HD-15

This three-story red brick Italianate structure is symmetrically divided into three bays with corresponding upper-story windows and divisions in the bracketed metal cornice, with Thomas Waters's name in the parapet.

48. Bockfinger-Flint Mercantile

1885. 1644–50 Market Street, HD-15

Stripped of its cornice and less ornate than its sister buildings, this mercantile shop maintains the scale and continuity of a rare intact row of late-nineteenth-century commercial buildings.

49. Columbia Hotel

1880, Frank Goodnow. 1981 renovation, SLP Architects.
1322–50 Seventeenth Street, southeast corner of Market Street, HD-15

Remnants of an ambitious pressed metal cornice, elegant brick corbelling, and stone lintels have survived two fires and much neglect of this four-story red brick edifice. James A. Duff, a Scottish entrepreneur representing British investors organized as the Colorado Mortgage and Investment Company, financed what was originally a stylish Italianate office building. It was converted to a hotel in 1892. Cornices and corbelling separate the four floors, while brick piers further break the facade into recessed storefronts and bays. After several decades as a flophouse with a first-floor tavern, the building was revamped for offices in the 1980s as part of Market Center.

50. Mattie Silks House

1886. 1990s remodel. 2009 Market Street, HD-15

Market Street roughly between Nineteenth and Twenty-First Streets served as Denver's red-light district from the 1870s until 1912, when reformers closed the district with its "brides of the multitude." Market Street was so notorious that property owners above Twenty-Third Street and on the Auraria side of Cherry Creek had their segments renamed Walnut Street. Mattie Silks came to Denver in 1876, where she outperformed and outlived her rivals, dying in 1929 at age eighty-three and buried in Denver's Fairmount Cemetery under the name Martha A. Ready. 2009 Market was one of several bordellos, most notably the 1942 Market House of Mirrors as well as 2015 Market, operated by Silks. The 2009 building was rehabilitated in the 1990s for use as a law office. All now converted to other uses, these are rare survivors of an endangered building type—the whorehouse.

Another of Silks's bordellos is the most notorious building in the LoDo District—the House of Mirrors. Silks's great rival, Madame Jennie Rogers, built it in 1886 at 1942 Market Street, the most elegant of the bordellos and the only known building in Denver specifically designed to be a brothel. When Jennie Rogers died in 1909, the building was purchased by Mattie Silks. She ran it until reformers closed down the red-light district in 1912. The former brothel became the Tri-State Buddhist Temple, then a warehouse, and most recently a special events venue.

51. Windsor Stables and Storefront–Blake Street Bath and Racquet Club

1886, John W. Roberts? 1978 renovation, William Saslow. 1732–72 Blake Street, southeast corner of East Eighteenth Avenue, HD-15

At this location stood a service building and stables for the Windsor Hotel (demolished 1959) two blocks away at 1800 Larimer Street. John W. Roberts, an architect who worked on New York City's Trinity Church, came to Denver in 1879 specifically to design Denver's finest hotel of the 1880s, and he probably worked on this structure as well. William Saslow renovated it in 1978 as one of the first residential-retail units in the then slummy Union Station neighborhood. Saslow renamed it the Blake Street Bath and Racquet Club after converting the rear stables area to a tennis court and swimming pool for residents of the units above the storefronts.

52. Barth Hotel

1882, Frederick C. Eberley. 1980s restoration, Long Hoeft Architects. 1514 Seventeenth Street, southwest corner of Blake Street, NR, HD-15

Built as the Union Wholesale Liquor warehouse, this structure became the Union Hotel in 1890. It was revamped and renamed the Elk Hotel in 1905, as a bronze plaque in the sidewalk reminds pedestrians. M. Allen Barth purchased the hotel in 1931 and renamed it the Barth. Fifty years later, Senior Housing Options, Inc., acquired the Barth and restored it as one of the few efforts to retain cheap, subsidized housing for the elderly poor being displaced by gentrification in what was Skid Row until the 1980s. This four-story red brick edifice features Italianate arched and paired upper-level windows, stone banding and window trim, and a prominent bracketed metal cornice.

53. Constitution Hall (site)

1865. 1870s addition. 1501–7 Blake Street, northwest corner of Fifteenth Street, HD-15

The original two-story red brick First National Bank had a street-level arcade matched by second-story round-arched windows. White sandstone arches with keystones adorned both openings. The Odd Fellows built a mansard third-story addition in the Second Empire mode in the early 1870s for use as their lodge hall. Delegates met there to draft a constitution for Colorado statehood in 1876. This landmark later became the Stores Restaurant Equipment Supply Company, which a disgruntled former employee burned down in 1977.

54. Barney Ford Building

1863, 1875, 1889, Frederick C. Eberley. 1983 restoration, James C. Morgan, Paul Foster, and Cab Childress. 1512–14 Blake Street, NR, HD-15

Only parts of Barney Ford's Restaurant, a two-story brick building, survive within this much altered structure, now three stories with square stone lintels and sills. Barney Ford, Colorado's best-known African American pioneer, became a successful businessman and a leading spokesman for his people. The son of a slave and a plantation master father, he escaped the South by way of the Underground Railroad and came to Colorado in 1860. Ford's original 1862 saloon and barbershop on this site was destroyed by the great fire of 1863. He replaced it with a new $9,000 structure boasting a basement barbershop, ground-floor restaurant, and upstairs saloon hall. Ford would appreciate the building's restoration for use as a restaurant.

55. Oxford Hotel

1891. 1902 additions, Frank E. Edbrooke. 1983 restoration, William Muchow and Associates. 1600–12 Seventeenth Street, southwest corner of Wazee Street, NR, HD-15

Denver's oldest operating hotel opened two years before Edbrooke's masterpiece, the Brown Palace Hotel, was completed at the other end of Seventeenth Street. The original

FIGURE 1.29. Oxford Hotel (Denver Public Library).

five-story red brick structure was built on a U plan, with a two-story addition (1902) on Wazee that used the same facade detailing.

To celebrate the repeal of Prohibition in 1933, the Oxford had Denver architect G. Charles Jaka design a Streamline Moderne cocktail lounge, the Cruise Room (1935). Flowing lines shape the front bar, booths, and ceiling. The walls are paneled with beaverboard bas-relief portraits by Denver artist Alley Henson of prominent people from various nations raising toasts in their own languages. The Oxford Hotel Annex (1912, Montana Fallis and Robert Willison), 1628 Seventeenth Street, is the same height as the hotel, but the entire facade is elaborately detailed white terracotta, an echo of the Belle Époque. Dana Crawford and Charles Calloway spearheaded the Oxford's restoration and 1983 reopening as a boutique hotel furnished with antiques.

56. Denver City Railway Company–Sheridan Heritage Building–Streetcar Lofts

1883. 1892 remodel, Harold and Viggio Baerresen. 1994 renovation, Urban Design Group. 1635 Seventeenth Street, corner of Wynkoop Street, NR, HD-15

The four-story false front of red brick with rhyolite trim exemplifies the architectural ambitions of the Gilded Age. This three-story horse car barn and corporate headquarters for an early-day streetcar firm poses as a grandiose stone and brick edifice. For much of the twentieth century the building served as the home of Hendrie and Bolthoff, one of the world's largest manufacturers of mining machinery. In 1994 a $9 million Sheridan Heritage project brought retail development to the ground floor with forty-three loft apartments above. Star-shaped tie rods help relate the top-story expansion to the original edifice.

57. Union Station

1881, William E. Taylor. 1895, Van Brunt and Howe. 1912, Aaron M. Gove and Thomas F. Walsh. 2014 hotel conversion, David Tryba Architects. 1701–77 Wynkoop Street, NR, HD-15

The centerpiece of LoDo is this Beaux Arts Italian Renaissance apparition at the lower end of Seventeenth Street. The New York tycoon Jay Gould and local entrepreneur Walter Scott Cheesman put together a multi-block parcel to give Denver a consolidated train station. Taylor, a Kansas City architect, planned the original depot, with a

FIGURE 1.30. Union Station (Tom Noel Collection).

new central section from the Kansas City firm of Van Brunt and Howe in 1895 after a fire. That firm switched from the Second Empire style to the more up-to-date Italianate mode. Their central hall was demolished in 1912, with an update and expansion of the central hall in the Beaux Arts mode. The 1880 wings remain Italianate in rusticated rhyolite with limestone trim. Union Station anchors Seventeenth Street, the "Wall Street of the Rockies," which since the 1880s has been lined with many of the city's tallest banks, hotels, and office buildings.

The depot's great hall still evokes the golden age of railroading, when Denver became the regional metropolis by reaching out to a vast Rocky Mountain rail hinterland. Rusticated pink-gray rhyolite from Castle Rock and pale gray sandstone trim from Morrison sheathed the original Second Empire edifice, the largest and most stylish building in Denver at the time. Gove and Walsh, a Denver firm that also designed many of the Wynkoop Street warehouses around Union Station, designed the 1912 Beaux Arts Neoclassical expansion. They used a granite exterior wainscoting that rises to a terracotta skin textured and colored to resemble the granite. Grand round-arched windows flood the main hall with natural light. Amtrak and the Regional Transportation District still offer rail passenger service here. A 2014 conversion to a luxury hotel named for preservationist Dana Crawford revitalized the station while retaining most of its historical integrity. The once vast maze of tracks west of the station has been converted to a multi-modal train, bus, bicycle, and pedestrian hub, with soaring overhead white fabric awnings in a state-of-the-art

FIGURE 1.31. John Wright Hickenlooper Jr. (shown here) and partners opened Colorado's first brew pub in the venerable John S. Brown Mercantile warehouse (Tom Noel Collection).

transit center designed by Skidmore Owings Merrill, the famous Chicago architectural team.

John S. Brown Mercantile–Wynkoop Brewing Company

1899, Aaron Gove and Thomas F. Walsh. 1988 restoration, Joe Simmons. 1634 Eighteenth Street, southeast corner of Wynkoop Street, NR, HD-15

The John S. Brown Mercantile warehouse rises in recessed window bays to fifth-story round arches that echo the large street windows. Exterior walls of the former wholesale grocery warehouse are red pressed brick, with sandstone trim and a quartzite foundation. The original interior was finished in Oregon pine and oak, with maple floors. In 1988 the building was remodeled as Colorado's first brewpub, with a second-floor pool hall. Pressed metal ceilings on the first and second floors help shield upper-level condominiums from the brewpub and pool hall hubbub below. John Wright Hickenlooper Jr. led the team that created this popular brewpub, from which he launched successful campaigns to become mayor of Denver (2002–10) and governor of Colorado (2011–present).

58. Littleton Creamery–Beatrice Foods Cold Storage–Ice House Lofts

1903, 1912, Aaron Gove and Thomas F. Walsh. 1916 addition, Frederick E. Mounjoy and Park M. French. 1998 restoration, Asset Investment Management. 1801 Wynkoop Street, NR, HD-15

Designed by a prominent Denver firm, this five-story building exemplifies early-twentieth-century industrial Renaissance Revival architecture, represented by the large stone voussoirs on the first floor. The intricate diamond-patterned polychrome brickwork along the fifth floor is echoed in Coors Field two blocks up north Wynkoop Street. Built in 1903 by the Littleton Creamery, the original five-story building produced butter in the basement, housed offices on the first floor, and used floors two through five as the largest cold storage facility in the Rocky Mountain region. In 1912 the Beatrice Creamery purchased the warehouse and added a 1912 five-story structure on the northeast side and a second 1916 five-story structure adjacent to the second addition. Beatrice Creamery used this location until 1979, when the warehouse closed. In 1998 it was renovated as the Ice House Lofts, for which unobtrusive windows were cut into the southwest elevation.

59. Spice and Commission Warehouse–Edward W. Wynkoop Building

1901, Aaron M. Gove and Thomas F. Walsh. 1980 renovation, Frank Zancanella. 1738 Wynkoop Street, HD-15

Dr. Emanuel and Joanne Salzman restored the four-story red brick Spice and Commission Warehouse, naming it for the pioneer sheriff Edward Wynkoop, who also gave his name to the street fronting Union Station. In 1980 the Salzmans and architect Frank Zancanella remodeled the interior for offices, the Salzman residence, and a roof garden. "When we converted this to LoDo's first loft, the area was Skid Row and mostly vacancies and vagrants," reports Dr. Salzman, former chief of radiology at Denver General Hospital. "There weren't enough people around to support a mugger. Joanne and I were impressed with my brother's loft in SoHo back in New York and decided to try the same thing here in Denver."

60. Hose Company No. 1

ca. 1883. 1963 Chestnut Street, southwest corner of Twentieth Street

Volunteer firefighters once tended horse and hose cars in one of Denver's oldest surviving fire stations. The Denver Fire Department became professional shortly after moving into this structure in 1884 and remained there until it moved to a new station in 1895. The red brick edifice with a corbeled cornice and twin, two-story arched bays is one of the few relics of the once teeming riverside neighborhood known as "the Bottoms," where shacks and shanties presented a fire hazard. Teeming once again in the 2000s, it is now an upscale area of pricey apartments, lofts, and retail businesses.

61. Moffat Station

1906, Edwin H. Moorman. 2101 Fifteenth Street, NR

This Neoclassical Revival brick box trimmed with lighter brick, concrete, limestone, and distinctive metal globe finials is a relic of David H. Moffat's railroad empire. With his Denver, Salt Lake, & Pacific Railroad (better known as the Moffat Road), he hoped to give Denver a line west through the mountains to the Pacific Coast. This dream earned Moffat the enmity of Union Pacific and Santa Fe Railroad barons, who did not want competition to erode their lucrative Colorado business. They squeezed Moffat out of Union Station, forcing him to build his own depot. The Moffat Road used this passenger and freight station until abandoning it in 1947, when the Denver & Rio Grande Railroad acquired the Moffat line. Moffat Station sat vacant and forlorn for decades, still ostracized from Union Station activity. Not until 2014 did Balfour at Riverfront Park restore the station as the social center of a multi-block residential development for independent living, assisted living, and nursing home care.

Auraria Area

Roughly bounded by Cherry Creek, West Tenth Avenue, and the South Platte River.

William Greeneberry Russell, his brothers Joseph Oliver and Levi, and a few other prospectors from Auraria, Georgia, founded Auraria City on November 1, 1858. They named their "city" with a Latin word for gold, the heavy metal they had found that summer in Cherry Creek and the South Platte River.

Their discovery launched the Colorado gold rush, a mass migration of an estimated 100,000 fortune seekers to what quickly became Denver City and Colorado Territory. Auraria's rival, Denver City, founded November 22, 1858, on the northeast bank of Cherry Creek, merged with Auraria in 1860. After the railroads arrived in the 1870s, Denver's oldest neighborhood evolved into a mixed residential, retail, and industrial area. During the 1970s it became a target of the Denver Urban Renewal Authority. Much of the Auraria neighborhood north of West Colfax Avenue was demolished to clear land for the 171-acre Auraria Higher Education Center, which houses the Community College of Denver, Metropolitan State University of Denver, and the University of Colorado Denver.

The Denver Landmark Preservation Commission, in one of its first major campaigns, used designation to save three Auraria churches, the Tivoli Brewery, and homes in what is now the Ninth Street Historic Park from urban renewal bulldozers. Historic Denver, Inc., a private preservation group founded in 1970, restored a full block of nineteenth-century homes on Ninth Street and donated the reconstructed block to what has become the most populous campus in Colorado, with more than 46,000 students.

HD-3 NINTH STREET PARK HISTORIC DISTRICT

Ninth Street between Champa and Curtis Streets, NR

One of Denver's oldest surviving residential face blocks consists of a corner store and thirteen middle-class dwellings with restored exteriors and renovated interiors now used for Auraria campus offices. The pavement of Ninth Street has been replaced with grass, but the original granite curbs and red sandstone sidewalks remain. Two of the dwellings are 1870s frame houses that pre-date early Denver ordinances mandating masonry construction. No one rich or famous lived in this typical nineteenth-century block complete with corner store, making it an unusual landmark district celebrating common folk.

The Knight House (1885), 1015 Ninth Street, with its mansard roof and tower, was the castle of Stephen Knight, a pioneer miller. His descendants, who became prominent in Denver banking, business, education, and political circles, helped restore one of Denver's best examples of the Second Empire style.

Another Second Empire model, the Witte House (1883), 1027 Ninth Street, retains its crested entry tower. The Madden-Schultz Duplex (1890, Jason J. Backus, builder), 1045–47 Ninth Street, is the simple two-story brick house of Eugene Madden, a Larimer Street saloonkeeper who served as the area's councilman from 1918 until his death in 1941. The Groussman Grocery (1906, Frederick C. Eberley), 1067 Ninth Street, is a two-story corner store with distinctive brickwork detail and globe finials. The Jewish family of Albert B. Groussman, who lived upstairs, operated this corner grocery, a typical cornerstone of nineteenth-century neighborhoods. Descendants helped fund restoration for what is now a campus café.

The Smedley House–Casa Mayan (ca. 1872), 1020 Ninth Street, a very early frame residence, retains its original bracketed eaves, but it is much altered and has a reconstructed porch. William Smedley, a Quaker dentist from Pennsylvania, built what later became the Casa Mayan restaurant, a social center for the Hispanic community. Ramon and Caroline Gonzales lived upstairs with their seven children, who helped run the street-level dining rooms. Casa Mayan was one of the first restaurants to introduce Mexican food, as well as music and dance, to non-Hispanics. Margaritas and Mexican culture served here helped bridge the chasm between Spanish- and English-speaking Denverites.

Restraint heightens the impact of detail on the Davis House (ca. 1873), 1068 Ninth Street, an Italianate dwelling with Carpenter Gothic porch woodwork. Houses at 1061, 1041, and 1024 Ninth Street are also Italianate. This handsome block from the past, with structures restored at twenty dollars per square foot, outshines the campus's bland newer brick buildings, erected for thirty dollars per square foot during the 1980s.

62. Golda Meir House

1911. 1146 Ninth Street, HD-3

This single-story flat-roofed duplex of pressed red brick with a corbelled and stepped parapet is a type so humble and common that it is generally overlooked. The restored dwelling, made significant by the residency of Golda Meir, a Jewish American who became the first female prime minister of Israel, was moved to Ninth Street from 1606–8 Julian Street in the working-class neighborhood of "Little Israel" along West Colfax Avenue.

FIGURE 1.32. Golda Meir, the first female prime minister of Israel, lived in this house, inspiring admirers to move the house to save and restore it (Tom Noel Collection).

63. Emmanuel Sherith Chapel–Student Art Gallery

1877. 1970s renovation, Gale Abels and Associates. 1201 Tenth Street, NR

Denver's oldest ecclesiastical edifice is a rhyolite Gothic Revival vernacular chapel built for an Episcopal congregation. In 1903 the chapel was purchased by some of the many East European Jews moving into the West Colfax neighborhood "Little Israel." A Star of David on the roof and a

Hebrew inscription over the entry commemorate the chapel's fifty-five years as a synagogue. Closed as a synagogue in 1958, it is now a student art gallery for the Auraria campus. This modest structure was dedicated Denver Landmark No. 1 in 1968, to be followed by more than 330 other landmarks.

64. St. Cajetan's Catholic Church

1926, Robert Willison. 900 Lawrence Street

The first church for Spanish-speaking Catholics in northern Colorado is this stucco and red tile edifice in the Spanish Colonial Revival style, with its curvilinear parapets, twin bell towers, and round arches. Millionaire flour miller John K. Mullen, whose house once stood here, donated both the site and $50,000 toward construction of the church. Although the church has been rearranged inside for use as an events center for the Auraria campus, it has been restored outside. With its no longer existing parish credit union, Ave Maria Health Clinic, and elementary school, St. Cajetan's tended to the economic, educational, and physical—as well as spiritual—health of the community until moving to a new location in southwest Denver in 1975. As the first major public building erected by and for Denver Hispanics, it is a tribute to what has become the city's largest ethnic minority.

FIGURE 1.33. St. Cajetan's Catholic Church celebrates Hispanic architectural traditions (Tom Noel Collection).

65. St. Elizabeth's Catholic Church

1898, Frederick W. Paroth. 1060 St. Francis Way, NR

Brother Adrian, one of the German Franciscans assigned to this parish, helped the architect design this replacement for a smaller brick predecessor on the same site. This Romanesque Revival church of rough-cut Castle Rock rhyolite has a dominant single corner spire soaring 162 feet. Behind a curving arcade and fountain are cloisters (1936, Jules Jacques Benoit Benedict) for the religious, with a private chapel and library retaining samples of the German stained glass and ornate woodwork gone from the modernized church sanctuary. Officially established as a German National Parish, St. Elizabeth's used the German language in many parish activities for Denver's largest foreign-born nineteenth-century immigrant group. The prayer garden and Gothic style monastery (1936, Jules Jacques Benoit Benedict) joined the church to the parish school (1890), which was replaced by the modern St. Francis Conference Center (1980, Marvin Hatami), with its contrasting expanses of glass and stark brick walls. The church remains active both as part of the Auraria campus and an active community parish, as well as a monument to Colorado's German pioneers.

66. Tivoli Union Brewery–Student Union

1881. 1890, many additions. 1980s renovation, Hellmuth, Obata, and Kassabaum. 2003–5 restoration, SLATERPAULL Architects. 900 block of Larimer Street, NR

This one-block complex is dominated by the seven-story mansard tower (1890, Frederick C. Eberley) of the Milwaukee Brewery. The attached West Denver Turnhalle Opera Hall (1882, Harold W. Baerresen) retains its horseshoe-shaped balcony and proscenium arch stage. The brewery expanded over the years to incorporate various businesses and surrounding structures, the oldest of which is the 1881 building at Tenth and Larimer Streets. The

FIGURE 1.34. Tivoli Brewery (Denver Public Library).

FIGURE 1.35. The Buckhorn Exchange Restaurant doubles as a wildlife museum of the Wild West (photo by Tom Noel).

bottling and storage building at the corner of Ninth and Walnut was a later addition. The complex operated as the Tivoli Union Brewery from 1900 until it closed in 1969. The Auraria Higher Education Center leased the brewery to private developers, who renovated the facility during the 1980s, creating a retail mall with a central sky-lighted atrium along with many sympathetic additions to fill the entire block. In 1991 students voted to use the Tivoli as their student center. In 2015 a reincarnated Tivoli Brewing Company opened in the old plant with a brew pub and beer garden.

67. Buckhorn Exchange Restaurant

1886. 1000 Osage Street, northeast corner of West Tenth Avenue, NR

In 1893, Henry H. Zietz moved his saloon from 2718 Market Street into this typical two-story brick commercial building. The Zietzes claimed to have brought the white oak front bar with hand-carved oak leaves and acorns from their family tavern in Essen, Germany. Three generations of Zietzes ran this legendary tavern, where Buffalo Bill and US presidents from Theodore Roosevelt to Ronald Reagan feasted on western delicacies, ranging from rattlesnake steaks to Rocky Mountain oysters.

Wildlife murals by Noel Adams decorate the exterior. The interior is jammed with several hundred stuffed animals, ranging from mythical jackalopes to a golden eagle, from prairie dogs to a whale phallus. In addition to doubling as a natural history museum, the Buckhorn is also packed with antique guns, trappers' tools, photographs, and antique furniture.

68. Byers Branch Library

1918, Ernest P. Varian and Lester E. Varian. 1992 restoration, Stanley Pouw Associates. 675 Santa Fe Drive, southwest corner of West Seventh Avenue

This exquisite Carnegie branch library was named for William Newton Byers, founder of the *Rocky Mountain*

News and Denver's greatest booster. The father-and-son Varian architectural team used concrete-covered brick and stone trim in a Spanish eclectic style. The single-room library is a large, finely crafted space, with a fireplace under a vaulted ceiling and with basement meeting, storage, and office space. Denver artist Carlota Espinoza painted the large mural *Pasado, Presente, Futuro* over the front desk, capturing the sweep of Hispanic history. As a center for English as a second language programs, this library in the Hispanic style has become a cornerstone for the Spanish-accented arts district on Santa Fe Drive.

69. West High School

1924–26, William Harry Edwards. 951 Elati Street

Facing Speer Boulevard across the generous expanse of Sunken Gardens Park, this Collegiate Gothic landmark exemplifies City Beautiful–era planning. On a four-block site between West Ninth and Eleventh Streets, the symmetrical four-story school is distinguished by a central seven-story tower. Constructed of light manganese brick trimmed with buff terracotta, its 1975 gymnasium and a 1978 wing are notable additions, along with a sympathetic 1990s swimming pool and outdoor patio connected by a three-story bridge. The original plan arranged rooms along subsidiary corridors radiating from a large central corridor, with natural lighting for all rooms. The main entry is adorned with Works Progress Administration Federal Art Project murals by Edward Chavez and Jenne Magafan. Flanking the auditorium doors are the 1933 *The Golden West* murals of Edmund L. Lambert, a graduate of West High.

HD-16 SPEER BOULEVARD HISTORIC DISTRICT

Speer Boulevard from University Boulevard to Irving Street, NRD

Mayor Robert W. Speer hired the nationally prominent Kansas City parkway planner George E. Kessler to create a 1907 Denver park and parkway master plan. Kessler's key diagonal, then called Cherry Creek Drive, followed Cherry Creek from East First Avenue west to the creek's confluence with the South Platte River and across the river to Irving Street in northwest Denver. Kessler's imaginative plan transformed the dump-lined, trash-strewn creek into a tree-lined boulevard, renamed Speer Boulevard in 1909. Subsequent planners, most notably landscape architect Saco R. DeBoer and architect-preservationist Paul Foster, have enhanced, expanded, and revived Kessler's plan.

The boulevard's 1988 landmark designation ended the street widening that kept devouring its grassy, tree-shaded edges. Restoration of the historic lighting, bridges, and landscaping on Speer stimulated a rejuvenation of the entire parkway and park system along City Beautiful lines. Speer Boulevard was re-celebrated during the 1980s with monumental pillars, an arched South Platte River bridge, and restored plantings. Pedestrian and cyclist ramps off the boulevard access a paved creek-side trail that stretches from Cherry Creek State Park to Denver's birthplace, Confluence Park. Creekfront Park (1992, Robert Karns and Bill Wenk) at Speer and Larimer, with water features and a path under Speer, connects the Auraria campus and Larimer Square. Although the Speer Boulevard district extends northwest into North Denver, the stretch between Zuni and Irving Streets scarcely resembles a parkway, as it is crowded by buildings instead of greenery.

70. Westside Courthouse

1922, James B. Hyder. 924 West Colfax Avenue at Speer Boulevard

Hyder, one of the first architectural graduates from the University of Colorado and a city architect at the time, designed this eclectic style, tapestry brick building with yellow mortar and terracotta trim. This building initially housed a jail as well as municipal courts until the new police headquarters and jail were built at 1245 Champa Street in 1941. This handsome brick building served as a courthouse until 1952, then it became a fire department building and still later the district attorney's office. Many prominent cases were heard here, including the "Spider Man" case. In 1998 the building was converted to the Bernie Valdez Hispanic Heritage Center, with various tenants.

2

Capitol Hill

CAPITOL HILL AREA

CHEESMAN PARK NEIGHBORHOOD

CITY PARK NEIGHBORHOOD

COUNTRY CLUB AREA

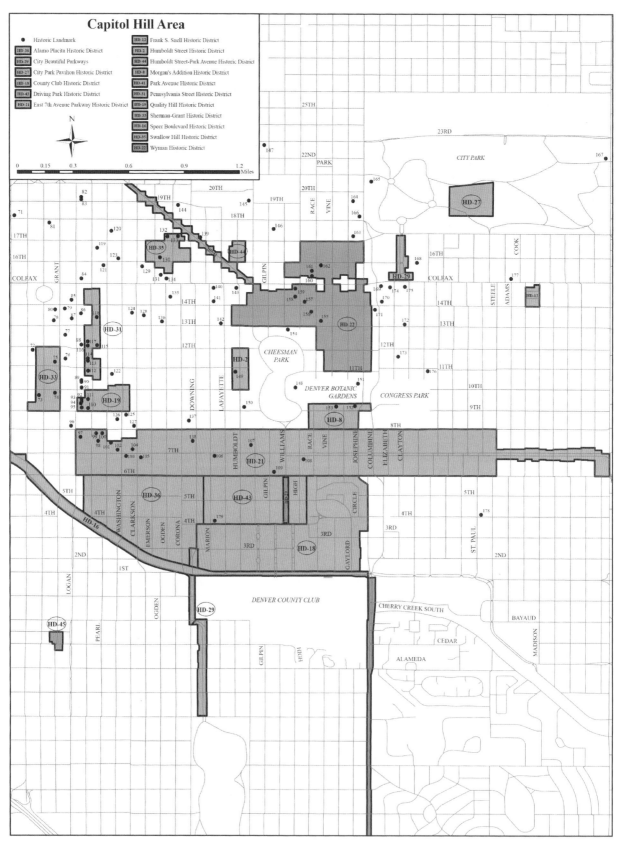

MAP 2.1. Capitol Hill area

Capitol Hill Area

Broadway to Colorado Boulevard between East Twentieth Street and Speer Boulevard and East First Avenue

Henry Cordes Brown homesteaded the hill east of Broadway in 1864. To attract land buyers, he donated part of Brown's Bluff in 1868 as the Colorado State Capitol site, hoping the capitol would be a magnet for his elite residential neighborhood. Although the gold-domed statehouse was not completed until 1908, Brown's dream came true: Colorado's movers and shakers decorated Capitol Hill with their exuberant masonry mansions beginning in the 1880s. These show homes flaunted various elements of the Queen Anne, Richardsonian Romanesque, Colonial Revival, and Neoclassical styles. Not only the mansions of the upper crust but also their churches, clubs, and schools arose along the tree-shaded sandstone sidewalks of Capitol Hill.

Greater Capitol Hill includes twenty historic districts and seventy-five individual landmarks. Capitol Hill United Neighborhoods, the largest and most active of Denver's neighborhood groups, has been a preservation watchdog for this area, which is under heavy development pressure. Much of the neighborhood's original nineteenth-century construction survives, although many mansions have been lost. After the silver crash of 1893, many large homes were converted to apartments and tuberculosis sanitariums. As apartment houses began to pop up alongside subdivided mansions, wealthier folks began building to the south and east. Today, many residences have been returned to single-family use or converted to offices. Others have been recycled as the eating, drinking, and lodging establishments that make Capitol Hill hospitable. To facilitate touring, individual landmarks and districts are organized by street, starting on the west with Broadway and moving east to Colorado Boulevard.

71. Trinity United Methodist Church

1888, Robert S. Roeschlaub. 1982 restoration and expansion, Seracuse, Lawler, and Partners. 1820 Broadway, northeast corner of East Eighteenth Avenue, NR, HD-38

The finest building designed by Colorado's first licensed architect is made of rhyolite from Castle Rock quarries. The light weight of this purplish-gray stone allowed Roeschlaub to design a 181-foot-high hexagonal corner steeple in stone without a single brace. The rough-faced rhyolite is trimmed

FIGURE 2.1. The soaring stone spire of Trinity United Methodist Church has sanctified the downtown skyline since 1888 (Tom Noel Collection).

in purplish sandstone, including three horizontal stripes in the steeple. This allusion to the Trinity is repeated in the triple-arched entry on Broadway and in Gothic windows arranged in sets of three. Except for these Gothic arches, the rose window, and the soaring steeple, the church might be called Richardsonian Romanesque.

Inside, Roeschlaub created a 1,200-seat sanctuary resembling a theater, where a large proscenium arch frames a 4,000-pipe Roosevelt organ, made by Theodore Roosevelt's cousin, Hilbourne Roosevelt. Electric lights on the arch, box seats, and a balcony lend opera hall drama. Of the many fine stained glass windows, the grand Resurrection window on the west wall is the most notable. The solid bronze and oak pulpit commemorates the church's most famous pastor, the Reverend Henry Buchtel, who also served as chancellor of the University of Denver and governor of Colorado.

In 1982 Trinity sold its air rights to a Toronto developer for a $2.7 million endowment that allowed for restoration of the church and construction of a subterranean office, education, and parking complex under a park on the north side of this Gothic gem. A 1926 addition was lost in the process, and the air rights remain unused.

72. St. Mark's Episcopal Church

1890, William A. Lang and Marshall R. Pugh. 1160 Lincoln Street, southeast corner of East Twelfth Avenue

Sister Eliza Barton's Mission of the Holy Comforter, which originally stood in a house on this corner, was replaced by Lang and Pugh's English Gothic edifice of Longmont sandstone. A corner bell tower collapsed, leaving a stubby base fronting the protruding buttresses, bays, gables, and miniature roof spire. The interior features clustered columns of red sandstone from which spring black ash ceiling beams that meet in Gothic arches. These high vaults frame an altar with a gold leaf triptych by Albert B. Olson, a Denver artist. The sanctuary end wall has seven tall Gothic window slits shaped like burning candles. Reincarnation as a nightclub has attracted throngs of youngsters to very early Sunday morning observances.

HD-33 SHERMAN-GRANT HISTORIC DISTRICT

East Ninth to East Twelfth Avenues between Sherman and Grant Streets

This roughly three-block district illustrates the transition from single-family residences to apartment buildings after 1893. Three early boom-era mansions with lush grounds, all individually landmarked, are represented by the Dennis Sheedy Mansion, the Henry M. Porter House, and the Crawford Hill Mansion. At the other end of the economic spectrum are nine quaint three-story 1930s apartment buildings named for literary celebrities in Poets Row. The row's curved corners, flat roofs, and glass brick windows are evidence that Denver was becoming modern during the Great Depression. Most of the Poets Row apartments were designed by Charles D. Strong, an architect and social activist. Metal and glass entries, ceramic and terracotta detailing give these modest apartments an Art Deco flair. Other district townhouses, terraces, and apartment complexes favor the Neoclassical Revival, Mission, and Art Moderne styles.

73. Crawford Hill Mansion

1906, Theodore Boal and Frederick L. Harnois. 1990 restoration, Peter Dominick Jr. 969 Sherman Street, southwest corner of East Tenth Avenue, NR, HD-33

Among the French Renaissance Revival elements of this stately brick home are the mansard roof and the symmetrical north facade with a trio of pedimented dormers flanked by ocular windows. Imposing Ionic columns support a two-story east portico with a third-floor balcony. Mrs. Crawford Hill, Denver's society queen, reigned here for decades. She snubbed Catholics and Jews and would be shocked that after her death in 1955 this mansion became the Jewish Town Club, before its restoration as law offices in 1990. This sparkling show home was built with the Hill family fortune made in the smelting industry, which darkened the skies of Black Hawk and north-central Denver. To wash off any smelter soot, the spacious grounds include a swimming pool.

FIGURE 2.2. Mrs. Crawford Hill leaving her mansion at 969 Sherman Street (photo by Harry Rhoads, Denver Public Library).

74. Henry M. Porter House

1913, Maurice Biscoe. 975 Grant Street, southwest corner of East Tenth Avenue, HD-33

After coming to Denver in 1859, the versatile and very successful entrepreneur Henry M. Porter built a telegraph, ranching, freight, real estate, mining, and retailing empire. Porter lived until 1937, becoming involved in many aspects

FIGURE 2.3. Dennis Sheedy Mansion (photo by Tom Noel).

of Denver's growth. Some of his fortune built Porter Memorial Hospital. His house, a red brick Georgian, is a study in understated elegance, with its modest red brick trim and red tile roof. Landmark designation rescued the Porter House in 1989 on the eve of the scheduled demolition of what remains a single-family residence.

75. Dennis Sheedy Mansion

1892, E. T. Carr. 1975 restoration, Dan Havekost. 1115 Grant Street, northwest corner of East Eleventh Avenue, NR, HD-33

Dennis Sheedy, a rancher, banker, smelter man, and businessman, had Carr, a Kansas architect, erect this Queen Anne style red brick residence with generous red sandstone trim. A broad, curving southeast corner porch capped by a tower and a north side porte-cochere distinguish this as does fine interior woodwork by carpenter John Joseph Queree. "A love of nature prompted me to furnish each

room with a distinctive wood," Sheedy explained, "and I carried out the idea to include the furniture."

Sheedy's sister back in Ireland, a Catholic nun, urged him to be philanthropic, reminding him of the biblical warning "It is easier for a camel to go through the eye of a needle than for a rich man to enter into the kingdom of God." Sheedy responded with generous donations to build the Immaculate Conception Cathedral and St. Joseph Hospital.

Four years after Sheedy's death in 1923, his home, with its grand music room, became a music school and boardinghouse for musicians and then, most recently, offices. The house and matching carriage house, renovated in the 1970s for business use, retain much of the original lavish decor, such as a sheepskin wall covering in the foyer and a buffalo hide on the breakfast room walls. Asymmetrical yet harmonious massing embraces porches, towers, and balconies in this three-story reminder that Grant Street was once Millionaires' Row.

76. Whitehead-Peabody House

1889, Frank E. Edbrooke. 1128 Grant Street

Dr. William R. Whitehead, a surgeon in the Confederate Army, later became a Denver City councilman and chairman of the Denver Board of Health. He first occupied the house later used by James H. Peabody during his term as governor (1902–4). Peabody used the state militia to crush the Western Federation of Miners, a union that was striking mines and smelters statewide in a campaign for an eight-hour workday and a minimum daily wage of three dollars. Peabody's illegal actions destroyed the union and also his chances for reelection. His scary tactics, as well as several strange occurrences in his former domicile, have given this house a reputation of being haunted. Several ambitious but short-lived restaurants and nightclubs were ultimately scared out by bizarre happenings. In 1994 this long-neglected, spooky Queen Anne house of red brick and rusticated red sandstone was restored for office use.

77. Creswell House

1889, John J. Huddart. 1244 Grant Street, NR

Joseph Creswell, whose Davis-Creswell Manufacturing Company made architectural steel, iron, and plumbing products, also operated the Colorado Mining and Marble Company. He used Manitou red-orange sandstone from the Red Rock Canyon quarries near Colorado Springs for his home, which displays Richardsonian Romanesque and Queen Anne elements. Ornate stone carving is the most distinguishing feature of this house. Sandstone is a soft rock that erodes quickly but can be carved easily, as demonstrated by the mythical stone beasts perched on the front gable including the eagle, a later addition.

78. Aromor Apartment Building

1926–27, Walter H. Simon. 225 East Thirteenth Avenue, northwest corner of Grant Street

Built to offer both long-term and short-term living to residents of Capitol Hill, this three-story apartment house represents the change from single-family residences to apartment complexes on the Hill in the early 1900s. Most notable for its grand Roman arched terracotta entrance, this structure's use of brick and terracotta throughout makes it a good representation of the Mediterranean style. It has been refurbished for low-income housing.

79. Scottish Rite Masonic Temple

1924, William N. Bowman. 1370 Grant Street, southeast corner of East Fourteenth Avenue

An imposing pedimented entry, curved corner, and large dome characterize this three-story Neoclassical monument. The brick and steel structure is clad in white terracotta blocks resembling limestone atop a base of Pikes Peak granite. The dome covers an immense interior auditorium with a double arched stage. Although a relative latecomer, the structure's style compliments the Neoclassical entourage around the nearby Colorado State Capitol. Scottish Rite Masons, who trace their origins to the eighteenth-century enlightenment in Europe, have been one of Colorado's most prominent fraternal groups.

80. First Baptist Church

1938, G. Meredith Musick. 230 East Fourteenth Avenue, southwest corner of Grant Street

Immense polished red granite columns support the pedimented entry portico of this red brick church trimmed with

FIGURE 2.4. First Baptist Church's Rev. Harold A. Malmborg (*left*) receives the church's landmark plaque from Denver Landmark Preservation commissioner Alan B. Fisher, 1986 (photo by Glenn Cuerden).

FIGURE 2.5. From its minaret to its interior Arabic inscriptions, this Moorish confection brings the Middle East to Denver (Tom Noel Collection).

Indiana limestone. The $253,711 edifice is in a T shape, with the sanctuary and vestibule forming the stem and classrooms and offices forming the crossbar. Elegant landscaping of the narrow street margins has enhanced the setting of this Georgian Revival church, which has a slender, distinctive spire. A 126-rank Aeolian-Skinner grand pipe organ adorns the sanctuary, and a cock crows atop the weather vane topping a majestic steeple.

81. El Jebel Temple–Rocky Mountain Consistory

1906, Baerresen Brothers. 1770 Sherman Street, southeast corner of East Eighteenth Avenue

A fanciful Moorish shrine with exotic onion domes, minaret tower, and a roof balcony, this five-story red brick building has contrasting creamy terracotta trim and, most notably, horseshoe-shaped window arches. Harold W., Viggio, Albert T., and William J. Baerresen, sons of a noted

Danish designer of ships and shipyards, established a successful architecture firm in Denver. Between 1884 and 1928 they designed and constructed many of the city's buildings, of which this is the most remarkable. This was the headquarters for Colorado's Shriners, the Thirty-Third Degree Masons who belong to the Ancient Arabic Order of the Mystic Shrine, before they moved into a new consistory next to the Willis Case Golf Course in northwest Denver. Among the many ornamental details is as inscription on the walls of the ballroom: "The Dream of the Architect— Baerresen Brothers." Since the 1990s, this exotic landmark has served as an events space.

82. Ross-Lewin Double

1891, Frank Kidder. 1912–18 Logan Street

An elegant example of late-nineteenth-century multifamily housing, this two-story red brick, eclectic style double was commissioned by George E. Ross-Lewin. After arriving in Denver in 1881, Ross-Lewin quickly became a prominent figure in the banking community and rose to vice president of First National Bank under President David H. Moffat. The double is symmetrical in design and includes bracketed eaves, Tuscan columns along a slightly curved porch, and brick voissier arches above the doors and side elevation windows. Perhaps Ross-Lewin's Neoclassicism inspired the grandiose Neoclassical twelve-story Tower on the Park next door at 1950 Logan.

83. Arcanum Apartments–Beldame Apartments
1907, Glen W. Huntington. 1904 Logan Street

Sporting Corinthian porch columns, this two-story red brick apartment building mixes Classical Revival and Colonial Revival elements. Its Latin-inspired name means "secret place," and the apartments inside may contain surprises.

84. Immaculate Conception Cathedral
1902–12, Leon Coquard, and Aaron M. Gove and Thomas F. Walsh. 401 East Colfax Avenue, northeast corner of Logan Street, NR

Denver's finest example of the French Gothic Revival style is clad in white Bedford, Indiana, limestone above a foundation of Colorado granite. The sanctuary, altar, and side altars are made of Carrera marble. Louis Coquard's original design, inspired by the great French cathedral at Amiens, was realized by the Denver firm of Gove and Walsh. St. John's Episcopal and the Immaculate Conception

FIGURE 2.6. Immaculate Conception Catholic Cathedral interior construction, 1911 (Archdiocese of Denver Archives).

Cathedrals underwent construction at the same time, and both took years to complete. Groundwater hampered St. John's construction, while lightning knocked down one spire of Immaculate Conception just after its erection. This inspired St. John's dean, Martyn Hart, to tell Bishop Nicholas C. Matz, "At least our troubles do not come from above." Another lightning strike in 1997 shattered Immaculate Conception's west spire, prompting critics to suggest that the heavens found fault with certain church dogmas. Denver architect David Owen Tryba restored the steeple using the original Indiana limestone.

Twin 210-foot-tall bell-tower spires flank a large rose window with stained glass angels playing classical instruments. The exquisitely detailed reredos, thirty feet high, is made of Carrera marble, as are the pulpit, much of the statuary, and the bishop's chair. Leonardo da Vinci's *The Last Supper* inspired the altar table bas-relief, and Bartolome Murillo's painting of the Immaculate Conception was the model for the central statue above the altar. Seventy-five exquisite stained glass windows were made by the F. X. Zetter Royal Bavarian Art Institute in Munich, which US bombers destroyed during World War II.

At the top of each interior column, a trinity of ribs springs from a cluster of marble wheat and grapes. These ribs support the Gothic vaulted ceiling, which soars sixty-eight feet over the slightly sloping 1,500-seat nave. The Vatican honored the cathedral by designating it a minor basilica in 1979. A $2.5 million restoration for the 1993 visit of Pope John Paul II added a bronze sculpture, the *Assumption of Mary*, in a meditation garden (1993, John Norris) on East Colfax Avenue, which is noted more for its sinners than its saints.

85. First Church of Christ Scientist

1906, Frederick J. Sterner. 1401–15 Logan Street, northwest corner of East Fourteenth Avenue

Smooth, white cast stone sheathes this Neoclassical temple, with its two-story Ionic-columned portico and huge domed, sky-lighted copper-clad roof behind a classical cornice. Inside, a sloping floor and huge sanctuary suggest a classical amphitheater. This $163,000 church features a large organ built by the Casavant Fréres Limitée of St. Hyacinth, Quebec. In 1928, an adjoining administration building and public reading room were built at 1415 Logan Street in a complimentary style.

FIGURE 2.7. Cuthbert-Dines House; rendering by architect Frederick J. Sterner (Tyson Dines III Collection).

86. Cuthbert-Dines House

1901, Frederick J. Sterner. 1350 Logan Street

Designed by a prominent Denver architect, this two-story Georgian Revival style brick residence exhibits large first-floor bay windows, a one-story south-facing solarium, and elaborate hooded entryway with a wrought-iron railing and a marble staircase that leads to a door framed by Ionic columns. Built by Lucas Montrose Cuthbert and his wife, Gertrude Hill Berger Cuthbert, daughter of US senator Nathaniel Hill, this 1901 home remained in the family until its 1923 purchase by Isabel A. and Tyson M. Dines, a prominent mining and railroad attorney. The Dines family stayed for seventy years until the house was purchased by Mary Louise Starkey. In 1993 Starkey converted the home into the Starkey International Institute for Household Management, a school that trains butlers, maids, and other household staff, as well as estate management professionals.

87. Denver Women's Press Club

1910, Ernest P. Varian and Lester E. Varian. 1325 Logan Street

George Elbert Burr, one of the country's foremost etchers of natural scenes, built this English style cottage and studio after settling in Denver in 1906. His life, landscapes, and nature etchings are discussed in Louise Combes Seeber's catalog, *George Elbert Burr, 1859–1939* (1971). After Burr moved to Phoenix in 1924, his home became the clubhouse of the Denver Women's Press Club, which had met in private homes since its 1898 founding. The ladies formed their own club after being excluded from the Denver Press Club (which is now struggling and begging women to join). This Tudoresque cottage has dark red brick walls with bracketed hoods over the entrance. The entrance hall has a low ceiling and a small open staircase to a balcony overlooking the two-story sky-lighted, vaulted-ceiling studio.

88. Baker-Plested Cottage

1886. 1208 Logan Street

Henry P. Baker, an agent for the Colorado Telephone Company, built and originally occupied the frame house that later became better known as the residence of journalist Dolores N. Plested. She worked for the *Trinidad Chronicle* and the *New York Times* and was a mainstay of the Denver Women's Press Club. Her simple cottage is the only wood dwelling in a neighborhood of larger masonry structures.

89. Daly House

1894. 1034 Logan Street

Thomas F. Daly founded the Capitol Life Insurance Company, which built the renaissance palace of an office building that still stands at 1600 Sherman Street. Daly's own two-story residence of rusticated red sandstone with a central bay thrust forward was restored in the 1970s. This eclectic edifice includes Craftsman style bracketed eaves, Romanesque Revival stone blocks, round-arched windows, and a third-story Queen Anne-ish front porch on a basic foursquare plan.

90. Stearns House

1896, Harry T.E. Wendell. 1030 Logan Street

For one of Denver's first Spanish Colonial Revival style domiciles, Wendell used modified Mission Revival elements and symmetrical massing for the home of Joel W. Stearns, president of the Mountain Electric Company. Radiating window voussoirs emphasize the round-arch window and door openings on the first floor. Quoins are of rusticated sandstone, while wrought iron is used for the balcony and gate, providing contrast with the light stucco skin of this two-story brick dwelling under a red tile roof with notable paired south-side Mission style chimneys. Converted to apartments in the 1940s, the building was restored in 1978.

91. Brind-Axtens Mansion

1908, Frederick J. Sterner and George H. Williamson. 1000 Logan Street, northeast corner of East Tenth Avenue

J. Fritz Brind, an Englishman, presided over the Insoloid Dynamite Fuse Company and held considerable stock in the Butterfly-Terrible Mining Company. His wife, Maria, was president of both the Old Ladies Home and the Denver Orphans Home. She was also the first woman to sit on the executive board of the Denver Charity Organization, which evolved into the United Way. The Brinds moved from their previous residence, a fine, extant stone home at 825 Logan Street, to this dwelling, which incorporates a variety of Mediterranean and Mission elements. Buff brick is used for the walls and the four tall chimneys that soar over the red tile roof and half-timbered dormers. The open beam timber trim is suggestive of Mission Revival, although the rectangular massing, windows, and balconies are more eclectic in what has is now an office building.

A prolific Denver architect, S. Arthur Axtens, lived here from 1956 until 1970 and used this structure as his studio and office. Among his works are the Streamline Moderne Dorset House Apartments (1937) across the street at 1001 Logan Street. Axtens's modernism is reflected in the Art Deco remodeling of the interior of the Brind Mansion, although the original marble and wood trim remains.

HD-19 QUALITY HILL HISTORIC DISTRICT

Roughly Logan to Washington Streets between East Ninth and Tenth Avenues

Quality Hill, according to the June 26, 1901, issue of the *Denver Times*, was a "most exclusive residential section." A fragment of this part of Capitol Hill, designated the Quality Hill Historic District, remains amid a variety of single- and multiple-family housing. The neighborhood raised $200,000 to help build the Quality Hill mini-park at Tenth and Pennsylvania, dedicated in 1986. The southwestern cornerstone is the Craig House, a trim, Neoclassical two-story townhouse at the northeast corner of East Ninth Avenue and Pearl Street (1914, Jules Jacques Benoit Benedict, 605 East Ninth Avenue). Dr. Alexander Craig's domicile has a hipped tile roof and broad, overhanging eaves above a dentiled cornice. The offset entry does not upset the generally symmetrical appearance of the stucco walls ascending from a dark brick base.

Both the Granada Apartments, 607–15 East Tenth Avenue, and the Cardenas Apartments, 707–15 East Tenth Avenue, are three-story 1925 apartment buildings designed by Walter Rice. They flaunt ornaments loosely based on Moorish and Spanish Colonial designs, such as iron balconies, curvilinear parapets, and arched bays whose white plaster contrasts dramatically with the red brick walls. Other apartment houses and residences, reflecting various styles and time periods, add diversity to this mixed district.

92. McKinley Mansion

1899: Frederick J. Sterner, 948–52 Logan Street, HD-19

The Georgian style estate housed notable residents such as Dr. Henry Buchtel, chancellor of the University of Denver and governor of Colorado.

93. Campbell House

1891, Ernest P. Varian and Frederick J. Sterner. 940 Logan Street, HD-19

Like the nearby McNeil House, this $20,000 show home was built by broker-speculator Fred A. Thompson and sold to Lafayette E. Campbell, an owner of the Mammoth Mining Company. Captain Campbell came to Denver to supervise construction of Fort Logan and stayed to supervise David Moffat's mines. Campbell also partnered with Nicholas C. Creede in tapping the rich silver mines of Creede. With its red brick and rich white frame trim, including prominent third-story dormers and an imposing semicircular entry portico, this a good vernacular example of Georgian Revival, with its symmetrical massing and side-lighted entry. Campbell House and 940 Logan Street next door were among the first Georgian Revival style dwellings built in Denver. "Just before we restored the house for office use," developer-realtor Mary Rae reported in 1975, "this place had seventy-five people living in it, with three old ladies residing on the landing."

94. McNeil House

1890, Ernest P. Varian and Frederick J. Sterner. 930 Logan Street, HD-19

John L. McNeil, a banker, lived here until 1915, when he sold the home to Lucien Hallet, whose father lived next door. Like many large Capitol Hill homes, it was converted to a rooming house during the Great Depression, then restored as a single-family residence in 1974 and subsequently converted to offices. An unusual combination of elements—a Palladian window, shed roof dormers, round entry porch, and polygonal bay windows—make this house easy to catalog as eclectic, although some consider it fits Georgian Revival style.

95. Hallet House

1892, Grable and Weber. 900 Logan Street, northeast corner of East Ninth Avenue, HD-19

Moses Hallet, a chief justice of the Colorado Territorial Court and later of the state supreme court, was also a judge on the US District Court for Colorado from 1877 to 1906. His residence of red pressed brick is dominated by a wraparound veranda, now enclosed. On the third story, the profusion of shingled gables, dormers, steeply pitched irregular rooflines, and massive smooth chimneys suggests the Shingle style. This well-kept home of Colorado's most distinguished pioneer jurist has been an apartment house and offices since the 1940s.

96. Sayre's Alhambra

1892. 801 Logan Street, northwest corner of East Eighth Avenue, HD-19

Hal Sayre came to Colorado in 1859 and adopted the long hair and buckskin suit of the West. As one of the state's first mining engineers, he did well in mining in Central City, a gold rush town he helped lay out. Sayre was president of Central City's Rocky Mountain Bank and fought with

FIGURE 2.8. Sayre's Alhambra (photo by Sandra Dallas Atchison from Denver Public Library).

the Colorado Volunteers at Sand Creek. Supposedly after a trip to Spain, he designed or helped design this twenty-five-room yellow brick house distinguished by ogee-arched transom cutouts inspired by the Alhambra in Granada, Spain. The south-facing front porch features an Arabesque arched arcade. Inside, the Moorish theme is continued in the cherry woodwork, along with paneling containing the hand-carved Sayre family crest and a fireplace in every room. Sayre fancied fast horses, which he stabled in the rear carriage house. He lived here until his death at age ninety-one in 1926. His wife, Elizabeth, stayed in the house until her death in 1937. Little altered, in the 1990s this structure, one of Colorado's few Moorish Revival style specimens, became one of the more dignified shelters for Denver's homeless, Providence House.

HD-21 EAST SEVENTH AVENUE PARKWAY HISTORIC DISTRICT

1914, Saco R. DeBoer. Logan Street to Colorado Boulevard roughly between East Sixth and Eighth Avenues, NRD

The district centered on East Seventh Avenue Parkway, Denver's largest historic district, comprises 927 buildings, from grand mansions and apartment houses on the west end to modest bungalows on the east end. At least sixty-four architects produced designs for residences in this district, which includes Albert J. Norton's 1900 residence at 661 Humboldt Street, Montana Fallis's 1909 residence at 622 Ogden Street, and Aaron M. Gove's 1911 house at 750 Marion Street

Seventh Avenue Parkway's median greenery is the design of Denver's foremost landscape architect, Saco R. DeBoer. Parkway median plantings range from larch trees to floral extravaganzas. Uniform tree lawns and setbacks help tie together this district of well-landscaped homes. Nancy Widmann, who spearheaded the landmark district designation, also produced a guidebook to the district.

97. Governor's Mansion

1908, Willis A. Marean and Albert J. Norton. 1980s restoration, Edward D. White Jr. 400 East Eighth Avenue, southeast corner of Logan Street, NR, HD-21

Walter Scott Cheesman, a real estate tycoon, businessman, and head of the Denver Union Water Company, died

FIGURE 2.9. Governor's Mansion, west facade (Denver Public Library).

before he could move into his new Georgian Revival mansion. The twenty-seven-room house became the home of his widow, Alice, and his daughter, Gladys, and her husband, John Evans II. Later, Claude Boettcher, who ran the huge industrial and commercial empire assembled by his father, Charles, bought the house. After his death, the Boettcher Foundation donated the dwelling to the state in 1958 for use as the governor's mansion, whose first floor is open to the public for free Tuesday tours.

A wrought-iron fence with cannonball finials on brick posts guards the formal dwelling. Deep-red brick walls are almost lost amid rich white wooden frosting under a hipped roof with prominent gabled dormers. The pedimented, dentiled cornice provides a strong shadow line. Massive two-story fluted Ionic columns guard the west-side portico. The north main entry has grouped columns supporting a porch that becomes a balustraded second-story balcony. Inside, the bar contains portraits of all of Colorado's governors, including John Wright Hickenlooper Jr., a brew pub entrepreneur who installed the first beer tap in a gubernatorial house in 2014. The south-side semicircular Palm Room conservatory has a marble floor and stone columns that match those on the portico that leads into the extensive yards and gardens bordered by Governor's Park.

FIGURE 2.10. (a) Despite Albert E. Humphreys's suicide and haunted house tales, the Grant-Humphreys Mansion is one of Denver's most popular special events venues. (b) As this window surround may suggest, Grant-Humphreys pioneered the use of terracotta instead of stone for trim (photos by Roger Whitacre).

98. Grant-Humphreys Mansion

1902, Theodore Boal and Frederick L. Harnois. 770 Pennsylvania Street, NR, HD-21

Denver's best-known Neoclassical residence has a monumental semicircular west portico supported by four two-story fluted Corinthian columns. Georgian balustrades on the first- and second-story porches and terraces are echoed by a rooftop balustrade. Built for James B. Grant, a smelter owner and Colorado governor (1883–85), the peach-hued brick house employs lavish terracotta trim in window surrounds, balustrades, cornices, corner pilasters, and friezes. This early use of terracotta as a substitute for decorative stonework set an example widely copied by other local architects and builders. Interiors are on a grand scale, featuring exotic woods, plaster trim, and a sunroom addition. The second owner, Albert E. Humphreys, an oil tycoon who later became embroiled in the Teapot Dome scandal, added a two-story ten-car garage, complete with a carwash and gas pump, for his fleet of Rolls-Royces. His suicide here and other macabre happenings have generated haunted house tales. In 1976 his son, Ira, donated the house to the Colorado Historical Society (History Colorado since 2009), which uses it as a house museum and rents it out for special events. Splendidly sited on the southwest corner of Capitol Hill, the building has an extensive lawn that flows west across a grassed-over block of Pennsylvania Street into Governor's Park.

99. Malo Mansion

1921, Harry James Manning. 500 East Eighth Avenue, southeast corner of Pennsylvania Street, HD-21

Oscar Malo married Edith Mullen and joined her father's flour-milling empire, which stretched from the West Coast to the Great Plains. This poor Irish immigrant became one of Colorado's most successful tycoon-philanthropists, as William J. Convery documents in his book *Pride of the Rockies: The Life of Colorado's Premier Irish Patron, John Kernan Mullen* (2000). Malo followed Mullen at the helm of the Colorado Milling and Elevator Company, producer of Hungarian Flour. One of the city's finest Spanish Colonial Revival mansions, this structure features white stucco walls, a red tile roof, and a triple-arch entry arcade. This twenty-three-room, two-story stucco villa exults in finely crafted detail, such as wrought-iron balconies and hand-painted rosettes on the overhanging eaves. Malo had Manning include rose patterns in stained glass throughout. A 1980s rear addition does not detract from this refined specimen. Built during Prohibition, it features a built-in bar hidden behind wood paneling in the library.

100. John Porter House

1923, Ernest P. Varian and Lester E. Varian. 777 Pearl Street, southwest corner of East Eighth Avenue, NR, HD-21

This is a rare Denver example of the Jacobean style, a Tudor variant characterized here by prominent gables that rise to the parapet and hide the roof behind it. Jacobean features include flattened pointed arches in the prominent entry porch, tapestry brick patterns, a steep-pitched roof, and tall ornate chimneys. John Porter was a successful businessman like his father, the tycoon Henry M. Porter. His tapestry red brick house became the residence of Catholic archbishop Urban J. Vehr, who installed a private chapel and an elaborate rose garden. This handsome house has been converted to offices.

101. Foster-McCauley-Symes–French Consulate House

1905, Frederick J. Sterner and George H. Williamson. 736–38 Pearl Street, HD-21

This Georgian Revival variant has a rounded front porch and double-pitched central Palladian dormer. Alexis C. Foster of the Causey Foster Securities Company built this three-story dwelling, later owned by Vance McCauley and then by US District Court judge J. Foster Symes. Following its use as the French Consulate, this residence was converted to private offices.

102. Wood-Morris-Bonfils House

1911, Maurice Biscoe and Henry H. Hewitt. 1987 renovation and expansion, Daniel J. Havekost. 707 Washington Street, northwest corner of East Seventh Avenue, NR, HD-21

A grand formal garden on Seventh Avenue was sacrificed for the 1987 addition of twenty-three condominiums, whose stucco walls, red tile roofs, balconies, and flattened arches echo the Mediterranean mode of the original dwelling. The distinctive two-story residence with balustraded terraces leading to the gardens was built for Guilford Wood, who made a fortune in the Cripple Creek gold mines. Subsequently, it became the home of *Denver Post* owner Helen Bonfils. She became one of Denver's greatest philanthropists, building Holy Ghost Catholic Church and helping many other Catholic institutions, but she is best-known for financing the Denver Performing Arts Complex and the Bonfils Blood Bank. She and others made substantial additions to one of Denver's finest Mediterranean style houses, which became the Mexican Consulate and was then converted to condos.

103. Ferguson-Gano House

1896, 1909 remodel, Theodore Boal and Frederick L. Harnois. 722 East Seventh Avenue, southeast corner of Washington Street, HD-21

This two-story eclectic style residence was built as the guest house for the estate of John A. Ferguson, whose even larger, now demolished mansion (also by Boal and Harnois) stood across the street at 700 Washington Street. George W. Gano, a prominent businessman involved in the upscale Gano-Downs Clothing Store, bought the guest house in 1909 and had Boal and Harnois remodel it.

104. Adolph Zang Mansion

1903, Frederick C. Eberley. 709 Clarkson Street, northwest corner of East Seventh Avenue, NR, HD-21

After outgrowing his extant townhouse at 1532 Emerson Street, Adolph Zang, son of the founder of the Zang Brewery, built this $108,000 Neoclassical Revival show home. A monochromatic mansion, its sedate gray brick and gray stone trim seem to snub more ostentatious neighboring residences. The two-story semicircular portico that proclaims the main entrance is supported by two massive Ionic columns. The front dormer in the hipped roof gives access to a small terrace from the third-floor ballroom. Behind splendid oak doors, the fantastic interior features painted and gilded ceilings, five ornate fireplaces, a Tiffany chandelier, and twelve varieties of beautifully carved woodwork. Look for Adolph Zang's monogram in the front leaded glass window, and note the stained glass window with a scene from Shakespeare's *Merchant of Venice* and another from *Romeo and Juliet*. The house and matching carriage house have been converted into offices. Zang became active in mining and real estate and was a major partner in building the Oxford Hotel after selling the Zang Brewery to a British corporation.

FIGURE 2.11. Adolph Zang Mansion (photo by Sandra Dallas Atchison, Denver Public Library).

105. Mitchell-Schomp House

1893. 680 Clarkson Street, southeast corner of East Seventh Avenue, HD-21

John Clark Mitchell, president of Denver National Bank, built this two-and-a-half-story house known as "Trails End" in an eclectic Mediterranean style. With a complementary 1915 wing by George L. Bettcher and landscaping by Jane Silverstein Ries, this large home retains its elegance. Various additions and disparate architectural elements have further contributed to its eclectic appearance. The Mitchells owned the house until 1945. Kay Schomp, who moved into the carriage house in 1949, subsequently acquired the main house. She explains: "We were sick about seeing so many Capitol Hill mansions destroyed. So we landmarked this one and had architect Daniel J. Havekost remodel it in 1973 to include apartments to get full use out of its 13,000 square feet."

106. Brown-Garrey-Congdon House

1912, Jules Jacques Benoit Benedict. 1987 restoration, Edward D. White Jr. 1300 East Seventh Avenue, southeast corner of Marion Street, HD-21

This narrow, 100-foot-long Chateau style townhouse is one of the finest of many splendid homes in the East Seventh Avenue Parkway Historic District. A steep, tiled roof with rounded dormers covers the two-story stuccoed masonry walls above a brick base and brick trim on tall, narrow window bays. A two-story semicircular conservatory bay overlooks the walled backyard garden.

Carroll T. Brown sold his house to mining heiress Anne Reynolds Garrey and her husband, George H. Garrey. Another legendary mining man, Tom Congdon, and his wife, Noel, later acquired this long, narrow landmark and found that "living in a house that's only 18 feet wide is a bit like living on a bus. We love it!"

107. Jane Silverstein Ries House

1935, Henry Eggers and Stanley Morse. 737 Franklin Street, HD-21

Jane Silverstein Ries, a longtime prominent Colorado landscape architect, transformed this house with her all-encompassing garden. Her campaign to replace lawns and "useless" banks with terraces and walled gardens is reflected in much of Denver's residential landscaping, as well as in her own home.

108. Kerr House

1925, Jules Jacques Benoit Benedict. 1900 East Seventh Avenue, southeast corner of High Street, HD-21

John G. Kerr, who once owned the travertine quarry at Wellsville near Salida, used its cream-colored stone to trim this Mediterranean Revival style house. An elaborate carved travertine entry leads to an interior with travertine floors. Kerr also owned a rhyolite quarry in Kerr Gulch near Howard in Fremont County that produced the extraordinary stone used to build another Denver landmark, the First Church of Christ Scientist, of which Kerr was a member.

Standart-Cleworth House

1925, Merrill H. Hoyt and Burnham Hoyt. 2025 East Seventh Avenue, northwest corner of Vine Street, HD-21

This beautifully proportioned Italian Renaissance Revival residence displays that style's low-hipped tile roof, symmetrical facade, and upper-story windows accented by small classical columns. The Hoyt brothers, in lengthy specifications for the brick home of insurance man Frederick W. Standart, required that the stucco have "one bushel of cattle hair per 100 square yards of plastering." They specified Bedford Indiana limestone, which is almost the same white as the stucco for the entry surround and window trim. Inside, round archways connect well-proportioned, generally symmetrical rooms adorned with painted glass and wrought-iron fixtures. Charles and Sheila Cleworth, owner-occupants since 1975, have maintained both the exterior and the interior in near original condition. "Thanks to the Hoyts' careful specs," noted Charles, a publisher and historic preservationist, "we've never even needed to repair or paint the stucco because it has all that hairy reinforcement!"

109. Church of the Ascension

1909–13, William E. Fisher and Arthur A. Fisher. 1918 addition. 1959 addition. 600 North Gilpin Street, northeast corner of East Sixth Avenue, HD-21

The congregation dates to a tent mission started by Mrs. Thomas Ward in 1904. As membership grew, it graduated to a small brick structure in 1909 that has grown over the years. This late Gothic Revival style church has a smooth buff brick skin, steep gabled roofs, Gothic arches, and stained glass windows by the famous four-generation firm of the Watkins family. The social and educational wing along Gilpin Street blends in well with neighboring residences thanks to its scale and many dormers. After a 2014 fire, the church restored much of the interior, engaging the Watkins Stained Glass Company of Denver to repair or replace stained glass windows done by Grandfather Watkins 101 years ago.

HD-36 ALAMO PLACITA HISTORIC DISTRICT

Bounded by Speer Boulevard and East Sixth Avenue between Logan and Downing Streets

Alamo Placita Park and its notable flowerbeds represents the centerpiece of this district. Designed by Saco R. DeBoer in 1927, the park was built on the site of one of Denver's city dumps. The architectural styles include bungalows, duplexes, and Denver squares as well as Tudor, Mission Revival, and Queen Anne residences of more modest proportions than those in the adjacent Country Club Historic District.

110. Clemes-Lipe-Sweeney House

1898, Franklin E. Kidder and Thielman R. Wieger. 1915 remodel. 901 Pennsylvania Street, northwest corner of East Ninth Avenue, HD-19

Constructed as a red brick home for James H. Clemes and his wife, Cora, in Queen Anne style with corner towers, this dwelling was radically remodeled, stuccoed, and expanded in 1915 when it became a duplex for brothers Walter E. and William C. Lipe, who also shared offices at the Lipe Brothers real estate firm. Robert F. "Bob" Sweeney, a publisher of Colorado small-town newspapers and a philanthropist, and his wife, Gerri, lived here from 1994 until 2012.

111. Taylor House

1900, Lester E. Varian and Frederick J. Sterner. 945 Pennsylvania Street, HD-19

The "House of Arches" is an eclectic edifice with distinctive porch arches repeated in the second- and third-story windows and the octagonal southwest corner tower, as well as in the arches of the octagonal central hall inside. Frank M. Taylor, a mining man, served on the boards of the Denver Museum of Nature and Science, the Denver Public Schools, and St. Luke's Hospital. In 1974 this residence was purchased and restored as the home of Colorado Outward Bound, part of a national organization that introduces city folk to the spiritual and physical advantages of outdoor recreation. After Outward Bound moved on, the office use continued.

HD-31 Pennsylvania Street Historic District

Pennsylvania Street roughly from East Colfax Avenue to East Tenth Avenue

Pennsylvania Street includes fine examples of single- and multi-family residences. Several prominent Denverites resided here, including legislator Thomas B. Croke, US senator Thomas Patterson, and Margaret "Molly" Brown. Architecturally, the styles of this district range from Foursquare and Craftsman to Italianate and Modern, showing the neighborhood's continual growth. There are fifty-one contributing buildings in this district, of which seven are individual Denver landmarks. One of the most notable of these is the Molly Brown House (1890, William A. Lang), 1340 Pennsylvania Street, now the celebrated house museum of Historic Denver, Inc. This historic district is one of the most intact and cohesive representations exhibiting the evolution of the Capitol Hill neighborhood from mansions to high-rise apartments.

112. Croke-Patterson-Campbell Mansion–Patterson Inn

1887, Isaac and Edgar J. Hodgson. 2013 restoration, Brian Higgins. 420 East Eleventh Avenue, southwest corner of Pennsylvania Street, NR, HD-31

Thomas B. Croke was a schoolteacher who invested in railroads and in an irrigated 3,500-acre farm that has become the suburb of Northglenn. His experimental farm proved remunerative enough to pay for this $100,000 mansion. Later, it became home to Thomas M. Patterson, owner of the *Rocky Mountain News* and a US senator, whose multifaceted career is examined in *Tom Patterson: Crusader for Change* (1995) by his great-granddaughter Sybil Downing and Robert E. Smith. Patterson's daughter, Margaret, and son-in-law, Richard C. Campbell, were the next owner-occupants. Several deaths here have inspired persistent rumors that this red sandstone chateau, with its creaky floors and squeaky doors, is haunted. After narrowly escaping demolition in the 1960s, the building was neglected by

FIGURE 2.12. Croke-Patterson-Campbell Mansion (photo by Louis McClure, Denver Public Library).

various short-term owners until 2013, when architect Brian Higgins bought and restored the chateau to recycle it as a bed and breakfast inn.

The Loire Valley chateau of Azay-le-Rideau (1520s) may have inspired this three-story edifice of Manitou red sandstone. The steep slate roof bristles with crockets, finials, roundel dormers, and corner turrets, although much carved sandstone decoration has disappeared on one of Denver's best examples of the French Chateau style. The irregular plan includes a Châteauesque carriage house connected to the house by a small courtyard in one of Capitol Hill's longest awaited and most spectacular restorations.

113. Butters House

1890, Frank E. Edbrooke. 1129 Pennsylvania Street, NR, HD-31

Like many westerners, Alfred Butters grew fat on the cattle business. He bought thousands of Texas longhorns at a few dollars a head and then drove them north to market where he sold the steers for thirty dollars a head. Butters became a businessman, banker, and state representative who lived in this eclectic dwelling with Neoclassical porch details. Its distinctive Palladian window is a Renaissance device that Edbrooke apparently introduced to Denver in this $14,000 residence. The house and carriage house have been restored for offices.

114. Fleming-Hanington House

1893, Edgar J. Hodgson. 1133 Pennsylvania Street, NR, HD-31

A retardaire two-story Greek portico fronts the four-square of Josiah M. Fleming, general manager of the Daniels and Fisher Stores. Fleming built this "Greek survival" house, with over-scale fluted columns and a classical pediment on the facade, for his daughter. From 1912 to 1924 this structure housed the family of Charles Hanington, a mining man who later became president of Mountain Motors Company. He was a civic activist who served as president of the Colorado Historical Society, the Denver Museum of Nature and Science, and the Denver School Board.

115. Dunning-Benedict House

1889, William A. Lang. 1200 Pennsylvania Street, northeast corner of East Twelfth Avenue, NR, HD-31

One of the finest houses of Denver's leading nineteenth-century residential architect embodies the asymmetrical massing, rough-faced masonry walls, and chunky stone arches of the Richardsonian Romanesque style. Three stories of rusticated gray rhyolite rise to gabled roofs and into four prominent chimneys. The balustraded entry porch has stout stone posts with foliated capitals. A crenelated parapet on a round corner tower is echoed by the crenelated balcony of a two-story south bay. The use of stained glass is extravagant, especially the large peacock window on the north wall. The two-story carriage house was connected to the dwelling by a later addition.

Walter Dunning, a realtor, commissioned this house, which illustrates William Lang's exuberance and penchant for eclectic historicist details from various periods. Mitchell Benedict, a state supreme court justice, bought the house in 1898, and his family lived here until the 1930s when the building was converted to apartments.

116. Keating House–Capitol Hill Mansion Bed and Breakfast Inn

1892, Reiche, Carter, and Smith. 1207 Pennsylvania Street, northwest corner of East Twelfth Avenue, NR, HD-31

This three-story Queen Anne dwelling features rough masonry walls of red-orange Manitou sandstone, a conical tower, and recessed upper-story porches. Built for businessman and realtor Jeffrey Keating and his wife, Mary, it was

FIGURE 2.13. Dunning-Benedict House (photo by Roger Whitacre).

later converted, like many Capitol Hill homes, into a boardinghouse, the Buena Vista Hotel. Following a restoration that returned to the original floor plan and interior woodwork, it reopened in 1993 as the Capitol Hill Mansion Bed and Breakfast Inn.

117. Robinson House

1906, Willis A. Marean and Albert J. Norton. 1225 Pennsylvania Street, HD-31

A low-pitched ceiling, wide overhanging eaves, half timbering, and exposed rafters lend Craftsman style distinction to this two-story brick dwelling, the home of William F. and Mary Byers Robinson. Mary was the daughter of William Newton Byers, founding editor of the *Rocky Mountain News*. Her husband worked for the *News* and then ran the *Leadville Democrat* before opening Robinson Printing Company, which he operated until his death in 1912. Today's Bradford-Robinson Printing Company is one of Denver's oldest printing and publishing houses. Mary continued to live in the house until an automobile accident ended her life in 1940, a sad fate for the little girl who first saw horse-and-wagon Denver in 1859.

FIGURE 2.14. The Molly Brown House is operated by Historic Denver, Inc., as a popular house museum (photo by Sandra Dallas Atchison).

118. Molly Brown House

1890, William A. Lang. 1340 Pennsylvania Street, NR, HD-31

The irrepressible wife of John J. Brown, a successful miner from Leadville, became the source of legend and of the Broadway play and movie *The Unsinkable Molly Brown*. Margaret "Molly" Brown was snubbed by Denver society as a vulgar parvenu. Snobs sniffed that Molly's mother, who lived with her, smoked a corncob pipe. In response, Molly educated herself and began traveling among the fashionable set in Europe and on the East Coast. Most notably, she survived the 1912 sinking of the ocean liner *Titanic*, but later, her house almost perished. After her death in 1932, the house became a bachelors' rooming house, a home for wayward girls, and then a target for demolition, the fate of a twin house that once stood next door to the north. Historic Denver, Inc., was formed in 1970 to rescue and restore this Queen Anne residence built of quarry-faced pink and gray rhyolite with red sandstone trim. As one of this country's best-known self-made women, Molly would probably be tickled to know that her home is now Denver's most popular house museum, restored from the anaglypta-covered hallways to the stone lions in front. Interiors are fussy and rich, with carved woodwork and a wealth of furnishings from the Brown era. The two-story carriage house has been converted to a visitor center and gift shop selling, among many other things, Kristin Iverson's book, *Molly Brown: Unraveling the Myth*, which recasts the bumpkin portrayed in the play and movie as a self-educated champion of women's and working-class rights.

119. Guerrieri-DeCunto House

1896, Frank Guerrieri?, builder. 1650 Pennsylvania Street, NR

Frank Guerrieri, an immigrant violinist from Paladello, Italy, arrived in Denver in 1876 and opened a liquor business with his brothers. In 1896 he built this house and moved in. Another business partner, Frank DeCunto, bought the house from Guerrieri in 1901 and lived there until 1919, when he sold it to yet another Italian immigrant with mercantile interests, David Serafini. This house, now used as offices, is a brick foursquare dressed up with a garland frieze, arched stone window lintels, wrought-iron balconies, and Corinthian porch columns.

120. Hayes Townhouses

1893, William A. Lang. 1926 alterations. 1732 and 1738 Pearl Street

These two, three-story sandstone townhouses designed by Denver's most distinguished nineteenth-century residential architect feature elaborate second-story oriel windows and Lang's characteristically fancy stonework.

121. Temple Emanuel Event Center

1899, John J. Humphreys. 1924 south addition, Thielman Robert Wieger. 1595 Pearl Street, southwest corner of East Sixteenth Avenue, NR

This large Moorish style synagogue once housed Colorado's oldest and largest Jewish congregation until that congregation moved to a new home, a National Register

FIGURE 2.15. Temple Emanuel Event Center (Tom Noel Collection).

landmark, at 51 Grape Street in 1961. The structure was saved from demolition by the City and County of Denver for use as an events center, then a Christian church. Ogee arches and other exotic influences in this beige brick building celebrate Judaism's Near Eastern origins. The facade features many Moorish elements, such as the minaret-like towers with walkways and copper domes. The domes are repeated atop two pavilions on the north and south sides. The central and north towers are octagonal and taller than the south tower, which fronts a rectangular addition with buttressed corners. Stone trim, striated brick banding, and a red tile roof enhance the composition. Floral and geometric motifs prevalent in Islamic architecture are evident in rows below the eaves, in the door panels, and in the stained glass windows, as well as in the interior carved wood paneling and stenciling. The 1,500-seat auditorium inside is paneled in dark oak and features a double-vaulted ceiling with decorative painting. Exotic ornament characterizes the interior and exterior.

FIGURE 2.16. A central soaring tower and rear addition never materialized on St. John's Episcopal Cathedral (a) (History Colorado), but the *reredos* by Arnold Ronnebeck (b) did go into the cathedral's St. Martin's Chapel (Denver Public Library).

122. Helene Apartments

1904, Samuel Hansen and George L. Bettcher. 1931 alterations. 1062 Pearl Street

A two-story brick apartment in the Moderne style flaunts Art Deco elements in its terracotta trim. The 1931 remodel added Moderne elements in an effort to keep up with modern times.

123. Huddart Terrace

1890, John J. Huddart. 625 East Sixteenth Avenue, northwest corner of Washington Street

John J. Huddart (1858–1930), an English-trained engineer and architect, started out in Denver as a draftsman with Frank Edbrooke, then established his own practice in 1887. In four decades of Colorado practice, he designed a great number and variety of buildings, including eight county courthouses. This two-story Queen Anne style brick and stone gem displays symmetrical protruding bays topped by shingled caps above recessed entries framed by Neoclassical columns.

124. St. John's Episcopal Cathedral

1911, Gordon, Tracy, and Swarthout. 1313 Washington Street between East Thirteenth and East Fourteenth Avenues and Clarkson and Washington Streets, NR

After an arsonist burned St. John's in the Wilderness at Twentieth Avenue and Welton Street, the congregation rebuilt this cathedral on a full-block site. The New York City firm that won a national architectural competition accommodated the surrounding residential neighborhood with a low, generously landscaped English Gothic Revival design clad in random-coursed Indiana limestone. The altar, altar screen, and *reredos*, all carved from oak, were salvaged from the earlier burned church. A taller central tower, transepts, and south additions included in the original design were never completed. The attached St. Martin's Chapel, a 1928 Gothic Revival design from Merrill and Burnham Hoyt, has fine wooden *reredos* by Denver sculptor Arnold Ronnebeck. A carillon of fifteen bells is housed in matching square, castellated towers flanking the north entrance. The fifty-one stained glass windows range from Gothic Revival to contemporary in style. A rosebush in the Eve window was added later when a seductive Eve proved distracting to churchgoers.

125. Kistler-Rodriguez House

1920, Jules Jacques Benoit Benedict. 700 East Ninth Avenue, southeast corner of Washington Street, NR

William H. Kistler, founder of the Kistler Stationery Company, lived in this impressive brick, terracotta-trimmed house until his death in 1936. Dr. Rene Alvarez Rodriguez, a prominent physician and civic activist, became the house's second owner. Dr. Rodriguez served as the consul for his native country, the Dominican Republic, and converted his residence to that country's consulate. He was a leading spokesman for Denver's Latin American community. This two-story eclectic style brick house has become even more eclectic with drastically modern rear additions. A dental group currently practices in this typically horizontal composition by Benedict.

126. Enos House

1891, Isaac Hodgson? 841 Washington Street

This red brick residence displays finely crafted details, such as the third-story central witch hat dormer and oriel window and a north-side port-cochere and rear carriage house. Charles W. Enos, a physician and surgeon specializing in eye and ear disorders, presided over the Denver Homeopathic College.

127. Cass-Friedman House

1899, Willis A. Marean and Albert J. Norton. 733 East Eighth Avenue, northwest corner of Clarkson Street

The dramatically stepped gable and dormer ends distinguish this as a rare Denver example of the Dutch Colonial Revival style. The tightly laid pressed red brick is trimmed with sandstone accents and banding. Generous windows, a conical corner tower, and distinctive chimneys provide residential ambiance for the home of Emogene Cass, widow of Dr. Oscar David Cass, a pioneer physician. Although trained in surgery, the doctor preferred finance and opened a gold brokerage after settling in Denver in 1860. Dr. Cass was a founder of the Hinckley Express Company and the Exchange Bank, two investment houses. Rabbi William S. Friedman of Temple Emanuel, the most prominent spokesman for his faith and a co-founder of the Charity Organization Society (now United Way), lived here after Cass. His home became an Episcopal commune headed by Bishop James Frey in the 1960s before its conversion to law offices in the 1990s.

128. Morey Middle School

1921, Arthur A. Fisher and William E. Fisher. 840 East Fourteenth Avenue between Clarkson and Emerson Streets and East Fourteenth and East Thirteenth Avenues

This Beaux Arts, Italian Renaissance style school features a central fountain court, round-arched windows, and a red tile roof. In addition to the two exterior entry murals, other murals by Louise Ronnebeck are in the auditorium, along with Robert Garrison's three polychrome statues: *Athena*, *Bust of a Youth*, and *Bust of a Girl*. This school, which includes a tiled basement swimming pool, indoor track, and a library with a vaulted ceiling and fine oak woodwork, was named for businessman and school board member Chester Morey. One of the first junior high schools constructed in Denver, it follows the City Beautiful tradition in occupying a generous one-block landscaped site with grand architecture, incorporating art to edify students and the public.

129. German House–Denver Turnverein

1921, George L. Bettcher. 1570 Clarkson Street, southeast corner of East Sixteenth Avenue, SR

Colorado's oldest ethnic club still holds meetings, parties, dance classes, and German-language performances open to all. The Turnverein, founded in Prussia around 1811 by Friedrich Ludwig Jahn, cherishes the slogan "A Sound Mind in a Sound Body." Turner is the German word for gymnast, while *verein* means union or association. Founded as a gymnastic club promoting exercise, sports, and fellowship, the Turnverein evolved into a social and cultural organization that included women and children. Popularly known as the German House, the club promoted German music, dance, drama, and art, as well as German food and drink. Germans were the largest foreign-born group in Denver during the

FIGURE 2.17. Denver Turnverein (photo by Tom Noel).

scantily robed woman dancing with a goat-footed satyr playing a lyre. Murals and German inscriptions in the basement rathskeller recall the Old Country. The upstairs hall, with its stage and bandstand, hosts dances, meetings, and fine arts programs. Built as a private social club, the Coronado Club, in 1921, the hall was purchased by the Turnverein in 1922. Although the landscaping and beer garden have been replaced by the parking lot, this handsome structure commemorates Denver's rich German culture.

HD-35 SWALLOW HILL HISTORIC DISTRICT

Emerson to Downing Street roughly between East Sixteenth and East Seventeenth Avenues

Named for George Ransom Swallow who platted the area, the district sports a notable collection of Queen Anne style residences designed by some of Denver's most prominent architects: Lang and Pugh, Varian and Sterner, James Murdoch, Frank Edbrooke, and others. Constructed between 1886 and 1910, the majority of these buildings were once home to prominent Denver families. Although many have been renovated into office spaces, the Swallow Hill Historic District was once entirely residential with the exception of St. Paul's Methodist Church. One of the most spectacular residences is the George M. Bailey Mansion. This three-story Queen Anne, an 1889 Lang and Pugh masterwork at 1600 Ogden Street, makes a spectacular cornerstone for the Swallow Hill Historic District.

nineteenth century, and this chapter flourished after opening its first hall on Market Street in 1865. The club built the Turn Halle, a large theater with a horseshoe-shaped balcony, in the Tivoli Brewery on the Auraria campus.

A Denver Turner, Robert Barth, became the first physical education teacher in the Denver Public Schools, and another member, Ruth Drumm Witting, was the first woman to direct exercise sessions over the radio. Although anti-German sentiment during World Wars I and II forced the Turnverein to adopt a much lower profile, it continued to welcome Teutons and to promote the German language and culture.

This fourth home of the Turnverein at Sixteenth and Clarkson Streets is a stucco building hinting at the Mediterranean Revival style, with its large fan-lighted windows, pedimented entry parapet, corner towerettes, and red tile roof. The terracotta entablature over the entry features a

130. Flower-Vaile House

1889, Robert G. Balcomb and Eugene R. Rice. 1610 Emerson Street, NR, HD-35

One of Swallow Hill's Queen Anne showplaces exults in whimsical massing and exuberant ornamentation on this three-story dwelling. Pressed brick with stone trim is sugar-coated with vergeboards that dramatize the multiple gables and dormers, especially at the octagonal entry porch. Here, the elaborate turned spindle porch posts spring into arches, a pattern repeated overhead on the second-story porch. Heavily rusticated stone window surrounds compete for attention with the double-decker porch on this hyperactive facade. This weighty show of opulence was restored in 1981 and converted from an apartment house to offices.

John S. Flower, a prominent Denver realtor and strong supporter of Mayor Robert W. Speer's City Beautiful

FIGURE 2.18. Zang Townhouse (photo by Tom Noel).

schemes, sold the house in 1890 to attorney Joel F. Vaile. Vaile's wife, Charlotte, authored children's books, including *The Orchard Girls*, *The Truth about Santa Claus*, and a fictional account of Colorado mining, *The M.C.C.* Balcomb and Rice also designed the Bouvier-Lathrop House (1890) next door at 1600 Emerson, another fussy facade that bulges beyond its rectangular plan and rusticated stone corseting.

131. Zang Townhouse

1889, William A. Lang. 1532 Emerson Street, NR, HD-35

Adolph J. Zang, who presided over Colorado's largest pre-Prohibition brewery, the Zang Brewing Company, commissioned this tall, narrow, two-story townhouse. Its rough-faced rhyolite facade climbs to a steep front gable and a slender corner oriel window with a steep conical cap. The parapeted front gable end is topped by a carved stone griffin that adds a Gothic shiver to the asymmetrical, dramatically vertical facade. Profuse floral adornment carved into the rhyolite lends an organic creepiness. Three more of William

Lang's townhouses (1889–90) survive two blocks west at 1624 and 1648 Washington Street and his own residence at 1626 Washington, whose facade sports a stepped gable.

132. Frank E. Edbrooke House

1893, Frank E. Edbrooke. 931 East Seventeenth Avenue, HD-35

Denver's style-setting architect of the late nineteenth century designed not only grand commercial edifices but also splendid residences, including this one, which he built for himself. This asymmetrical Queen Anne is given a fine sense of proportion by the repeated rooflines and details such as the grouped columns on the first- and second-story porches. Note the front window trimmed with raised brick courses that accentuate the arches. Stone banding at the sill level is skillfully incorporated into the porch balustrade, and a second-story band becomes the common sill of three windows that paraphrase Andrea Palladio. The 1896 Edbrooke-designed house next door at 941 East Seventeenth Avenue has been converted to a spa.

133. Aldine-Grafton Apartments

1890, James Murdoch. 1980 remodel. 1001–21 East Seventeenth Avenue, northwest corner of Ogden Street, HD-35

These classy townhomes were built as the Aldine Family Hotel by Albert Brewster and renamed the Grafton by subsequent owner Katherine Grafton Patterson, wife of Colorado US senator Thomas M. Patterson. These six townhomes have two-story brick bays with recessed two-tiered porches and third-story dormers with conical turrets protruding from a mansard roof. During the Great Depression the Grafton sank to subdivision into thirty apartments. A 1979–80 remodeling turned one of Capitol Hill's most architecturally rhythmic multi-family buildings into condominiums.

HD-41 PARK AVENUE HISTORIC DISTRICT

Park Avenue from East Colfax Avenue to East Twentieth Avenue between Washington and Franklin Streets

Celebrating Denver's first boulevard (1873), this district encompasses only the public right-of-way and triangle parks along Park Avenue. It presaged Mayor Robert W. Speer's much larger plan for parkways and boulevards.

FIGURE 2.19. Aldine-Grafton Apartments (photo by Roger Whitacre).

134. Ogden Theatre

1917, Harry W.J. Edbrooke. 935 E. Colfax Avenue at Ogden Street, NR

After Thomas Edison and George Eastman developed motion picture film, the golden age of movie houses arrived in the 1910s and 1920s. Even small neighborhood theaters like the Ogden put on architectural airs. Otherwise a simple, functional, two-story brick box, the Ogden wears a fanciful facade framed by twin octagonal towers complete with false windows, a geometric frieze, and a red tile roof. The polychromatic terracotta, garlands, swags, and other Beaux Arts details suggest the visual escapes the movies inside provided. J. A. Goodridge and John Thompson hired Frank Edbrooke's nephew and protégé, Harry, who gave the edifice a vaguely Mediterranean flair.

A 1993 exterior restoration was accompanied by a remodeling of the interior, with nightclub tables and seating, three bars, and a dance floor. The original forty-five-foot oak stage and domed ceiling stayed. The original stenciling, Neoclassical terracotta trim, and Corinthian columns have been restored to preserve a grand setting worlds away from the bleak shoeboxes of modern multiplex theaters.

FIGURE 2.20. These two unidentified 90s rockers are among the young people who have patronized the Ogden Theatre since its 1993 conversion to a live theater and nightclub (photo by Glenn Cuerden).

FIGURE 2.21. Emerson School (Photo by Tom Noel)

135. Emerson Elementary School

1885, Robert S. Roeschlaub. 2012 restoration, SlaterPaull. 1420 Ogden Street, northeast corner of East Fourteenth Avenue, NR

The most impressive feature of this school, as Francine Haber, Kenneth R. Fuller, and David N. Wetzel note in their book *Robert S. Roeschlaub*, is "a windowless wall consisting of nothing more than band courses and a large white Indiana limestone sundial within an ornamental arch." As in other Roeschlaub schools, the central public court allows easy inspection of the classrooms angled off of it. This two-story red brick school rises into a steeply pitched roof punctuated with dormers, gables, and elaborate chimneys. Closed as a school in 1979 as a result of declining enrollments, it was sold to a group of nonprofits that opened it as the Frank McGlone Senior Center. After

restoration in 2012, the school reopened as a center for preservation agencies, including Colorado Preservation, Inc., Historic Denver, Inc., and the National Trust for Historic Preservation, outfits interested in practicing what they preach: the most efficient building is a recycled one already built. Emerson Elementary School is also a LEED Gold certified showcase demonstration of how preservation can be energy-efficient.

136. The Cornwall

1901, Walter E. Rice. 1317 Ogden Street, northwest corner of East Thirteenth Avenue, NR

William T. Cornwall built and lived in this stylish gray brick apartment house, whose Mediterranean Revival mode is reflected in the balconies, column capitals, cornices, architraves, friezes, wrought iron, and terracotta trim. Rice, a developer, engineer, and inventor as well as an architect, built his own terracotta studio in the basement. There, he made the trim and the tiles covering the corner towers of the roof garden, with its open promenades and fourth-floor penthouses. This handsome, stylish, and striking structure was restored and revamped into condominiums in the mid-1970s.

137. Corona School–Dora Moore Elementary School

1889, Robert S. Roeschlaub. 1909 addition, David Dryden.
1993 restoration and additions, Stanley Pouw and Associates.
846 Corona Street between East Eighth and East Ninth
Avenues, NR

In 1975, when the school board announced plans to demolish this elementary school, students helped persuade the Denver Landmark Preservation Commission and the Denver City Council to declare this Romanesque Revival gem the first locally landmarked school. Roeschlaub,

Colorado's leading institutional architect of the nineteenth century, designed at least a dozen Denver schools, including three other Denver landmarks: Emerson Elementary School at East Fourteenth Avenue and Ogden Street, Stevens Elementary at 1140 Columbine Street, and Wyatt Elementary School, 3620 Franklin Street.

Symmetrical composition, generous exterior detail, and the interior court plan distinguish this as Roeschlaub's most beautiful school. The square corner entry towers are topped by bell-shaped domes with nipple finials. The brick walls blend into rich layers of stone and terracotta trim that include cherubs as role models for schoolchildren. Two large additions, each reflecting its own era, complement the original without crowding the full-block site. Originally called the Corona School, the school was renamed in 1938 for a longtime principal.

FIGURE 2.23. Governor Ralph Carr sometimes bicycled from his Downing Street home to work at the Colorado State Capitol (*Denver Post* photo).

138. Governor Ralph L. Carr Residence

1905. 747 Downing Street, HD-21

Ralph Lawrence Carr, governor of Colorado from 1939 to 1943, used as his residence and home office this modified foursquare enhanced with an Ionic column front porch and central dormer. Carr courageously defended Japanese

FIGURE 2.22. Corona School–Dora Moore Elementary School (photo by Tom Noel).

Americans during World War II and, to show his trust, he recruited a housekeeper, Wakako Domoto, from the Amache Japanese Relocation Center at Granada in southeastern Colorado. His defense of a hated minority led him to lose a close 1944 US Senate race, but he was honored posthumously with the Ralph L. Carr Colorado Judicial Center (2013, Fentress Architects), 1300 Broadway.

139. Rosenzweig House

1882, Charles L. Dow, builder. 1129 East Seventeenth Avenue, northwest corner of Park Avenue between Downing and Marion Streets, NR

Charles L. Dow, a contractor, built numerous Denver houses and briefly lived in this one. Leopold Rosenzweig, a Russian Jew who moved to Denver for his health, later occupied the house. His daughter, Frances, became a Wagnerian soprano who performed under the name Frances Rose. When she retired, she lived here until her death in 1956. Publisher Charles "Cal" Cleworth restored this and neighboring residences, including the tiny, steep-roofed 1882 cottage at 1732 Downing Street, and converted them to a distinctive office complex that includes the two-story carriage house, barn, and coal shed. The two-and-a-half-story Italianate main house has an Eastlake style porch at the west-side entrance, a dentiled frame cornice, and bracketed eaves under a hip roof. Also on the site are a gabled barn and a coal shed.

140. The Colonnade

1902, Charles Quayle. 1984 alterations. 1210 East Colfax Avenue, southeast corner of Marion Street

A distinctive three-story colonnade facade with fluted Neoclassical columns and granite bases may have inspired the name. The building also features a flat roof with hipped projecting bays, hipped dormers, ornate bracketed eaves, and a cornice above a frieze with medallions, garlands, and egg and dart trim. The original facade remains intact behind 1984 alterations that covered it with glass. Among the first luxury apartment buildings in Denver, this $100,000 showplace is illuminated with leaded and frosted glass and an interior courtyard. As the pioneer generation aged and lost money in the 1893 silver crash, many left their Capitol Hill mansions for prestigious apartment houses such as this. The Colonnade is now rejuvenated as lofts.

141. Wolcott School Apartments

1898, Frederick J. Sterner?. 1400–14 Marion Street, northeast corner of East Fourteenth Avenue

The Wolcott School for Girls, once an elite Capitol Hill private academy, reflects the Renaissance Revival mode, with balconies and groupings of round-arched windows. The alley bridge connection to the 1906 three-story addition is reminiscent of Venice. Three buildings are united by shared access and architectural details, most notably round-arch windows. Anna Louise Wolcott, sister of US senator Henry R. Wolcott, founded the school for the offspring of Denver's power elite. Anna Wolcott became the first woman regent of the University of Colorado in 1910 and was active in musical, educational, and social circles. After Wolcott's marriage to Frederick J. Vaille, Mary Kent Wallace ran the Wolcott School. She left in 1922 to open the Kent School for Girls. Shortly afterward, the Wolcott School closed to become apartments.

142. Doyle-Benton House

1896, Frank Houck. 1301 Lafayette Street, northwest corner of East Thirteenth Avenue

James Doyle, a prospector and original partner of the Portland Mining Company in Cripple Creek, made millions from that golden jackpot. He lived in this two-and-a-half-story brick Denver Square from 1896 to 1905. As mining declined and agriculture boomed in Colorado, this house underwent an ownership change during the early 1900s. In 1907 Frank Benton, founder of the Frank Benton Land and Livestock firm, purchased the residence, which remained in the Benton family until 1971. The building was then converted into a four-unit apartment house until returned to a single-family home in 2004. The home is an early example of foursquare architecture, represented in its boxy shape with centralized dormer, tapered Ionic columns, and a hipped roof. A first-story Palladian window, carriage house, and corbeled chimney further distinguish this residence.

143. Hamilton Apartment Building

1908, William Cowe and George F. Harvey Jr. 1475 Humboldt Street, southwest corner of East Colfax Avenue

This dignified three-story red brick apartment structure has a Mission Revival style curvilinear parapet and prominent bracketed eaves. A recessed entry, wrought-iron balconies, and large angled windows in the three bays enliven this little-altered landmark.

HD-44 HUMBOLDT STREET–PARK AVENUE HISTORIC DISTRICT

Humboldt Street between East Sixteenth and Seventeenth Avenues

This one-block historic district, anchored by three fine stone townhouses at the southeast corner of Humboldt Street and Sixteenth Avenue, contains a mix of residences including modest cottages, elegant Queen Annes, apartment houses, and mostly congenial infill.

144. Tammen Hall

1932, Merrill H. Hoyt and Burnham Hoyt. 1010 East Nineteenth Avenue, southeast corner of Ogden Street

Henry Heye Tammen and Agnes Reid Tammen donated $100,000 to help build this eight-story buff brick, Art Deco style building designed in a U-shape with a second-story balcony. Tammen, co-founder and longtime co-publisher of the *Denver Post,* also bequeathed $2 million to the hospital. His wife continued her charitable work there until her death in 1942. The building features a symmetrical facade, with Roman arched bays decorated with narrow horizontal bands and pyramidal red tile roofs. This structure housed the Children's Hospital's nurses' residence and training school until 1953. When Children's Hospital moved to Aurora in 2007, nearby St. Joseph Hospital bought the old site, including Tammen Hall, which it plans to restore for office use.

145. Catherine Mullen Nurses' Home–Mullen Building

1933, Temple Hoyne Buell. 1895 Franklin Street

Ella Mullen Weckbaugh donated this building to St. Joseph Hospital in memory of her mother, Catherine Smith Mullen. The jagged parapets and columns of rich brown and red bricks rise into leaf-like clusters at the top, suggesting an organic, bushy-like parapet. The protruding brown and red brick plumes contrast dramatically with the blond brick structure. The well-preserved interior also makes this one of Denver's finest Art Deco monuments, with richly

FIGURE 2.24. Inside and outside, the Mullen Building retains its original Art Deco shine (exterior photo by Tom Noel, interior photo by Glenn Cuerden).

detailed tile mosaics for the floors and bas-relief geometric ornament plastered into the ceilings and walls. Once the dormitory and school for nursing students, the building now houses the St. Joseph Hospital Foundation.

146. 1750 Gilpin Building
1893, Josiah S. Briean. 1750 Gilpin Street

The Mouat Lumber and Investment Company built this elegant Queen Anne residence in 1893 for speculation. Denver architect Josiah S. Briean later designed this two-and-a-half-story red brick building with sandstone banding and foundation. It features a steeply pitched cross-gabled roof, bracketed eaves, a recessed second-story porch, and a tower-like bay on the north side. The interior retains detailed woodwork and the original fireplaces with oak mantle and decorative tile. During the 1960s the residence was converted to offices for nearby St. Joseph Hospital.

147. Walter-Bierly House
1888. 2259 Gilpin Street, southeast corner of East Twenty-Third Avenue

John Walter, a sheepman who founded the Standard Meat Company, built this two-and-a-half-story brick home with a matching carriage house. His family lived here until the 1940s. The windows with hooded lintels, Eastlake style front porch framing, and symmetrical composition suggest the Italianate style. The steep-pitched roof, however, is more Queen Anne in style and may be a later addition. Walter's grandson, Justin W. Brierly, a lawyer, Denver Public Schools administrator, and executive manager of the Central City Opera House Association, also lived here.

Cheesman Park Area

Walter Scott Cheesman arrived in 1859 and became Denver's biggest real estate tycoon, property owner, and taxpayer. One of his most notable land assemblages created Union Station and the railyards. Among many other enterprises, he is best-known for founding the Denver Union Water Company and nearly monopolizing water service until the city bought his firm in 1918. The park named for him was originally Denver's pioneer cemetery, Mount Prospect. Reborn as Congress Park in 1890, it was renamed for Cheesman and more elegantly landscaped in 1907. Many fine surrounding residences, including modern high-rise

deluxe apartments and condominiums, make Cheesman Park a favorite residential area as well as one of the city's most popular parks.

148. Cheesman Park Memorial Pavilion
1910, Willis A. Marean and Albert J. Norton. 1000 High Street, NR

This Colorado Yule marble memorial commemorates pioneer business tycoon Walter Scott Cheesman, with a viewing platform reminiscent of the Greek Parthenon. Surrounded by formal gardens and a reflecting pool, the classical columned pavilion crowns the hill at the east end of Cheesman Park (1898, Reinhard Schuetze). Once the city cemetery, this urban park features curvilinear walks and drives and perimeter trees bordering an expanse of lawn that carries the eye to the mountain view. Cheesman Esplanade, as the full-block grassy median strip between Williams and High Streets is called, connects the park with East Seventh Avenue Parkway.

FIGURE 2.25. In this aerial view of Cheesman Park Memorial Pavilion, ca. 1920, Mount Calvary Catholic Cemetery occupies what is now the well-fertilized Denver Botanic Gardens (photo by Humphreys Aviation).

HD-2 HUMBOLDT STREET HISTORIC DISTRICT
Humboldt Street between East Tenth and Twelfth Avenues, NRD

On the west side of Cheesman Park, twenty-six large homes comprise the residential enclave sometimes termed Humboldt Island. Built between the 1890s and the 1920s, the dwellings vary in style, but nearly all were architect-designed. Langdon E. Morris Jr., in his book *Denver*

Landmarks (1979), contends that this district reflects "that unfortunate period when architects were timidly seeking new forms" and lacks "the vigor and design sense of the preceding High Victorian era." If most of these homes lack daring, they do exemplify the conservative tastes and interest in fine craftsmanship of Denver's wealthy elite.

The Dencla-Walker-White House (1898, Harry T.E. Wendell, 1151 Humboldt Street) is a distinctive Georgian Revival, with a walled garden and eyebrow second-story dormers. At 1050 East Tenth Avenue on the southeast corner of Humboldt Street, the imposing mansion of Frederick G. Bonfils was demolished in 1969 and replaced by a fifteen-story apartment house. After public protest failed to stop this high-rise, Denver passed an ordinance to protect Cheesman Park's mountain view from further encroachments. Bonfils, a former Kansas City con man, and Henry Heye Tammen, a former bartender whose Tuscan villa (1907, Edwin Moorman) is at 1061 Humboldt, made the *Denver Post* the most lucrative—and sensational—newspaper ever published in the Rockies. These two self-made millionaires along with the Stoibers, mining millionaires from Silverton, gave Humboldt Island a reputation as the address for Denver's nouveau riche.

The Brown-Mackenzie-McDougal House (1903, Eugene R. Rice, 1100 Humboldt Street, northeast corner of East Eleventh Avenue) is an eclectic design pairing an oriel window and double Gothic arch window with a wrought-iron balcony over an unrelated entry canopy, added later. Nearly every window is a different size and design, and the massing is irregular, as if Rice set out deliberately to provide an alternative to the foursquares from which his plan derives. His unpredictable composition is unified by a heavy red tile hipped roof with dormers, gables, and knob finials.

The Thompson-Henry House (1905, Baerresen Brothers, 1070 Humboldt Street, southeast corner of East Eleventh Avenue) features Palladian windows and a grand semicircular portico with eight fluted Corinthian columns fronting this peachy brick Georgian Revival dwelling trimmed in white terracotta. A second-story pedimented porch door and third-story Palladian-influenced dormer further distinguish one of the first Denver homes erected with steel beams. On the north side, four immense two-story Ionic columns support a third-story balustraded porch beneath an ocular window.

The Stoiber-Reed-Humphreys Mansion (1907, Willis A. Marean and Albert J. Norton, 1022 Humboldt Street) is the

FIGURE 2.26. Stoiberhof has been restored, from its third-story dormers to its basement swimming pool and bowling alley, 1908 (photo by Charles S. Price, Denver Public Library).

showiest of all in this parade of show homes. Lena Stoiber's twelve-foot-high stone wall makes it difficult to see the nine lot grounds and formal Renaissance Revival mansion built by her husband, Edward G. Stoiber. He struck it rich at Silverton's Silver Lake mine and, like many other mining millionaires, gravitated to Denver. The high wall, at least in legend, was Lena's way of spiting snooty neighbors who gossiped about her past in Silverton's notorious red-light district. After Stoiber's death she married Hugh Rood, who perished on the *Titanic* in 1912. Lena then sold the thirty-room mansion to Mrs. Verner Z. Reed. When Mrs. Reed built her Tudor mansion at 475 Circle Drive, she sold the mansion to Ruth Boettcher Humphreys, who succeeded Mrs. Crawford Hill as the queen bee of Denver society.

149. Sweet-Miller House

1906, Frederick J. Sterner and George H. Williamson. 1075 Humboldt Street, southwest corner of East Eleventh Avenue, HD-2

Colorado governor William E. Sweet, a Progressive, unsuccessfully took on the Ku Klux Klan, which ousted him from office in 1924. The governor's two-and-a-half-story Georgian Revival home, where his widow, Joyeuse, lived until her death in 1962, is distinguished by a full-length front porch under a balustraded balcony and by a variety of Palladian-themed windows. Kent Miller, an attorney, purchased the home in 1984 and restored the classical interior elements, such as fluted columns, arches, and ceiling moldings. The alternating red and brown brick extends to the fence posts for the front-yard garden.

150. The Waldman
1922, William E. and Arthur A. Fisher. 1515 East Ninth Avenue, northeast corner of Humboldt Street

David M. Waldman had Fisher and Fisher, the most ubiquitous early-twentieth-century Colorado architects, also design his Acacia Apartments (1922), 429 East Fourteenth Avenue, and the Bernard (1923), now the Cardwell, 850 Humboldt Street. A distinctive wrought-iron and glass canopy welcomes residents to the elegant Mediterranean style Waldman on the west side of Cheesman Park. The three-and-a-half-story stucco building above a raised dark-brick basement rises to a rooftop belvedere. Waldman lived in one of the forty-two apartment units here, which range from 600 square feet to 3,900 square feet.

151. Boettcher Conservatory, Denver Botanic Gardens
1964, Victor Hornbein and Edward D. White Jr. 1005 York Street

Despite the convention that landmarks should be at least fifty years old to be considered for National Register listing and at least thirty years old for a Denver landmark designation, the Denver Landmark Preservation Commission designated this futuristic structure only nine years after its completion. The Boettcher Conservatory is made of faceted Plexiglas panels between interlaced concrete arches in an inverted catenary curve that arcs fifty feet above tropical gardens. Around 2,000 horticultural species are cultivated amid waterfalls and pools constructed in a sloped, naturalistic environment inside the humid, warm conservatory. The Boettcher Foundation, whose money came largely from the Ideal Cement Company, funded this complex and encouraged the use of concrete throughout. Even the lampposts in the surrounding walks and gardens are concrete "trees" with globe lights posing as fruits. Denver architect David Owen Tryba designed a 2009 expansion, including a parking garage topped by the Mordecai Children's Garden, a visitor center, and newly opened greenhouses that invite

FIGURE 2.27. Boettcher Conservatory, Denver Botanic Gardens (photo by Tom Noel).

visitors inside.

HD-8 MORGAN'S ADDITION HISTORIC DISTRICT

East Eighth to East Ninth Avenues between York Street and Cheesman Park

Samuel B. Morgan subdivided what had been the south edge of the Mount Calvary Catholic section of City Cemetery (now the Denver Botanic Gardens). Between 1910 and 1930, some of the city's most prominent and wealthy families constructed grand homes here. The forty-five homes showcased in this district are mostly revival styles by leading architects that are purer and more confident than the eclectic homes across Cheesman Park in Humboldt Island. The Sullivan House (1926, Jules Jacques Benoit Benedict, HD-8) at 801 Race Street offers an unusually stark, almost abstract Eighth Avenue facade, contrasting with the building's colonnaded west facade and Benedict's more typical Renaissance Revival palace at 817 Race Street, the Neusteter-Chenoweth House (1921). Jules Jacques Benoit Benedict's 1922 home for Dr. James J. and Ruth Porter Waring, 910 Gaylord Street, with its Juliette balcony, is particularly charming, as is Benedict's 800 Race Street (1920) villa. The Livermore-Benton House (1911, Maurice Biscoe and Henry H. Hewitt) at 901 Race Street exemplifies the Colonial Revival style, as do the neighboring Dines House (1931, Harry James Manning), 900 Race Street, and the Daniel Millet House (1920, William E. and Arthur A. Fisher), 860 Vine Street. This district's homes, bordering the Denver Botanic Gardens on the north side of East Ninth Avenue, are perhaps Denver's finest parade of mansions.

152. Denver Botanic Gardens House

1926, Jules Jacques Benoit Benedict. 909 York Street, northwest corner of East Ninth Avenue, NR, HD-8

Elements from the Beaux Arts and Tudor styles enhance this eclectic show home, which sports irregular massing, brick and stucco walls, oriel and grouped windows, and a steep pitched roof of green tiles. The house sits behind a tree-shaded garden and courtyard at the southeast corner of the Denver Botanic Gardens. Exquisitely furnished, it boasts the usual Benedict hallmark, a carved stone fireplace. The main staircase, with its wrought-iron balustrade, winds gracefully up from the entry. A second stairway,

FIGURE 2.28. Denver Botanic Gardens House (photo by Tom Noel).

hidden behind shelves in the library, leads down to the wine cellar and up to the master bedroom. Constructed for Richard C. Campbell, the business manager of the *Rocky Mountain News*, this mansion was purchased in 1958 by Mrs. James J. (Ruth Porter) Waring, who lived next door at 910 Gaylord Street in an exquisite 1924 Beaux Arts house also by Benedict. She gave this mansion to the Denver Botanic Gardens for use as its headquarters.

153. Petrikin Estate

1917, Aaron M. Gove and Thomas F. Walsh. 2109 East Ninth Avenue, northeast corner of Vine Street, HD-8

Built by the president and chairman of the board of the Great Western Sugar Company, William Petrikin, this three-story Colonial Revival brick structure remained the residence of William and his wife, Eloise, until 1945. Their house is one of the most grandiose of the show homes in the Morgan's Addition, which was once a part of City Cemetery, now occupied by Cheesman Park and the Denver Botanic Gardens. Gove and Walsh designed this formal mansion on a half-block site on the south edge of the Denver Botanic Gardens. Extensive gardens behind the brick and wrought-iron fence greet visitors, as do twin two-story fluted Ionic columns framing a Neoclassical fenestrated entry. Gove and Walsh also planned the Sugar Building, Great Western's corporate office, at 1350 Sixteenth Street, southeast corner of Wazee Street.

HD-22 WYMAN HISTORIC DISTRICT

Roughly from East Seventeenth to East Eleventh Avenues between York and Franklin Streets

This large district of 547 structures covers roughly the same area as John H. Wyman's original 1882 addition to the City of Denver. Wyman paid $3,000 for his fifty-one-block tract in 1866 and sold it twenty years later for $300,000. The main artery began as a dirt trail known as the Kansas City Road. It was renamed Colfax Avenue in honor of US representative Schuyler Colfax, who supported Colorado statehood and subsequently became vice president under Ulysses S. Grant. Colfax resigned in the wake of publicity about his role in Grant administration scandals. Colfax Avenue, too, has had its share of scandals.

Streetcars originally enabled Denverites to move out of downtown and build fine homes in the Wyman Addition. This section of Capitol Hill attracted mansion builders such as Senator Lawrence C. Phipps Sr., probably the richest man in Colorado. Streetcars later pushed beyond the Wyman Addition to the Cheesman Park, Country Club, Park Hill, and Montclair neighborhoods, carrying wealthy homeowners with them. Many of the large old homes were converted to boardinghouses or tuberculosis sanitariums. Only five of the many original Colfax Avenue mansions survive today, and four of them are hiding behind storefronts. The 1400 blocks of High and Vine Streets and the 1300 and 1500 blocks of Race Street still exude opulence, with their stout and merry Victorians. New tree plantings and restorations of old landmarks are reviving the entire Wyman Historic District. Notable rebirths such as the Castle Marne Bed and Breakfast, the Milheim House, and the Holiday Chalet Victorian Hotel have inspired the rehabilitation of other antique houses for single-family residences or offices. Designation as a Denver Landmark District in 1994 led to district guidelines and incentives that have furthered the dramatic turnaround in this riches-to-rags-to-riches neighborhood.

154. Tears-McFarlane House

1896, Frederick J. Sterner. 1290 Williams Street, southeast corner of East Thirteenth Avenue, NR

Daniel W. Tears, an attorney with offices in the Equitable Building, commissioned this Georgian Revival dwelling on the north edge of Cheesman Park. Third-story pedimented dormers behind a balustrade distinguish this red brick house whose rounded entry porch, supported by grouped columns, is topped by a balcony. Note the terracotta keystones in the radiating brick voussoirs. After Tears died in 1922, this became the home of William and Ida Kruse McFarlane, a prominent Central City family. She taught English at the University of Denver, co-founded the Central City Opera House Association with Anne Evans, and started a dance academy in the basement of this large home. On the north-side stairway landing, the big stained glass window is attributed to Tiffany. Restored in 1978 as a community center with an added large south-side meeting room, the structure has served as the Capitol Hill United Neighborhoods Community Center since 2006.

155. Pope-Thompson-Wasson House

1894, Harry T.E. Wendell. 1320 Race Street, HD-22

Gatepost pineapples, a symbol of welcome and hospitality, give this eclectic Mediterranean style residence its nickname, the Pineapple House. The distinctive diamond-pane front window is arched in greeting, like the doorway. Broad sheltering eaves and a second-story balcony also reach out to welcome passersby to this smiling yellow brick home with pleasingly asymmetrical proportions.

156. Adams-Fitzell House

1892, Franklin E. Kidder and John J. Humphreys. 1359 Race Street, HD-22

This rare Denver example of a Shingle style cottage has a broad-eaved conical cap on the corner tower. A polygonal dormer over the recessed entry porch, north- and south-side bays, and the steep-pitched roof also distinguish this dwelling. The rustic stone base extends upward into the tall chimney and porch posts for the overhanging second floor.

Note the rhyolite details such as the radiating door and window sills, the irregular polygonal chunks of rhyolite in the skin, and the pedestrian bench built into the sidewalk steps. Craftsman elements include the curled and twisted wrought-iron porch railing, the saw-tooth hemline to the second-story shingling, and the exposed porch roof beams. George H. Adams, a cattle and mining man, originally owned the house. Grant R. Fitzell, the second owner, was followed by his daughter as the home's owner.

FIGURE 2.29. Sykes-Nicholson-Moore House (photo by Roger Whitacre).

157. Sykes-Nicholson-Moore House

1897, Ernest P. Varian and Frederick J. Sterner. 1410 High Street, northeast corner of East Fourteenth Avenue, HD-22

The Reverend Richard E. Sykes, minister of First Universalist Church, commissioned this two-and-a-half-story brick Georgian Revival mansion. The second owner, Meredith Nicholson, wrote his mystery novel, *The House of a Thousand Candles* (1905), using this house as a setting. The book became the basis of a Broadway play and two movies. The house received a later addition on the south side, a semicircular two-story solarium that echoes the curve of the entry porch. The well-preserved interior is notable for its golden oak woodwork and a mantelpiece carved with words from Ralph Waldo Emerson, "The ornament of a house is the guests who frequent it." After a stint as the residence of Harold Willis Moore of the Benjamin Moore

Paint Company, it became a rooming house, then a halfway house, and later the ashram of the Guru Maharaja Ji, who turned the yard into a huge vegetable farm. After the guru left, the "House of a Thousand Candles" sputtered. It was rekindled in 1989 by the Starkey Institute for Household Management, which trained servants here until 1994 when it moved to another Denver landmark, the Cuthbert-Dines House, leaving 1410 to other professional office uses.

158. Watson House

1894, Frederick J. Sterner. 1437 High Street, HD-22

Ionic columns and pilasters and a third-story Palladian window distinguish the subsequently remodeled Colonial Revival home built for George H. Watson Jr. This block of High Street has many architectural treasures. The Clarence H. Olmsted House (1892, David W. Dryden?), 1460 High, has a great gambrel gable, and the Bohm Mansion (1895, Colorado Realty and Construction), 1820 East Colfax Avenue, has been recycled as the Holiday Chalet Victorian Hotel.

159. Peter McCourt House

1896, Colorado Realty and Construction. 1471 High Street, NR, HD-22

A two-story porch with full-height Ionic columns fronts this exuberant brick foursquare with Colonial Revival aspirations. The facade is embellished by balustraded second- and third-story balconies. Peter McCourt, brother of Elizabeth "Baby Doe" McCourt Tabor, managed the Tabor Grand Opera House for his brother-in-law, Horace Tabor, and orchestrated the Silver Circuit, which brought national theater companies to mining town opera houses. In McCourt's theatrical home, the interior boasts golden oak woodwork, a Tiffany chandelier, and an electric lamp borne by a statue of Mercury, not to mention the gilded claw feet of the bathtub. Dormers extend from all four sides of the third story, as do four flared chimneys on what is now an apartment house.

160. Milheim House

1893. 1515 Race Street, HD-22

John Milheim, a Swiss immigrant, opened the still-standing Colorado Bakery and Saloon building at 1444 Market Street. His wife, Mary, lived in this house until her death in 1930. The exterior embellishments and exquisite original woodwork look back to the Queen Anne era. Shortly

FIGURE 2.30. Milheim House (photo by Tom Noel).

before its scheduled demolition in 1989, this two-and-a-half-story red pressed brick foursquare was moved from 1355 Pennsylvania Street. Ralph Heronema acquired the house for next to nothing but spent $400,000 to transport the 583-ton structure seventeen blocks and replant it on its new foundation. After a brief stint as a bed and breakfast, it currently houses the Lighthouse Writers Workshops.

161. Chappell House

1895, Frank S. Snell?. 1555 Race Street, NR, HD-22

Reflecting the shift from Victorian exuberance to more cautious Neoclassical styles after the silver crash of 1893, this two-and-a-half-story red brick domicile has a symmetrical massing asserted by a corner tower. Delos Allen Chappell, a very wealthy owner of coal mines, water works, hydro-electric plants, and banks, dwelled here amid a dignified interior of original hardwood trim. Since 1936 this has been the home of the Unity Temple of Practical Christianity. Fanciful finials, wide bracketed eves, an eyebrow dormer, and radiating brick voussoirs adorn this house, located on a block of notable residences.

162. Raymond House–Castle Marne

1890, William A. Lang. 1572 Race Street, southeast corner of East Sixteenth Avenue, NR, HD-22

Lang's robust stone detailing embellishes this three-story castle of pink and gray rusticated rhyolite. Rich detailing is exemplified by a fanciful column supporting the keystone of the transom arch on the parlor window beside the carved golden oak entry. On the north side, in another typical Lang detail, stone trim frames a round stained glass window above two round-arched portals, whose awkward junction is disguised with a stone bouquet. Exquisite stonework even characterizes the nine fluted chimneys. Rough-hewn stone balustrades crown the porch and the southwest pentagonal corner tower. Note the three front porch capitals carved with the three stages of a lotus plant coming into bloom. On the north side, the large stained glass peacock window in the stairway was restored by Watkins Stained Glass of Denver with some pieces left over from their original work.

Real estate developer Wilbur S. Raymond built this Richardsonian Romanesque style edifice with Queen Anne overtones on three lots. With two-story 1920 additions, the house was converted to the Marne Apartments. James Peiker and his family bought this show home in 1988 for

FIGURE 2.31. Raymond House–Castle Marne, ca. 1892 (Denver Public Library).

$184,000 and have spent more than $400,000 lovingly restoring and refurnishing it as a bed and breakfast, the Castle Marne. This spectacular revival, complete with a matching carriage house, helped spark the renaissance and landmarking of the Wyman Historic District. Lang's finest domestic design served as the show home for the Wyman Addition.

163. Baerresen-Freeman House

1904, Baerresen Brothers. 1718 Gaylord Street

This English Colonial Revival house under a gambrel roof offers a plethora of Neoclassical elements. Designed by Baerresen Brothers for the oldest of the four brothers, Harold, it achieved harmony by topping the triple Ionic

entry columns with pairs of balcony balusters that are a diminutive version of the front porch balustrade. The domicile's second owner, William R. Freeman, gained fame as the man who helped salvage the Denver, Salt Lake, & Pacific Railroad after the death of its president, David H. Moffat. The house has been restored and converted to offices.

164. Pearce-McAllister Cottage

1899, Frederick J. Sterner. 1880 Gaylord Street, NR

Harold V. Pearce, one of many British investors in Colorado railroads, mining, and smelting, managed the Argo, Denver's first major smelter. He married the daughter of Dr. William A. Bell, vice president of the Denver & Rio Grande Railroad. The couple occupied the house until they

FIGURE 2.32. At the Pearce–McAllister Cottage, a cast iron cat prowls the roof (photo by Tom Noel).

returned to England in 1907. Henry McAllister, general counsel for the D&RG, purchased the house, and his family donated it to the Colorado Historical Society in 1971, along with many furnishings. It now houses the Denver Museum of Miniatures, Dolls, and Toys.

Sterner used the Dutch Colonial mode for this two-story brick house, which Pearce built as a wedding present for his bride. The plan is a modified T, with a two-story servants' wing at the rear. The wood-shingled gambrel roof with three evenly spaced shed dormers overhangs a full-length entry porch. The offset doorway is flanked by sidelights and pilasters. A glazed conservatory was added to the southeast corner around 1926. The distinctive gambrel form is repeated in the carriage house.

165. Graham-Bible House

1893. 2080 York Street, NR

This shingled cottage displays a Queen Anne irregular plan, fancy cutout verge boards, and a curved north-side

porch under a conical roof, but a shingled skin suggests the Shingle style. Built as the official residence of the superintendent of City Park, it first housed Superintendent Alexander J. Graham and later housed longtime park superintendent James A. Bible.

FIGURE 2.33. Graham-Bible House (photo by Tom Noel).

FIGURE 2.34. The date of completion of the Frank Smith Mansion (a), one of Denver's French style show homes, is hidden amid second-story ornamentation (b), 1986 (photos by Glenn Cuerden).

166. Frank Smith Mansion

1902, William E. Fisher and Daniel Riggs Huntington. 1801 York Street, northwest corner of East Eighteenth Avenue, NR

High chimneys, ornate rounded dormers in a steep pitched roof, and elaborate voussoirs give a French Beaux Arts flair to this three-story $45,000 mansion built by Frank L. Smith, a mining man. Gray brick over a steel frame is ornamented with white terracotta under tiled hipped roofs. The letter S appears repeatedly in the plasterwork, making it clear that the family wanted to be remembered. The most impressive of a row of notable residences along

the west edge of City Park, this Beaux Arts mansion and its prominent matching carriage house served a long stint as a boardinghouse before a 1980s restoration as offices.

City Park Area

HD-17 CITY PARK PAVILION HISTORIC DISTRICT

Roughly Milwaukee to St. Paul Streets between East Nineteenth and East Twentieth Avenues, NRD

City Park, Denver's largest (317 acres) and most elaborate park, contains notable buildings, striking sculpture, a zoo, and the Denver Museum of Nature and Science. Harry Meryweather, a city civil engineer, laid out the park in the Olmsted tradition, using a romantic, informal plan of looping drives and walks around manmade lakes. Reinhard Schuetze, Denver's first landscape architect, further refined the plan, which ranges from dense tree planting and shrub massing to grassy expanses. George E. Kessler, the Olmsted Brothers, and Saco R. DeBoer also had a hand in shaping City Park. The pavilion (1896) and the Floating Bandstand (1896, Fisher and Humphreys; 1929 remodel, Charles Francis Pillsbury) at the west end of Ferril Lake were designated a district and restored in the 1990s.

FIGURE 2.35. The pavilion and Floating Bandstand anchoring the west end of City Park's Ferril Lake were restored during the 1990s for a second century of use, including free band concerts (Denver Public Library).

167. Fire Station No. 18–Denver Police Gang Unit

1912, Edwin H. Moorman. 2205 Colorado Boulevard, north-west corner of East Twenty-Second Avenue

Located on the east edge of City Park, this fire station is disguised as a bungalow to blend in with the most common house type in the Park Hill neighborhood across the boulevard. Edwin Moorman's design bristled with porticos, pergolas, gabled projections, and extended, bracketed Craftsman rafter ends. The simpler building actually erected retains the dark red Harvard brick, columned pergola, Palladian window, and many Craftsman details. During the 1980s a new station No. 18 was built, and this building was converted to an office for the Denver Police Gang Unit.

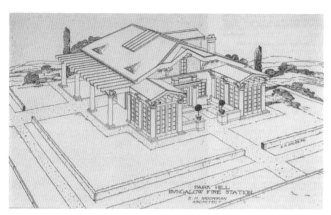

FIGURE 2.36. Park Hill Fire Station No. 18 poses as a bungalow (*Denver Municipal Facts*, April 6, 1912).

168. East High School

1925, George H. Williamson. 1545 Detroit Street to City Park Esplanade between East Colfax and East Seventeenth Avenues

Sited on the south side of City Park, East High exemplifies the City Beautiful dream of showcasing public schools set on parks and parkways. Such school buildings taught lessons in fine design. A seven-story bell tower vaguely reminiscent of Philadelphia's Independence Hall distinguishes this landmark. Mottled red brick trimmed with pale gray terracotta sheathes this eclectic adaptation of the English Jacobean style. The four-story H-plan building is remarkable for its 25 percent wall-to-window ratio, designed to maximize natural light. Minimal interior remodeling has left in

FIGURE 2.37. East High School (photo by Tom Noel).

place the gray Ozark marble of the main lobby, the statue of East High's mascot, an angel, and a replica of Michelangelo's statue *David*. A recent $350,000 restoration turned the clock tower into a museum and refreshed the Renaissance style library with its fine mural, *The Travels of Marco Polo the Venetian*, by Hugh Weller, as well as recapturing the original grand entrance, auditorium, and landscaping. For decades the East High Angels led the state in most academic endeavors. Several additions, including temporary buildings, do not enhance the four-block complex.

169. Austin Apartments

1904, Audley W. Reynolds. 2400 East Colfax Avenue, southeast corner of Josephine Street, SR

A faint echo of the Italian Renaissance Revival style is seen in this three-story brick building with round-arch top-floor windows and recessed balconies. Pharmacist Frank A. Austin erected the structure and opened his drugstore in the corner storefront. A $1 million 1995 rehabilitation restored the commercial storefronts and the upstairs apartments as affordable housing, with vintage oak woodwork and skylights.

170. Bosworth House

1899, Ernest P. Varian and Frederick J. Sterner. 1400 Josephine Street, northeast corner of East Fourteenth Avenue

From 1902 to 1947, this was the home of Mrs. Leora Bosworth, widow of Joab Bosworth, founder of the Denver Fire Clay Company, a leading supplier of decorative brick and masonry trim. Mrs. Bosworth, a civic and social activist, founded the Monday Literary Club. She bequeathed the home to the Denver branch of the American Association of University Women in 1947. The AAUW sold the house in 1966 to the Assistance League of Denver, a local chapter of a national charity, which in 1990 restored the house for its offices. The rusticated red sandstone Queen Anne house is asymmetrical but unified by evenly pitched roofs of dormers and gables with ornate verge board.

171. Gates House

1892, H. Chaten. 1365–75 Josephine Street, southwest corner of East Fourteenth Avenue

One of Denver's best examples of the Richardsonian Romanesque style, this house drew inspiration from the

FIGURE 2.38. Gates House (photo by Tom Noel).

work of Henry Hobson Richardson. It has the typical massive blocks of stone, enormous Romanesque arches, shingled upper stories, oriel and recessed windows, and an asymmetrical plan. Rhyolite is used for both the building's first-floor skin and its towering chimneys.

Russell Gates founded the Russell Gates Mercantile Company, which had stores throughout east-central Colorado. Gates, who ran as a Republican mayoral candidate in 1897, built the house for $16,000. It became the Castle Apartments from the 1920s until the 1970s, when it was restored as an office and a residence. In 1995 the 6,313-square-foot mansion went on the market for $680,000 and became a private residence once again.

172. Benson-Orsborn House

1893. 1305 Elizabeth Street, northwest corner of East Thirteenth Avenue

Builder and owner Lorenzo Benson constructed the "brick barn" (now the garage) in 1890 and the main house in 1893 but disappeared shortly thereafter. George E. and Jeannette B. Orsborn, who lived here from 1922 until 1953, practiced medicine as the husband-and-wife firm of Orsborn and Orsborn and were also active and respected in civic circles.

This Queen Anne style residence sparkles after a 1996 restoration by residents Jeff and Lisa Kipp. The grand entry porch is topped by a second-story open balcony and a third-story closed octagonal tower. A generous bay window with a distinctive flattened arch adorns the facade, as does a second-story oriel window. The red brick house has red sandstone trim that is outshone by the splendid exterior wood trim, such as the verge board, paired Tuscan porch columns, and geometric shingle work above the tower and oriel windows. The interior retains much fine, original woodwork and second-story beveled glass windows. Fine details include ornate verge board and a well-preserved interior with elaborate oak woodwork. The brick barn has been converted to a residence.

173. Stevens Elementary School

1901, Robert S. Roeschlaub. Early 1990s condo conversion, Charles Nash. 1140 Columbine Street

The last of many schools designed by Roeschlaub is relatively modern in its simplicity and in the generous banks of windows that flood the interior with light. This multi-gabled building is buff brick, with sparse Neoclassical sandstone trim and a crowning cupola. Opened as the George Washington Clayton School, it was renamed in honor of its first principal, Eugene C. Stevens. Charles Nash remodeled the school in the early 1990s, adding attic decks and skylights to recycle it as a condominium complex that retains chalkboards, playground, and other souvenirs of its school days.

174. Fifth Church of Christ Scientist

1929, Harry W.J. Edbrooke. 1477 Columbine Street, southwest corner of East Colfax Avenue

This immense three-story 24,000-square-foot, Italian Renaissance style church is a dignified Neoclassical monument accented with carved stone trim, designed by an architect who started out with his uncle Frank, the city's foremost nineteenth-century architect. Placed on a granite foundation, this light buff-colored brick structure features large arched windows, terracotta trim, and a large foyer consisting of beautiful terrazzo flooring. Since the 1990s the building has been used as a church, for daycare, as a counseling center, and for civic events.

175. Bonfils Memorial Theater–Lowenstein Theater–Tattered Cover Bookstore

1953, John K. Monroe. 2006 addition, Josh Comfort. 2006 interior redesign, Semple Brown Design. 1475 Elizabeth Street, southwest corner of East Colfax Avenue

Commissioned in 1949 by Helen Bonfils, *Denver Post* heiress, in memory of her parents, Frederick G. and Belle Bonfils, this building celebrates Helen's first love—the-

FIGURE 2.39. Bonfils Memorial Theater was renamed the Lowenstein Theater for the late Henry Lowenstein, who ran it, crafted many productions, and guided many women and minorities to stage success (Tom Noel Collection).

ater—although she also owned and operated *The Denver Post* and pursued many other philanthropic causes. This tall, single-story Art Moderne style theater is constructed of tawny brick with buff-colored terracotta and red sandstone trim. It opened in 1953 as the Bonfils Memorial Theater and home of the Denver Civic Theater, founded in 1929. It closed in 1984 following the opening of the Denver Performing Arts Complex and its Bonfils Theater. In 1986 the theater was renamed the Lowenstein Theater in honor of the longtime designer and producer Henry Lowenstein, who kept it in use for local productions. In 2006 the theater went through a major rehabilitation by the St. Charles Town Company, LLC, which converted the interior for use by Denver's largest local independent bookseller, Tattered Cover, and a restaurant.

FIGURE 2.40. Fire House No. 15 (Denver Public Library).

176. Fire House No. 15

1903, John J. Huddart. 1991 house conversion, Ron Abo. 1080 Clayton Street, southeast corner of East Eleventh Avenue

To the dismay of the neighborhood, the Denver Fire Department announced that it was abandoning this handsome Beaux Arts, residential-scale firehouse in 1985 because of its deteriorating condition. To the rescue came Nathaniel and Kathleen Fay, who bought and restored it, with the help of architect Ron Abo, as a private residence with a king-size garage. The Fays did this project with the first

use of the State Income Tax Credit, a 1991 provision that allows owners of designated landmarks tax credits for restoration expenses up to $50,000. In 1995 the Fays restored the limestone trim, re-pointed the buff brick walls, and made structural repairs.

"We love living in this firehouse and keeping it a part of the neighborhood," reported Kathy Fay. "Our two kids love it, too, especially since we bought our bright red 1949 Ford-Pirsch fire truck. They can slide down the fire pole to breakfast or to sit in the truck." Subsequent owners have divided the former fire station into two residential units. In 2014 Philae Dominick, widow of architect Peter Dominick, renewed the north unit and added extensive landscaping.

177. Bluebird Theater

1914, Harry W.J. Edbrooke. 3315–17 East Colfax Avenue, northeast corner of Adams Street, SR

Flying away from a pornographic past, the Bluebird has been restored in more ways than one. Originally built as the Thompson Theater, its speckled beige brick Beaux Arts Mediterranean Revival facade has urn lamp finials and a prominent marquis that culminates in a neon bluebird. Decorative patterns in the brickwork are notable. As in many theaters, the fanciful facade is flanked by the plain brick side and rear walls. Denver theater tycoon Harry Huffman acquired the theater in 1922 and renamed it the Bluebird. Ralph Batschelet, who managed the neighborhood theater for Huffman, promoted Depression-era patronage with "Bank Night" and "Deluxe Country Store" giveaways of cash and commodities. The Bluebird turned to skin flicks in 1974 and, to the relief of protesting neighbors,

FIGURE 2.41. Bluebird Theater (photo by Tom Noel).

closed in 1987. With city and neighborhood support, Christopher C. Swank restored the theater as a cabaret. The Bluebird is once again swanky, with both video and live performances. Inside, the stage was extended to cover the orchestra pit, but the proscenium arch survives, along with its fresco of cherubs admiring a cartouche that reads "JET" for the original builder, John E. Thompson.

HD-12 SNELL'S SUBDIVISION HISTORIC DISTRICT

East Colfax to East Fourteenth Avenues between Cook and Madison Streets

Frank Snell, a Denver native, was never licensed as an architect but was an active builder. His Snell Addition (1905–11) comprises a local district of twenty-five houses. Most are foursquare variations, varying in brick color and detail. The one-block development, with two alley streets (Colfax A and Colfax B Places) and large "back-yard" houses, is a rare early Denver experiment in small lots and high density. Five rows of residential house remain within the block, with the East Colfax Avenue face block converted to commercial uses.

The Arps House (ca. 1905, Frank Snell), 3422 Colfax A Place, is typical of the district's scheme of large houses on tiny lots. It was the home of Denver historian Louisa Ward Arps, whose thoroughly researched, well-written books on Colorado include *Denver in Slices* (1959). The architect-developer built Snell House (ca. 1905, Frank Snell), 3421 Colfax A Place, for himself, with dormer windows on three sides of the third floor. Snell maintained that large yards were undesirable "junk catchers." He contended that many people would rather not spend their time caring for large lawns, an idea ahead of its time. Not until the 1980s did many Denver homebuyers begin to show a preference for smaller lots, condos, and lofts.

178. Harman Town Hall–Greenleaf Masonic Temple

1891, Franklin E. Kidder. 400 St. Paul Street, northeast corner of East Fourth Avenue

Edwin Preston Harman and his wife, Louisa, purchased a 360-acre tract in 1871 between University and Colorado Boulevards and East Sixth Avenue and Cherry Creek. As Denver boomed during the 1880s, the Harmans incorporated their farm as the town of Harman in 1886. Their little country town erected this ambitious town hall to oversee its municipal policemen, fire department, dog-catcher, and school. After Harman was annexed to Denver in 1895, this structure became a Denver police and fire station. In 1934 the Lawrence N. Greenleaf Masonic Lodge purchased the two-story red brick building for its neighborhood temple. The building features raised brick courses that highlight the voussoirs of the round-arched second-story windows beneath a bracketed cornice. A dramatic contemporary addition rises to a rear third story and provides a north-side courtyard and office spaces.

Country Club Area

HD-43 DRIVING PARK HISTORIC DISTRICT

Located between Fourth and Sixth Avenues and from half a block east of Downing Street to half a block east of High Street, this district originated with the Denver Gentlemen's Driving Association. In 1880 several prominent Denver men created this association and bought land here to build a private horse riding and racing club. When they realized that as a result of Denver's growth and expansion this land was worth more for development, they sold the land in 1888. This historic district now encompasses over 300 residences, the majority of which are contributing, and displays distinctive architectural styles of the late nineteenth and early twentieth centuries.

179. Benjamin Brown House

ca. 1889, Robert G. Balcomb and Eugene R. Rice. 1898–1900 several additions. 1930s addition. 1960s addition. 410 Marion Street, HD-43

Commissioned by Benjamin Brown, a native-born West Virginian and prominent Denver banker, this two-story stucco-over-brick mansion has a rusticated foundation with wood shingle gables and a gabled roof. Joined at the rear of the main structure is an ornate two-story carriage house with a cupola. Originally built in Queen Anne style, the structure has received various additions. Although the original style can only be seen from the facade, the mansion still displays several defining architectural elements of this style, such as brackets, elaborate dentils, cornices, gables, and a circular porch.

HD-18 COUNTRY CLUB HISTORIC DISTRICT

Between East First and Fourth Avenues from Downing Street to University Boulevard

This residential district contains some of Denver's grandest homes by leading early-twentieth-century architects. William and Arthur Fisher collaborated with Frederick Law Olmsted Jr. to design Country Club Place (1909), which stretches from Franklin to Race Streets between East First and East Fourth Avenues. This original subdivision has extra-long and wide blocks with landscaped medians. For the entry gateways on East Fourth Avenue, the Fishers used stucco and red barrel tile, suggestive of Spain. The Fishers maintained that the Spanish Colonial Revival style was most appropriate for Denver, with its dry, sunny climate. Subsequent subdivisions are Park Club Place (1905), from Franklin to Downing Streets between East Fourth and East First Avenues, and the Circle Drive area (1930s) between East Fourth and East Sixth Avenues from University Boulevard to Race Street.

Burnham and Merrill Hoyt's versatility is evident in their impressive Tudor style residence for Donald Bromfield (1927), 100 Gaylord Street, as well as in Burnham's fine International style Maer House (1940), 545 Circle Drive. Jules Jacques Benoit Benedict designed various Beaux Arts–influenced revival style houses, including the Arthur House (1932), 355 Gilpin Street; the Ellis House (1912), 1700 East Third Avenue; the Huff House (1912), 120 Humboldt Street; and the McFarland House (1927), 476 Westwood Drive. Temple Hoyne Buell designed the Châteauesque Bard House (1929) at 100 Vine Street. Many Country Club residences are architect designs, including modern homes by and for architects such as Paul Atchison at 160 Humboldt Street (1956), James Sudler at 180 High Street (1976), and Robert Fuller, 2244 East Fourth Avenue (1977). Although not individually landmarked, the following residences in the Country Club Historic District may be of interest.

Bridaham House

1905, Frederick J. Sterner and George H. Williamson. 350 Humboldt Street, HD-18

Greek Revival had gone out of style by the 1860s but continued to be used on retardaire banks, churches, and post offices. This rare Colorado residential example of "Greek Survival" sits on three lots behind an iron fence with brick piers topped by concrete cannonball finials. Behind an entry court balustrade, the two-story portico is supported by six enormous Tuscan columns and has triglyphs on the frieze. Lester Burbank Bridaham ran what he claimed was the largest wholesale drug company between the Missouri River and the West Coast.

Biscoe House

1908, Maurice Biscoe. 320 Humboldt Street, HD-18

Maurice Biscoe, a Beaux Arts–trained architect, came to Denver to represent the New York firm of Gordon, Tracy, and Swarthout in the construction of St. John's Episcopal Cathedral. He stayed in the Mile High City to design fine residences, including his own, a two-story L-plan house in Mediterranean Revival style, with modest but pleasing detail. Biscoe also designed the Sinsheimer House (1917), 190 High Street, an Italian Renaissance Revival villa. Biscoe later joined the Boston firm of Andrews, Rantoul, and Jones, where he eventually became a partner.

Speer House

1912, Willis A. Marean and Albert J. Norton. 300 Humboldt Street, northeast corner of East Third Avenue, HD-18

Mayor Robert W. Speer was involved in developing the Country Club area with Frederick Ross and others. This neighborhood embodies the mayor's City Beautiful scenario with tree lawns and generous public spaces, such as median strips and wide setbacks fronting residences. The mayor lived in this expanded Denver Square, with wide bracketed eaves and a wraparound porch with entries on both streets. Kate Speer, the mayor's widow, lived here until her death in 1954.

William E. Fisher House

1910, William E. Fisher. 110 Franklin Street, HD-18

Architect Fisher designed his own house in the Spanish style, which he and his brother, Arthur, considered appropriate for Denver's climate. The three-story Spanish Colonial Revival abode, with stucco walls, a red tile roof, and wide bracketed eaves, is oriented to the south-side garden with a pillared entry. The Fishers ran Denver's most prolific architectural firm from 1905 to 1937, when William committed suicide in this house. The Fisher firm planned the large blocks and wide medians and tree lawns of the Country Club neighborhood where many other Fisher designs are found, including Arthur Fisher's 1909 residence at 128 Gilpin Street.

FIGURE 2.42. Mrs. Verner Z. (Mary Dean) Reed, her dog, and her mansion (Denver Public Library).

Reed Mansion

1931, Harry James Manning. 475 Circle Drive, HD-18

Colorado's grandest Tudor Revival mansion is a towering composition of steep-pitched slate roofs, four immense ornate chimneys with multiple clay pots, and numerous dormers and gables. The glazed tapestry brick walls with limestone trim and half-timbered gable ends soar above two-and-a-half acres of walled gardens, with a separate garden house designed by Saco R. DeBoer. Don't miss the squirrel statues flanking the entry gates on the circular drive. A greenhouse, terrace, fountain, swimming pool, and interior elevator were added in 1955–56. Mary Reed

commissioned the house shortly after the death of her husband, Verner Z. Reed, who made fortunes in both Cripple Creek gold and Salt Creek, Wyoming, oil. The high style Tudor Revival design helped popularize vernacular Tudor Revival. Marketed as "English bungalow," this mode became one of the most popular local styles of the 1930s. Other large Tudor types by Manning are the nearby dwellings at 150, 160, and 210 Vine Street. Mary Reed blessed the city not only with this splendid mansion but also with buildings on the University of Denver campus and with the Margery Reed Mayo Day Care Center, a Denver landmark, for less fortunate children in Five Points.

3

Northeast Denver

CURTIS PARK HISTORIC DISTRICTS

BALLPARK HISTORIC DISTRICT

FIVE POINTS HISTORIC CULTURAL
   DISTRICT

CLEMENTS ADDITION HISTORIC DISTRICT

LAFAYETTE STREET HISTORIC DISTRICT

EAST PARK PLACE HISTORIC DISTRICT

CLAYTON COLLEGE HISTORIC DISTRICT

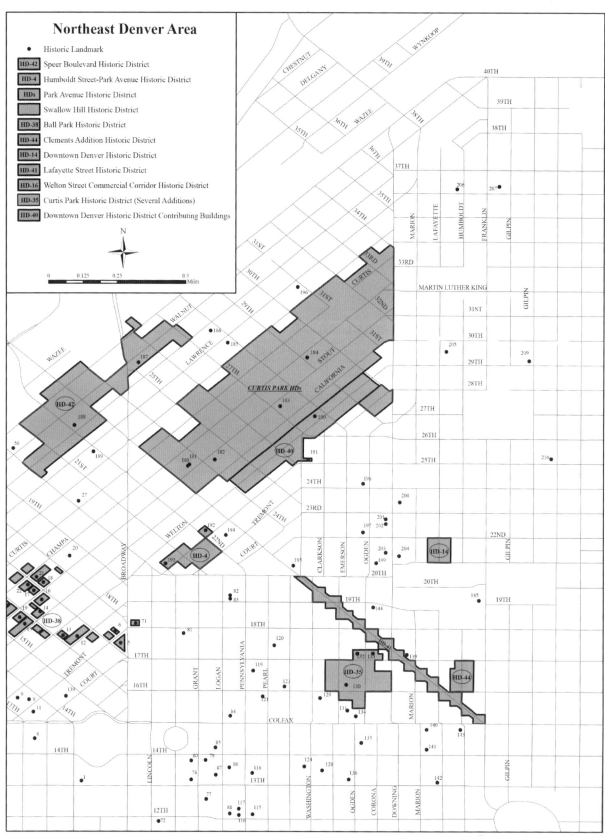

MAP 3.1. Northeast Denver area

Northeast Denver, bounded by Twentieth Avenue and Twentieth Street on the south, the South Platte River on the west, I-70 on the north, and York Street on the east, is one of the oldest and least altered sections of Denver. Initially developed along numerous streetcar lines that took the middle and upper classes out of the core city, the area later attracted many people of color, including blacks, Asians, and Hispanics.

The housing stock is mostly two-story brick, detached dwellings in Italianate, Queen Anne, Bungalow, and Foursquare styles. The foursquares are so common that these boxy, symmetrical houses with central attic dormers and classically columned front porches are widely known as Denver Squares. Between the 1930s and the 1980s, this area declined. During the 1970s, however, preservationists and realtors discovered what a fine housing stock remained, and wealthier folks began returning. Residents of all races pride themselves on living in a racially mixed neighborhood. The architectural styles are also varied, and a remarkable number of the original, sturdy residences and churches remain.

The initial non–Native American Indian settlement was Curtis Park, which sprouted up around the city's first streetcar line that ran from Seventh and Larimer Streets down Sixteenth Street and then out Champa Street to Twenty-Eighth Street There, prominent Denverites began building fashionable suburban homes, many of which survive as notable Italianate and Queen Anne examples. The area also included Five Points, named for the five-way intersection of Washington Street, Welton Street (north- and southbound), East Twenty-Sixth Avenue, and Twenty-Seventh Street. After 1900 this became a predominantly African American neighborhood, with some Asians and Hispanics. Today, the Curtis Park–Five Points area is making a comeback, with a population that is roughly a third black, a third brown, and a third white. Its history is celebrated with the Five Points Historic Cultural District.

Curtis Park Historic Districts

NRD, HD-25 (HAS GROWN, WITH SEVEN ADDITIONS THROUGH HD-52; SEE APPENDIX A)

The seven additions to the Curtis Park District over the years have expanded its boundaries to roughly Downing Street on the northeast, Curtis Street on the northwest, Twenty-Fourth Street on the southwest, and California Street on the southeast. The neighborhood is named for

Denver's first municipal park, Curtis Park (1868), located at Thirtieth to Thirty-Second Streets between Arapahoe and Champa Streets. This park, renamed Mestizo-Curtis Park in 1990, was a donation from real estate developer Samuel S. Curtis. As Denver's first streetcar suburb, Curtis Park blossomed after the 1871 completion of the horse car line from downtown along Champa. Streetcars offered fast and cheap connections to downtown jobs, shopping, and amusements, coaxing Denverites out to what was then suburbia.

Initially a haven for those with the means to afford the suburbs, during the early 1900s Curtis Park evolved into a core city working-class neighborhood that attracted minorities. This neighborhood has been a melting pot where African, Anglo, German, Irish, Japanese, Jewish, Mexican, and Scandinavian Americans have established homes and businesses.

The David Crowell House (1873; 1977 restoration, Brian Congleton), 2816 Curtis, is a small frame cottage and perhaps the oldest structure in the area. Other clapboard dwellings are found at 2915 Curtis and 2826 and 2828 Stout Streets. At 2445 California Street is one of Denver's rare Second Empire designs, with a mansard roof and hooded and pedimented dormers. Among the grander Italianate homes is that of department store founder John Jay Joslin (1880), 2915 Champa Street. A more typical Italianate house belonging to Dr. Justina Ford, a prominent black physician, was moved to 3091 California Street and restored as the Black American West Museum. Since the 1970s, this vintage neighborhood has been rejuvenated. The Curtis Park face-block project rehabilitated forty-one houses in the district, winning a national AIA Honor Award for Historic Denver, Inc., and preservation architects Gary Long and Kathy Hoeft. The project rescued two nineteenth-century brick workers' cottages by moving them to Twenty-Eighth and Curtis Streets, renovating the interiors, and selling them to low-income buyers. Determined neighborhood residents and preservationists have even restored the sandstone sidewalks and tree lawns in this unusually intact and livable neighborhood within the shadows of downtown skyscrapers.

180. Nagel House

1889, Frederick C. Eberley. 1990s renovation. 2335 Stout Street, HD-52

Built for watchmaker Peter Nagel and his wife, Clara Kaub Nagel, the daughter of Frank and Babette Kaub, owners of the adjacent residence, this two-story brick Queen

FIGURE 3.1. Huddart/Lydon House (photo by Roger Whitacre).

found under the eaves and at the top of the entry porch, as well as the centered triangular pediment.

182. Huddart/Lydon House

1891, John J. Huddart. 2418 Stout Street, HD-26

Cole Lydon was a conductor for the Denver & Rio Grande Railroad. Like many other Curtis Park pioneers, he moved to Capitol Hill when it became the more fashionable neighborhood. Lydon's house was purchased in the early 1990s by William A. West, a University of Colorado at Denver professor of Victorian literature. West's interest in all things Victorian led him to Curtis Park and its huge inventory of nineteenth-century homes. He wrote a book on the area and championed the Curtis Park Historic District, where his other restorations include the Italianate cottage and gardens at 2826 Curtis Street.

John Huddart, a prolific nineteenth-century Denver architect, was trained in England as an engineer. He designed the Lydon residence in his typically eclectic style. Stepped Dutch side parapets and steep shingled gables, a second-floor oriel window, and a third-story dormer give this narrow house a picturesque verticality further enhanced by the finials. Red pressed brick, carved and smooth stone trim, fish-scale shingles, and floral bas-relief in the gables are among the notable details.

183. Kinneavy Terrace

1889, John J. Huddart. 2700–14 Stout Street, northeast corner of Twenty-Seventh Street, HD-48

This eclectic two-story Queen Anne style row house retains its exquisite brick and woodwork and its three large towers, but the ornate covered entryways that once marked the five residence bays are gone.

184. Anfenger House

1884. 2900 Champa Street, northeast corner of Twenty-Ninth Street, HD-50

Louis Anfenger, a Bavarian-born Jewish pioneer, became a state representative and a founder of National Jewish Hospital and Temple Emanuel Synagogue. He built this large house, in which he raised eight children. Louis's son Milton was a state senator and prominent attorney who helped establish Denver's early professional baseball club, the Denver Bears. Louis's grandchildren include the

Anne style dwelling has seen some rough times. After withstanding two serious fires, the structure sat abandoned for several years and faced near demolition before it was renovated in the 1990s.

181. Kaub House

1885. 2343 Stout Street, HD-52

This two-story classic Italianate style residence is a rare gem in Curtis Park, as it is one of only a handful of structures that retains a near-original interior. The home was originally built for Bavarian-born immigrant Frank Kaub, a Denver Pacific Railroad machinist and engineer. Staying close to their parents, two of his daughters built homes on the same block, at 2335 Stout Street and at the corner of Stout and Twenty-Fourth Streets, respectively. The most notable features of this residence are the ornate brackets

FIGURE 3.2. Anfenger House (photo by Roger Whitacre).

historian Marjorie Hornbein. The Anfenger House has a low hipped roof with wide eaves, a two-story bay, and long, narrow windows with lintels, making it a good example of the Italianate style that prevails in Curtis Park. The house boasts seven fireplaces and a large third-floor attic. After condemnation and a narrow escape from the wrecking ball, the house was restored outside and inside.

185. Margery Reed Mayo Day Nursery

1926, Harry J. Manning. 1128 Twenty-Eighth Street, southeast corner of Lawrence Street

The philanthropist Mary Dean Reed commissioned this state-of-the-art facility for Denver's oldest child day-care center and nursery. Reed dedicated it to her young daughter, who suffered an untimely death. She hired architect Harry J. Manning, who designed her mansion at 475 Circle Drive, to design a nursery scaled for children, with a zoo-animal bas-relief and a terracotta monkey frieze. This progressive nursery served children of all races and religions

FIGURE 3.3. The Sisters of Charity of Cincinnati cared for Curtis Park–area kids with games like Ring around the Rosie (top left) at the Margery Reed Mayo Day Care Center (bottom) (Denver Public Library).

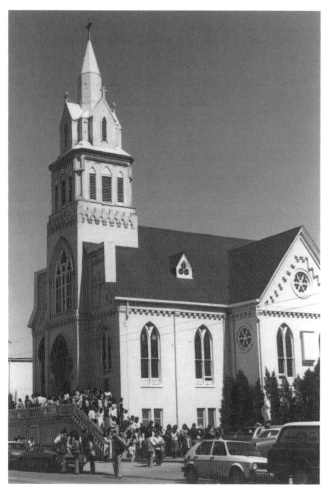

FIGURE 3.4. Sacred Heart Catholic Church, Denver's oldest operating house of worship, before restoration in 1979 (photo by Tom Noel).

when the Catholic Sisters of Charity of Cincinnati staffed the location. In 1995 the Archdiocese of Denver closed this two-story structure, as the center had fallen into disrepair. A State Historical Fund grant several years later helped restore the exterior and interior for a reopening as a still much-needed daycare center.

186. Sacred Heart Catholic Church

1880, Emmett Anthony. 2760 Larimer Street, southwest corner of Twenty-Eighth Street, NR

This traditional cruciform church has a tall steeple centered above the Larimer Street entrance. A poor immigrant Irish and Italian congregation used wood trim instead of stone and even a wooden altar painted white to look like marble. They replaced the failing masonry steeple with a diminutive wooden one. The church slowly

deteriorated until 1999, when a near miracle happened—a seventy-five-ton crane crowned the church with a new twenty-five-foot-high gilded aluminum steeple, a replica of the original.

Inside and outside, the church went through restoration and enhancement that repaired and re-pointed the brick and renewed the woodwork. Carlota Espinoza painted the large ceiling mural, which hides the scar where a skylight collapsed. Through such creative solutions, a congregation that is now largely Hispanic has kept Sacred Heart alive as the oldest ecclesiastical edifice in Denver used regularly for religious services.

Father Edward Barry, S.J., the third pastor of Sacred Heart Catholic Church, was an amateur architect who allegedly designed the Sacred Heart School (1890), 2840 Lawrence Street. This two-story brick school has large well-lit classrooms clustered around a two-story auditorium. A brick parapet hides the flat roof. Round transoms atop the windows echo the round-arch entry under a round niche for a statue of the Sacred Heart of Jesus. The high school closed in 1939, although the elementary school remained open until 1978. The similarly styled convent next door, at 2844 Lawrence Street, is now a shelter for homeless and single women.

Ballpark Historic District

HD-42

Named for its proximity to Coors Field, home of the Colorado Rockies National League baseball club, the Ballpark Historic District stretches from Twentieth to Twenty-Seventh Avenues and from Blake to Lawrence Streets. This eclectic district features commercial buildings, multi-family housing, bars, hotels, and warehouses. With the opening of Coors Field in 1995, the district was created to prevent the spread of parking lots and to promote the recycling of old buildings in what is evolving into an entertainment and residential district.

187. Benjamin Moore Paint Company

1925, with three major construction phases ending in 1945. 2500 Walnut Street, northeast corner of Broadway Street, HD-42

A twenty-foot-high neon sign that reads Benjamin Moore Paints on top of the building makes this landmark easy to find. The three-story red brick structure has vibrant white tile and stucco trim, hinting at the Art Deco style. It is a cornerstone of the old warehouse district that has been repurposed as apartments, offices, and retail outlets.

188. Burlington Hotel

1890, Frank E. Edbrooke. 2201 Larimer Street, northwest corner of Twenty-Second Street, NR, HD-42

By the 1960s, this three-story red brick Romanesque Revival hotel had become Denver's deadliest skid row flophouse, where men were killed for spare change and a few drops of cheap booze. A narrow U-shaped design gives this hotel a central light well. Developer Rick Borman pursued landmark designation in 1994 as the first step in his proposed rehabilitation of this long-neglected but still salvageable mainstay of upper Larimer Street. It is now a funky retail anchor for the Ballpark Historic District.

189. Savage Candy Company

1910, Wilmott and Stoddard. 2158–62 Lawrence Street, southeast corner of Twenty-Second Street, HD-42

The Nathan W. Savage Candy Company, founded in Pueblo in 1888, built this Denver factory where sixty-five employees made a complete line of candy, ranging from children's penny treats to chocolate extravaganzas. The typical two-story red brick commercial building with storefronts is distinguished by fancy brickwork, including a corbelled brick parapet and an angled corner entry beneath a roofline pediment. The building was rehabilitated in 1995 for use by the Sobriety House, an institution "dedicated to the resurrection and renewal of lives gone shabby and dissolute."

Five Points Historic Cultural District

HD-40

Located roughly from Twenty-Fourth to Thirtieth Streets between California Street and Glenarm Place

This area was the commercial heart of the African American community known as Five Points. Between 1920 and 1950, with segregation laws in place, Welton Street was the "main street" of black Denver, with its restaurants, hotels, grocery and drug stores, clubs, and everything else the African

American community needed to survive. The most recognizable structure is the Rossonian (originally Baxter) Hotel (1912, George L. Bettcher), 2650 Welton Street, the anchor of the neighborhood. Nationally prominent black jazz musicians played here during the 1920s to the 1940s, attracting even white audiences. This historic district is unique in Denver in being designated a historic cultural district.

190. Douglass Undertaking Building

ca. 1891. 1916 remodel, Merrill H. Hoyt and Burnham Hoyt. 2745 Welton Street, HD-40

Neoclassicism was more than an elitist style for grand public buildings. Here it shines in an old cottage the Hoyt brothers converted to a classy storefront with a pedimented and pilastered facade. The urn recessed in the tympanum was the logo of a black businessman, Jonathan R. Contee, whose undertaking parlor was converted in 1957 to a livelier use—a billiard hall. La Paz Billiard Hall's Spanish name is indicative of the growing Hispanic presence in what was once a predominantly black neighborhood. From across the street you can see that this business, like most of its neighbors, is a storefront added to an old house. The mortuary may have been named in honor of Frederick A. Douglass, the famous mulatto abolitionist.

FIGURE 3.5. Douglass Undertaking Building, 1981 (photo by Tom Noel).

191. Fire Station No. 3

1931, C. Francis Pillsbury. 2500 Washington Street, HD-40

Reflecting a trend that attempted to blend fire station design with the surrounding residential architecture, this corner building has Spanish Revival elements in a variegated brick structure with terracotta trim. Fire Station No. 3 was Denver's all-black station from its dedication in 1931 until the fire department was desegregated in 1958.

Clements Addition Historic District

HD-4

Roughly Twentieth to Twenty-Second Streets between Tremont and Glenarm Places, NRD

This district is a fragment of the Alfred Clements Addition to the City of Denver. Vulnerably sited on the fringe of the Central Business District, this is one of Denver's oldest intact residential remnants. Amid restored houses and row houses, the greatest treasure is a Ralph Adams Cram church, St. Andrews Episcopal. Kingston Row (1890, Arthur S. Miller) is an ornate three-story red brick terrace with a Queen Anne front and a simpler "Mary Jane" rear. At either end of the six row houses are units incorporating round towers topped with slate roofs and finials. Fussy facade fenestration includes round-arched windows, diamond-paned dormer windows, and curved glass in the towers.

192. Clements Rowhouse

1884. 2201–17 Glenarm Place, northwest corner of Twenty-Second Street, NR, HD-4

In Denver, a wide-open western town with plenty of room to grow, multi-family attached housing is rarer than in most cities. Even in the poorest neighborhoods, single-family detached houses are the norm. An exception is this splendid two-story brick Italianate row house with two-story bays, Eastlake incised stone window trim, and an elegantly bracketed and mansarded cornice.

Thomas House

1883, William Quayle. 2104 Glenarm Place, NR, HD-4

This house was designed by William Quayle for Hugh H. Thomas, who, with partner George A. Gano, owned the Gano and Thomas Furniture Store. The house was treated to a 1975 restoration by owner-occupants Kay and Bill James, who highlighted Quayle's fine detail work, from the elaborate brick chimneys to the sandstone belt coursing, from

FIGURE 3.6. Clements Addition Streetscape, 2100 block of Tremont Place (photo by Roger Whitacre).

the wooden columns of the three porches to the carved stone lintels of windows grouped in twos or threes. The first-floor rooms boast Eastlake woodwork and thirteen-foot-high ceilings. Quayle, who opened a Denver office in 1880, later worked with his brothers Charles and Edward, who were also architects. In 1900 William moved to San Diego, where his work became more prominent. Like many other Quayle houses and schoolhouses, this home reflects his eclectic combination of stylistic elements.

FIGURE 3.7. St. Andrews Memorial Episcopal Chapel (photo by Thomas H. Simmons).

193. St. Andrews Memorial Episcopal Chapel

1908, Ralph Adams Cram. 2015 Glenarm Place, northwest corner of Twentieth Street, NR, HD-4

Ralph Adams Cram, a high-church Anglican and devotee of John Ruskin, was a leading exponent of the Gothic Revival style. This nationally prominent Yankee architect, whose initial partner was Bertram G. Goodhue, designed this small Gothic Revival church on an L plan using a skin of dark red Harvard brick with limestone trim and a slate roof. The interior, dominated by tall brick Gothic arches, has a timbered ceiling and diamond-paned windows with leaded amber glass and wooden Gothic tracery. The only Colorado work by Cram, it resembles his much larger St. George's Chapel in Newport, Rhode Island. Works of art include Edwardian *reredos* by Albert Byron Olson and a Byzantine Revival statue of the Virgin by Marion Buchan. Jules Jacques Benoit Benedict designed the 1928 parish house next door at 2013 Glenarm Place.

194. Ebert Elementary School

1924, Frederick E. Mountjoy and Frank W. Frewan. 1993 classroom, lunch room, and library addition, Murata Outland. 410 Park Avenue West at Tremont Place

Concrete moldings with lion heads, human heads, garlands, and a floral frieze enliven this two-story Renaissance Revival building of light yellow brick. Congenial additions have not detracted from this unusually elegant, symmetrical school named for Frederick J. Ebert, a pioneer mining engineer, forester, rancher, surveyor, and state senator. In the library, polychromatic terracotta tiles around the fireplace depict fairy-tale characters.

195. Shorter African Methodist Episcopal Church

1925, Prince Hall Masons. 119 Park Avenue West at Washington Street

In 1886 the Shorter African Methodist Episcopal Church built a church on this site that stood until 1925, when it was destroyed in a fire allegedly set by the Ku Klux Klan. Later that year the congregation erected the current structure. The three-story red brick, eclectic Mission Romanesque style church includes a spacious auditorium, gymnasium, nursery, reading rooms, and many additional multi-use spaces. The structure now houses the Denver-based Cleo Parker Robinson Dance, an organization Parker Robinson founded in 1970 that is dedicated to cross-cultural dance arts rooted in African American traditions.

196. Epworth Church/Community Center

1915, W. P. Houdy. 1130 Thirty-First Street, southeast corner of Lawrence Street

The Epworth Church/Community Center and, subsequently, Goodwill Industries of Denver did religious, humanitarian, and community work in this three-level Renaissance Revival brick building. A symmetrical composition, it features classic columns, round arches, stained glass windows with biblical scenes, and a central octagonal dome. The church is attached to offices and a gymnasium. The Methodist deaconess Melissa Briggs, whose tent mission evolved into this church, bicycled around town collecting broken toys, clothing, and other items to restore for distribution to the poor. Her Epworth Goodwill Mission evolved into today's Goodwill Industries of Denver. The Epworth complex also served as the Curtis Park Community Center until 1966. In 1979 the Epworth Church moved to the High Street Community Center. For the next nine years Goodwill Industries used the building for its work repairing and recycling donations for sale. As Goodwill grew, it moved to larger quarters at 2257 Larimer Street. After being abandoned for over two decades, this imposing structure was acquired in 2013 by developer-preservationists Larry Nelson and Ruth Falkenberg. She reports, "We were impressed by the rich humanitarian history of this landmark and hope to bring it back as a beautiful and useful part of the Curtis Park neighborhood."

197. Scott Methodist Church–Sanctuary Lofts

1892, Franklin E. Kidder. 1995 rehabilitation, Norman Coble. 2201 Ogden Street, northwest corner of East Twenty-Second Avenue, NR

Built originally as Christ Methodist Episcopal Church, this structure was renamed for a pioneer black Methodist bishop, Isaiah B. Scott, after an African American congregation bought the church in 1927. Gothic arches prevail on a structure whose bulky massing and rusticated stone skin are otherwise more Romanesque. Gray rhyolite walls are trimmed in red sandstone on an elaborate exterior on which the pressed metal crockets and finials have been painted red to match the sandstone. The simpler interior sanctuary has little ornament other than the colored glass

FIGURE 3.8. Scott Methodist Church–Sanctuary Lofts (photo by Tom Noel).

windows in floral and geometric patterns and the cast-iron support columns. The 190-foot-tall wooden steeple, the tallest in town when erected, was removed from the stone corner bell tower following 1976 wind damage. In 1995 this landmark church, whose congregation built a new church at 2880 Garfield Street, was rehabilitated as the Sanctuary Lofts.

198. Zion Baptist Church

1893, Frank H. Jackson and George F. Rivinius. 933 East Twenty-Fourth Avenue, northwest corner of Ogden Street

Colorado's oldest black congregation, Zion Baptist, was established by former slaves in 1865. In 1911 that flock bought this edifice, originally built as Calvary Baptist Church. The Reverend Wendell T. Liggins, pastor from 1941 until his death in 1991, was a famed orator and civic activist who made this a popular and influential church. A rusticated rhyolite structure trimmed in the same gray stone,

FIGURE 3.9. At Zion Baptist Church, the Rev. Wendell T. Liggins cuts an anniversary cake for Colorado's first black congregation (photo by Burnis McCloud, Denver Public Library).

this church exemplifies the Richardsonian Romanesque style. Inside, distinctive stained glass windows brighten an interior dominated by dark ceiling beams and woodwork.

199. Wolf House

ca. 1900, Harold W. Baerresen and Viggio Baerresen. 2036 Ogden Street

Known for several important commercial buildings and their masterpiece structure, the 1907 Moorish Revival El Jebel Temple, prominent Denver architects Harold W. and Viggio Baerresen of the Baerresen Brothers also designed residential structures. This two-story Denver Square boasts a hipped roof with the typical central attic dormer but an unusual off-center front porch with six ornate Tuscan columns and wide bracketed eaves. Jacob L. Wolf was the longtime owner/occupant.

200. Holmes House

1893, James Murdoch. 2330 Downing Street

Dr. Clarence F. Holmes, Denver's most prominent African American dentist, was a spokesman for his people and spearheaded the formation of a Denver chapter of the National Association for the Advancement of Colored People (NAACP). Holmes and his family lived in this boxy eclectic Victorian from 1943 to 1970.

201. Gebhard/Smith House

1883. 2253 Downing Street, southwest corner East Twenty-Third Avenue

Henry Gebhard, a founder of the Denver Stockyards, where he ran a packinghouse and the Stockyards National Bank, also helped establish Denver's National Western Stock Show in 1906. His Italianate house, with a distinctive

FIGURE 3.10. Gebhard/Smith House (photo by Tom Noel).

two-story northwest corner bay, ornate brackets, and chimneys, was restored in the 1980s by Dr. Charles Brantigan for his medical offices. Elaborate woodwork characterizes the front porch and the large roof brackets beneath a hipped roof. Incised geometric patterns adorn the wood trim and stone lintels. This is one of the most notable houses in the San Rafael National Register Historic District, which extends from East Twentieth to East Twenty-Sixth Avenues between Clarkson and Downing Streets.

202. McBird-Whiteman House

1880, Matthew John McBird. 2225 Downing Street

This Victorian house with a distinctive third-story mansard tower was moved to this site in 1993 from 2023 Lafayette Street to accommodate expansion of the hospital district. Architect Matthew John McBird presumably designed this house, where he lived from 1880 until his death in 1903. Later owners Charles and Kathleen Brantigan arranged the move and renovated the brick abode to revive Second Empire elements, such as the keystone-arch double windows and pedimented third-story tower windows of what is now a medical office.

FIGURE 3.11. The McBird-Whiteman House on the move, 1993 (photo by Charles Brantigan).

203. Thomas Hornsby Ferril House

1889, Franklin Goodnow?. 2123 Downing Street, NR

Thomas Hornsby Ferril, Colorado's premier poet laureate, lived here from 1900 until his death in 1988. His great-aunt, Mrs. John Palmer, built this typically eclectic red brick Victorian house with geometric Eastlake trim. Ferril's poetry, however, is far from typical in capturing Colorado's past, with its fragile communities and vanishing landmarks, as these lines from "House in Denver" demonstrate:

In the morning I could stand

A long time watching my father disappear

Beyond the sunflowers which you noticed farther

In the morning. Now tall buildings interfere

In piles of shining masonry, but are there

Walls yet to come no more secure than these?

My city has not worn its shadows long

Enough to quiet even prairie bees.

204. American Woodman's Life Building

1950, Gordon D. White. 2100 Downing Street, northeast corner of East Twenty-First Avenue

The American Woodmen, founded in Denver in 1901, became the leading Colorado fraternal organization that sold insurance to African Americans. The group's sleek headquarters is an example of Streamline Moderne architecture, with curved corners, horizontal bands of windows, and its skin of white terracotta. The structure remained in use by the organization until it closed in 1993, and it has since been diligently restored, inside and outside, to its moderne origins as the home of Humphries Poli Architects.

Lafayette Street Historic District

HD-14

The 2100 block of Lafayette Street includes residential offerings from the Baerresen brothers, Henry Dozier, and William A. Lang. Dozier planned the 1890 Queen Annes at 2115 and 2123 Lafayette Street. The Baerresen brothers designed the John Crook House (1891), 2150 Lafayette, with its third-story pedimented and eyebrow dormers capping a Queen Anne composition. More modest one-story Queen Anne cottages at 2122 and 2126–28 Lafayette add diversity to this block, whose district designation became the first firm boundary between an antique residential neighborhood and the ever-expanding hospital district.

Foster-Brantigan House

1890, William A. Lang. 2105 Lafayette Street, northwest corner of East Twenty-First Avenue, HD-14

This cornerstone of the Lafayette Street Historic District is a three-story Queen Anne with verge board and shingle trim. Ernest LeNeve Foster, a mining engineer, first resided here. Following a 1980s restoration by Kathleen and Charles Brantigan, the house once again sparkles with the rejuvenation of its curved leaded and stained glass windows, the original tile on all three fireplaces, cast-brass doorknobs, anaglyptic wall coverings, and picture moldings.

205. Cody House

1892, Arthur Hughes, builder. 2932 Lafayette Street

William F. "Buffalo Bill" Cody, the most famous Coloradan of all, died here in his sister's house on January 10, 1917. Cody had an illustrious career as a Pony Express rider, army scout, Indian fighter, and buffalo-meat supplier for railroad construction teams. Buffalo Bill became even better known for his Wild West Show, which toured the United States and Europe, delighting millions with reenactments of western adventures. This two-story red brick Queen Anne with a two-story front porch is a less impressive tribute than the Buffalo Bill Grave and Museum atop Lookout Mountain in a Denver Mountain Park.

206. Annunciation Catholic Church

1907, Frederick W. Paroth. 3601 Humboldt Street, northwest corner of East Thirty-Sixth Avenue, NR

This Romanesque Revival cornerstone of the Cole neighborhood is the heart of a parish compound that includes a school, convent, and rectory. Since 1970 the Capuchins (the Franciscan Order of Friars Minor) have staffed this parish. They worked with parish volunteers to give the church a facelift, acquired the corner grocery at Thirty-Eighth and Humboldt Street as a parish center, and replaced the old school with low-income apartments. A projected massive steeple atop the church's corner bell tower never materialized, but this red brick church with its glorious rose window over a triple-arched entry is still an inspiring sight. Inside, Annunciation is wonderfully old-fashioned, with stained glass windows from Munich and a twenty-foot-high Carrara marble high altar guarded by six-foot-tall angels. The nave is adorned with golden oak pews and scagliola columns that burst into florid capitals supporting ornate arches that carry the ribs of the high vaulted ceiling.

207. Wyatt Elementary School

1887, Robert S. Roeschlaub. 3620 Franklin Street, northwest corner of East Thirty-Sixth Avenue

The Hyde Park Elementary School was renamed for George W. Wyatt, a longtime principal, after his death in 1932. This three-story Richardsonian Romanesque edifice is more playful and less symmetrical than most Roeschlaub schools. The steep-pitched billowing roof and bell-cast corner entry tower, framed between an eccentric tall chimney and a round tower, distinguish the red brick school with generous red sandstone and red terracotta trimming. Closed in 1982, it has evolved into the Wyatt-Edison Charter School.

FIGURE 3.13. Wyatt Elementary School, 1982 (photo by Roger Whitacre).

208. Elyria Elementary School

1924. Wilson and Wilson. 4725 High Street

Designed in the Spanish Colonial Revival style, with Mission and Mediterranean decorative elements, this Elyria neighborhood landmark has a red tile roof over a U-shaped school that reaches out to this working-class neighborhood. After the elementary school closed in 1980, the one-story beige brick building was rehabilitated in 1989 as El Centro Su Teatro, a 100-seat theater. In 2012 the building found new life as housing for veterans after Su Teatro, a flourishing

FIGURE 3.12. (a) Archbishop James V. Casey celebrates Annunciation Catholic Church's restoration with a solemn high mass, 1982. (b) The Annunciation Window is one of the church's F. X Zettler Royal Bavarian Art Institute stained glass masterpieces from the famous Munich studio obliterated by US bombing during World War II (both photos by James Baca).

Hispanic theater group, moved to larger quarters at 721 Santa Fe Drive.

209. Schulz-Neef House

ca. 1881. 1739 East Twenty-Ninth Avenue between Williams and High Streets

German immigrant R. Ernst Schulz, a bookkeeper for the German National Bank, built this splendid two-story Gothic Revival residence. In 1883, soon after its construction, the Neef family of beer-brewing fame purchased the house at public action and lived there until 1945. After a brief stint as a fourplex apartment house, it returned to a single-family home. With elaborate ornamental woodwork, pointed finials, and a steeply gabled roof, this Denver example of Gothic Revival architecture is a highlight of the Whittier neighborhood.

210. Miller House

1902. 2501 High Street, northwest corner of East Twenty-Fifth Avenue

Byron L. Miller, a businessman and realtor who became a building inspector, erected this house and lived here for at least three decades. Paired round-arch windows recessed in rusticated rhyolite walls distinguish this eclectic style house. The stonework is notable, especially on the entry porch, with its paired polished stone columns atop the stone porch wall.

East Park Place Historic District

HD-23

2000 block of East Park Place between Vine and Race Streets and East Twenty-First and Twenty-Second Avenues

The East Park Place Historic District contains eight single-family homes, of which seven are foursquares. Four of these structures were designed by Denver architect and developer Frank S. Snell. Here at Park Place, as in the Snell Addition Historic District, Snell experimented with smaller yards and denser housing patterns. Snell had hoped to build sixteen homes in this block but went out of business in 1907. The block is notable for its early ethnic diversity, with a Chinese family arriving in 1949 and black families after 1952.

Clayton College Historic District

HD-34 CLAYTON COLLEGE HISTORIC DISTRICT

Roughly bounded by Martin Luther King Boulevard, Colorado Boulevard, Madison Street, and Bruce Randolph Avenue, NRD

Established by George Washington Clayton, a highly respected Denver real estate tycoon, this campus opened in 1911 as an orphanage for white males but is now open to all sexes and races. Clayton was a county commissioner and a Denver city councilman, and he helped found Denver water and power utilities. He died in 1899 without children and left much of his $2 million estate to found this institution, modeled after Girard College in his native city of Philadelphia. It contained dormitories, educational facilities, and a farm where the boys raised their own food. This richly endowed orphanage provided unusually well-staffed and organized programming on a large site, including what is now the Park Hill Golf Course. Constructed between 1909 and 1913 from a design by leading Denver architects Maurice Biscoe and Henry Hewitt, the Mediterranean Revival style campus in uniform red sandstone is distinguished by gabled dormers, hipped roofs, stone quoins, arched windows, and spacious landscaping on a hilltop site. It has evolved into the Clayton Early Learning Center, with various early learning programs, including research and training, as well as daycare and schooling for underserved children from birth to age five.

FIGURE 3.14. Clayton College (photo by Tom Noel).

4
Northwest Denver

HIGHLANDS AREA

WEST COLFAX AREA

GLOBEVILLE AREA

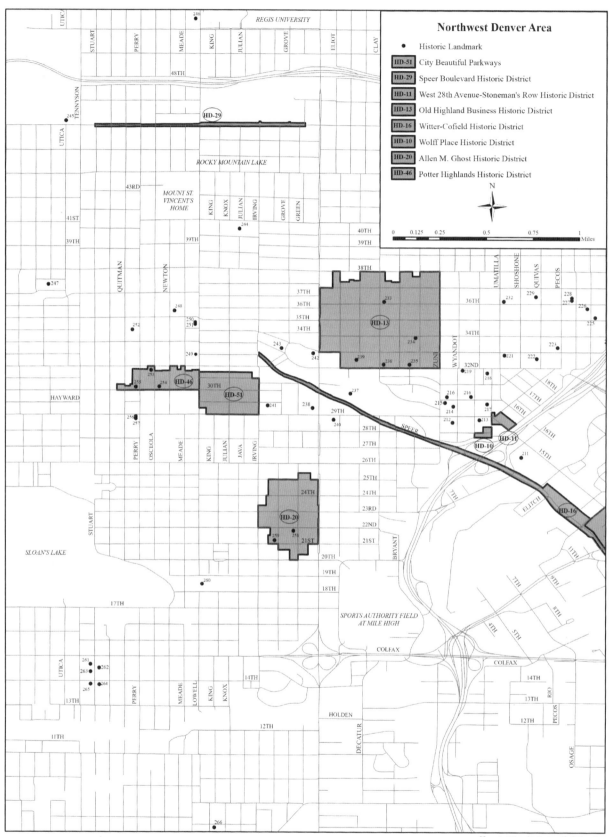

MAP 4.1. Northwest Denver area

Northwest Denver is bounded on the east by the South Platte River, on the north by Fifty-Second Avenue and the city limits, on the west by Sheridan Boulevard and the city limits, and on the south by West Sixth Avenue. This quadrant traces its origins to December 14, 1858, when Denver founder William H. Larimer Jr. waded across the South Platte River to stake out "Highland" on the bluff northwest of Denver, which Larimer had founded a month earlier. Separated from the rest of the city by the South Platte River and, after 1870, by railroad tracks, northwest Denver did not flourish until the 1880s.

The initial wave of English, Scottish, and Irish settlers began after General William J. Palmer and Dr. William A. Bell of the Denver & Rio Grande Railroad platted the Highland Park Addition in 1875. Curving streets with Scottish names still characterize this National Register Historic District, also known as Scottish Village. Between the 1890s and 1920s, North Denver experienced a high tide of Italian immigrants. They turned part of the area into Little Italy, but Hispanics became the most numerous new ethnic group after 1940. The ethnic peoples of northwest Denver have given it a colorful collection of churches, restaurants, commercial blocks, and dwellings. Here, one still gets a feel for nineteenth-century neighborhoods, with their corner stores, churches, schools, and other essentials within walking distance.

Spared the intense development of Lower Downtown, the Central Business District, and Capitol Hill, northwest Denver retains many original structures. Church spires, not high-rise apartments and office towers, still crown the skyline. Since the 1990s North Denver has been discovered by a younger generation appreciative of the substantial brick homes, neighborhood businesses within walking distance, and wealth of ethnic eateries. The area is now threatened by overdevelopment—many single-family homes are being demolished for modern multi-story apartments crowding their sites. Faced by boxy new site-filling multi-family residences, North Denverites have come to cherish their many landmarks.

Highlands Area

West Sixth Avenue to I-70 between the South Platte River and Sheridan Boulevard

211. Denver Tramway Co. Powerhouse–Forney Transportation Museum–Recreational Equipment, Inc.

1901, Stearns Rogers Co. 1416 Platte Street near Fifteenth Street

This Neoclassical temple of technology, bordering Confluence Park at the junction of Cherry Creek and the South Platte River, has red brick walls with roundel windows and corbeled arches. This coal-fed power plant generated electricity to move Denver's trolleys. Converted to a transportation museum by J. Donovan Forney in 1968, it housed automobiles, trucks, buses, railway rolling stock, and streetcars. The building survived the 1965 South Platte River flood, whose devastation inspired a cleanup of the Platte and the 1976 opening of Confluence Park. This park and the greenway of trails leading to it have sparked a renaissance of the area surrounding the power plant.

Recreational Equipment, Inc. (REI) bought the neglected edifice and completed a spectacular restoration in 2000. Extensive landscaped grounds now surround the three-story brick Neoclassical structure. Inside, a cavernous, sky-lighted atrium includes a large climbing wall. During the day, the restored industrial-sized arched windows light this huge sporting goods emporium.

HD-11 OLD HIGHLAND HISTORIC BUSINESS DISTRICT

Fifteenth Street between Central and Boulder Streets

Fires and demolitions have erased much of the original North Denver commercial district that arose along the first streetcar line to cross the river and the railroad tracks. These brick and stone relics represent sturdy nineteenth-century neighborhood commercial complexes. Robert A. Wilson, a civil engineer, helped design the now gone Marquis Block (1889), 2501–9 Fifteenth Street, and the Slockett Block (1890), 2535 Fifteenth Street. Newer construction of unsympathetic design has diminished this district.

HD-10 West Twenty-Eighth Avenue– Stoneman's Row Historic District

1891–93. West Twenty-Eighth Avenue between Vallejo and Umatilla Streets, NRD

Three stonemasons who prospered in Denver's 1880s building boom erected the nine structures in this district for their families. Balcomb and Rice created 2753–55 Umatilla and 2112–14, 2118–20, and 2140 West Twenty-Eighth Avenue; Baerresen Brothers designed 2122 West Twenty-Eighth Avenue; and J. H. Barnes planned 2128 West Twenty-Eighth Avenue. These flat-roofed dwellings share a repetition of Richardsonian elements, such as triangular roof pediments, yet they have enough variety of texture and materials to avoid monotony. Smooth and rusticated sandstone and rhyolite facing, combined with the weight of the Romanesque Revival elements, make these small brick units seem larger than they are. They overlook the Platte Valley and downtown from a bluff now scarred by blatant new postmodern construction.

212. Conine-Horan House

1892, Solomon A. Layton? and Frank P. Fryburger?, builders. 2839 Wyandot Street

John Conine, a lumber merchant, and his wife, Martha, originally lived here. She was a leading suffragist instrumental in earning Colorado women the right to vote in 1893. Capitalizing on that nation-leading achievement, she won a seat in the Colorado House of Representatives in 1896. An ardent reformer, Conine fought political corruption and crusaded for libraries, public drinking fountains (to discourage people from going to saloons), playgrounds, and public ownership of utilities.

The next owner of this red sandstone–fronted townhouse was William P. Horan, a native of Greenfield, Massachusetts, who came to Denver in 1887. He resided here with his wife, Elizabeth, and their children from 1896 to 1908. Horan, a graduate of the Egyptian School of Embalming, opened a mortuary in downtown Denver in 1890. He climbed to the top of the trade with state-of-the art funeral practices such as motorized hearses, which he introduced to Denver in 1912. Horan served for many years as Denver city coroner. Some charged that Horan, a devout Democrat, helped maintain the list of "dead names" used by the political machine of Mayor Robert W. Speer. "These people were good Democrats," Horan supposedly

FIGURE 4.1. Conine-Horan House, 2014 (photo by Tom Noel).

said. "Why should they be denied the vote just because they're underground?"

After Horan's death in 1930, his children continued to run what became W. P. Horan and Sons, which survives to this day as the Horan and McConaty Funeral Service. The Conine-Horan House, a survivor of a block of similar 1890s residences, commemorates one of Denver's best-known Irish Catholic businessmen. Rectangular-cut, quarry-faced red sandstone and an ornate tin parapet front the two-story red brick townhouse. Note the new townhouse to the south incorporating historic design elements.

213. Wheeler Block

1894, Louis M. Wood. 2150 West Twenty-Ninth Avenue, southeast corner of Vallejo Street

This large five-story corner commercial edifice has a grand parapet and sunburst nameplate in the pediment. The sandstone-trimmed brick edifice has distinctive arches below the elaborate pressed metal frieze, parapet, and central pediment. Charles A. Wheeler, who lived nearby at West Twenty-Eighth Avenue and Wyandot Street, was

FIGURE 4.2. Wheeler Block before restoration, 1995 (photo by Thomas H. Simmons).

FIGURE 4.3. Tallmadge and Boyer Terrace (photo by Tom Noel).

an accountant and organizer of the Colorado & Southern Railroad. He built this apartment house and meeting hall as a home for societies such as the Daughters of America and the Knights of Pythias. After a 1902 foreclosure, the Wheeler Block became the Mountain View Apartments, then served as a tuberculosis sanitarium, a nursing home, and apartments before restoration in the 1990s as offices.

214. Tallmadge and Boyer Terrace

1889. 2925–59 Wyandot Street, southwest corner of West Thirtieth Avenue

Realtors Charles E. Tallmadge and John C. Boyer built the two-story 1889 terrace in the Queen Anne style, with walls of decorative red brick with rusticated red sandstone trim and Eastlake wooden spool work on the gabled porch entries. The homes are set back from the attached corner store and have their own little lawns. In 1996 the eight terrace units were renovated for ongoing residential use.

Tallmadge and Boyer also commissioned the Tallmadge and Boyer Block (1891, Wenzel Janisch and Edwin Miller; 2926 Zuni Street, NR). Elaborate red brick and red sandstone characterize this commercial block, now residential. Rising three stories to a triple-bracketed cornice and wide frieze, the block has both arched and parapeted corbelling over the top-floor windows. Among many other businesses, the block housed a neighborhood newspaper, the *Highlands Chieftain*.

215. Romeo Block

1889, Baerresen Brothers. 1994 restoration, David Fox and Larry Arbuthnot. 2944–58 Zuni Street, southeast corner of West Thirtieth Avenue, NR

A corner oriel bay window crowned with a flattened dome dramatizes this two-story red brick, stone-trimmed commercial structure, as do second-story bay windows, recessed first-floor entry bays, and handsome transoms. The Romeo Block was named for liquor dealer Louis M. Weiner's son, Romeo S. Weiner, who built it with his partner, Sam Barets. Barets brought in Denver's largest shipment of whiskey to that date—9,000 gallons of "Quaker City" rye whiskey—in 1899. This corner commercial block was elegantly restored as a fourteen-unit apartment in 1994 by developers David Fox and Larry Arbuthnot. Their $1 million project removed a stucco facade, replaced a rear wall, and repaired or replaced brick, stone, and tinwork to resurrect an unusually fine edifice.

FIGURE 4.4. Romeo Block (photo by Thomas H. Simmons).

FIGURE 4.5. Asbury Methodist Church (Kidder and Humphreys architectural rendering, Denver Public Library).

216. Asbury Methodist Church

1890, Franklin Kidder and John J. Humphreys. 2205 West Thirtieth Avenue, northwest corner of Vallejo Street

Located on a prominent hillside visible from downtown, this $75,000 edifice of rusticated gray rhyolite was named for Bishop Francis Asbury. The church is reminiscent of Henry H. Richardson's Trinity Church (1879) in Boston, with its arched entry at the base of a square corner bell tower with four turrets. Stone pilasters grouped at the corners divide the tower's narrow, arched openings. Round-arched tripartite window bays center the street elevations. Horizontal red sandstone bands and arches contrast well with the gray rhyolite and visually hold the large expanses together. Inside, elaborate stained glass with geometric and floral patterns illuminates the renovated pipe organ (1875), said to be the oldest in continual use in Colorado. Reflecting the ethnic evolution of North Denver, the original Scotch-Irish flock was replaced by a Korean congregation and then by the Sanctuary Church, which added a contemporary clock tower on the west side.

217. Crescent Hand Laundry Building

ca. 1891, James A. Hamman, builder. 1996 restoration, Murphy Stevens. 2323–29 West Thirtieth Avenue

Originally occupied by William W. Bewley's coal, hay, and feed store, this structure housed the Crescent Hand

Laundry from 1902 to 1916. Later occupants included a restaurant and other businesses. Renovations failed to halt the decline of the building, which had become dilapidated and run down by 1995, when Carey Bringle and Susan Proctor bought it. With the aid of the nonprofit Potter Highlands Preservation Association, the owners obtained a $16,875 State Historical Fund grant toward a $92,015 restoration. Re-pointing, cleaning, stone repair, and paint removal have returned the antique facade to its original design and retrofitted the interior with four loft apartments.

FIGURE 4.6. Fager Residence (photo by Thomas H. Simmons).

218. Fager Residence

ca. 1884. 2947 Umatilla Street

Charming simplicity radiates from this tiny clapboard front-gable cottage with a central brick chimney. The frame porch gingerbread includes squared columns and decorative brackets. This rare example of frame construction within the Denver city limits has two tiny rear additions. Sarah J. Fager, a fifty-nine-year-old widow from Tennessee, bought the land and built this house around 1884. Later owners added the porch and a chicken coop to this dignified, little-altered, working-class residence.

FIGURE 4.7. All Saints Episcopal Church–Chapel of Our Merciful Savior (photo by Tom Noel).

219. All Saints Episcopal Church–Chapel of Our Merciful Savior

1890, James Murdoch. 2222 West Thirty-Second Avenue, southeast corner of Wyandot Street, NR

A soaring steeple on a buttressed corner bell tower and a steep gable roof distinguish this red brick Gothic Revival chapel with an adjacent rectory. Built originally as All Saints Church, it was renamed after that congregation moved to a larger church at 3650 Yates Street in 1961. Rusticated rhyolite trims the entrance centered beneath a rose window. Inside, the original carved wooden statues, pulpit, baptismal font, and pews survive under hammered ceiling beams set in a herringbone pattern. Elsie Ward Hering, a Denver

student of Augustus Saint-Gaudens, sculpted the marble angel that holds a scalloped holy water basin. Installation of a cell phone station hidden in the tower helped pay for enhancements to the church and grounds.

220. Cowie House

1888, Alexander Johnstone Cowie, builder. 3147 Umatilla Street

Alexander Johnstone Cowie, a Scottish stonemason and city sidewalk inspector, probably built his own brick cottage. Its polychromatic stone facade features a rhyolite base and quoins with floral medallions carved into the stone door frame. Fish-scale shingling adorns the front bay window and gable. Originally, this two-lot site was part of Acacia Cemetery, established in 1866 by the Denver Masons and the Order of Odd Fellows. That cemetery, bounded by West Twenty-Ninth and West Thirty-Second Avenues between Tejon and Zuni Streets, was vacated in the early 1880s and the bodies removed so the bone yard could be developed for livelier residential purposes.

221. Cole-DeRose Apartment House

1895. 1940–46 West Thirty-Third Avenue, southeast corner of Tejon Street

Linus C. Cole, a New Yorker who came to Denver in 1892, constructed this two-story red brick Neoclassical townhouse, where he also lived. The Doric-columned entry porches and central frieze above a second-story porch are distinctive. Cole also built and operated an adjacent corner grocery store that no longer stands. The DeRose family, a prominent North Denver Italian clan who lived here and operated the grocery, purchased the Cole complex in 1916. The grocery disappeared in the 1970s, replaced by garages.

222. Fox-Schlatter House

1888. 3225 Quivas Street

Edward L. Fox's modest one-story brick cottage gained national fame in 1895 when Francis Schlatter made it the center of his ministry of public healing. Schlatter lived with the Foxes and stood on a makeshift platform in their front yard to treat hundreds who flocked there daily. During his two-month ministry, Schlatter attracted some 80,000 people. Trainloads of sick people came to Denver on special Union Pacific Railroad trains. They disembarked at

FIGURE 4.8. Crowds gathered at the home of Francis Schlatter as word spread of his miraculous healing powers, 1895 (photo by W. A. White, Library of Congress).

Union Station to board a special North Denver–bound Denver Tramway Company trolley car marked "This Car for the Healer." Schlatter disappeared mysteriously on the night of November 13, 1895. Rumors slowly drifted back to town that his skeletal remains had been found in Mexico, where he may have died of starvation. The Fox house is all that survives of Schlatter's amazing ministry. John Varone bought the house from Fox's widow, Mary, in 1912 and built his extant grocery store on the corner of West Thirty-Third Avenue and Quivas Street.

223. St. Patrick's Catholic Church

1910, Harry James Manning and Frances C. Wagner. 3301–25 Pecos Street, northwest corner of West Thirty-Third Avenue, NR

As one of Colorado's first Irish parishes, St. Patrick's promoted Celtic culture, including Denver's now-huge St.

Patrick's Day Parade. The parade began in the 1880s as a parish festival that included mass and musical entertainment. The festival was held in collaboration with the Daughters of Erin and the Ancient Order of Hibernians. It ended in church, not a saloon.

Father Joseph P. Carrigan built this parish complex, inspired by his tour of eighteenth-century California missions. The fine Mission style design includes smooth cast-stone blocks with raised mortar joints. The red barrel tile roof features a curvilinear parapet and a pair of copper-domed towers. The church, sacristy, a two-story rectory, and a small library are guarded by an arcaded passageway. Stucco walls and exposed beams carry the Mission style inside the church. In 1989 the parish was closed and became Our Lady of Light Monastery for Capuchin Poor Clare nuns, noted for their twenty-four-hour prayer vigils and their heavenly cookies. A block away, at 3233 Osage Street, the original red brick Romanesque St. Patrick's

FIGURE 4.9. St. Patrick's twin domes have been gilded, but otherwise the church is little altered; ca. 1911 (Tom Noel Collection).

Catholic Church (1883) was converted to the parish school and then to the Original Mexican Café before conversion to residences.

224. Our Lady of Guadalupe Catholic Church

1948, John K. Monroe. 1990 addition. 3559 Kalamath Street, southwest corner of West Thirty-Sixth Avenue

Started as a storefront mission, this ministry has evolved into a parish complex whose murals and architectural details honor both the Spanish and Aztec traditions. Spanish-speaking Theatine priests named the church for the patroness of Mexico, whose life-size statue occupies the niche over the arched doorway. John K. Monroe, who followed his mentor, Jules Jacques Benoit Benedict, as Denver's Roman Catholic archdiocesan architect, designed this $66,500 church. Spanish Mission Revival style is apparent in the red tile roof, prominent curvilinear parapet, domed bell tower, round arches, and arcaded courtyard. The 1990 south wing of the church, which seats 180, reflects the growing congregation and the prominence of what was once a tiny mission chapel.

Carlota Espinoza painted the interior mural (1975) of Nuestra Señora de Guadalupe, who appeared to a poor Indian boy, Juan Diego, on a hill near Mexico City in 1531. Juan Menchaca painted an older series of murals depicting the Stations of the Cross. This church has been a center for

FIGURE 4.10. Our Lady of Guadalupe Catholic Church (photo by Thomas H. Simmons).

economic, political, and social activism to improve the lot of Denver Hispanics. It also perpetuates mariachi masses, the Christmastime Las Posadas ceremony, and other traditional Hispanic rituals.

225. Hannigan-Canino Terrace

1890. 3500 Navajo Street, at the northeast corner of West Thirty-Fifth Avenue, NR

Although single-family housing has always dominated even the poorest neighborhoods in Denver, perhaps a hundred terraces such as this were built in working-class neighborhoods. Ten two-story apartments are divided by basement-to-parapet brick firewalls. This rhythmic composition of red brick is topped with a flat roof and stepped corbeled cornices. Ten bays are separated by pilasters, and all the door and window openings have segmental arches. Each apartment contains a living room and small kitchen

FIGURE 4.11. Italian immigrants built Our Lady of Mount Carmel Catholic Church (photo by Tom Noel).

on the first floor, with a closed stairway leading to upstairs bedrooms. Built without bathrooms and central heat, the units have been individually remodeled to include these conveniences.

Irish immigrant Frank Hannigan built these units at a time when many of his countrymen were coming to Denver. Joseph Canino remodeled the corner unit as a storefront and small apartment in 1935 to accommodate his meat market and family. That year he bought the entire building for around $3,500. Second owner Canino represented a later wave of Italian immigrants. These two ethnic groups slowly improved their economic conditions and moved on, succeeded by Hispanics and a most recent wave of new urbanists.

226. Our Lady of Mount Carmel Catholic Church

1904, Frederick R. Paroth. 3549 Navajo Street, southwest corner of West Thirty-Sixth Avenue, NR

Still reigning over the neighborhood once known as Little Italy, Mount Carmel was Colorado's first Italian parish church. The Romanesque Revival design in brick has twin towers capped by copper domes. A large rose window is centered in the front gable above raised brick courses that circle the window and form arches above the entry niche for the white marble statue of Our Lady of Mount Carmel above a triple Roman arch entry. The 1,000-pound bell, the heartbeat of Italian North Denver, once regulated neighborhood life, as church bells did in the Old Country. The interior is decorated with marble statues brought from Italy and with ceiling and wall murals. From the alley behind

the church, proud craftsmanship can be seen in the red brick chimneys with blond brick insets in the shape of a cross. The cornerstone honors the founding pastor, Father Mariano Felice Lepore, who was mysteriously murdered a year before his church opened.

227. Frank Damascio House

1895, Frank Damascio. 3611–15 Osage Street

Frank Damascio, one of Colorado's many Italian stonemasons, helped build the Brown Palace Hotel, the Immaculate Conception Cathedral, and other Denver landmarks. In his eclectic family home, he used alternating courses of rusticated granite and smooth red sandstone. Two expansive Roman arches frame a recessed corner porch. Small decorative turrets frame each side of the front facade. Stone posts reinforce the wrought-iron fencing around this double house, later converted to a convalescent hospital by Frank's daughter, Elisa Damascio Palladino.

228. Cerrone's Grocery

1893, Frank Damascio. 3617 Osage Street

Frank Damascio and his partner, Horace Palladino, opened their North Denver Mercantile Company in this building of Damascio's design, a single-story brick rectangle with fifteen-foot ceilings. Fluted pilasters rise above the roof to bracket a corbeled cornice. From the 1920s to the 1990s, the Cerrone family operated one of Denver's last old-fashioned neighborhood groceries, with its original flagstone entry, hardwood floor, wooden display cabinets, and a meat-chopping block guarded by a statue of the Blessed Virgin.

229. Bryant-Webster Elementary School

1931, G. Meredith Musick and J. Roger Musick. 3635 Quivas Street, NR

The brothers, both prominent Denver architects, designed this two-story gem named for the earlier Bryant and Webster Schools it replaced. Three-dimensional brickwork with an opalescent glaze duplicated Native American designs, as did plumes and pendants and sunbursts. Distinguished features of this elementary school include its vertical emphasis, straight-headed sash windows, a flat roof, and a bold tower entrance. This fine example of "Pueblo Deco" style honors Hopi, Navajo, and Pima Indians of the

FIGURE 4.12. Bas-relief Native American motifs adorn the tower of the Bryant Webster Elementary School (photo by Tom Noel).

Southwest by mimicking their art. Slightly protruding triangular bays showcase the subtly contrasting, protruding brickwork.

230. Horace Mann Middle School

1931 and 1956 addition, Temple Hoyne Buell. 1994 addition, Hoover, Berg, Desmond. 4130 Navajo Street between West Fortieth and Forty-Second Avenues

Horace Mann was a Massachusetts legislator and Antioch College president who became a nationally noted advocate of free coeducational schools for all. He also championed better training and pay for schoolteachers. Denver honored Mann with one of its more unusual schools, a brick mason's tour de force with beige bricks that seem to grow out of the structure organically, like ivy. Architect Buell claimed "I dreamed up Horace Mann sitting one day on my porch watching sun and shadows on brickwork. For this school,

FIGURE 4.13. The facade of Horace Mann Middle School (a) is enlivened by ornate bricks that contain the name of architect Temple Hoyne Buell (b) (photos by Tom Noel).

we employed only brick and all the effects we could create with it—classical, Gothic, Renaissance and modern." Buell also employed the Art Deco style, as reflected in the vertical brick stacks, stepped massing, and crenelated roofline. The

H-plan school occupies a full block, with generous landscaping and recreation facilities extending to Lipan Street and including Ciancio Park.

231. Smedley Elementary School

1902 with 1911 addition, David W. Dryden. 1950s Moderne addition. 1994 addition, Ramon F. Martinez. 4250 Shoshone Street between West Forty-Second and Forty-Third Avenues

Dentist William Smedley was an early school board president whose residence is preserved in Auraria's Ninth Street Historic Park. He gave his name to this two-story red brick school with a raised basement characterized by a quiet Neoclassicism. David W. Dryden, who also designed North High and many other Denver schools, planned both the 1902 original building and the 1911 addition. Straight window lintels and relatively sparse Neoclassical

FIGURE 4.14. Smedley Elementary School (photo by Tom Noel).

ornamentation typify this early-twentieth-century idea of a modern school building. A 1950s north-side Moderne addition nearly doubled the school's size. Faced with plans to demolish and replace Smedley Elementary in the early 1990s, teachers, students, and neighbors rallied to pursue landmark designation and a sensitive south-side 1994 addition that has made the school young again.

FIGURE 4.15. Fire Station No. 7 (photo by Thomas H. Simmons).

232. Fire Station No. 7

1909, Glen Wood Huntington. 3600 Tejon Street, northeast corner of West Thirty-Sixth Avenue

This fire station's predecessor, with slits in its medieval corner watch turrets, survives at West Thirty-Second Avenue and Erie Street. It became the Tivoli Terrace Night Club and, later, the Denvue Apartments. In part because fire horses had trouble on such a steep hill, No. 7 moved to this replacement station. North Denver native and lifelong politician Dennis Gallagher recalls that the firefighters in this pressed red brick with light stone trim station used their horse-drawn wagon to take Mother Frances Cabrini, the first US citizen to be canonized as a saint, and her nuns on Sunday picnics. "My dad," Gallagher adds, "and other old-time smoke eaters told me that whenever they were out with the nuns, North Denver was miraculously protected from any kind of blaze." After the fire company moved to newer quarters in 1975, the firehouse was rehabilitated as retail shops in the downstairs bays with condominiums upstairs. Much of the original firefighting apparatus has been retained. Note the extravagant corbelled frieze with broad bracketed eaves and the original twin pedimented garage doors.

HD-13 POTTER HIGHLANDS HISTORIC DISTRICT

Roughly Zuni Street to Federal Boulevard between West Thirty-Second and West Thirty-Eighth Avenues, NRD

The Reverend Walter M. Potter, who established the First Baptist Church of Denver in 1864, bought a 320-acre North Denver site. He died in 1866 and willed the property to the Baptist Home Missionary Society, which sold it to various developers of Potter Highlands. This venerable neighborhood, now a large historic district with 667 buildings, is a fairly intact ensemble of late 1800s dwellings. Tree lawns and flagstone sidewalks front evenly set-back homes. Large Queen Anne style residences, like the Mouat House, now the Lumber Baron Bed and Breakfast (1890; 1994 restoration, David Anderson), 2555 West Thirty-Seventh Avenue, and the Sayre-Brodie House (1886), 3631 Eliot Street, showcase products from Mouat's lumber company and Brodie's Lyons sandstone businesses. Interspersed throughout the district are plainer Queen Anne examples, as well as foursquares, classic cottages, and bungalows.

The Edbrooke Foursquares (ca. 1904, Frank E. Edbrooke), 2501, 2511, and 2521 West Thirty-Second Avenue, were constructed as a family complex for John W. Prout, a mining man and geologist in the first graduating class of Colorado School of Mines. The small rear yards were joined and had a common carriage lot and driveway, which helps explain the lack of garages. These early foursquares, with little ornamentation other than the Tuscan porch columns and bracketed cornices, represent Edbrooke's shift from embellished Victorian designs to Neoclassicism. One of the more modern homes is Milton House (1916, Glen W. Huntington), 3400 Federal Boulevard, a Prairie style residence with a flat roof, overhanging eaves, window bands, and ribbon windows. The Highlands Masonic Temple (1927, Merrill H. Hoyt), 3550 Federal Boulevard, is an example of starved Neoclassicism occupying a full landscaped block.

233. Amos B. Hughes House

1913, Home Construction Company, builder. 3600 Clay Street, corner of northeast West Thirty-Sixth Avenue, HD-13

This Craftsman home was built for Amos B. Hughes, a Denver policeman and later the proprietor of the Orient Hotel in downtown Denver. This distinctive home retains many of its original Craftsman features, including six-foot-tall casement windows, half-timbered gables, and generous overhanging eaves. One of the notable features of this home is the Art Nouveau stained glass windows in the dining room.

234. Hugh McKay House

1891. 3359 Alcott Street, southeast corner of West Thirty-Fourth Avenue, HD-13

Hugh McKay, a Scottish immigrant involved in mining and construction, used rough-faced rhyolite for his sturdy house. The second story hunkers down under broad sloping eaves, and its small windows squint into Colorado's brilliant sunshine, which dazzled immigrants from grayer, wetter places. A Scottish thistle is carved into one first-floor window lintel, and the interior has fine turned woodwork and stained glass. The steep-pitched roof and prominent dormers are repeated in the matching carriage house. Anne McKay, the builder's daughter, kept the house and barn in nearly original shape for decades after his demise.

FIGURE 4.16. Stonemason Hugh Mckay's craftsmanship extends from the retaining wall to the chimney (Photo by Thomas H. Simmons)

235. Henri Foster House

1874. 2533 West Thirty-Second Avenue, HD-13

Henri R. Foster, who helped develop the town of Highlands and served as the first town clerk, built this show home for the new Denver suburb, which stretched from Zuni Street to Sheridan Boulevard between West Colfax and West Thirty-Eighth Avenues. Foster also helped develop adjacent Highland Park, with its curvy streets with Scottish names. Highland Park, also known as Scottish Village, is a residential National Register Historic District bounded by

Zuni on the east, West Thirty-Second on the north, Clay Street on the west, and West Dunkeld Place on the south. Foster led the fight against annexation of Highlands and Highland Park, but financial problems related to the 1893 depression led voters to approve annexation by Denver in 1896.

Foster was a director of Riverside Cemetery, a trustee of the Colorado School for the Deaf and the Blind in Colorado Springs, and an organizer of the now demolished Boulevard Congregational Church. His house has tall, paired Italianate windows, but the steep, double-pitched roof and newer porch on this L-plan house cloud the issue of style on one of the oldest dwellings in North Denver.

236. Henry Lee House

1890. 2653 West Thirty-Second Avenue, northeast corner of Clay Street, HD-13

Henry Lee, a state senator and state representative, first introduced legislation to create Sloan's Lake Park and City Park. A pioneer who came to Denver in 1864, he established the Pioneer Seed Company and a farm implement firm that offered chilled-steel plows capable of breaking the tough prairie sod. He experimented with these plows on his large farm, which is now part of Crown Hill Cemetery. On a spacious site, he built this Queen Anne on one of Denver's few carriage blocks, with the center of the block reserved for residents' horses and carriages. Verge boards accent the steep-pitched front gable, and fish-scale shingle trim also distinguishes this house. A wraparound porch displays the red sandstone used to trim this pressed red brick domicile.

237. North High School

1911 and 1913 addition, David W. Dryden. 1959 gymnasium, pool, and classrooms, Charles Gordon Lee. 1983 auditorium, cafeteria, and classrooms, Haller and Larson. 1983 and 1993 classroom additions, Oz Architecture. 2000 master plan and skylight restoration, Humphries Poli Architects. 2960 Speer Boulevard

Constructed during the City Beautiful movement in Denver, this school and West, East, and South High Schools were built as model schools. Considered one of the most noteworthy works of renowned Denver architect David W. Dryden, the $335,000 school borrows from Beaux Arts classicism for its ionic columns, recessed arched portals, finials, and an overall ornate facade that climaxes in a rooftop

balustrade. The original school and mechanical arts wing have endured many additions, including a sensitive ca. 2000 restoration by Humphries-Poli Architects, who restored the grand central skylight.

238. St. Dominic's Catholic Church

1926, Robert Willison. 2905 Federal Boulevard, northwest corner of West Twenty-Ninth Avenue

The Dominican Fathers founded St. Dominic's parish in 1889 and began saving their money for the day they could move out of various temporary homes to this magnificent English Gothic structure. It took three years to build the $270,000 gray stone church, which became the centerpiece of a parish complex that included a rectory, convent, and parish school. St. Dominic's hosted Denver's first parish credit union in the diocese to help parishioners get through the Great Depression.

239. St. Elizabeth's Retreat Chapel

1897, Frederick J. Sterner. 2835 West Thirty-Second Avenue, HD-13

This Georgian Revival chapel is reminiscent of Christopher Wren's London churches, which Sterner admired. He designed it for the Oakes Home, a tuberculosis sanitarium. Inside the chapel, dark wood and red brick walls under a coffered ceiling are illuminated by colored and stained glass. The Poor Sisters of St. Francis acquired the site in 1943 and converted it to a retirement home. Adjacent Neoclassical buildings of the Oakes Home were demolished to build housing, including a fourteen-story 1988 high-rise and a garden for a senior residence, rechristened the Gardens at St. Elizabeth's.

240. Queree House

1888, Joseph John Queree. 2914 West Twenty-Ninth Avenue

Joseph John Queree, a Scottish immigrant remembered as one of Denver's finest carpenters, adorned his own brick house—as well as many Denver mansions—with his exquisite woodwork. An octagonal tower entrance with a bell-cast roof distinguishes this small one-story, flat-topped cottage. Red brick corbelling and arches provide sedate trim. Queree's daughter, Pearl, lived here for many years while working as a teacher and principal for the Denver Public Schools.

FIGURE 4.17. St. Elizabeth's Retreat Chapel (photo by Tom Noel).

FIGURE 4.18. This unusual window gave the House with the Round Window its name (photo by Thomas H. Simmons).

242. Woodbury Branch Library

1912, Jules Jacques Benoit Benedict. 1992 restoration, David Owen Tryba. 3265 Federal Boulevard, southeast corner of Highland Park Place

This beautifully proportioned Italian Renaissance villa in miniature adorns the northeast corner of Highland Park. Roger W. Woodbury, first president of the Denver Public Library board, suggested the Florentine style for this branch library, where his portrait hangs above one of two original fireplaces. The library sits atop a full basement and is sheathed in beige-speckled brick trimmed with elaborate terracotta window surrounds, pilasters, and medallions. Triple arches grace the central entry. Inside, the ceiling's ornately carved open trusses and silver birch decking shine after a 1992 restoration that undid many "improvements"

241. House with the Round Window

1890, William W. Monetelius and Raymond J. Walker, builders. 3240 West Hayward Place

This story-and-a-half Queen Anne brick cottage has an eccentric round window in the decorative front bay. Fish-scale and diamond-pane shingles trim the round window gable and a higher gable hovering over it. Sandstone trim on the brick walls and fine stained, beveled, and leaded glass add to this romantic scenario. Oscar L. Edgecomb, a clerk for the Denver & Rio Grande Railroad, originally owned this residence, which was restored by owner Henry L. Cato. A simple bracketed roof porch shelters a discrete off-center entry.

FIGURE 4.19. Woodbury Branch Library (photo by Thomas H. Simmons).

to resurrect the original inspired design. Tryba, a Denver architect, did restoration and added a rotunda at the rear that opens to an outdoor terrace. In this two-floor addition, he used the same large-arch portals that distinguish the original facade of this branch library, originally funded in part by the Andrew Carnegie Foundation.

243. Bosler-Yankee House

1875, John G. Weller. 3209 West Fairview Place, northwest corner of Grove Street

This once elegant but often remodeled Italianate has lost its dominant square entry cupola but has kept much of its other ornamentation while becoming a test case of demolition by neglect. Ambrose Bosler, a Highlands town founder who established and operated the Union Ice Company at Rocky Mountain Lake, built this huge home for $14,000. William H. Yankee, vice president of North Denver Bank, bought the house in 1888. In 1915 it became a sanitarium, where Dr. John H. Tilden prescribed diets and bed rest as a cure for everything from tuberculosis to obesity. Yankee began remodeling and Tilden continued the process, which diminished the onetime mansion as well as its once expansive gardens. A recent restoration has resurrected the generous original porches. Subsequently, the owner raised the roof, leaving the building open to the elements and beginning a prolonged battle with the landmark commission in a case that led the city to seize the property to save it in 2015.

244. Skinner Middle School

1922, W. Harry Edwards. 1992 wing, Murata Outland Associates. 3435 West Fortieth Avenue between Irving and King Streets

A Collegiate Gothic style characterizes this E-plan school, which retains some of Saco R. DeBoer's original landscaping and arboretum. On the brownish brick two-story structure over a raised basement, light terracotta dramatizes the roof parapet, half-arch entry transom, and foliated "S" shields. Among many surviving original interior features is an elegant oak and beveled glass home economics classroom, where students practiced formal entertaining. Elizabeth Hope Skinner was the charismatic oratory and drama teacher for whom this school is named. A 1992 east wing, designed by Kevin Sullivan of Murata Outland Associates, used similar brick, window treatments, and detailing to complement the original edifice.

FIGURE 4.20. Skinner Middle School (photo by Tom Noel).

245. Smiley Branch Library

1918, Park French of Mountjoy, French, and Rewe. 1994 restoration, David Owen Tryba. 4601 West Forty-Sixth Avenue at Utica Street in Berkeley Lake Park

Akin to surrounding homes, this English cottage style branch has a one-story residential appearance. Decorative patterns enhance ornate red brick under a red tile roof. The buttressed corners and entry are highlighted by angled brick courses, and the round arch of the entry is repeated in the fan-lighted windows. Tryba added an elevator and a basement entrance that replicate the original exquisite brick patterns. A notable triple-stack chimney for the restored fireplace confirms that master masons erected this library and perhaps the cobblestone restrooms nearby in the park. The library is named for a teacher, William H. Smiley, who rose to become Denver's superintendent of schools. In

FIGURE 4.21. Smiley Branch Library (photo by Thomas H. Simmons).

1979 this branch opened a unique toy library whose items could be checked out and, it was hoped, returned in good condition.

246. Berkeley School

1894 and 1906 addition, David W. Dryden. 1923 addition, Glen Wood Huntington. 5025–55 Lowell Boulevard

The oldest surviving school in northwest Denver was abandoned in 1976. Landmarking by both the Denver Landmark Preservation Commission and the National Register of Historic Places in 1996 facilitated the restoration of the school as a residence. The original one-story two-room red brick school, with an open bell tower over the entrance, has arched openings and bracketed wide eaves, giving it a Craftsman style feeling. As the Berkeley neighborhood flourished, a much larger red brick two-story school on a raised basement arose on the south side of the

1894 building. The new school and a discreet 1923 north addition blend well in what is now a harmonious residential complex.

247. Elitch Theater

1890, Charles Herbert Lee and Rudolph Liden. 2007 rehabilitation, Oz Architecture. 2015 restoration, Humphries Poli Architects. West Thirty-Seventh Place between Utica and Vrain Streets, NR

This rustic wooden theater is one of the few surviving structures of Elitch Gardens Amusement Park, which occupied the site bounded by West Thirty-Eighth and Thirty-Sixth Avenues between Tennyson and Wolff Streets until 1995. John and Mary Elitch opened the park and the theater in 1890. John, a handsome vaudeville actor and athlete, made the theater his main concern until his 1891 death during a vaudeville tour in San Francisco. Mary Elitch then

FIGURE 4.22. Elitch Theater (photo by Carl Sandberg).

ran the theater and gardens with the help of her second husband, Thomas Long, until her death in 1936.

Elitch's, Denver's oldest, largest, and best-known amusement park, moved to a new Auraria site in 1995. The Mulvihill-Gurtler family, owners since 1936, left the theater behind on its original site. This unusual frame playhouse claimed to be the country's oldest continually operating summer-stock theater when it closed in 1987. Among the hundreds of nationally prominent actors and actresses to tread its stage were June Allyson, Sid Caesar, Douglas Fairbanks Jr., Tammy Grimes, Julie Harris, Van Johnson, Grace Kelly, Myrna Loy, Jane Powell, Vincent Price, Lynn Redgrave, Debbie Reynolds, Ginger Rogers, and Mickey Rooney.

Architecturally, the theater is frame, with Stick- and Shingle style elements. It evolved over the years from the original circular frame building into an octagon two stories high, with a hexagonal shingle roof crowned by a turret and flagpole. The sides, each forty-three feet wide, are of wood-drop siding painted gray with white trim. A two-story addition (ca. 1900) forms a vestibule or outer lobby, with two enclosed stairways to the balcony. Quaint and unique,

this remarkable landmark awaits creative reuse. As part of the ongoing restoration, the nearby carousel pavilion was redone and linked to the theater with a grassy open space.

248. John Brisben Walker House
1885, David Cox Sr. 3520 Newton Street

Reversing the standard Denver pattern of brick houses trimmed with stone, this gray stone house is trimmed in red brick. Asymmetrical Queen Anne massing includes an angled southeast bay facing downtown Denver. Neighborhood stonemason David Cox Sr. built this two-and-a-half story residence for John Brisben Walker, a northwest Denver developer who also owned Red Rocks and sold the land to the city for use as an amphitheater and a mountain park. Walker also developed Denver's Berkeley neighborhood, where he donated the land for Regis University. Walker later moved to New York City, where he owned *Cosmopolitan* magazine before selling it to William Randolph Hearst. Although Walker built the house, it became the home of his brother, Bolivar.

249. Beth Eden Baptist Church

1931, William N. Bowman. 3241 Lowell Boulevard

This red brick Tudor Revival has that style's steep-pitched roof, half timbering, and multiple grouped windows. It replaced an 1891 predecessor on this site, survived the loss of a larger addition, and was narrowly saved by a 2014 designation. This rare designation despite the owner's objection came after a prolonged fight between neighbors protesting intense development in West Highlands and a developer who wanted to raze the church and put in three five-story apartment buildings.

250. Cox "Gargoyle" House

ca. 1889, David Cox Sr. 3425 Lowell Boulevard

Stonemason David Cox Sr. designed and built his two-story home and decorated it with fanciful carved creatures. Constructed of alternating broad and narrow courses of rusticated sandstone block, the dwelling exemplifies Cox's craftsmanship. Note the stone balustrade of the porch, the grouped porch columns with carved capitals, the carved stone of the gable panel and finial, the floral friezes and dragon downspouts, and the faces topping the window spandrels.

FIGURE 4.23. Cox "Gargoyle" House (photo by Thomas H. Simmons).

251. Cox House

1903, David Cox Sr. 3417 Lowell Boulevard

Next door to his own Gargoyle House, stonemason Cox erected a foursquare with eighteen-inch-thick wall panels of dressed buff sandstone for his daughter. Stone stringcourses circle the structure at several levels, with the first-floor course intersecting the cap of the porch's stone balustrade. From its rusticated red sandstone foundation to its wide bracketed eaves, this home exemplifies fine craftsmanship.

252. Edison Elementary School

1925, Robert K. Fuller. 1950 addition. 1993 addition, Bennett, Wagner, and Grody. 3350 Quitman Street

Designed in Collegiate Gothic style by a leading Denver architect, this two-story symmetrical red brick school with light-colored terracotta trim boasts a grand three-story tower entrance. Before receiving several additions, the original school consisted of twenty rooms, a library, gymnasium, auditorium, office, clinic, and lunch room. In 1949 the school received funding to build a small addition on the northeast side of the building, which is virtually indistinguishable from the original structure. In 1993 a considerably larger addition was built to accommodate growing enrollment. These sensitive additions maintain the original character with the same materials and design elements, such as the distinctive pediments. Occupying a full block, the school boasts both student and community gardens, an updated playground, and many new trees planted by students and parents.

HD-46 WOLFF PLACE HISTORIC DISTRICT

Roughly West Thirtieth to West Thirty-Second Avenues between Lowell Boulevard and Quitman Street

In the late 1860s Hiram G. Wolff, a pioneer settler in Highland, established a farm and Sunnyside Nursery. To water his farm and the neighborhood, Wolff built the area's first ditch. His Highland Ditch started on Clear Creek near Golden and remained in the family until 1970, when they sold it to the Adolph Coors Brewing Company. As his real estate and nursery empire prospered, Wolff moved from his foursquare at West Thirtieth Avenue and Newton Street across the street to an also extant larger home (1891) at 3000 Newton Street. Wolff began developing Wolff Place in the late 1880s and sold part of it to John Kernan Mullen as the wooded hilltop site for the Mullen Home for the Aged. Designed by Harry James Manning and completed in 1918 on a spacious ten-acre site stretching from Lowell Boulevard to Newton Street between West Twenty-Eighth and West Twenty-Ninth Avenues, the home is ably run to this day by the Little Sisters of the Poor. The adjacent Wolff Place residential subdivision contains a few near-mansions, such as Wolff's home at 3000 Newton and the Herman Heiser House, 3016 Osceola Street, as well as many more modest homes built after the silver crash of 1893.

253. Highlands United Methodist Church

1896 and 1922 addition, Arthur S. Wilson. 1925 additions. 1950 addition, Harry Wells. 3131 Osceola Street, southwest corner of West Thirty-Second Avenue, HD-46

Organized in 1892, the Highlands United Methodist Church built a church structure on this site in 1896. That small original red brick church did not survive a fire but has a much larger 1925 replacement in the current structure. This vernacular Gothic Revival two-story light gray brick church has a distinctive front gable roof and front corner towers. The 1950 Educational Wing smoothly carries on the brick color, bond, and style of the mother church. The original 1906 parsonage survives at 3920 West Thirty-Second Avenue.

254. Herman Heiser House

1893, Matthew Woulter. 1989 restoration, David Cole. 3016 Osceola Street, northeast corner of West Thirtieth Avenue, HD-46

Herman H. Heiser, a custom saddler, placed his HH monogram in the front-porch tiles of his two-story Queen Anne residence. Particularly impressive is the entry porch, with its beveled and leaded glass sidelights and transom beneath a second-story porch under a bell-cast roof. A tower rises at the southwest corner to another bell-cast roof. Decorative brickwork and bas-relief ornaments include lions' heads at the base of the tower. Interior woodwork, paneling, and doors showcase different woods in each room. A 1989 restoration added a three-car garage, detailed to match even the narrow mortar joints of the house. Compare this show home with the tiny clapboard cottage (1885) nearby at 2972 Osceola. The diversity of housing types in North Denver has promoted economic diversity.

FIGURE 4.24. Herman Heiser House (photo by Thomas H. Simmons).

255. William Moses House

1895. 4001 West Thirtieth Avenue, northwest corner of Perry Street, HD-46

William E. Moses, an attorney, realtor, Civil War veteran, and active officer of the Colorado-Wyoming chapter of the Grand Army of the Republic, died in this house in 1929. He had selected a fine hilltop site for his Queen Anne residence, an asymmetrical design with a third-story ballroom opening onto a hexagonal balcony tower. The wide bracketed eaves and flared roof are echoed in the single front dormer. The prominent second-story oriel window wears zinc Adamesque garlands. The generous round-arch entry is highlighted with a stone band. This red brick dwelling with restrained stone and frame trim is shaded by one of the largest and oldest red oaks in Denver.

HD-51 ALLEN M. GHOST HISTORIC DISTRICT

West Twenty-Ninth to West Thirty-First Avenues between Julian Street and Lowell Boulevard

Originally known as Kountze Heights, this land was sold to Allen M. Ghost, a real estate investor and developer, in 1887. Ghost advertised his streetcar neighborhood as high ground, with easy access and great views of Denver. Of the 206 structures in this district, all but 2 are residential. This residential district primarily includes bungalows, classic cottages, foursquares, and Queen Anne styles, with some Craftsman, Dutch Colonial Revival, and Tudor Revival. These residences vary from small one-story cottages to large multi-lot two-story buildings and some infill.

256. Lobach House

1894, Joseph Vetter, builder?. 2851 Perry Street

See next entry.

257. Frank E. Woodbury House

1894, Joseph Vetter, builder?. 2841 Perry Street

The Lobach and Frank E. Woodbury Houses are nearly identical twins; they share the same plan, rich verge board, and gables framing elaborate second-story Palladian-inspired windows. They differ in the Adamesque trim decorating the gables and pedimented entries to wraparound porches supported by clusters of Tuscan columns. Rough stone foundations and window banding adorn these one-story brick Queen Anne cottages, which even have similar stained glass sidelights and transom lights in their elaborate front windows. Reflecting an obsolete custom of families living in proximity, these homes were built for the intermarried families of Eugene Lobach and Frank E. Woodbury. Frank ran the *Denver Evening Times* after buying it from his father, Roger Woodbury. Frank also organized the Rocky Mountain Savings Bank and helped found the Denver Athletic Club. His wife, Grace Lobach Woodbury, was a concert pianist, composer, and music teacher.

HD-20 WITTER-COFIELD HISTORIC DISTRICT

Federal Boulevard to Irving Street between West Twentieth and West Twenty-Fifth Avenues

Of the 216 buildings in this district, most are single-family residences in a neighborhood named for the two men who platted it in 1875: attorney-developer Daniel Witter and developer Joseph B. Cofield. Queen Anne dwellings, ranging from cottages to large, elaborate homes, reflect the most common architectural style. Most of the homes built after 1910 are modest bungalows.

258. Frederick W. Neef House

1886. 2143 Grove Street, NR, HD-20

Frederick W. Neef of the Neef Brothers Brewing Company built this exquisite Queen Anne, the finest gem in the Witter-Cofield Historic District. Eastlake verge board on the entry porch is repeated on the two-story front bay and in the main front gable of this asymmetrical brick house. Among the exuberant and varied details are an attic oriel window tucked under the front gable and stained glass transoms in a variety of ornate window surrounds.

259. Half-Moon House

ca. 1892. 3205 West Twenty-First Avenue, northwest corner of Hooker Street, HD-20

This dramatic Queen Anne is named for the conspicuous half-moon openings in the porch woodwork. A third-story

FIGURE 4.25. Frederick W. Neef House (Tom Noel Collection).

FIGURE 4.26. Half-Moon House (photo by Tom Noel).

front gable with an oriel window sweeps down to cover the second-story balcony and to become a roof for the wrap-around corner porch. The profuse wooden trim in Eastlake patterns and the unusual asymmetry distinguish the

well-preserved house of Stanley M. Barrows, a real estate developer who specialized in Jefferson County farmlands. Timothy Wirth and his wife, Wren, restored the house and matching carriage house in the 1970s before he moved to Washington, DC, as a US representative and, later, senator for Colorado.

260. Lake Middle School

1926, Merrill H. Hoyt and Burnham Hoyt. Various additions.1820 Lowell Boulevard

Crowning a hill overlooking Sloan's Lake, this Tudor castle has an entrance guarded by two copper cupolas. Fanciful brickwork and detailing make this one of Denver's most regal schools. Masons used more than 100 different shapes and sizes of bricks. Numerous arches and beams continue the medieval theme inside the school. The expansive $829,000 building covers a 3½-block park-like setting designed by landscape architect M. Walter Pesman. New classrooms, a technology center, and other additions do not mar this pretty picture.

FIGURE 4.27. Sloan's Lake provides both a setting and a name for Lake Middle School (Denver Public Library).

West Colfax Area

261. Voorhees House

1890, Lang and Pugh. 1471 Stuart Street, southwest corner of West Colfax Avenue, NR

Ralph Voorhees, a real estate developer and state legislator, commissioned William A. Lang and his partner, Marshall R. Pugh, to design picturesque show homes at 1389, 1390, 1435, 1444, and 1471 Stuart Street for his West Colfax subdivision. Rusticated rhyolite, elegant shingling, deeply recessed sets of round and rectangular ribbon windows, irregular massing, and heavy stone arches and lintels add distinction to these residences. Most are asymmetrical and culminate in third-story towers, steep-pitched gables, and rustic stone chimneys. Voorhees's own $25,000 three-story house at 1471 Stuart Street, which hides behind a three-story front bay, was restored by Dr. John Litvak as his medical offices.

These five spectacular Stuart Street mansionettes were show homes for a fine residential district that never developed, thwarted by the 1893 silver crash and the propensity of Denver's wealthy to build on the east side, leaving the west side to many immigrants such as the East European Jews who settled along West Colfax Avenue.

262. Spangler House

1890, Lang and Pugh. 1444 Stuart Street, NR

This splendid Shingle style home is covered by shingles on the top two stories above a buff sandstone ground floor. Jane Spangler, the widow of Sheriff Mike Spangler, lived here, across the street from his sister, Mrs. Ralph Voorhees. Max Schradsky, a Jewish Russian who had been part of the Cotopaxi Colony in southern Colorado, later acquired this house. A policeman and Democratic Party captain, Schradsky represented the growing number of Jewish Immigrants moving into the West Colfax neighborhood after 1893, earning it the moniker Little Israel.

263. Frank Smith Mansion

1890, Lang and Pugh. 1435 Stuart Street, NR

Frank W. Smith bought this rusticated buff sandstone Romanesque Revival dwelling with varied deep-set windows. A three-story tower, finials, and a minaret give it a churchlike verticality. South-side stained glass window slits

FIGURE 4.28. The Spangler House is one of Denver finest Shingle style residences (photo by Roger Whitacre).

FIGURE 4.29. The Frank Smith Mansion showcases some of architect William Lang's most exuberant stonework (photo by Tom Noel).

follow the interior staircase upward. Rich details include the tower's open porch, flora patterns carved into the stone, massive stone block construction, and an eyebrow window at the tippy-top.

264. Kenehan House

1890, Lang and Pugh. 1390 Stuart Street, southeast corner of West Fourteenth Avenue, NR

Roady Kenehan, an Irish-born blacksmith active in the Denver Horseshoers Union, rose through the ranks to become a labor leader. He also jumped into politics, serving on the Denver City Council and as state auditor and state treasurer. After his death Elizabeth McNulty, a teacher at nearby Glen Park School, lived here with two aunts for many years. Displaying architectural versatility, William A. Lang and his partner designed this as a Queen Anne alternative to the Richardsonian Romanesque and Shingle styles they employed for the neighboring homes. Note the acanthus leaf-bracketed tiny second-story corner porch and pagan green man carving supporting the north-side bay window.

Two mini–north-side porches are among the other whimsical details with which Lang endowed his designs. Like many other large homes, this became an apartment house during World War II when housing was in short supply but was returned to a single-family residence in 1994.

265. Bliss House

1892, Lang and Pugh. 1389 Stuart Street, southwest corner of West Fourteenth Avenue, NR

Dr. Gerald Bliss, a Civil War veteran and member of the honor guard for President Abraham Lincoln's funeral, lived here for almost fifty years. For his dwelling, Lang and Pugh departed from their usual Richardsonian Romanesque proclivities in this Queen Anne dwelling. A northwest corner tower incorporates a third-story covered porch, and a southwest bay sweeps downward to shelter the recessed entry porch. The north side has a glassy tower and an open third-story porch under a bell-cast cap.

266. Seventh Avenue Congregational Church

1931, William Norman Bowman. 678 King Street, southeast corner of West Seventh Avenue

This red brick Gothic Revival church is distinguished by a prominent square corner bell tower with battlements, which houses the narthex. Featuring steep gabled roofs and arched stained glass windows, it is one of the oldest existing churches in the Villa Park neighborhood.

Globeville Area

Globeville is bordered by the South Platte River on the east, East Fifty-Second Avenue on the north, I-25 on the west, and I-70 on the south. This industrial area grew up around the Globe Smelter. The many smelters in the area are gone, but numerous humble homes remain, providing some of the most affordable housing in Denver. This immigrant neighborhood has long been neglected and has been carved up by the city's two major freeways. It has undesignated landmarks in its Polish Catholic, Russian Orthodox, and Slovenian Catholic churches.

267. Globeville School

1925, Willis A. Marean and Albert J. Norton. 5100 Lincoln Street

This former Denver Public School was a melting pot of children of the immigrant laborers who fueled Denver's once-dominant smelting industry. The two-story rectangular building with a red brick facade is an eclectic mixture of Tudor Revival, Collegiate Gothic, and Arts and Crafts style architecture. Embellished with decorative wood brackets that support a large overhanging symmetrical hip roof, the school's defining features are the two white terracotta octagonal pilasters capped with an octagonal capital and a finial that frame the entrance facade. Laradon Hall, a private institution for children with severe learning disabilities, bought the abandoned school in 1951. It now consists of classrooms for the Laradon complex of housing and employment assistance for the developmentally disabled, with facilities stretching north past East Fifty-Second Avenue.

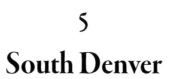

5

South Denver

BAKER AREA

WASHINGTON PARK AREA

BELCARO AREA

PLATT PARK AREA

UNIVERSITY PARK AREA

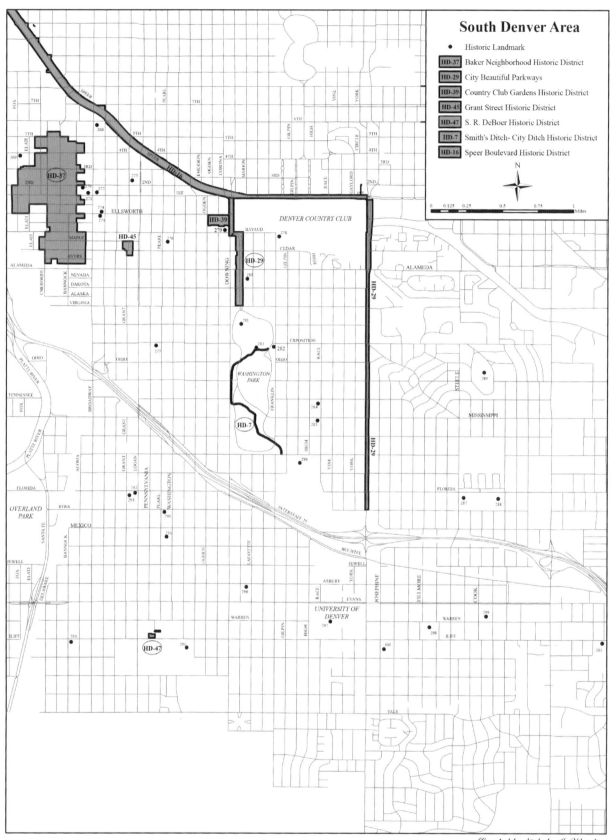

Created by Nicholas J. Wharton

MAP 5.1. South Denver area

For this guide, the South Denver area is defined as everything within the city limits south of Cherry Creek and Sixth Avenue. The town of South Denver, incorporated in 1886 and annexed to Denver in 1893, occupied the smaller area bounded by Alameda Avenue and Yale Avenue on the south, between Colorado Boulevard and the South Platte River. That town sprouted along the Broadway tracks as the largest of Denver's streetcar suburbs. This middle-class, white, predominantly Protestant community resisted annexation to the big city to the north until 1893. South Denver's town hall was the landmarked house of Mayor James Fleming at 1510 South Grant Street.

One of South Denver's oldest and finest mansions, the Thomas B. Field House, 2340 South Washington Street, is one of two Denver landmarks demolished by fire (the other is Constitution Hall, 1501 Blake Street, in LoDo). One undesignated landmark is one of the most prominent buildings in southwest Denver, Edbrooke's Old Main, an edifice with a soaring bell tower on the Teikyo-Loretto Heights College campus on South Federal Boulevard. University Hall on the University of Denver campus, a fine Richardsonian Romanesque Revival stone fortress by Robert S. Roeschlaub, is another undesignated jewel.

Baker Area

Roughly Sixth Avenue and Speer Boulevard on the north, Downing Street on the east, Alameda Avenue on the south, and Santa Fe Drive on the west

268. Leeman Auto Company

1932, Raymond Harry Ervin. 1934 addition. 1999–2000 rehabilitations. 550 Broadway Street, southeast corner of East Sixth Avenue

Claiming to be the "largest new and used car dealer in the West," Leeman featured a DeSoto-Plymouth automobile showroom, as well as a maintenance facility and a used car lot. Located on the busy intersection at Sixth Avenue and Broadway, this one-story brick and terracotta building was constructed in an L-shaped plan. The structure's verticality expresses the Art Deco style and is exemplified by high corner parapets, buttresses, and the decorative use of contrasting russet-colored wire-cut brick. To court prospective buyers, architect Ervin used the modern style and materials to create a state-of-the-art showroom to shine on new motor vehicles. Exposed steel

arched trusses support the intersecting barrel roofs of this structure. The 1999–2000 rehabilitations project replaced and replicated doors and windows, restored paint and stucco, and removed non-contributing additions. The Broadway Central retail complex that opened in 2000 features an outdoor patio for the dining establishments in the complex.

HD-37 Baker Neighborhood Historic District

Roughly bounded by West Fifth Avenue, Fox Street, West Alameda Avenue, and Bannock Street, NRD

The name was borrowed from Baker Junior High School, which is named for James Hutchins Baker, a president of the University of Colorado (1875–92). The district is located on land originally settled by the family of *Rocky Mountain News* editor William Newton Byers. The neighborhood consists predominantly of late-nineteenth and early-twentieth-century Queen Anne homes with some terraces, classic cottages, foursquares, Edwardians, bungalows, and Dutch Colonial Revivals. Among the various notable non-landmarked structures is St. Peter and St. Mary Episcopal Church (1891, Boal and Harnois), 126 West Second Avenue and Acoma Street, a Richardsonian Romanesque rhyolite structure. The Denver district is slightly smaller than the National Register Historic District, which stretches from West Fifth to West Alameda Avenues between Broadway and Fox Streets.

269. Mary Coyle Chase House

1891. 532 West Fourth Avenue

This modest story-and-a-half brick dwelling has a fish-scale–shingled front gable with a sunburst peak and a wooden-columned front porch. Mary Coyle grew up in this Queen Anne–ish house of a working-class, story-telling Irish family. Beautiful, bright, and ambitious, she became one of the first woman reporters for the *Rocky Mountain News*, where she met and married editor Robert Chase. She also began writing plays. Her Pulitzer Prize–winning play, *Harvey* (1944), introduced the world to an imaginary six-foot-tall rabbit. This became one of the longest-running plays in Broadway history and was made into a popular movie starring Jimmy Stewart. Chase continued to write for the wire services and did publicity work for various social

FIGURE 5.1. Mary Coyle Chase is shown here with her best-known character, the six-foot rabbit Harvey. Chase is the only Coloradan to win a Pulitzer Prize. Irish folktales of pookas, mischievous spirits often appearing in animal form, inspired her prize-winning play *Harvey,* which features the giant rabbit (*Rocky Mountain News,* Denver Public Library).

causes, including labor unions, alcoholic rehabilitation, and New Deal programs. With profits from *Harvey,* Chase and her husband bought a grand Tudor mansion at 505 Circle Drive in the Country Club neighborhood.

270. Fire Station No. 11

1936, C. Francis Pillsbury. 40 West Second Avenue

Originally opened at 301 West Cherokee Street in 1903, Station No. 11 moved to this location in 1936. Pillsbury, who designed other residential style fire stations in Denver, gave this three-bay, red tapestry brick firehouse Art Deco piers that rise into a parapet. Horizontal and vertically stacked maroon bricks give this Works Progress Administration project a modernistic facade that retains the original stainless steel lamps, Art Deco signage, and big doors.

271. First Avenue Hotel

1906, Charles Quayle. 2009 renovation, Alvarez Morris Architects. 101–15 Broadway Street, northwest corner of West First Avenue

Typical of early-twentieth-century commercial buildings, this one is Neoclassically inspired, with a bracketed cornice and broad eaves hovering over a symmetrical four-story arrangement. The Fleming Brothers, leading South Denver developers, had architect Charles Quayle, the son of architect William Quayle, design this edifice with generous glass storefronts below hotel units. One of the largest buildings in South Denver, it was restored during the 1980s as a cornerstone of Broadway's revitalization but awaits new uses.

272. Mayan Theater

1930, Montana S. Fallis. 1985 restoration, Midyette-Seieroe Architects. 110 Broadway Street

In a fierce preservation struggle, this theater came within a whisker of demolition in 1984. Denver mayor Federico Peña saved the day by siding with preservationists against developers, an unusual mayoral move. He helped rescue this rare surviving example of only six known US pre-Columbian motif movie houses. For the first time in its history, the city designated a landmark despite the owner's protest. The theater's technicolor terracotta ornamentation and hand-painted and stenciled walls were rejuvenated inside and out, including the marquee facade's terracotta Mayan chief. Vibrantly colored Aztec and Mayan motif polychrome trim furthers the Mayan Deco design. This exotic facade, made largely by Julius P. Ambrusch of the Denver Terra Cotta Company, fronts an older red brick theater, the homely Queen Theater, built around 1915.

FIGURE 5.2. Mayan Theater (photo by Tom Noel).

FIGURE 5.3. South Broadway Christian Church (photo by Tom Noel).

273. Arthur E. Pierce House

1892, Robert G. Balcomb and Eugene R. Rice. 1930 addition. 1946 addition. 24 East Ellsworth Avenue

Arthur E. Pierce, a Denver pioneer who arrived in 1858, opened the town's first bookstore, newsstand, and library. In 1892 Arthur and his wife, Ada, commissioned Balcomb and Rice to design this two-story Queen Anne style house. Unfortunately, the Pierces never lived in this home, likely because of the silver crash of 1893. They lived elsewhere and rented the residence until they sold it in the late 1910s.

274. South Broadway Christian Church

1891, J. E. Miller and Walter J. Janisch. 23 Lincoln Street, northwest corner of East Ellsworth Avenue

The dominant element of this Richardsonian Romanesque church is a massive square stone bell tower crowned with a crenelated parapet enhanced by an engaged smaller round tower. The church's rough-faced rhyolite walls are highlighted by carved stone adorning the gable peaks, buttress caps, and recessed entrance. Decorative wood accentuates the steep peaks of rhythmic rows of gables and dormers in this eye-catching medieval monument. Exquisite details range from the triple-arch stone entry to fine stained glass windows in one of Denver's most picturesque edifices.

275. Sherman Elementary School–Art Students League of Denver

1893, Henry Dozier. 1920 bungalow annex. 200 Grant Street, northeast corner of East Second Avenue

This school was named for General William T. Sherman, Yankee Civil War hero. The two-and-a-half-story building is clad in smooth red-orange sandstone above the rusticated stone basement level. Sandstone is also used for the arch fronting the recessed entry in a protruding bay. By 1920, overcrowding led to construction of the bungalow annex to the north. The neighborhood fought the Denver Public Schools' plan to close, sell, or demolish this school. After closing in 1982, the building was preserved with landmark designation and recycled in 1987 as the home of the Art Students League of Denver, with 24,000 square feet of studios and offices.

HD-45 GRANT STREET HISTORIC DISTRICT

Roughly bounded from Maple Avenue to Cedar Avenue along Grant Street, the district includes thirteen houses and the Grant Avenue Methodist Episcopal Church (1907). This district of middle-class residences includes Colonial Revival, Foursquare, and Shingle style examples.

276. Byers Junior High School–Denver School of Science and Technology

1922, Harry J. Manning and William N. Bowman. 150 South Pearl Street

Built on a full-block site that once included the last home of William Newton Byers, the founding editor of the *Rocky Mountain News*, Byers Junior High School is a vernacular example of Collegiate Gothic design. This two-and-a-half-story wire-cut buff brick structure with terracotta trim is built in a E design to allow natural light and fresh air into each classroom. *Architectural Forum* praised the school as one of the forty best-designed schools in the nation. In the 1980s the school became an alternative learning center, then the Denver School of the Arts until closing in 2005. In 2014 the school was modernized for use as the Denver School of Science and Technology's Byers Junior High School.

FIGURE 5.4. Byers Junior High School (photo by Tom Noel).

277. Lincoln Elementary School

1891, T. D. Robinson. 1904 addition. 1929 addition. 1995 addition. 710 South Pennsylvania Street to Pearl Street between East Exposition and East Ohio Avenues

The 1891 original school on this site was demolished in 1929. Today, the 1904 three-story brick addition and the two-story 1929 addition comprise the primary portions of the school. Both additions are distinguished by ornamental brickwork, Romanesque arches, and large double-hung windows. The third addition in 1995 includes a one-story entry, lunch room, and administrative structure. All three additions are distinguishable by different-colored and differently finished brick, but they all include a signature curvilinear parapet.

278. Grant House

1925, Merrill H. Hoyt and Burnham Hoyt. 100 South Franklin Street, southeast corner of Bayaud Avenue

This two-story stucco-over-brick show home was the residence of Mary Grant, the widow of Colorado governor James B. Grant. After his death, Mrs. Grant sold their 777 Pennsylvania Street mansion to Albert E. Humphreys Sr. and commissioned the prominent Denver firm of Hoyt and Hoyt to design this Beaux Arts classical house overlooking the Denver Country Club. Key features of this L-shaped home, many of which also characterize the Grant-Humphreys Mansion, are a two-story Corinthian column semicircular entry, a balustraded roof parapet, and arched transoms over most first-floor doors and windows, as well as expansive terraces.

HD-39 COUNTRY CLUB GARDENS HISTORIC DISTRICT

1940, William E. Fisher, Arthur A. Fisher, and Walter L. Hubbell. Roughly Ellsworth to East First Avenues between South Downing and South Ogden Streets

As the first multi-unit Denver project of the Federal Housing Administration, this innovative project embodied garden city planning principles. The ubiquitous firm of Fisher and Fisher designed this two-block complex with five apartment houses in the Streamline Moderne style. Beige tile banding on the red brick underlines the streamlined horizontality. Clean lines and elegant simplicity,

FIGURE 5.5. Country Club Gardens (photo by Glenn Cuerden).

FIGURE 5.6. Steele Elementary School went through the usual landmarking process of a public hearing (photo by Tom Noel).

exemplified by the balconies, give this complex a contemporary feeling. The extensive grounds, the design of landscape architect M. Walter Pesman, distinguish this from most apartment complexes. As this fashionable area on the west side of the Denver Country Club began to sprout high-rise apartments in the 1970s, Country Club Gardens was designated a historic district to spare it from demolition. A new threat arrived in 2016 when twenty percent of the district was demolished to build two thirty-story residential towers that darkened the once spaciously landscaped gardens.

279. Norman Apartments

1924, William Norman Bowman. 99 South Downing Street, northwest corner of East Bayaud Avenue

Bowman, a prominent Denver architect who made this building his home, used Spanish Colonial Revival and Colonial Revival elements on an otherwise modern building. Arranged as two six-story wings set at right angles, the complex consisted of forty-eight luxurious apartments with elegant entry halls, nine-foot ceilings, mahogany trim and doors, and maid, chauffeur, and laundry service in the "Aristocrat of Apartments." In 1983 the New Height Group purchased the property and converted it to condominiums. Landmarking forestalled a proposed demolition of what is one of Denver's best-preserved examples of 1920s luxury apartment living.

280. Steele Elementary School

1913, David W. Dryden. 1929, Merrill H. Hoyt and Burnham Hoyt. 320 South Marion Street Parkway

Colorful terracotta trim and mosaic tile roofs on twin pyramidal towers lend an exotic Art Deco flair to this buff brick and stucco school, which is well-sited on the parkway entrance to Washington Park. Dryden's original 1913 school was completely different, a typical Neoclassical edifice. Stripped to its structural elements by the Hoyts, the school was reconstructed with Deco style flat roofs, decorative panels, stringcourses, and faux balconies. The school is named for Robert Wilbur Steele Sr. (1820–1901), a pioneer jurist who became chief justice of the Colorado Supreme Court.

Washington Park Area

Roughly bounded by Cherry Creek on the north, University Boulevard on the east, I-25 on the south, and Downing Street on the west

This trendy turf is centered on one of Denver's most popular parks and the surrounding residential neighborhood. Reinhard Schuetze, a European-trained landscape architect, originally laid out the park, the city's third largest (after City Park and Sloan's Lake). Saco R. DeBoer laid out the extensive flower gardens on the west side of the park near Ohio Avenue in 1913. Created in 1898, Washington Park originally had a sandy beach on the north side of Smith Lake and became the city's favorite swimming hole. Less happily, Smith Lake was the scene of an ugly race riot when African Americans and white sympathizers tried to integrate the beach in 1932. Polio scares ended the swimming in the 1950s, but the landmarked bathhouse survives from Denver's sandy beach days. Sailing and boating are still promoted at its landmarked boathouse. The surrounding residential neighborhood of Wash Park, as it is popularly called, originally predominantly contained bungalows, many of which have been scraped or pop-topped to build much bigger homes as this area became one of the city's most fashionable places in which to live.

HD-7 SMITH'S DITCH–CITY DITCH HISTORIC DISTRICT

1865, in Washington Park, NR

Denver's first major irrigation ditch has the second-oldest water right on the upper South Platte River. This ditch made possible the greening of the semiarid Mile High City, which averages only fourteen inches of precipitation a year. The Capitol Hydraulic Company, incorporated on February 21, 1860, began the twenty-seven-mile-long canal named for John W. Smith, who completed it in 1865. Washington Park's Smith Lake is also named in his honor. Washington Park also contains Grasmere Lake on its south end.

Smith's Ditch begins as a diversion of the South Platte River in Waterton Canyon southwest of Littleton (the first four miles of the ditch are now inundated by Chatfield Reservoir). It flows for fifteen miles through Englewood, enters Denver through Harvey Park, and flows through Washington Park to Capitol Hill. Dug by hand and by horse-drawn scrapers,

the ditch was originally an open, unlined canal three feet wide on the bottom and seven feet wide at the top. It fed hundreds of lateral canals that ran along the streets of Denver, enabling Denverites to plant trees, lawns, and gardens and thereby transforming the city into an oasis. Smith spent $10,000 to build what the city bought in 1875 for $60,000 and extended to City Park, where it fills Ferril Lake. The ditch is now buried except in Washington Park, where it feeds both lakes. Denver historian Louisa Ward Arps, in her book *Denver in Slices* (1959), observes that City Ditch is "the oldest working thing in Denver."

281. Washington Park Bathhouse

1912. South Downing Street and East Center Avenue

This bathhouse recalls Smith Lake's past days as a swimming hole, where a sandy beach and this bathhouse were installed in 1912. Fears of polio and pollution ended the swimming in 1957. Ice skating continued a little longer, with two fireplaces in the bathhouse making it a warming hut. Low-pitched roofs and wide bracketed eaves characterize this two-story stucco bathhouse, which has changing rooms on either end. In 1996 this neglected structure underwent a $600,000 rehabilitation as offices, meeting rooms, a reading room, and headquarters for Volunteers for Outdoor Colorado, an organization dedicated to protecting and enhancing outdoor recreation and natural resources.

282. Eugene Field House

ca. 1880. 701 South Franklin Street, NR

Denver's first major preservation project, spearheaded by Margaret Tobin "Molly" Brown, may have been the 1927 campaign to spare this tiny clapboard house from being demolished to make room for a gas station. Molly led the crusade to move the poet's home from 307 West Colfax Avenue to Washington Park, where it was later converted to a branch of the Denver Public Library. Eugene Field was a journalist and poet noted for *A Little Book of Western Verse* and his poem "Wynken, Blynken, and Nod." That children's poem inspired the sculpture fountain (1919, Mabel Landrum Torrey) of three children sailing off to sleep in a wooden shoe just northwest of the cottage. Field lived in this simple frame residence while working as a reporter and managing editor of the *Denver Tribune* from 1881 to 1883, before moving to Chicago. His cottage is now the District City Park Rangers office.

FIGURE 5.7. Washington Park's beach, with the boathouse (*left*) and pavilion, early 1950s (Denver Public Library).

283. Washington Park Boathouse and Pavilion

1913, Jules Jacques Benoit Benedict. 1987 restoration, Anthony Pellechia Associates.

The boathouse on the south shore of Smith Lake has a two-story lakefront facade with an open pavilion over enclosed boat storage. The upper-level pavilion serves as a picnic, gathering, and special events venue. In winter, the boathouse served as a warming house for ice skaters. The boathouse's mix of Prairie style, Italianate, and Arts and Crafts elements is outlined with electric lights to create a dreamy nocturnal reflection. Boats can still be rented here, as can bicycles.

284. Neahr House

1894. 1926 addition. 1017 South Race Street

One of the earliest houses built in the Washington Park area was first owned by Charles M. Clayton, a stonecutter by profession, who may have designed and built this striking stone house. Will C. Neahr, an employee of the Denver Machine Shop who later worked as a page at the Denver Public Library, subsequently owned the house. It is an eclectic mix of classic front-porch columns with an otherwise rustic structure of gray rhyolite and Manitou orange sandstone. This one-and-a half-story house has stout stone chimneys, three prominent dormers, and a distinctive front porch built entirely of stone except for the roof. A sympathetic second-story rear addition doubles the size of this handsome classic cottage.

285. Myrtle Hill School–Washington Park School Annex–Myrtle Hill Lofts

1928, Harry J. Manning. 2008 renovations and additions, Studio K2. 1125 South Race Street between East Tennessee and East Mississippi Avenues

This two-story Beaux Arts Classical schoolhouse was the final addition to the 1906 Washington Park Elementary School that stood on the site for almost 100 years. The school displays exuberant terracotta trim and elaborate friezes, arches, medallions, and wide bracketed eaves. The original Myrtle Hill School was renamed Washington Park Elementary School in 1923. It remained open until 1982 and was then leased to the Denver Academy, a private school that closed in 2000. In 2005 the property was purchased by a developer who planned to raze the school. Extensive negotiation with the neighborhood led to a compromise that allowed new loft development in the 1928 school but demolition of the rest of the property for construction of townhomes and single-family residences. With similar brickwork and horizontal emphasis, the new residences relate well to the old landmark.

286. South High School

1926, William E. Fisher and Arthur A. Fisher. 1963 addition, Charles Gordon Lee. 1983 addition, MCB Architects. 1700 East Louisiana Avenue to East Iowa Avenue between South High and South Race Streets

The Denver School Board set high design standards in the 1920s, granting Denver's leading architects artistic freedom, a policy that proved its worth in South High. For this splendid school on the south edge of Washington Park, the Fishers drew inspiration from the Basilica of St. Ambrogio in Milan. This three-story Italian Renaissance Revival school has polychromatic brick walls trimmed in yellowish terracotta under a red tile roof. A monumental edifice, it is enlivened by fanciful brickwork in a variety of colors and patterns. The main entrance has a loggia of five arches with griffins perched above, keeping an eye on students. The large clock features a clock face with zodiac signs rather than numerals. Denver sculptor Robert Garrison decorated the school with bizarre animals, such as one symbolizing final exams perched atop the third-story main-entry columns. Over the main entry a bas-relief satirizes a squabbling teachers' meeting. Inside the school's study hall Garrison

placed a crowing rooster to keep students awake, a parrot promoting memory, an owl symbolizing study and wisdom, and a penguin symbolizing deportment.

Belcaro Area

Roughly bounded by South University Avenue on the west, Cherry Creek on the north, Colorado Boulevard on the east, and East Evans Avenue on the south

287. Cory Elementary School

1951, Victor Hornbein. 1550 South Steele Street, southeast corner of East Florida Avenue

Victor Hornbein's horizontal composition, with its asymmetrical yet harmonious layers of projecting flat roofs, is reminiscent of Frank Lloyd Wright's Usonian style. Hornbein, although inspired by Wright, developed his own unique style geared to Colorado's high, dry, sunny climate. Walls of banded glass windows capture abundant natural light and mountain views under prominent projecting eaves that keep out the high, hot summer sun. Brick walls serve as both the exterior and interior finish. This school is named for John Jerome Cory (1890–1945), a Denver teacher who became principal of South High, then assistant superintendent of Denver junior and senior high schools and the Emily Griffith Opportunity School.

FIGURE 5.9. Cory Elementary School (photo by Thomas H. Simmons).

288. Merrill Middle School

1953, Temple Hoyne Buell. 1551 South Monroe Street, southwest corner of East Florida Avenue

Louise A. Merrill was a teacher and founding principal at Byers Junior High, whose burgeoning student population was divided to fill this modern flat-roofed L-shaped school.

FIGURE 5.8. South High School (photo by Tom Noel).

FIGURE 5.10. Phipps Mansion (Belcaro) (Denver Public Library).

Warm tawny brick trimmed in white limestone extends to expansive one- and two-story wings, adding to the horizontality of this iconic 1950s structure. The entrance is sheltered by a boxy modern clock tower and an overhanging second-story that exhibits the school's distinctive ribbon windows.

289. Phipps Mansion (Belcaro) and Tennis Pavilion
1932, Charles Adams Platt with William E. Fisher and Arthur A. Fisher. 3400 Belcaro Drive

Belcaro (Italian for "beautiful loved one") is what US senator Lawrence C. Phipps called his 33,123-square-foot Georgian mansion, Denver's grandest residence. On the hilltop of what was once a much larger estate, the eight-acre grounds surround a fifty-four-room house surmounted by eight massive chimneys.

Platt, a New York architect and a premier designer of fine country houses, began work on the $301,063 house before his death in 1933. His architect sons, William and Geoffrey, completed the house, with William and Arthur Fisher as supervising Denver architects. The poured concrete building is clad in hand-pressed red brick with dressed Indiana limestone trim and a slate roof. Beyond the entry, with its columns and broken pediment, are a reception area and stair hall finished in Colorado travertine from Wellsville. The oak paneling of the billiard room was transplanted from a Jacobean house in London. The paneled dining room and other interior fixtures were also brought from England.

The ivy-covered Tudor Revival tennis house on the north side of the mansion was designed by John Gray of Pueblo, the initial project architect replaced by Platt. The glass-and-tile-roofed 423,000-cubic-foot structure is, like the mansion, clad in brick and Indiana limestone. Exposed steel beams appear in the barrel vault over the court. A loggia entrance is trimmed in artistic wrought iron. The tennis house has a two-bedroom second-floor apartment, dressing rooms, kitchen, soda fountain, and fireplace lounge. A large Allen Tupper True mural in the lounge depicts Phipps family members skiing at the Winter Park Ski Area, which they helped develop.

Lawrence C. Phipps, a millionaire vice president and treasurer of Carnegie Steel in Pittsburgh, moved to Denver for his family's health. He served as a US senator (1918–30) and invested successfully in many local ventures. In 1931 the Phipps family's Belcaro Realty and Investment Company began developing the area surrounding the mansion as one of Denver's poshest residential enclaves. After Phipps's 1958 death, his widow donated the mansion and the tennis house to the University of Denver (DU) for use as the Lawrence C. Phipps Memorial Conference Center. DU sold the complex in 2010 for around $9.2 million to philanthropist Tim Gill and his partner, who made it their home.

Platt Park Area

Roughly bounded by Louisiana Avenue on the north, South Downing Street on the east, East Iliff Avenue on the south, and Broadway on the west

290. Cameron United Methodist Church

1909–13, Thomas T. Barber. 1600 South Pearl Street, southeast corner of East Iowa Avenue

Originally organized as the Fleming's Grove Methodist Church in 1888, the church was renamed thanks to a generous donation from the Cameron family. That first church, converted to a private residence, survives a block to the east, at the southwest corner of 1601 South Washington Street and East Iowa Avenue. The present 1909 church is an eclectic mix of crenelated square towers, Romanesque rounded arches, steep-pitched gabled roofs, and a domed sanctuary. Local artist Frank Watkins of Denver's Watkins Stained Glass, a company founded in 1881 and now in its fourth generation of ownership, created and installed the

four stained glass windows in the sanctuary. Many meeting rooms helped make this church a community center.

291. Grant Middle School

1952, Gordon D. White. 1751 South Washington Street, southwest corner of East Mexico Avenue

An asymmetrical composition, steel girder and concrete construction, smooth exterior surfaces, flat roofs, and horizontal window bands make this an example of 1950s modern school design. On this site stood Grant Elementary School (1890), which was enlarged in 1893 to become South High School until the current South High was constructed in 1926. The old school, with 1907 and 1924 additions, was demolished in 1952 to be replaced by this school, which is named for President Ulysses S. Grant. A whimsical sculpture garden includes the planets and a cow jumping over the moon.

292. Sarah Platt Decker Branch Library

1913, Willis A. Marean and Albert J. Norton. 1993 restoration, David Owen Tryba. 2009 renovation, Oz Architects. 1501 South Logan Street, southwest corner of East Florida Avenue

This fanciful recreation inspired by Anne Hathaway's cottage in Stratford-on-Avon, England, has a green tile roof with two ornate chimneys with multiple stacks. The walls of this L-shaped residential style library are tapestry wire-cut brick with creamy terracotta trim. Denver artist Dudley Carpenter painted two interior murals, *The Pied Piper of*

FIGURE 5.11. Sarah Platt Decker Branch Library (photo by Tom Noel).

Hamlin and *The Lady of the Lake with the Sword Excalibur.* Inglenook seating by the fireplaces and a high, open-beam, vaulted ceiling make this a cozy neighborhood haven. The basement harbors another inglenook fireplace and Marie L. Woodson's mural *There Is No Frigate Like a Book,* as Emily Dickinson titled one of her poems. The library is named for a nationally prominent clubwoman who presided over the Colorado Board of Charities and Corrections and the National Federation of Club Women. She championed causes ranging from the creation of Mesa Verde and Rocky Mountain National Parks to women's suffrage to branch libraries.

293. James Fleming House

1882. 2013 restoration, Hoehn Architects. 1510 South Grant Street, southeast corner of East Florida Avenue

James Alexander Fleming, the four-term mayor of South Denver, used his home as the town hall for the largest of Denver's streetcar suburbs. Fleming sold his house to South Denver in 1891 for ongoing use as a town hall with a library on the second floor, a jail in the basement, and a fire department in the barn. When the town faltered financially during the 1893 crash, it was annexed to Denver in 1894.

Denver converted this two-story rhyolite dwelling with three prominent round, conical-capped towers to a community center and dedicated its one-block grounds as Platt Park. In 2011 the Queen Anne style house became the home of the Park People, a civic-minded group dedicated to maintaining and enhancing Denver parks. Having outgrown the Eugene Field House in Washington Park, they gave Fleming House a restorative $850,000 facelift and moved their offices here to continue their city-wide improvements. The building is open to the community for public use and special events. Fleming House also houses one of the Park People's success stories, Denver Digs Trees, which plants around a thousand trees each year to enhance the urban forest.

294. John Collins United Methodist Church

1900. 1930 removal of steeple. 1950s alterations. 2320 South Bannock Street, southeast corner of West Warren Avenue

The Reverend John Collins, a bewhiskered Englishman who came to Colorado in 1872, established many Methodist churches, including Cameron, Littleton, Washington Park, and Valverde as well as this namesake structure. This small,

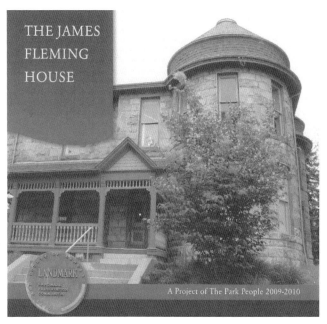

FIGURE 5.12. James Fleming House (Park People).

red brick vernacular Gothic Revival structure sits on a brick and rhyolite foundation in an I-shaped floor plan. The cross-gabled roof has a distinctive large, square three-story bell tower on the northeast corner. In the early 1930s the steeple of the tower was removed for repairs; however, with the onset of World War II, funds were not available to replace it. Additional 1950s alterations capped the tower and dressed up the entrance with a sandstone veneer.

HD-47 DeBoer Historic District

515 East Iliff Avenue

Saco R. DeBoer, Denver's most celebrated landscape architect and city planner, purchased this site in 1918 and had architect Lester E. Varian design a Tudor home with a tower that served as his office and his logo. DeBoer landscaped the large grounds and over the years added other modest buildings. A plan to demolish all structures on the site and build eleven new residences sparked protest that culminated in the 2007 designation of much of the DeBoer property as a historic district. The three surviving structures include an 1876 farmhouse, 501 East Iliff; the Tudor Revival towered structure where DeBoer lived and worked, at 515 East Iliff; and the large Mediterranean style studio-residence of John Thompson, 2260 South Piñon

Court. The remainder of the site has been developed as housing.

295. Nursery Building

1923, Ernest P. Varian and Lester E. Varian. 888 East Iliff Avenue in Harvard Gulch Park

Children, not plants, were nourished in this one-story care center. Together with a gym and a boiler room, this is a remnant of what used to be the State Home for Dependent and Neglected Children, which occupied the Thomas Field House site (1893), 2340 South Washington Street at East Iliff Avenue. Field, a railroad construction engineer, also served as Denver city treasurer. He built an 11,600-square-foot residence on this eighty-acre site. Following his death, from 1902 to 1971 the Field House served as the main building of the State Home for Dependent and Neglected Children. The Georgian Revival three-story brick and stone landmark was vacant when fire destroyed it in 1987. The surviving nursery, distinguished by its curvilinear parapets in the Mission Revival mode, has been converted to Colorado State University's Cooperative Extension Service office for Denver County. The towering nearby smokestack rises from the children's home's power plant, which now houses the Harvard Gulch Golf Club, a city park open to the public.

University Park Area

East Louisiana Avenue on the north, South Colorado Boulevard on the east, East Iliff Avenue on the south, and South Downing Street on the west

The University of Denver, with its copper-spired Ritchie Events Center, crowns this part of South Denver. The un-landmarked Tihen Tower of Pope John Paul XXIII Catholic Seminary anchors another of the large campuses here, as does South High's ornate Renaissance Revival tower.

296. Asbury Elementary School

1925, Temple Hoyne Buell. 1948 and 1975 additions. 1320 East Asbury Avenue between South Marion and South Lafayette Streets

Temple Buell, the son of a prominent Chicago family, was gassed during World War I. That war injury, compounded by tuberculosis, led him to move to Denver. He went there

to die, but the sunny, salubrious climate and Buell's bon vivant nature enabled him to fool—and outlive—his doctors. He died in 1990 at age ninety-four and was eulogized as one of Colorado's most successful and prominent twentieth-century architects. Like other early Buell schools, this is an example of Collegiate Gothic, complete with lion gargoyles and shields carved over the doors. This two-story brownish-red, wire-cut brick, L-shaped school has two tasteful small additions that match the original style.

297. Evans Memorial Chapel

1878. University of Denver Campus, East Warren Avenue and South University Boulevard on campus

In memory of his daughter, Josephine Evans Elbert, who died at a young age in 1868, former territorial governor John Evans built this $13,000 chapel at the southwest corner of West Thirteenth Avenue and Bannock Street, diagonally across from the Byers-Evans House. This Gothic Revival edifice of Morrison sandstone was later augmented by the larger adjacent Grace Methodist Episcopal Church (1887). Frederick J. Sterner designed Grace in the same Gothic Revival style, using similar brownish sandstone. The University of Denver (DU) acquired the site and demolished the larger church in 1959 for a parking lot but kept the Evans Chapel wing. Each stone was numbered, disassembled, and then reassembled in the Harper Humanities Gardens in the heart of the DU campus.

298. Chamberlain Observatory

1890, Robert S. Roeschlaub. 2930 East Warren Avenue, southeast corner of South Fillmore Street in Observatory Park, NR

Humphrey B. Chamberlain, a wealthy real estate promoter and amateur astronomer, gave this observatory to the University of Denver. Its skin of random, rusticated red sandstone blocks topped by a silvery iron dome is an elegant combination of forms and colors. Roeschlaub's prototype was an 1887 observatory for Carleton College in Minnesota. In Denver he added lateral gabled wings and a protruding entrance bay and had Chamberlain's name carved into the stone nameplate over the Romanesque arch entry. Chamberlain enriched the city and the university by donating the park as well as one of the nation's finest observatories, but he died in dire straits, a victim of the silver crash of 1893. His still active observatory is open to the

FIGURE 5.13. Chamberlain Observatory (photo by Tom Noel).

public during astronomical events. A nearby mini-observatory in the same style adds to this picturesque centerpiece for Observatory Park.

299. Fitzroy Place–Warren-Iliff Mansion

1892, Frank E. Edbrooke. 2160 South Cook Street, northeast corner of East Warren Avenue

Edbrooke designed this mansion for the bishop of the Methodist Episcopal Church, Henry White Warren, and his wife, Elizabeth Iliff Warren. She came west as a Singer Sewing Machine salesperson and met and married cattle king John Wesley Iliff. After he died at a young age, she married Bishop Warren. They named their place for her hometown in Ontario and had Edbrooke design this three-story Arizona red sandstone mansion in an exuberant Queen Anne style. Irregular massing includes protruding corner bays, a generous round-arch entry, prominent

FIGURE 5.14. Fitzroy Place–Warren-Iliff Mansion (photo by Tom Noel).

dormers, and chimneys. Distinctive roofing and the rusticated stonework help unify the imposing exterior. In an irregular maze of thirteen rooms, the residence contains thirteen fireplaces. A carriage house designed in the same style occupies what was once a full-block site. It is included in the landmark boundary, but the nearby Shingle style cottage (1890) is not. In 1967 the residence became the Randall School, a private prep school, and in 1975 it became another private academy, Accelerated Schools. Plans to demolish the house and develop the square block site inspired designation as a Denver Landmark in 2007. The vacant north half of the block that once provided a spacious setting for Fitzroy Place has sprouted with new residences.

300. Holland House

1933, Eugene G. Groves. 2340 South Josephine Street

To "ensure economy and permanency," Groves patented a pre-cast concrete construction system for Holland House that eliminated the need for all wooden structural elements. The residence contains concrete studs and beams, concrete floors, and concrete stucco over wire mesh walls. Located originally on four lots and sitting nearly thirty feet back from the street, this one-story three-bedroom two-bath concrete structure of highly original design includes built-in concrete kitchen countertops, tables, seating, and beds. Groves's signature domed ceiling provides interesting acoustic effects in the living room. Other surviving concrete houses by Groves are at 2733 West Forty-First Avenue (1935) and his own home at 330 Birch Street (1938).

301. Bethesda Chapel and Gateway–Denver Academy

1926 and 1930, Harry James Manning. 4400 East Iliff Avenue, southeast corner of South Birch Street

This chapel and corner gateway are signature structures on the spacious Bethesda campus, once a renowned tuberculosis sanatorium. The original campus buildings display a traditional stepped Dutch gable style using red brick with buff brick trim under red tile roofs. The ornate gate served as the main entrance to the campus until 1980, when it was turned into a pedestrian entry. The chapel remains intact, with an entrance tower capped by a copper cupola, although the interior has been remodeled to serve as the campus library. In 2001 this elegant sanitarium became the

FIGURE 5.15. Fort Logan Field Officers Quarters (photo by Tom Noel).

Denver Academy, a private school that has recycled the stylish old buildings with respect.

302. Fort Logan Field Officers Quarters

1889, Frank J. Grodavent. 1995 restoration, Edward D. White Jr. 3742 West Princeton Circle

In 1887 the US Congress authorized an army fort on the southwestern outskirts of Denver, and Lieutenant General Philip H. Sheridan arrived to select a site along what is still called Sheridan Boulevard. After first mistakenly occupying private land, the army found the right site on the south bank of Bear Creek. Fort Logan was named for John A. Logan, a Union Army Civil War general. The post was closed in 1946, and in 1960 Governor Stephen L.R. McNichols acquired part of the site and converted it to the Fort Logan Mental Health Center. The state center shares approximately 550 remaining acres with other organizations, including Fort Logan National Cemetery (1949). The Field Officers Quarters has been restored as a museum by the Friends of Historic Fort Logan. Civilian architect Frank J. Grodavent designed this house and other officers' quarters arranged in a crescent on the west side of the fort's parade grounds. This large three-story Queen Anne style brick house trimmed in granite sports a third-story balcony in the corner hexagonal tower and corbelled chimney caps.

6

East Denver

Hilltop area

Montclair area

Park Hill area

Lowry area

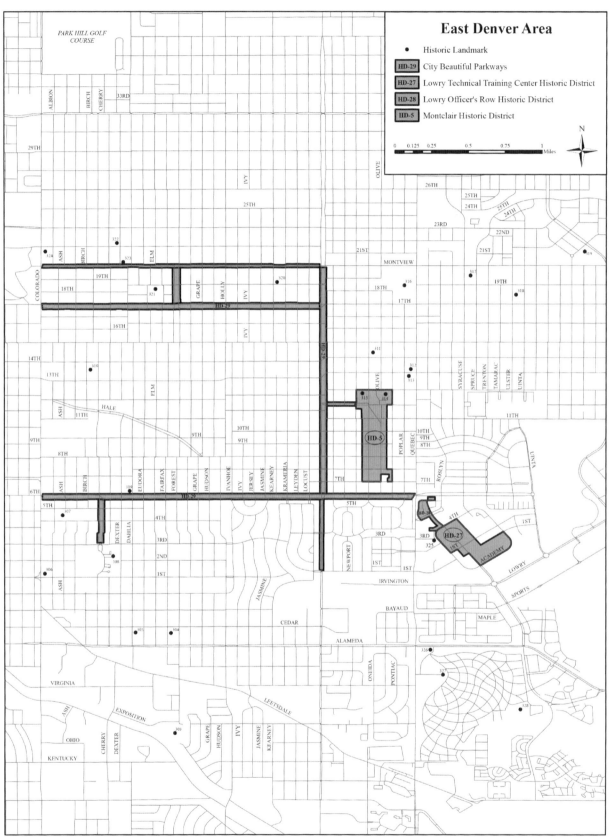

MAP 6.1. East Denver area

East of Colorado Boulevard, south of East Twenty-Third Avenue, west of Valentia Street, and north of East Kentucky Avenue

East Denver is a relatively prosperous residential area through which the landmarked parkway system provides a touring route. East Seventeenth Avenue Parkway, East Sixth Avenue Parkway, Montview Boulevard, and Clermont, Forest, Monaco, and Richthofen Parkways are interconnected greenways lined by homes that reflect popular architectural styles of the past 100 years. Richthofen Parkway leads to Montclair, an 1885 suburban town with subsequent infill, annexed to Denver in 1902. This relatively heterogeneous historic district resembles a catalog of residential styles from the 1880s to the 1990s. Two historic districts on what until 1994 was Lowry Air Force Base commemorate the tremendous impact of the military on Denver's development.

HD-29 CITY BEAUTIFUL PARKWAYS HISTORIC DISTRICT

1900s–1920s: George Kessler, Reinhard Schuetze, Saco R. DeBoer, and others

Denver aspired to become a City Beautiful, a dream pursued most aggressively by Mayor Robert W. Speer (1904–12, 1916–18). This crusade did much to uplift architecture, landscape architecture, public spaces, and public buildings. With a desire to create an elegant urban setting with ample green space, citizens, architects, and government officials alike began to plant lawns, gardens, and trees. To help further this idea, in 1894 Denver created a plan titled the "Park and Boulevard System of Denver." This plan proposed a city-wide system of parks and parkways, and a determined Mayor Speer would catapult Denver into becoming a beautiful city. East Denver wound up with many parkways, which often inspired notable private homes with their own distinctive landscaping.

303. Four Mile House

1859. Additions. 1976 restoration, Edward D. White Jr. 715 South Forest Street and East Exposition Avenue, NR

Denver's oldest extant building is this hewn ponderosa pine log cabin, refined over the years with clapboarding, a later frame wing, and a two-story brick addition. Built as a farmhouse that became a traveler's rest stop along Cherry Creek and the Smoky Hill Trail, it rests on a giant ax-hewn cottonwood log. With the help of drawings by the Historic American Buildings Survey, the house has been restored as a living history museum and farm on a seven-acre site. Among the reconstructed outbuildings is a three-hole privy complete with a window and roof vent. The City of Denver owns this retreat to the rural past, operated by Four Mile Historic Park, Inc. This bucolic setting, complete with farm animals, is a welcome escape from the surrounding modern developments.

Hilltop Area

304. Amter Residence

1951–53, Joe Lort. 222 South Fairfax Street

Designed by a Modernist architect, a second-generation student of Frank Lloyd Wright, this residence displays defining elements of Wright's Usonian style. Telltale elements include the horizontal orientation, ribbon windows, low-sloping roofs with overhanging eaves, and wood and stone exterior materials without applied ornament. Additional interior elements include built-in furniture and storage, indirect lighting instead of exposed light fixtures, and gravity heat from the floor instead of radiators. This is a survivor in the Hilltop neighborhood, which is losing its Modernist heritage with pop-tops and scrape-offs for much larger neo-traditional style Mc-mansions.

FIGURE 6.1. Four Mile House (Tom Noel Collection).

305. Joshel House

1951, Joseph P. Marlow. 220 South Dahlia Street, NR

Marlow, an admirer of Wrightian design, reduced this International style house to the basics. A wide, recessed carport on the northwest corner incorporates the main entrance, combining porch, garage, and porte cochère. The two-story south elevation is largely glass, opening the house to sunlight. Marlow set the split-level house with a single flat-roof plane into the south-facing hillside, protected on the north and west by evergreens. Historic Denver, Inc., retains a facade easement not only on the house but on the entire yard, whose north-border evergreens provide a windbreak and privacy, the same treescaping Marlow used for his own International style house (ca. 1949) at the southeast corner of Oneida Street and East Twelfth Avenue. Current owners are respectfully restoring the Joshel House and grounds.

306. Epiphany Episcopal Church

1941, S. Arthur Axtens. 1960 addition, Walter Simon. 100 Colorado Boulevard, northeast corner of East First Avenue

The Epiphany Episcopal Church congregation, founded in 1896, moved to this location in 1941. Denver architect S. Arthur Axtens designed this $60,000 two-story stone-studded church in a subtle Art Deco style, with a skin of sparkling quartz aggregate. A distinctive sixty-foot-high tower rises out of a combination of rectangular forms. The minimal ornamentation included a quiet recessed frieze and inset crosses. The north wing and the Jean Agnes Carroll Memorial Chapel have slightly different but equally restrained ornamentation.

307. Steck Elementary School

1930, S. Arthur Axtens. 1942 additions, S. Arthur Axtens. 1995 addition, Hans Kahn. 425 Ash Street

Named for Amos Steck, a pioneer state senator, county court judge, and the second mayor of Denver, this two-story brick elementary school is designed by a Denver architect known for his building at the former Colorado Woman's College, now the Denver campus of Johnson and Wales University. Axtens built residential, ecclesiastical, and commercial buildings throughout the Denver area. This Art Deco style school displays a vertical emphasis in

beige wire-cut brick, with polychromatic brick trim and terracotta accents in geometric shapes. Steck shares athletic fields with Roscoe C. Hill Middle School to the east.

308. George Cranmer House

1917, Jules Jacques Benoit Benedict. 1920 addition, Burnham Hoyt. 200 Cherry Street, NR

Denver's most exuberant architect designed this Italian Renaissance villa for George E. Cranmer, Denver's visionary manager of parks from 1935 to 1947. His wife, Jean Chappell Cranmer, a founder of the Denver Symphony Orchestra, often housed and entertained its musicians here. The two-story stucco-clad brick residence with rhyolite trim is situated on the east edge of Cranmer Park, with a panoramic view of the Front Range of the Rocky Mountains. A hipped tile roof, stucco chimneys, and an elaborate pedimented stone main entrance cap the asymmetrical facade. Many of the interior details were also designed by Benedict, including the iron chandeliers in the arched ceiling, the massive stone living room fireplace, and the sunroom with Palladian windows that are echoed in the trim of the interior walls of this well-preserved show home.

FIGURE 6.2. George Cranmer House (photo by Glenn Cuerden).

309. Dugal Farmhouse

ca. 1891. 1907 addition, R. H. Lewis. 1918–19 additions. 4775 East Sixth Avenue, northwest corner of Dahlia Street

Perhaps the first residence built on East Sixth Avenue Parkway, this two-story farmhouse has several sympathetic additions that give it a Prairie style feeling. The original structure had Victorian elements, with the later addition of a Prairie style facade. The first story is brick beneath a wood-shingled upper story. A second-story shingled addition covers a port cochere. Louis Dugal, a successful Canadian-born Denver lawyer, built this house and lived in it until 1917. This 3,500-square-foot house on a 19,000-square-foot lot started as a quaint farmhouse that grew into an elegant manor.

310. Milo A. Smith House

1890. 1891–1922 additions, Milo A. Smith. 1360 Birch Street, NR

Milo A. Smith, a developer of early Denver subdivisions and streetcar lines, built this eclectic residence in 1890, later making multiple renovations and additions to showcase his property. The result is Queen Anne styling in the multi-gabled roof, Tuscan columns in the now enclosed wraparound porch, and Craftsman details in the windows. During the 1910 renovation the exterior of the home was stuccoed and the enclosed entry porch became a permanent addition, as a cement foundation was poured. The interior of the home retains the original hardwood floors, staircases, wood trim, fireplaces, and mantles. The three-car garage built in 1919 replaced the original carriage house.

Montclair Area

HD-5 MONTCLAIR HISTORIC DISTRICT

Roughly Olive and Oneida Streets between Seventh and Twelfth Avenues

A German émigré, Baron Walter B. von Richthofen, founded and promoted Montclair as a suburban town in 1885. The core of that neighborhood is an unusual Denver historic district of scattered large Victorian homes on one-block tracts infilled with many more modest and recent residences. The older houses were built as show homes to attract homebuilders, but the silver crash of 1893 froze development for decades. Basement excavations and unfinished homes were reoccupied by prairie dogs.

The neighborhood is a catalog of area styles from the 1880s to the present, with a preponderance of 1950s brick houses incorporating bungalow and ranch house elements. The three-story brick house (1897; 1987 restoration) at 740 Olive Street was the home of architect Harlan Thomas, who served as a Montclair mayor.

The Richthofen Fountain (1901, Harlan Thomas); Richthofen Parkway and Oneida Street, NR, was erected by Baroness Louisa von Richthofen to commemorate her husband, the baron. This fountain of pinkish, black-flecked Pikes Peak granite later became her ash repository. In addition to the name "Richthofen," the fountain is incised with a line from Samuel Taylor Coleridge's poem "The Rime of the Ancient Mariner": "He Prayeth Well Who Loveth Well Both Bird, and Man, and Beast."

Notable features of the Montclair District are its so-called TB houses. Between 1907 and 1911, Charles M. Kittredge and Dennis Tirsway built these unusual houses at 928, 940, and 956 Olive Street and 791 Newport Street. Other, considerably altered models are at 725, 737, 920, and 928 Newport. These single-story homes are a reminder that Denver became one of America's most health-conscious cities following the 1893 silver crash. Health care became a major industry as asthmatics, tuberculars, and other lung disease patients began a new rush to Colorado. They came for the high, dry, sunny atmosphere, nationally prescribed as a cure for the deadliest disease of that time: tuberculosis. By 1900 Denver was filled with sanitariums, hospitals, and rest homes. Many old mansions became boardinghouses for members of the "one-lunged army."

The TB houses, designed to give patients more light and fresh air, were side-gabled, with screened side porches at either end and open interiors with minimal interior walls. Subsequent owners have often enclosed the sleeping porches. The house plans are surprisingly modern in their emphasis on bringing the outdoors inside. Ten-foot ceilings, many windows, and large doorways made for a bright, open house, in contrast to the bungalows built at the time.

311. Fire Station No. 14

1937, C. Francis Pillsbury. 1426 Oneida Street

This station occupies the site of the old Montclair Town Hall and fire station prior to Montclair's annexation to Denver in 1902. Pillsbury, a Denver architect, designed this building for the Federal Administration of Public Works to harmonize with residential architecture. It resembles the Tudoresque cottages popular in the 1920s and 1930s in its tapestry brick facade with tile trim, steep-pitched side-gabled roof, and central projecting entry bay with a prominent doorway under a half-timbered gable.

FIGURE 6.3. The Stanley School (a) boasted of having Denver's first public school kindergarten (b) (Tom Noel Collection).

312. Stanley School–Montclair School–Paddington Station Preschool

1891, John J. Huddart. 1991 addition, David Owen Tryba. 1301 North Quebec Street, northwest corner of East Thirteenth Avenue, NR

Built to accommodate the flourishing Montclair neighborhood, this two-story red brick school trimmed in red sandstone reflects the Romanesque Revival style. Young admirers of Henry M. Stanley, the renowned explorer of "Dr. Livingston, I presume" fame, petitioned to have the school renamed Stanley School. After Montclair's 1902 annexation to Denver, the Denver Public Schools renamed it the Montclair School. Replaced by a newer Montclair School in 1948, this building narrowly escaped demolition to become a private school in 1983. The British Primary School (BPS) thrived here before moving to larger quarters in the redeveloped Lowry area. BPS, however, left its Paddington Station Preschool in this building.

The main recessed entrance features a rounded sandstone arch with voussoirs, dentils, and carved keystone. The structure has retained its original doors and original one-over-one double-hung sash windows with transoms. Much of the interior has also remained unaltered, including the classroom doors, bead board wainscoting, and trim. In 1895 a red sandstone annex with flared hipped roof was added to the west to house a gymnasium and what is thought to have been Colorado's first kindergarten. A 13,500-square-foot 1991 addition replaced the previous addition but incorporated some of its red brick trim and sandstone lintels. Distinguished by Postmodern architectural design that is sympathetic to the original school, the new addition houses more classrooms, a library, a multipurpose room, and meeting rooms.

313. St. Luke's Episcopal Church

1890, James Murdoch. Several additions. 1256–70 Poplar Street, southeast corner of East Thirteenth Avenue

Rusticated rhyolite walls pierced by lancet windows and a square corner tower with a tall, shingled steeple distinguish this church. Despite additions, St. Luke's, with its small buttresses, fine stonework, and large rose window, remains a good example of English Gothic Revival. The parapeted gable ends are topped by stone Celtic crosses. A columbarium, St. Michael's yard, has been installed in the west-side

FIGURE 6.4. St. Luke's Episcopal Church, 1910 (Denver Public Library).

courtyard. Notable stained glass windows portray St. Luke as an evangelist and a physician.

314. Richthofen Castle

1887, Alexander Cazin. 1910 addition, Maurice Biscoe. 1924 addition, Jules Jacques Benoit Benedict and Maurice Biscoe. 7020 East Twelfth Avenue, southwest corner of Pontiac Street, NR

Baron Walter von Richthofen erected this rhyolite castle as the show home of Montclair, his suburban real estate scheme. Cazin, a fellow German, probably designed this mock medieval fortress, with its three-story crenelated turrets. On the northwest corner note the red sandstone bust of Frederick Barbarossa, the medieval ruler who first tried to unify Germany. Edwin Hendrie, who purchased the castle as his home in 1903, had Maurice Biscoe remodel the

FIGURE 6.5. Baron Walter von Richthofen (Tom Noel collection).

FIGURE 6.6. Richthofen Castle, 1887 (photo by William Henry Jackson, History Colorado).

original prickly Prussian affair in 1910 with Tudoresque additions. Biscoe added a half-timbered west wing, red tiled the roof, and remodeled the interior for Hendrie's daughter, Gertrude, and her husband, William W. Grant. In 1924 the Grants had Benedict design the south wing. Inside the thirty-eight-room castle is an entry hall with dark oak paneling and hand-tooled leather walls and a parquet-floored music room that seats 150. The gatehouse to the east was converted to a separate residence, 1177 Pontiac Street. Low-slung modern homes now surround the castle, a private residence that still dominates the Montclair neighborhood. In 2012 new owners began restoring the castle and also reunited it with the gatehouse, which had been converted to a separate residence.

315. Molkery/Montclair Civic Building

ca. 1888, Alexander Cazin. 1909 remodel, Fred W. Amter. 2004 restoration, SlaterPaull. 6820 East Twelfth Avenue between Newport and Oneida Streets, NR

Modeled after German and Swiss health spas, this building started out as a Molkery (German for "milk house"), with cattle stabled in the basement. Tuberculosis patients housed upstairs lounged on the open-air sun porches, drank fresh milk from the cattle below, and breathed the barnyard effluvium, then thought to be good for the lungs. This care apparently failed, and the building briefly became an insane asylum before reincarnation in 1910 as one of Denver's first community centers. The rhyolite foundation and first story are topped by a shiplap-sided second story. Porches on

FIGURE 6.7. The Molkery has evolved from a tuberculosis sanitarium (a) into the Montclair Civic Building (b). A 2004 restoration brought back the chimney and the cupola, among other missing or damaged elements (photos by Tom Noel).

three sides are now enclosed on the west. Bavarian-inspired wooden trim on the facade also adorns a balcony over the entry. The 2004 restoration brought back four chimneys and a cupola lost in a 1920s windstorm and fully restored the landmark inside and out for community use.

Park Hill Area

East of Colorado Boulevard, south of I-70, west of Quebec Street, and north of East Colfax Avenue

Sited on a hill east of City Park, this residential area varies from mansions along East Seventeenth Avenue Parkway and Montview Boulevard to multi-family low-income housing in the north section. Historically, the neighborhood was one of Denver's most prestigious, but it is best known as a neighborhood that accepted integration, one of the first communities in the country to promote blacks and whites living side by side.

316. Treat Hall–Centennial Hall

1889, Frank H. Jackson. 1800 Pontiac Street, NR

Designed in the Richardsonian Romanesque style, this first building of Colorado Woman's College was named for the college's first president, Jay Porter Treat. It initially housed faculty, students, a dining room, and classrooms. The rusticated gray rhyolite walls are enlivened by contrasting lavish red stone banding, quoins, and trim surrounding the round-arched windows. The massive entry arch, steep-pitched roof, and Châteauesque dormers add charm to this imposing monolith. A four-story gray brick north addition

FIGURE 6.8. Treat Hall–Centennial Hall (photo by Nicholas J. Wharton).

dominates but borrows the red sandstone trim of the original for its round-arch window trim. Colorado Woman's College was purchased in 1982 by another private school, the University of Denver, and converted to its Park Hill campus. In 2001 the University of Denver sold the campus, which has since housed the Denver campus of Johnson and Wales University, a culinary school. Following major 2015 restorations, Treat Hall was renamed Centennial Hall.

317. Ashley Elementary School

1930, John M. Gardner and Eugene F. Evans. 1951 addition, Arthur S. Axtens. 1914 Syracuse Street, northeast corner of East Nineteenth Avenue

This school is named for Eli Melville Ashley (1833–1909), a man with bushy eyebrows and a bushy goatee who presided over the Western Chemical Company. He also headed the Denver Chamber of Commerce and served on the Denver School Board, where he helped achieve a consolidated Denver School District. Axtens's addition of a hallway and additional classrooms uses the same zigzag blonde brick patterns, ornate iron railings, and vertical window pattern employed by Gardner and Evans on a fine Art Deco structure. The ornate Art Deco entrance is especially notable on the L-shaped building, whose grounds occupy a full block.

318. Greeters of America

1900, Peter Maider, builder. Various additions. 1740–60 Ulster Street

The Greeters of America, an organization of hotel employees, established its national home for indigent, ill, and retired members in these two houses. The first, 1740 Ulster, had been constructed in 1900 as a cottage with a gambrel roof and fish-scale shingled second-story facade. The Greeters built the larger brick residence at 1760 Ulster in the late 1920s, with decorative brick panels in the front porch and half-timbered gables. The newer building was once connected to the older house by a breezeway, no longer standing. Both buildings are now private residences. This unimposing brick complex blends well with the surrounding residential area.

319. Hangar 61–Ideal Basic Cement Company Corporate Hangar

1959, Arthur A. Fisher, William E. Fisher, and Rodney Davis. Engineered by Milo Ketchum. 8695 East Twenty-First Avenue

This innovative architectural and engineering feat borders the former Stapleton International Airport. The 9,400-square-foot concrete hanger was built to house

FIGURE 6.9. An old hangar is now a spectacular new church (photo by Tom Noel).

a Fairchild F-27 turbo-prop airliner owned by the Ideal Basic Cement Company. The building soars to 33 feet at the apex of a diamond-shaped barrel-vaulted roof, and the thin shell concrete hangar spans 160 feet with no center supports. After Stapleton closed in 1995, replaced by Denver International Airport, this hangar sat empty. Colorado Preservation, Inc., acquired the hangar when it looked as though it would be demolished and restored it with developer Larry Nelson. It is one of the few traces of the old Stapleton Airport complex, now recycled as a church.

320. Kappler-Cannon-Fieger House

1912, George L. Bettcher. 1980 addition. 1904 Kearney Street, northeast corner of East Nineteenth Avenue

This quaint Park Hill "bungalow" is actually a large Craftsman house that sits on four lots and includes gardens, a fountain, and a swimming pool. This once south-facing home has been reoriented to face west, with the original foyer becoming a music room. The residence was built by investment banker Otto H. Kappler, a German immigrant who lived there until his death in 1920, when the president and manager of Windsor Farm Dairy, Hugh Brown Cannon, purchased the house. Between 1979 and 2014 the residence housed Henry Fieger, a neurosurgeon, and his wife, Jill Hilton Fieger. They built a 900-square-foot addition in 1980. The now 5,000-square-foot home has fourteen rooms, four fireplaces, crystal sconces, sculptured brass doorknobs, and original Tiffany lighting.

321. Park Hill Elementary School

1901. 1912 addition. 1928 remodel and addition, Frederick E. Mountjoy and Frank W. Frewan. 1968–69 addition, Phillips-Carter-Reister. 5050 East Nineteenth Avenue between Elm and Fairfax Streets

Medallion busts of Beethoven and Shakespeare are part of the blue, white, and gold terracotta trim for this school in Mediterranean Revival style. In 1928 Mountjoy and Frewan added a gymnasium on the west side of the building and an auditorium on the east. These additions match the stucco building mass, terracotta detail, and red tile roof of the original 1901 school (architect unknown). In 1968–69 architects Phillips-Carter-Reister designed the kindergarten wing and cafeteria as a horizontal massing that compliments the vertical nature of the 1901 three-story

FIGURE 6.10. The 1901 original Park Hill Elementary School and its 1912 addition (a) and the school's fearless baseball team (b) (Tom Noel Collection).

central building but lacks the grace and exquisite detail of the original school.

322. St. Thomas Episcopal Church

1908, Harry J. Manning. 2201 Dexter Street, northwest corner of East Twenty-Second Avenue

One of Denver's best examples of Spanish Colonial Revival style has a Churrigueresque entry surround of cast stone. Its keystone with an embossed cross caps the arched doorway beneath a stained glass window crowned by a wreath framing the ark of salvation. A stepped three-arch bell tower, stucco walls, and red tile roof characterize the church. Sympathetic auxiliary buildings flow from the main building, helping to form a cloister courtyard fronted by a covered arcade. Inside on either side of the altar, *reredos* feature tile shields depicting the twelve apostles. This low, stylish church blends well with the surrounding residential neighborhood.

FIGURE 6.11. St. Thomas Episcopal Church (Tom Noel Collection).

323. Park Hill Branch Library

1920, Merrill H. Hoyt and Burnham Hoyt. 1994 restoration, David Owen Tryba. 4705 Montview, northeast corner of Dexter Street

This Italian Renaissance Revival style branch library honors Montview Boulevard's grand residential scale. The Andrew Carnegie Foundation helped fund this $27,000 branch, a stucco one-story building under a red tile roof. Rich details include an entry cartouche featuring the lamp of learning and Acanthus-encrusted balusters that divide the diamond-paned front windows. An unfortunate 1964 remodeling was happily undone in a 1994 restoration. Once again, the interior radiates natural light and spaciousness, with dark woodwork and ceiling beams for contrast. The cast-stone fireplace is adorned with a bas-relief ship inspired by Samuel Taylor Coleridge's poem "The Rime of the Ancient Mariner."

FIGURE 6.12. Park Hill Branch Library (photo byTom Noel).

324. Margaret Long House

1908. 2070 Colorado Boulevard

Margaret Long, MD, the daughter of a Massachusetts governor who also served as secretary of the US Navy, graduated from Smith College and the Johns Hopkins Medical School. She became a fast friend of classmate Dr. Florence Sabin, with whom she formed a social club, the Anti-Matrimonial Alliance. Neither woman ever married, making medicine their one true love. After Margaret's sister died from tuberculosis, she moved to Denver in 1905. On a prominent site facing City Park, she constructed her home in the Dutch Colonial style with Classical Revival elements. Reflecting the impact of tuberculosis on Denver architecture, Long added a large open-air front porch topped by a third-story deck. Yet another rear deck reflects her

FIGURE 6.13. Dr. Margaret Long leaving her house on one of her motoring expeditions to explore Colorado trails (photo by Louis McClure, Denver Public Library).

belief that Colorado's fresh air and sunshine were curative. Professionally, Dr. Long worked and conducted research at Denver General Hospital. In addition, she helped found the Sands House Sanitarium in Edgewater, Colorado, a facility that served poor women and girls who had tuberculosis; the building still stands at 5261 West Twenty-Sixth Avenue. After she retired, Margaret turned to writing substantial history books, including *The Smoky Hill Trail* (1953) and *The Santa Fe Trail* (1954). She died in 1957.

Lowry Area

HD-27, LOWRY TECHNICAL TRAINING CENTER HISTORIC DISTRICT, AND HD-28, LOWRY OFFICERS' ROW HISTORIC DISTRICT

Quebec to Dayton Streets between East Alameda and East Eleventh Avenues

The base was established on the site of the Agnes C. Phipps Memorial Sanatorium, a large and lavish tuberculosis complex opened in 1904 by Lawrence C. Phipps and named for his mother, a TB victim. The City of Denver purchased the 1,866-acre site in 1937 and donated it to the Army Air Corps, the predecessor of the US Air Force, for an air base and aviation-training center. It was named for Denverite Francis B. Lowry, who had been shot down over France during World War I. The commanding officer moved into the hospital superintendent's house, 7100 East Sixth Avenue Parkway (1904, Aaron M. Gove and Thomas F. Walsh), the only sanitarium structure still standing. These Denver architects designed the sanitarium in the Mission style, with open sleeping porches and arcades in stuccoed buildings flaunting curvilinear parapets and red tile roofs.

The air base grew a great deal during World War II as a major US training station for bombardiers, artillerymen, and aerial photographers. During the Cold War, the base continued to thrive and became the first home of the US Air Force Academy before it moved to its Colorado Springs campus. More than 600 structures dotted the site, and 1.5 million men and women were trained or stationed at Lowry over the years.

On September 30, 1994, the US Air Force decommissioned Lowry, which was converted to a commercial and mixed-use residential neighborhood. Two historic districts were created.

The Lowry Officers' Row Historic District contains sixteen houses (including the former commander's 1904

house) along Rampart Way and East Fourth and East Sixth Avenues. The Lowry Technical Training Center Historic District consists of Building 349 (the original 3,600-bed brick barracks, which became the Administrative Building); Buildings 379 and 380, Art Deco edifices used for classrooms; and two large aircraft hangers, Buildings 401 and 402. Hanger 401 has been adaptively reused as the Wings over the Rockies Museum, 7711 Academy Boulevard. Hanger 402, 7581 Academy Boulevard, has been reincarnated as storage, offices, the Laughing Latte Coffee Shop, and the Lowry Beer Garden.

325. Lowry Chapel No. 1–Eisenhower Chapel
1941. 293 Roslyn Street, NR

This standard frame military-design chapel is strategically located next to the Officers' Row and the Lowry Technical Training Center Historic Districts. Lowry Air Force Building 27 is a rare surviving example of a simple, low-budget, ship lap-sided military chapel. This humble, little-altered edifice gained fame as a place where President Dwight D. Eisenhower and his wife, Mamie, attended services during his visits to Denver between 1953 and 1955. Easily recognizable by its prominent spire, this is a survivor on a base where three other identical chapels were demolished during the early 1970s.

326. Fairmount Cemetery Gate Lodge
1890, Henry T.E. Wendell. 7200 East Alameda Avenue

This Richardsonian Romanesque stone gatehouse served as the original grand entry for Colorado's most populous

FIGURE 6.14. Fairmount Cemetery Gate Lodge (Denver Public Library).

FIGURE 6.15. Fairmount Cemetery Ivy Chapel (photo by Tom Noel).

arboretum. Schuetze, Colorado's first landscape architect, subsequently designed or redesigned many Denver parks. At Fairmount, where he is buried, Schuetze achieved the goal of great cemetery parks: landscaping designed to look as if it was not designed. Many well-known Coloradans reside in this necropolis, and a number erected stately private mausoleums as their final earthly homes. Frank E. Edbrooke probably designed his own private Neoclassical mausoleum, as did Temple Hoyne Buell, whose polished granite crypt has elaborate wrought-iron doors guarded by gilded maidens. The Gate Lodge's Gothic arch entry reflects a similar large portal on the nearby Ivy Chapel.

327. Fairmount Cemetery Ivy Chapel

1890, Henry T.E. Wendell. 1995 restoration. 430 South Quebec Street within Fairmount Cemetery

This delicate late French Gothic Revival stone chapel has a multiple-arch grand entry, flying buttresses, and spires in a vertical composition that makes it one of Denver's best Gothic monuments. Gray sandstone serves as both skin and trim but was being eroded by the ivy, which had to be removed to restore the stone.

328. Fairmount Mausoleum

1930, Frederick E. Mountjoy and Francis W. Frewan. 430 South Quebec Street within Fairmount Cemetery

Located near the southeast corner of the cemetery, Fairmount Mausoleum is one of the largest mausoleums in the United States. Constructed of concrete and reinforced steel, this large Greek style temple has a granite veneer. The interior has rich Alabama white marble walls, Tennessee pink marble floors, and one of the largest collections of stained glass in Colorado. The community mausoleum houses thousands and is equipped with its own chapel, flower shop, numerous private rooms, and soft recorded music to create a celestial atmosphere.

cemetery. Fairmount's founders promised to abandon the "mournful effects of the old style cemetery" in favor of a romantic cemetery park, for which the US prototype was Mount Auburn Cemetery in Cambridge, Massachusetts. Fairmount's developers recruited Reinhard Schuetze, a native of Holstein, Germany, who had studied landscape architecture and engineering at the Royal Academy in Potsdam. Schuetze planted more than 4,000 trees in Fairmount, which is still the state's largest and most diverse

7

Denver Mountain Parks

Daniels Park

Dedisse Park

Red Rocks Park

Nestled in the mountains outside Denver's city limits, the Denver Mountain Parks are city-owned and operated. Other municipalities have undertaken similar projects, but the variety and vastness of Denver's mountain parks are noteworthy. These forty-six parks encompass roughly 14,000 acres in Clear Creek, Douglas, Grand, and Jefferson Counties. Among other attractions, they contain buffalo and elk herds in Genesee Mountain Park, an outdoor amphitheater in Red Rocks Park, and the Winter Park Ski Area.

Mayor Robert W. Speer made mountain parks part of his City Beautiful agenda and helped persuade voters to approve a 1912 city charter authorizing the acquisition and development of land outside the city limits. Given the task to plan a string of parks, Frederick Law Olmsted Jr., the nation's premier parks planner, surveyed the future parks on horseback before providing a master plan.

The first mountain park, Genesee, was acquired by the city in 1912 in efforts to save Genesee Mountain forests from being sold to a sawmill. A subsequent acquisition included Lookout Mountain (1917), where Buffalo Bill's grave and a museum were installed in 1918. Mayor Benjamin Franklin Stapleton and his energetic and resourceful manager of improvements and parks, George E. Cranmer, expanded and polished the park system, building Red Rocks Amphitheatre and the Winter Park Ski Area by 1941. While the entire Denver Mountain Park system is on the National Register of Historic Places, only three specific sites have been designated Denver Landmarks.

Daniels Park

HD-24 FLORENCE F. MARTIN RANCH HISTORIC DISTRICT

ca. 1920s. Twenty-one miles south of Denver in Daniels Park, 8615 Daniels Park Road, NR

Florence F. Martin, born in Sydney, Australia, into a prominent family, became a world-traveling socialite. She met William Cooke Daniels, the Denver Daniels and Fisher Stores Company department store magnate, and became fast friends with Daniels and his wife, Cicely. The Daniels gave Martin property in Daniels Park, twenty-one miles south of Denver in Douglas County. There, Martin assembled a 2,400-acre ranch. Her large house burned, leaving only ruins, but a barn, round tiled silo, bunkhouses, chicken houses, pump houses, other outbuildings, and a

reservoir survive. The site is gated, with no public access. Tours can be arranged with Denver Mountain Parks at (720) 865-0900.

Upon her death in 1957, Martin donated the entire ranch to the city of Denver for use as a mountain park, with the stipulation that the park be named for William Cooke Daniels. The Martin Ranch is architecturally notable for its use of native stone foundations, with upper walls of tongue and groove or shingle siding, in a ranch complex displaying both rustic- and Craftsman style elements. The 160-acre core of the ranch comprises the historic district. Adjacent Daniels Ranch parcels were also donated to Denver over the years as part of a largely failed effort to put together a greenbelt of mountain parks in the foothills around the city. In recent years the Castle Pines subdivision has grown to border the eastern boundary of the park.

The majority of Daniels Park is dedicated as a preserve for a buffalo herd; however, on the west side of the park the Tall Bull Memorial Grounds are devoted to Native American religious uses. In addition, the Denver Parks and Recreation Department built a rustic style picnic shelter, designed by prominent Denver architect Jules Jacques Benoit Benedict, of massive fieldstones with built-in benches around a central fireplace. This pubic amenity is situated on a high ridge, with superb views of the South Platte Valley and the Front Range of the Rockies.

Dedisse Park

329. Evergreen Lake Warming House

1934, Civilian Conservation Corps. Twenty-seven miles west of Denver, south shore of Evergreen Lake, NR

A grassy hillside flows onto the roof of this round log shelter dug into the south bank of a picturesque mountain reservoir. Massive logs with corner saddle notching form a low-slung shelter angled to fit the contour of the lake's shoreline. The use of peeled logs and the rustic style may have been suggested by the nearby Keys on the Green Clubhouse and Restaurant, a rustic design for the Denver Mountain Parks golf course bordering the west edge of Evergreen Lake. Reminiscent of sod-roofed log dugouts, this Warming House provides a wonderful example of discreet, contextual mountain resort architecture.

This unobtrusive earth-sheltered structure was built as a warming house, skate rental shop, and snack bar for ice skaters who flocked to the Denver Mountain Park. The

Warming House offered hot chocolate and had loud-speakers that broadcast classical music for the skaters. The Warming House proved to be too small, and the Civilian Conservation Corps constructed a mirror-image addition on the east side of the structure, which shares the boardwalk and pier. As Evergreen Lake and the surrounding wetlands attract numerous visitors, naturalists, and bird enthusiasts, the Warming House has been restored and converted to the Evergreen Nature Center. The Warming House, Evergreen Lake, and Keys on the Green Clubhouse are part of the Dedisse Park National Register Historic District.

Red Rocks Park

330. Red Rocks Outdoor Amphitheatre

1941, Burnham Hoyt. Fifteen miles west of Denver, in Red Rocks Park near the junction of Highways 8, 26, and 74, NR, NHL

For its 1957 centennial exhibit featuring each state's finest twentieth-century design, held at the National Gallery of Art in Washington, DC, the American Institute of Architects selected Red Rocks Outdoor Amphitheatre as Colorado's best. This acoustically superb outdoor theater at 6,000 feet above sea level is formed by massive sandstone slabs and metamorphic rocks tilted upward by volcanic action. In May 1945 *Architectural Forum* praised "the admirable restraint with which architect Burnham

Hoyt has preserved the original flavor of a majestic setting." Collaborating with nature, Hoyt used local juniper trees as landscaping and native red sandstone for everything from drainage canals to walls. Instead of blasting away rocks to conform to the theater footprint, he shaped the theater to fit between the rocks. The wonderful simplicity of this design has been marred by subsequent stage covering that partially blocks the view of Denver and the High Plains. The surrounding 1,640-acre Red Rocks Park offers hiking trails through dramatic foothills scenery. Red Rocks is notable for its history as well as its superb design, having hosted many celebrated performers, from the Beatles to U-2.

331. Indian Concession House

1931, Wilbert R. Rosche. Fifteen miles west of Denver, in Red Rocks Park near the Amphitheater, NR

Now known as the Trading Post, this two-story Southwestern style structure mixes a Mission Revival parapet and Pueblo Revival vigas, a combination as common as intermarriage between Hispanics and Native Americans. This elegant structure set in a cactus garden contains a visitor's center, café, and museum.

FIGURE 7.2. The Red Rocks Trading Post, concession house, and museum opened in 1931 as the Indian Concession House, with many Native American artifacts, curios, and souvenirs (Tom Noel Collection).

FIGURE 7.1. Red Rocks Outdoor Amphitheatre exemplifies how architecture can yield to the natural environment by including native junipers and rock formations (photo by Tom Noel).

Appendix A

Denver Landmarks by Designation Number

1. Emmanuel-Sherith Chapel, 1201 Tenth Street
2. Constitution Hall, 1501–7 Blake Street (demolished)
3. Governor's Mansion, 400 East Eighth Avenue
4. St. John's Episcopal Cathedral, 1313 Washington Street
5. Immaculate Conception Cathedral, 401 East Colfax Avenue
6. Byers-Evans House, 1310 Bannock Street
7. Trinity United Methodist Church, 1820 Broadway Street
8. First Baptist Church, 230 East Fourteenth Avenue
9. First Church of Christ Scientist, 1401–15 Logan Street
10. Daniels and Fisher Tower, 1101 Sixteenth Street
11. Denver Women's Press Club, 1325 Logan Street
12. Four Mile House, 715 South Forest Street
13. Zion Baptist Church, 933 East Twenty-Fourth Avenue
14. St. Elizabeth's Catholic Church, 1060 St. Francis Way
15. South Broadway Christian Church, 23 Lincoln Street
16. Evans Memorial Chapel, University of Denver campus
17. St. Mark's Episcopal Church, 1160 Lincoln Street
18. Scott Methodist Church–Sanctuary Lofts, 2201 Ogden Street
19. St. Cajetan's Catholic Church, 900 Lawrence Street
20. Molly Brown House, 1340 Pennsylvania Street
21. The Navarre, 1725 Tremont Street
22. Frank Smith Mansion, 1801 York Street
23. Pope-Thompson-Wasson House, 1320 Race Street
24. Denver Tramway Co. Powerhouse–Forney Transportation Museum–Recreational Equipment, Inc., 1416 Platte Street
25. Pearce–McAllister Cottage, 1880 Gaylord Street
26. Tivoli Union Brewery–Student Union, 900 Auraria Parkway
27. Buckhorn Exchange Restaurant, 1000 Osage Street
28. US Mint, 320 West Colfax Avenue
29. Tears-McFarlane House, 1290 Williams Street
30. Odd Fellows Hall, 1543–45 Champa Street
31. Denver City Cable Railway Building, 1801 Lawrence Street
32. Richthofen Castle, 7020 East Twelfth Avenue
33. Croke-Patterson-Campbell Mansion–Patterson Inn, 420 East Eleventh Avenue
34. Foster-McCauley-Symes–French Consulate House, 736–38 Pearl Street
35. Sacred Heart Catholic Church, 2760 Larimer Street
36. Thomas Hornsby Ferril House, 2123 Downing Street
37. Asbury Methodist Church, 2205 West 30th Avenue
38. Herman Heiser House, 3016 Osceola Street
39. Queree House, 2914 West Twenty-Ninth Avenue
40. McKay House, 3359 Alcott Street
41. Cox House, 3417 Lowell Boulevard
42. Cox "Gargoyle" House, 3425 Lowell Boulevard
43. Miller House, 2501 High Street
44. John Brisben Walker House, 3520 Newton Street
45. Cheesman Park Memorial Pavilion, 1000 High Street
46. Denver Botanic Gardens House, 909 York Street
47. Boettcher Conservatory, Denver Botanic Gardens, 1005 York Street
48. Eugene Field House, 701 South Franklin Street
49. Red Rocks Outdoor Amphitheatre, Red Rocks Park
50. Molkery/Montclair Civic Building, 6820 East Twelfth Avenue
51. James Fleming House, 1510 South Grant Street
52. Dennis Sheedy Mansion, 1115 Grant Street
53. Denver Fire Station No. 1, 1326 Tremont Place
54. Hallet House, 900 Logan Street
55. Campbell House, 940 Logan Street
56. McKinley Mansion, 948–52 Logan Street

57. Clemes-Lipe-Sweeney House, 901 Pennsylvania Street
58. Taylor House, 945 Pennsylvania Street
59. Hitchings Block, 1620 Market Street
60. Liebhart-Lindner Building, 1624 Market Street
61. McCrary Building, 1634–38 Market Street
62. Waters Building, 1642 Market Street
63. Bockfinger-Flint Mercantile, 1644–50 Market Street
64. Columbia Hotel, 1322–50 Seventeenth Street
65. US Post Office and Federal Building–Byron White Federal Courthouse, 1823 Stout Street
66. St. Elizabeth's Retreat Chapel, 2835 West Thirty-Second Avenue
67. St. Andrews Memorial Episcopal Chapel, 2015 Glenarm Place
68. Half Moon House, 3205 West Twenty-First Avenue
69. Voorhees House, 1471 Stuart Street
70. Frank Smith House, 1435 Stuart Street
71. Raymond House–Castle Marne, 1572 Race Street
72. Bliss House, 1389 Stuart Street
73. Bosworth House, 1400 Josephine Street
74. Malo Mansion, 500 East Eighth Avenue
75. John Porter House, 777 Pearl Street
76. Adams-Fitzell House, 1359 Race Street
77. Corona School–Dora Moore Elementary School, 846 Corona Street
78. Mary Coyle Chase House, 532 West Fourth Avenue
79. Dunning-Benedict House, 1200 Pennsylvania Street
80. Keating House–Capitol Hill Mansion Bed and Breakfast Inn, 1207 Pennsylvania Street
81. Treat Hall–Centennial Hall, 1800 Pontiac Street
82. St. Luke's Episcopal Church, 1256–70 Poplar Street
83. Frederick W. Neef House, 2143 Grove Street
84. Creswell House, 1244 Grant Street
85. Daly House, 1034 Logan Street
86. McNeil House, 930 Logan Street
87. Fairmount Cemetery Gate Lodge, 7200 East Alameda Avenue
88. Fairmount Cemetery Ivy Chapel, 430 South Quebec Street
89. Spangler House, 1444 Stuart Street
90. Baker-Plested Cottage, 1208 Logan Street
91. The Cornwall, 1317 Ogden Street
92. Sykes-Nicholson-Moore House, 1410 High Street
93. Watson House, 1437 High Street
94. Kerr House, 1900 East Seventh Avenue
95. Grant-Humphreys Mansion, 770 Pennsylvania Street
96. Frank Damascio House, 3611–15 Osage Street
97. St. Thomas Episcopal Church, 2201 Dexter Street
98. Phipps Mansion (Belcaro) and Tennis House, 3400 Belcaro Drive
99. Adolph Zang Mansion, 709 Clarkson Street
100. All Saints Episcopal Church–Chapel of Our Merciful Savior, 2222 West Thirty-Second Avenue
101. Our Lady of Mount Carmel Catholic Church, 3549 Navajo Street
102. St. Patrick's Catholic Church, 3301–25 Pecos Street
103. Equitable Building, 730 Seventeenth Street
104. Gates House, 1365–75 Josephine Street
105. Ideal Building–Denver National Bank–Colorado Business Bank, 821–27 Seventeenth Street
106. Rosenzweig House, 1129 East Seventeenth Avenue
107. Walter-Bierly House, 2259 Gilpin Street
108. Stearns House, 1030 Logan Street
109. Wells Fargo Building, 1338 Fifteenth Street
110. Frank E. Edbrooke House, 931 East Seventeenth Avenue
111. Kenehan House, 1390 Stuart Street
112. Frank E. Woodbury House, 2841 Perry Street
113. Lobach House, 2851 Perry Street
114. Thomas Field House, 2305 South Washington Street (demolished)
115. Mitchell-Schomp House, 680 Clarkson Street
116. Zang Townhouse, 1532 Emerson Street
117. Guerrieri-DeCunto House, 1650 Pennsylvania Street
118. William Moses House, 4001 West Thirtieth Avenue
119. Gebhard/Smith House, 2253 Downing Street
120. Henry Lee House, 2653 West Thirty-Second Avenue
121. Kistler-Rodriguez House, 700 East Ninth Avenue
122. Henri Foster House, 2533 West Thirty-Second Avenue
123. Clements Rowhouse, 2201–17 Glenarm Place
124. Mattie Silks House, 2009 Market Street
125. Baerresen-Freeman House, 1718 Gaylord Street
126. Fleming-Hanington House, 1133 Pennsylvania Street
127. Butters House, 1129 Pennsylvania Street
128. Flower-Vaile House, 1610 Emerson Street
129. Wheeler Block, 2150 West Twenty-Ninth Avenue
130. Cerrone's Grocery, 3617 Osage Street
131. Lowry Chapel No. 1–Eisenhower Chapel, 293 Roslyn Street
132. Wolcott School Apartments, 1400–14 Marion Street
133. Denver City Railway Company–Sheridan Heritage Building–Streetcar Lofts, 1635 Seventeenth Street
134. Chappell House, 1555 Race Street

135. Peter McCourt House, 1471 High Street
136. Masonic Temple, 1614 Welton Street
137. Denver Athletic Club, 1325 Glenarm Place
138. Barney Ford Building, 1512–14 Blake Street
139. Curry-Chucovich-Gerash House, 1439 Court Place
140. Kettle Building, 1422–26 Larimer Street
141. Congdon Building, 1421–25 Larimer Street
142. Barnum Building, 1412 Larimer Street
143. Sussex Building, 1430 Larimer Street
144. Clayton Building–Granite Hotel, 1456–60 Larimer Street
145. Crawford Building, 1437–41 Larimer Street
146. Gallup-Stanbury Building, 1445–51 Larimer Street
147. Lincoln Hall, 1413–19 Larimer Street
148. McKibben Building, 1411 Larimer Street
149. Gahan's Saloon–Miller Building–Ted's Montana Grill, 1401–7 Larimer Street
150. Spice and Commission Warehouse–Edward W. Wynkoop Building, 1738 Wynkoop Street
151. Denver Gas and Electric Building–Insurance Exchange Building, 910 Fifteenth Street
152. Oxford Hotel, 1600–12 Seventeenth Street
153. Bosler-Yankee House, 3209 West Fairview Place
154. Mayan Theater, 110 Broadway Street
155. Emerson Elementary School, 1420 Ogden Street
156. Sarah Platt Decker Branch Library, 1501 South Logan Street
157. Anfenger House, 2900 Champa Street
158. Philip Milstein (1907–93), Denver's only human landmark
159. Wood-Morris-Bonfils House, 707 Washington Street
160. Hotel Hope, 1404–6 Larimer Street
161. Barth Hotel, 1514 Seventeenth Street
162. Windsor Stables and Storefront–Blake Street Bath and Racquet Club, 1732–72 Blake Street
163. Fire House No. 15, 1080 Clayton Street
164. Hose Company No. 1, 1963 Chestnut Street
165. Sweet-Miller House, 1075 Humboldt Street
166. First Avenue Hotel, 101–15 Broadway Street
167. Denver Press Club, 1330 Glenarm Place
168. Temple Emanuel Event Center, 1595 Pearl Street
169. Brind-Axtens Mansion, 1000 Logan Street
170. Hannigan-Canino Terrace, 3500 Navajo Street
171. Neusteter Building, 720 Sixteenth Street
172. Wyatt Elementary School, 3620 Franklin Street
173. Milheim House, 1515 Race Street
174. Central Bank, 1100–1108 Fifteenth Street (demolished)
175. Paramount Theater, 1621 Glenarm Place

176. Harman Town Hall–Greenleaf Masonic Temple, 400 St. Paul Street
177. Scottish Rite Masonic Temple, 1370 Grant Street
178. Brown Palace Hotel, 321 Seventeenth Street
179. Boston Building–Boston Lofts, 822–30 Seventeenth Street
180. Park Hill Branch Library, 4705 Montview Boulevard
181. Byers Branch Library, 675 Santa Fe Drive
182. Smiley Branch Library, 4501 West Forty-Sixth Avenue
183. Woodbury Branch Library, 3265 Federal Boulevard
184. Crawford Hill Mansion, 969 Sherman Street
185. Guaranty Bank Building, 815 Seventeenth Street
186. Ferguson-Gano House, 722 East Seventh Avenue
187. Annunciation Catholic Church, 3601 Humboldt Street
188. Henry M. Porter House, 975 Grant Street
189. Greeters of America, 1740–60 Ulster Street
190. Moffat Station, 2101 Fifteenth Street
191. Fort Logan Field Officers Quarters, 3742 West Princeton Circle
192. East High School, 1545 Detroit Street
193. Cass-Friedman House, 733 East Eighth Avenue
194. Robinson House, 1225 Pennsylvania Street
195. Stevens Elementary School, 1140 Columbine Street
196. Denver Municipal Auditorium–Ellie Caulkins Opera House, 920 Fourteenth Street
197. South High School, 1700 East Louisiana Avenue
198. Twentieth Street Bathhouse/Gym, 1101 Twentieth Street
199. Brown-Garrey-Congdon House, 1300 East Seventh Avenue
200. Smedley Elementary School, 4250 Shoshone Street
201. Jane Silverstein Ries House, 737 Franklin Street
202. West High School, 951 Elati Street
203. Ashley Elementary School, 1914 Syracuse Street
204. Ebert Elementary School, 410 Park Avenue West
205. Huddart/Lydon House, 2418 Stout Street
206. Douglass Undertaking Building, 2745 Welton Street
207. Cody House, 2932 Lafayette Street
208. McBird-Whiteman House, 2225 Downing Street
209. Whitehead-Peabody House, 1128 Grant Street
210. Burlington Hotel, 2201 Larimer Street
211. Grant Middle School, 1751 South Washington Street
212. Skinner Middle School, 3435 West Fortieth Avenue
213. Romeo Block, 2944–58 Zuni Street
214. Denver Dry Goods Building, 700 Sixteenth Street
215. Bluebird Theater, 3315–17 East Colfax Avenue
216. Denver Tramway Company–Hotel Teatro, 1100 Fourteenth Street

217. House with the Round Window, 3240 West Hayward Place
218. Morey Middle School, 840 East Fourteenth Avenue
219. Denver Public Schools Administration Building, 414 Fourteenth Street
220. Chamberlain Observatory, 2930 East Warren Avenue
221. Graham-Bible House, 2080 York Street
222. Washington Park Bathhouse, South Downing Street and East Center Avenue
223. Nursery Building, 888 East Iliff Avenue
224. Golda Meir House, 1146 Ninth Street
225. First National Bank–American National Bank–Magnolia Hotel, 818 Seventeenth Street
226. Park Hill Elementary School, 5050 East Nineteenth Avenue
227. Ogden Theatre, 935 East Colfax Avenue
228. Joshel Residence, 220 South Dahlia Street
229. Cory Elementary School, 1550 South Steele Street
230. Merrill Middle School, 1551 South Monroe Street
231. Washington Park Boathouse and Pavilion
232. Indian Concession House, Red Rocks Park
233. Evergreen Lake Warming House, Evergreen Lake Park
234. Savage Candy Company, 2158–62 Lawrence Street
235. Fire Station No. 3, 2500 Washington Street
236. Holmes House, 2330 Downing Street
237. Asbury Elementary School, 1320 East Asbury Avenue
238. Hayden, Dickinson, and Feldhauser Building–Colorado Building, 1617 California Street
239. Austin Apartments, 2400 East Colfax Avenue
240. El Jebel Temple–Rocky Mountain Consistory, 1770 Sherman Street
241. Steele Elementary School, 320 South Marion Street Parkway
242. Fager Residence, 2947 Umatilla Street
243. Tallmadge and Boyer Terrace, 2925–59 Wyandot Street
244. Fire Station No. 7, 3600 Tejon Street
245. Our Lady of Guadalupe Catholic Church, 3559 Kalamath Street
246. German House–Denver Turnverein, 1570 Clarkson Street
247. Horace Mann Middle School, 4130 Navajo Street
248. Sherman Elementary School–Art Students League of Denver, 200 Grant Street
249. Cowie House, 3147 Umatilla Street
250. Fox-Schlatter House, 3225 Quivas Street
251. Cole-DeRose Apartment House, 1940–46 West Thirty-Third Avenue

252. Conine-Horan House, 2839 Wyandot Street
253. Elitch Theater, West Thirty-Seventh Place
254. Benson-Orsborn House, 1305 Elizabeth Street
255. Sayre's Alhambra, 801 Logan Street
256. Crescent Hand Laundry Building, 2323–29 West Thirtieth Avenue
257. Elyria Elementary School, 4725 High Street
258. Aldine-Grafton Apartments, 1001–21 East Seventeenth Avenue
259. George Cranmer House, 200 Cherry Street
260. Fire Station No. 14, 1426 Oneida Street
261. Fire Station No. 11, 40 West Second Avenue
262. Fire Station No. 18–Denver Police Gang Unit, 2205 Colorado Boulevard
263. Hover-Bromley Building, 1348 Lawrence Street
264. Berkeley School, 5025–55 Lowell Boulevard
265. Bryant-Webster Elementary School, 3635 Quivas Street
266. North High School, 2960 Speer Boulevard
267. Margery Reed Mayo Day Nursery, 1128 Twenty-Eighth Street
268. St. Dominic's Catholic Church, 2905 Federal Boulevard
269. Lake Middle School, 1820 Lowell Boulevard
270. Enos House, 841 Washington Street
271. Byers Junior High School–Denver School of Science and Technology, 150 South Pearl Street
272. Edison Elementary School, 3350 Quitman Street
273. Littleton Creamery–Beatrice Foods Cold Storage–Ice House Lofts, 1801 Wynkoop Street
274. Huddart Terrace, 625 East Sixteenth Avenue
275. Milo A. Smith House, 1360 Birch Street
276. Shorter African Methodist Episcopal Church, 119 Park Avenue West
277. Benjamin Brown House, 410 Marion Street
278. Cuthbert-Dines House, 1350 Logan Street
279. Helene Apartments, 1062 Pearl Street
280. Kinneavy Terrace, 2700–14 Stout Street
281. Fifth Church of Christ Scientist, 1477 Columbine Street
282. Arthur E. Pierce House, 24 East Ellsworth Avenue
283. Nagel House, 2335 Stout Street
284. Kaub House, 2343 Stout Street
285. Lincoln Elementary School, 710 South Pennsylvania Street
286. Ross-Lewin Double, 1912–18 Logan Street
287. Westside Courthouse, 924 West Colfax Avenue
288. Grant House, 100 South Franklin Street
289. Highlands United Methodist Church, 3131 Osceola Street

290. Hayes Townhouses, 1732 and 1738 Pearl Street
291. Seventh Avenue Congregational Church, 678 King Street
292. Arcanum Apartments–Beldame Apartments, 1904 Logan Street
293. Steck Elementary School, 425 Ash Street
294. Epworth Church/Community Center, 1130 Thirty-First Street
295. Dugal Farmhouse, 4775 East Sixth Avenue
296. Leeman Auto Company, 550 Broadway Street
297. Amos B. Hughes House, 3600 Clay Street
298. Bethesda Chapel and Gateway–Denver Academy, 4400 East Iliff Avenue
299a. Ten-Winkel Apartments, 404–10 West Twelfth Avenue
299b. Carpenter Gothic Houses, 1173–79 Delaware Street
300. The Colonnade, 1210 East Colfax Avenue
301. Aromor Apartment Building, 225 East Thirteenth Avenue
302. 1750 Gilpin Building, 1750 Gilpin Street
303. Evans School, 1115 Acoma Street
304. Hamilton Apartment Building, 1475 Humboldt Street
305. Norman Apartments, 99 South Downing Street
306. Cameron United Methodist Church, 1600 South Pearl Street
307. Neahr House, 1017 South Race Street
308. Globeville School, 5100 Lincoln Street
309. Church of the Ascension, 600 Gilpin Street
310. Wolf House, 2036 Ogden Street
311. Union Station, 1701–77 Wynkoop Street
312. Fairmount Mausoleum, 430 South Quebec Street
313. Doyle-Benton House, 1301 Lafayette Street
314. Tammen Hall, 1010 East Nineteenth Avenue

315. Catherine Mullen Nurses' Home–Mullen Building, 1895 Franklin Street
316. Baur's Confectionary Company, 1512–14 Curtis Street
317. John Collins United Methodist Church, 2320 South Bannock Street
318. Myrtle Hill School–Washington Park School Annex–Myrtle Hill Lofts, 1125 South Race Street
319. Kappler-Cannon-Fieger House, 1904 Kearney Street
320. Schulz-Neef House, 1739 East Twenty-Ninth Avenue
321. Stanley School–Montclair School–Paddington Station Preschool, 1301 Quebec Street
322. Fitzroy Place–Warren-Iliff Mansion, 2160 South Cook Street
323. Hangar 61–Ideal Basic Cement Company Corporate Hangar, 8695 East Twenty-First Avenue
324. Epiphany Episcopal Church, 100 Colorado Boulevard
325. Petrikin Estate, 2109 East Ninth Avenue
326. Amter Residence, 222 South Fairfax Street
327. American Woodman's Life Building, 2100 Downing Street
328. Governor Ralph L. Carr Residence, 747 Downing Street
329. Benjamin Moore Paint Company, 2500 Walnut Street
330. Holland House, 2340 South Josephine Street
331. The Waldman, 1515 East Ninth Avenue
332. Bonfils Memorial Theater–Lowenstein Theater–Tattered Cover Bookstore, 1475 Elizabeth Street
333. Margaret Long House, 2070 Colorado Boulevard
334. Beth Eden Baptist Church, 3241 Lowell Boulevard
335. Nicoletti–Gulliver-Lynch House, 227 South Lincoln Street

Appendix B

Denver Historic Districts by Designation Number

HD-1 Larimer Square Historic District

HD-2 Humboldt Street Historic District

HD-3 Ninth Street Park Historic District

HD-4 Clements Addition Historic District

HD-5 Montclair Historic District

HD-6 Civic Center Historic District

HD-7 Smith's Ditch / City Ditch Historic District

HD-8 Morgan's Addition Historic District

HD-9 No District Number 9

HD-10 West Twenty-Eighth Avenue–Stoneman's Row Historic District

HD-11 Old Highland Historic Business District

HD-12 Snell's Subdivision Historic District

HD-13 Potter Highlands Historic District

HD-14 Lafayette Street Historic District

HD-15 Lower Downtown Historic District

HD-16 Speer Boulevard Historic District

HD-17 City Park Pavilion Historic District

HD-18 Country Club Historic District

HD-19 Quality Hill Historic District

HD-20 Witter-Cofield Historic District

HD-21 East Seventh Avenue Parkway Historic District

HD-22 Wyman Historic District

HD-23 East Park Place Historic District

HD-24 Florence F. Martin Ranch Historic District

HD-25 Curtis Park "B" Historic District

HD-26 Curtis Park "A" Historic District

HD-27 Lowry Technical Training Center Historic District

HD-28 Lowry Officers' Row Historic District

HD-29 City Beautiful Parkways Historic District

HD-30 Curtis Park "C" Historic District

HD-31 Pennsylvania Street Historic District

HD-32 Curtis Park "D" Historic District

HD-33 Sherman-Grant Historic District

HD-34 Clayton College Historic District

HD-35 Swallow Hill Historic District

HD-36 Alamo Placita Historic District

HD-37 Baker Neighborhood Historic District

HD-38 Downtown Denver Historic District

HD-39 Country Club Gardens Historic District

HD-40 Five Points Historic Cultural District

HD-41 Park Avenue Historic District

HD-42 Ballpark Historic District

HD-43 Driving Park Historic District

HD-44 Humboldt Street–Park Avenue Historic District

HD-45 Grant Street Historic District

HD-46 Wolff Place Historic District

HD-47 Deboer Historic District

HD-48 Curtis Park "E" Historic District

HD-49 Curtis Park "F" Historic District

HD-50 Curtis Park "G" Historic District

HD-51 Allen M. Ghost Historic District

HD-52 Curtis Park "H" Historic District

Appendix C

Denver Landmark Preservation Commissioners*

Archuletta, Lena (1984–87)

Arndt, Helen Millet (1967–83)

Atchison, Philip (1967–69)

Barry, Joseph B. (1974–85)

Bershof, James F. (2000–2012)

Bishop, Tina

Buchanan, Brad

Catherwood, Jean (1986–92)

Christman, Abigail (2014–2016)

Corbett, Kathleen (2013–)

Duckett-Emke, Andy (2012–)

Elfenbein, Sharon (2010–16)

Falkenberg, Ruth (1979–91)

Ferril, Thomas Hornsby (1972–78)

Fisher, Alan (1967–78)

Flores, Philip A. (1991–?)

Foster, Paul (1983–88)

Fuller, Mrs. (Frances Walker) Pierpont (1967–79)

Gibson, Barbara (2006–14)

Goldstein, Martin (2009–)

Greenblatt, Sarah

Hart, Gerald T. (1967–74)

Hiraga, Eric (2010–12)

Hoeft, Kathy (1990–92)

Holdorf, Ryan (2012–)

Hornbein, Marjorie (1986–92)

Hornby, Barbara Sudler (1992–?)

Humphries, Dennis (2006–14)

Jordy, Charles (2010–)

Leonard, Stephen J. (1994–2011)

Maiz, Chris

Mazzula, Fred M. (1967–81)

McCarthy, Sarah

McConnell, Carla (2006–11)

Milstein, Philip (1967–84, 1987–90)

Morgan, James C. (1978–92)

Morris, Langdon East, Jr. (1972–83)

Noel, Thomas J. (1983–94)

Norgren, Barbara S. (1979–91, 1993–20??)

Nunnally, Sharon L. (1992–9?)

Pouw, Stanley (1991–92)

Rogers, John

Root, Robert (1992)

Rosenman, Seth (1992–95)

Schneider, Roslyn Yamashita (1990–94)

Shalkey, Edward (2008–12)

Stearns, Robert L. (1967–72)

Sudler, James A. (1967–72)

Swett, B. Storey (1992)

Vigil, Lance (2012–13)

Walter, Douglas (2014–)

White, Edward D., Jr. (1969–92)

Zimmer, Amy (2012–)

* Please pardon this incomplete list. If you can supply names and dates of service, please contact tom.noel@ucdenver.edu.

Appendix D

Lost and Undesignated Denver Landmarks

Aladdin Theater (1926; Frederick W. Ireland Jr.), 2010 East Colfax Street (demolished 1984)

Albany Hotel (1885–1930s; remodel and expansion Burnham Hoyt), Seventeenth and Stout Streets (demolished 1977)

Apollo Hall (1859; Libeus Barney), 1425 Larimer Street (burned down 1892)

Arapahoe County Courthouse (1883; Frederick C. Eberley), Sixteenth Street and Court Place (demolished 1933)

Arapahoe School (1872), Eighteenth and Arapahoe Streets (demolished 1955)

Archer Home–Denver Municipal Dispensary (1875), Thirteenth and Welton Streets (demolished 1925)

Argo Smelter (1878; Robert S. Roeschlaub), Vasquez Boulevard and I-70 (demolished 1910)

Ashland School (1874–82; William Quayle; 1894 addition), West Twenty-Ninth Avenue (demolished 1975)

Bancroft Block (1880; Robert S. Roeschlaub), Sixteenth and Stout Streets (demolished 1902)

Barth Block (1882; Robert S. Roeschlaub), 1210 Sixteenth Street (demolished 1946)

Bennett-Chappell House (1880s; A. Quayle), 1300 Logan Street (demolished 1970)

William D. Bethell–Lawrence Phipps House (1893; Theodore D. Boal), 1154 East Colfax Avenue (demolished ca. 1925)

Charles Boettcher House (188?; John J. Huddart), 1201 Grant Street demolished 1953)

Charles Boettcher II Home (1922; Jules Jacques Benoit Benedict?), 777 Washington Street (demolished 1963)

Boettcher School (1940; Burnham Hoyt), 1900 Downing Street (demolished 1992?)

Brinton Terrace (1882; Ernest P. Varian and Frederick J. Sterner), 23–37 East Eighteenth Avenue, northwest corner; 1803–7 Lincoln Street (demolished 1956)

Broadway School (1875; Robert S. Roeschlaub), 1300 Broadway Street (demolished 1923)

Henry C. Brown–Horace A.W. Tabor Mansion (1870s), Seventeenth and Broadway Streets (demolished ca. 1903)

John Sidney Brown House (189?), 909 Grant Street (demolished 1968)

Byers-Porter House (1883), 1510 Sherman Street (demolished ca. 1919)

Cactus Club (1925; Burnham Hoyt), 441 Fourteenth Street and Glenarm Place (demolished 1969)

California Building (1892; Frank E. Edbrooke), Seventeenth and California Streets (demolished 1961)

John F. Campion House (ca. 1900; Aaron M. Gove and Thomas F. Walsh), northeast corner of East Eighth Avenue and Logan Street (demolished 1963)

Central Bank (1911; Jules Jacques Benoit Benedict), 1100–1108 Fifteenth Street, corner of Arapahoe Street (demolished 1990)

Central Presbyterian Church (1875; Robert S. Roeschlaub), Eighteenth and Champa Streets (demolished by fire ca. 1906 after being moved to East 23rd Avenue and Ogden Street)

Chamber of Commerce Building (1884; Frank E. Edbrooke), Fourteenth and Lawrence Streets (demolished 1967)

Cheesman Block (1881), Seventeenth and Larimer Streets (demolished 1971)

Chever Block (1879; Robert S. Roeschlaub), 1701 Larimer Street (demolished 1971?)

John B. Church Residence (1890; Robert S. Roeschlaub), 900 Pennsylvania Street (demolished 1965)

William Church "Castle" Residence (1890; William A. Lang and Marshall R. Pugh), 1000 Corona Street (demolished 1965)

Clark, Gruber and Company Bank and Mint (1860), Sixteenth and Market Streets (demolished 1909)

Club Building (1892; Frank E. Edbrooke), 1725–39 Arapahoe Street (demolished 1955)

Colorado National Bank (1882; William H.J. Nichols and Leo Canmann), 1701 Larimer Street (demolished 1939)

Constitution Hall (1865, 1870s additions), 1501–7 Blake Street (burned down 1977)

Continental Oil Building (1927; William North Bowman), 1755 Glenarm Place and Eighteenth Street (demolished 1976)

Cooper Building (1895; Frank E. Edbrooke), Seventeenth and Curtis Streets (demolished 1970)

Curtis and Clarke Building (1874), 1644–50 Larimer Street (demolished ca. 1964)

Delgany School (1885; Robert S. Roeschlaub), Twenty-First and Delgany Streets (demolished 1917)

Denham Theater, 635 Eighteenth and California Streets (demolished 1974)

Denver City Hall (1883; William H.J. Nichols), Fourteenth and Larimer Streets (demolished 1937)

The Denver Club (1889; Ernest P. Varian and Frederick J. Sterner), Seventeenth Street and Glenarm Place (demolished 1953)

Denver High School (1889; Robert S. Roeschlaub), Nineteenth to Twentieth and Stout to California Streets (demolished 1929)

Ebert School (1880; Robert S. Roeschlaub), Twenty-Second and Logan Streets (demolished 1924)

Eleventh Street School (1861, 1873 addition), Eleventh and Lawrence Streets (became the Washington School and was demolished 1884?)

Ernest and Cranmer Building (1890; Frank E. Edbrooke), Seventeenth and Curtis Streets (demolished 1963)

Essex Building (1887; Frank E. Edbrooke), 1617 Lawrence Street (demolished ca. 1970)

John Evans House (186?), Fourteenth and Arapahoe Streets (demolished ca. 1910)

John Evans II House (1911; William E. Fisher and Arthur A. Fisher), 2001 East Alameda Avenue, northeast corner of Race Street (demolished ca. 1968)

John A. Ferguson Mansion, East Seventh Avenue, corner of Washington Street (demolished ?)

First Baptist Church (1883; Frank E. Edbrooke), 230 East Fourteenth Avenue (demolished 1937)

Donald K. Fletcher Mansion (1892), 1575 Grant Street (demolished 1961)

Gettysburg Cyclorama Building (1886), 1726 Champa Street (demolished 1906)

Gilpin School (1881; Robert S. Roeschlaub), Twenty-Ninth Street between Stout and California Streets (demolished 1951)

Golden Eagle Dry Goods (1880; Frank E. Edbrooke), 1600 Lawrence Street (demolished 1971)

Peter Gottesleben Residence (1888; Robert S. Roeschlaub), 1901 Sherman Street (demolished ?)

Grant Smelter Stack (1892), 4100 Arkins Court (demolished 1950)

Guldman-Bonfils Mansion (1912; Aaron M. Gove and Thomas F. Walsh), 1500 East Tenth Avenue, southeast corner of Humboldt Street (demolished 196?)

Haish Manual Training School (1888; Robert S. Roeschlaub), Fourteenth and Arapahoe Streets (demolished 197?)

Nathaniel P. Hill Residence (1881; Robert S. Roeschlaub), Fourteenth and Welton Streets (demolished 1934)

Holzman House (1890; Ernest P. Varian and Frederick J. Sterner), 1772 Grant Street (demolished 19?)

Lafayette Hughes Mansion (1920s; William E. Fisher and Arthur A. Fisher), Polo Club (demolished 192?)

Hyperbolic Parabaloid (1958; I. M. Pei), Sixteenth Street and Court Place (demolished 1996)

Interstate Trust Building (1891; Frank E. Edbrooke), 1132 Sixteenth Street, corner of Lawrence Street (demolished 1970)

Iron Building (1891; John W. Roberts), Seventeenth and Arapahoe Streets (demolished 1969)

Charles M. Kittredge Mansion (1893; John J. Huddart), East Eighth Avenue and Oneida Street (demolished 1956)

Charles B. Kountze Home (1875; William H.J. Nichols), Fourteenth and Welton Streets (demolished ?)

Charles B. Kountze Mansion (1882; A. W. Fuller), 1601 Grant Street, northwest corner of East Sixteenth Avenue (demolished 1959)

Lafayette (Maria Mitchell) School (1898–1901; Robert S. Roeschlaub), Lafayette Street and 1335 East Thirty-Second Avenue (burned down 1970)

Longfellow School (1882; Robert S. Roeschlaub), Thirteenth and Welton Streets (demolished 1956)

Majestic Building (1894; Frank E. Edbrooke), Sixteenth and Broadway Streets (demolished 1977)

Markham Hotel (1882; Frank E. Edbrooke?), 1654 Lawrence Street, corner of Seventeenth Street (demolished 1969)

John McMurtrie–John Good Mansion (1892; Issac Hodgson), 1007 Pennsylvania Street (demolished 1965)

McPhee Block (1890; Frank E. Edbrooke; 1920 remodel as the C. A. Johnson Building), Seventeenth Street and Glenarm Place (demolished 1975)

Metropole Hotel and Broadway Theater–Cosmopolitan Hotel (1890; Frank E. Edbrooke), Eighteenth and Broadway Streets (demolished 1984)

Metropolitan Building, 1612 Court Place (demolished ca. 1978)

Mining Exchange Building (1891; Kirchner and Kirchner), Fifteenth and Arapahoe Streets (demolished 1963)

Moffat House, Fourteenth and Curtis Streets (demolished 192?)

Moffat Mansion (ca. 1900; Harry Manning), northeast corner of East Eighth Avenue and Grant Street (demolished 1972)

Morey-Guggenheim House (189?; Aaron M. Gove), 1555 Sherman Street, southwest corner of East Sixteenth Avenue (demolished 1953)

John K. Mullen House (1898), 896 Pennsylvania Street (demolished 19?)

New Isis Theater (1912; Robert S. Roeschlaub), 1716–26 Curtis Street (demolished 1954)

Old Post Office, Customs House, and Federal Building (1892), Arapahoe and Sixteenth Streets (demolished 1965)

Orpheum Theater (1903; Marean and Norton; 1930, demolished and rebuilt as the New Orpheum Theater), 1537 Welton Street (demolished 1967)

Paddock–H. Wolcott Residence (ca. 1890; Harry Ten Eyck Wendell), 1751 Glenarm Place (demolished 1925)

Palace Theater, Fifteenth and Blake Streets (demolished ?)

Patterson Block (1924), Seventeenth and Welton Streets (demolished 1975)

Thomas M. Patterson Residence (1883; Robert S. Roeschlaub), Seventeenth and Welton Streets (demolished ca. 1923)

Pearce Mansion–Democratic Club, 1712 Sherman Street (demolished ?)

Pioneer Building (1888), 1501 Larimer Street (demolished 1971)

Quincy Block (18??; Frank E. Edbrooke), 1012 Seventeenth Street, corner of Arapahoe Street (demolished ?)

Railroad Building (1888), 1511 Larimer Street (demolished 1971)

Republic Building (1928; George Meredith Musick Sr.), Sixteenth Street and Tremont Place (demolished 1981)

Robert S. Roeschlaub Residence (1880; Robert S. Roeschlaub), West Colfax Avenue and Delaware Street (demolished ?)

Platt Rogers Mansion (1884; Ernest P. Varian), East Colfax Avenue, corner of Washington Street (demolished ca. 1957)

Security-Midland Bank (1927; William E. Fisher and Arthur A. Fisher), Seventeenth and California Streets (demolished 1993?)

Shorthorn Building (1889; Frank E. Edbrooke), Twenty-Third and Larimer Streets (demolished 199?)

Skyline Park (1973; Lawrence Halprin and Associates), Arapahoe Street between Fifteenth and Eighteenth Streets (demolished 2000)

Sloan's Lake Depot (1890; Robert S. Roeschlaub), Sheridan Boulevard and West Twenty-Fifth Avenue (demolished 19??)

Sopris Duplex (1886; Robert S. Roeschlaub), 1337 Stout Street (demolished 19??)

St. Leo's Church (1898?), Tenth Street and West Colfax Avenue (demolished 1965)

Strand–State Theater (1914; 1925 modernization as the State Theater), 1630 Curtis Street (demolished 1953)

Tabor Block (1879; Willoughby Edbrooke and Frank E. Edbrooke), Sixteenth and Larimer Streets (demolished 1972)

Tabor Grand Opera House (1880; Willoughby Edbrooke and Frank E. Edbrooke), Sixteenth and Curtis Streets (demolished 1964)

Tabor Mansion, 1260 Sherman Street (demolished 1968)

Charles S. Thomas House (1882; 1892 expansion and remodel; Frederick Sterner), 1609 Sherman Street (demolished 1960)

Times Building (1881; Robert S. Roeschlaub), 1547–72 Arapahoe Street (demolished 19??)

Tuxedo Place (1880; Robert S. Roeschlaub), East Colfax Avenue, northeast corner of Downing Street (demolished 1???)

Twenty-Fourth Street School (1879; Robert S. Roeschlaub), Twenty-Fourth and Walnut Streets (burned down 1934)

Uncle Dick Wootton's Hall (1859; Richens L. Wootton), Eleventh and Walnut Streets (demolished ?)

Union Block (1882; Robert S. Roeschlaub), Sixteenth and Arapahoe Streets (demolished 1963)

Unity Temple (1887; Frank E. Edbrooke), Nineteenth and Broadway Streets (demolished ?)

Welcome Arch (1906; Mary Woodsen), Seventeenth and Wynkoop Streets (demolished 1931)

West Court Hotel (1911; Robert Willison and Montana Fallis), 1415 Glenarm Place (demolished 1982)

Whittier School (1883; Robert S. Roeschlaub), Marion Street between East Twenty-Fourth and East Twenty-Fifth Avenues (demolished 1974)

Windsor Hotel (1880–1960), Eighteenth and Larimer Streets (demolished 1959)

Wolfe Hall (1867), Seventeenth and Champa Streets (demolished 1888)

Roger W. Woodbury Mansion (1889; Leonard Cutshaw), 2501 Woodbury Court (demolished 1958)

B. F. Woodward Residence (1889; Frank E. Edbrooke), 1530 Sherman Street (demolished 2007)

Wyman Elementary School (1890; Robert S. Roeschlaub), East Seventeenth Avenue and Williams Street (demolished 1975)

Zang Brewing Company (1859; many additions), Sixth to Ninth Streets between Platte and Water Streets (demolished ?)

Bibliography

General Works

Arps, Louisa Ward. *Denver in Slices*. Denver: Sage Books, 1959, 1983 and 1998 reprints. Foreword by Thomas J. Noel. 274 pages. Maps, illustrations, endnotes, index.

Barnhouse, Mark A. *Lost Denver*. Charleston, SC: Arcadia, 2015. 127 pages. Illustrations.

Brettell, Richard B. *Historic Denver: The Architects and the Architecture, 1858–1893*. Denver: Historic Denver, Inc., 1973. 240 pages. Index, bibliography, notes, illustrations.

Bretz, James. *The Mansions of Denver: The Vintage Years*. Boulder: Pruett, 2005. 207 pages. Illustrations, bibliography, maps, index.

Chandler, Mary Voelz. *Guide to Denver Architecture*, 2nd ed. Golden, CO: Fulcrum, 2013. 324 pages. Index, black-and-white photographs, maps.

Chandler, Roger A. *Fentress Bradburn Architects*. Washington, DC: Studio Press, 1995. 223 pages. Bibliography, appendixes, color and black-and-white illustrations.

City Club of Denver. *Art in Denver*. Denver: Denver Public Library, 1928. 59 pages. Illustrations, index.

Dallas, Sandra. *Cherry Creek Gothic: Victorian Architecture in Denver*. Norman: University of Oklahoma Press, 1971. 292 pages. Illustrations, map.

Davis, Sally, and Betty Baldwin. *Denver Dwellings and Descendants*. Denver: Sage Books, 1963. 250 pages. Illustrations bibliography, index.

Denver City and County. Check the website (www.denvergov.org) for information on the Denver Landmark Preservation Commission and for the latest list of landmarks and historic districts.

Denver Landmark Preservation Commission. *Design Guideline for Landmark Structures and Districts*. Denver: Denver Planning Office, 1995. 54 pages. Illustrations.

Denver Landmark Preservation Commission. Files of individual and district nominations in the Denver Public Library's Western History and Genealogy Department and in the Denver Community Planning and Development Office.

Denver Municipal Facts. Denver: City and County of Denver, 1909–31. (Initially a weekly, then a monthly magazine)

Etter, Don D. *Denver Going Modern: A Photographic Essay on the Imprint of the International Style on Denver Residential Architecture*. Denver: Graphic Impressions, 1977. 132 pages. Illustrations, index.

Etter, Don D. *Denver's Park and Parkway System National Register Nomination*. Denver: Colorado Historical Society, 1986. 23 pages. Illustrations.

Forest, Kenton, Gene McKeever, and Raymond McAllister. *History of the Public Schools of Denver: A Brief History and Complete Building Survey*. Denver: Tramway, 1989. 64 pages. Illustrations, bibliography.

Goodstein, Phil. *Denver Streets: Names, Numbers, Locations, Logic*. Denver: New Social Publications, 1994. 144 pages. Maps, illustrations, bibliography, index.

Haber, Francine, Kenneth R. Fuller, and David N. Wetzel. *Robert S. Roeschlaub: Architect of the Emerging West, 1843–1923*. Denver: Colorado Historical Society, 1988. 168 pages. Illustrations, endnotes, index.

History Colorado, Office of Archaeology and Historic Preservation. *National and State Register of Historic Properties*. Denver: History Colorado. Frequently updated online at http://www.historycolorado.org/OAHP. This office also has extensive files on designated and potential Colorado and Denver landmarks.

Kohl, Edith Eudora. *Denver's Historic Mansions*. Denver: Sage Books, 1957. 268 pages. Illustrations.

Leonard, Stephen J., and Thomas J. Noel. *Denver: Mining Camp to Metropolis*. Niwot: University Press of Colorado, 1990,

1994 reprint. 544 pages. Maps, illustrations, endnotes, appendixes, bibliography, index.

McAlester, Virginia, and Lee McAlester. *A Field Guide to American Houses*. New York: Knopf, 2014. 848 pages. Illustrations, index.

Morris, Langdon East, Jr. *Denver Landmarks*. Denver: Charles W. Cleworth, 1979. 324 pages. Maps, illustrations, index.

Murphy, Jack A. *Geology Tour of Denver's Buildings and Monuments*. Denver: Denver Museum of Natural History and Historic Denver, Inc., 1995. 96 pages. Illustrations, bibliography, index.

Musick, G. Meredith, Sr. *Wayfarer in Architecture*. Denver: Privately printed, 1976. 100 pages. Illustrations.

Noel, Thomas J. *Buildings of Colorado*. New York: Oxford University Press, 1997. 669 pages. Illustrations, index, glossary of architectural terms, bibliography, maps.

Noel, Thomas J. *Colorado Catholicism and the Archdiocese of Denver, 1857–1989*. Niwot: University Press of Colorado, 1989. 468 pages. Maps, illustrations, bibliography, index.

Noel, Thomas J. *Guide to Colorado Historic Places: Sites Supported by the Colorado Historical Society's State Historical Fund*. Englewood, CO: Westcliffe, 2007. 391 pages. Photos, maps, index.

Noel, Thomas J., and Barbara S. Norgren. *Denver: The City Beautiful and Its Architects*. Denver: Historic Denver, Inc., 1987, 1993 reprint. 248 pages. Illustrations, bibliography, glossary of architectural terms, index, biographical dictionary of Denver architects.

Noel, Thomas J., and Amy B. Zimmer. *Showtime: Denver's Performing Arts, Convention Centers and Theatre District*. Denver: Denver Theatres and Arenas, 2008. 144 pages. Over 400 color and black-and-white photos, index, sources.

Paglia, Michael, and Diane Wray Tomasso. *Photos by Kathleen Roach: The Mid-Century Modern House in Denver*. Denver: Historic Denver, Inc., 2007. 96 pages. Illustrations, maps.

Paglia, Michael, Rodd L. Wheaton, and Diane Wray Tomasso. *Denver: The Modern City*. Denver: Historic Denver, Inc., 1999. 96 pages. Maps, sources, index.

Pearson, Michelle. *Historic Denver Landmarks for Children and Families*. Denver: Historic Denver, Inc., 2007. 96 pages. Maps, sources, index.

Pearson, Michelle. *Historic Sacred Places of Denver*. Denver: Historic Denver, Inc., 2004. 96 pages. Maps, sources, index.

Smiley, Jerome C. *History of Denver: With Outlines of the Earlier History of the Rocky Mountain Country*. Denver: Times-Sun Publishing, 1901. 978 pages. Illustrations, index, maps.

Wilk, Diane. *A Guide to Denver's Architectural Styles and Terms*. Denver: Denver Museum of Natural History and Historic Denver, Inc., 1995. 96 pages. Illustrations.

Zimmer, Amy B. *Denver's Historic Homes: Images of America*. Charleston, SC: Arcadia, 2013. 127 pages. Photos.

Central Denver Neighborhoods

Bakke, Diane, and Jackie Davis. *Places around the Bases: A Historic Tour of Coors Field Neighborhood*. Englewood, CO: Westcliff, 1995. 177 pages. Map, illustrations, index.

Ballast, David Kent. *Denver's Civic Center: A Walking Tour*. Denver: City Publishing, 1977. 30 pages. Maps, illustrations.

Barnhouse, Mark A. *Denver's Sixteenth Street*. Charleston, SC: Arcadia, 2010. 127 pages. Black-and-white photographs, map.

Brenneman, Bill. *Miracle on Cherry Creek: An Informal History of the Birth and Rebirth of a Neighborhood*. Denver: Central Bank and Trust, 1973. 130 pages. Illustrations, bibliography.

Etter, Don D. *Auraria: Where Denver Began*. Boulder: Colorado Associated University Press, 1972. 99 pages. Maps, illustrations.

Everett, Derek R. *The Colorado State Capitol: History, Politics, Preservation*. Boulder: University Press of Colorado, 2005. 244 pages. Photos, appendixes, endnotes, bibliography, index.

Gibson, Barbara. *The Lower Downtown Historic District*. Denver: Denver Museum of Natural History and Historic Denver, Inc., 1995. 96 pages. Illustrations, index.

Goodstein, Phil. *How the West Side Won: The History of West Denver*. Denver: New Social Publications, 2015. 474 pages. Photos, maps, bibliography, index.

Noel, Thomas J. *The Denver Athletic Club 1884–1984*. Denver: Denver Athletic Club, 1983. 106 pages. Illustrations, bibliography, index.

Noel, Thomas J. *Denver's Larimer Street: Main Street, Skid Row, and Urban Renaissance*. Denver: Historic Denver, Inc., 1982. 196 pages. Maps, illustrations, index.

Noel, Thomas J. *Growing through History with Colorado: The Colorado National Banks, 1862–1987*. Denver: University of Colorado at Denver, Colorado Studies Center, 1987. 160 pages. Illustrations, bibliography, index.

Pierson, Francis J. *Getting to Know Denver: Five Fabulous Walking Tours: Experiencing Denver's History through Architecture*. Denver: Charlotte Square, 2006. 211 pages. Photos, maps, appendix, index.

Capitol Hill Neighborhoods

Arps, Louisa Ward, and Bernice East Peters. *Cemetery to Conservatory and a Jubilee History of Denver Botanic Gardens, 1951–1976*. Denver: Denver Botanic Gardens, Inc,, 1980. 72 pages. Index, notes and references, illustrations, map.

Bakemeier, Alice Millett. *Country Club Heritage: A History and Guide to a Denver Neighborhood.* Foreword by Barbara Hornby Sudler. Denver: Heritage, 2000. 234 pages. Index, sources, endnotes, photos, maps.

Beck, Rhonda, and Diane Gordon. *Northwest Congress Park Neighborhood.* Denver: Historic Denver, Inc., 2004. 96 pages. Maps, illustrations, bibliography, index.

Goodstein, Phil. *Denver's Capitol Hill: One Hundred Years of Life in a Vibrant Urban Neighborhood.* Introduction by Thomas J. Noel. Denver: Life Publications, 1988. 182 pages. Index, photos, drawings, appendixes, notes.

Goodstein, Phil. *The Ghosts of Denver: Capitol Hill.* Denver: New Social Publications, 1996. 538 pages. Photos, bibliography, index.

Grinstead, Leigh A., Steve Grinstead Fletcher, and Gheda Gayou. *Molly Brown's Capitol Hill Walking Tour.* Denver: Historic Denver, Inc., 1995. 104 pages. Map, illustrations, bibliography.

Murphy, Jack. *A Geology Tour of Denver's Capitol Hill Stone Buildings.* Denver: Historic Denver, Inc., 1997. 96 pages. Maps, illustrations, bibliography, index.

Simmons, Laurie, and Thomas H. Simmons. *East Colfax Avenue.* Denver: Historic Denver, Inc., 2007. 96 pages. Map, sources, index.

Student, Annette L. *Historic Cheesman Park Neighborhood.* Denver: Historic Denver, Inc., 1999. 96 pages. Maps, index, sources.

Widmann, Nancy. *The East Seventh Avenue Historic District.* Denver: Historic Denver, Inc., 1997. 96 pages. Maps, sources.

Wilk, Diane. *The Wyman Historic District.* Denver: Denver Museum of Natural History and Historic Denver, Inc., 1995. 96 pages. Illustrations.

Zimmer, Amy B. *Denver's Capitol Hill Neighborhood: Images of America.* Charleston, SC: Arcadia, 2009. 127 pages. Index, photos.

Northeast Denver Neighborhoods

Etter, Carolyn, and Don Etter. *The Denver Zoo.* Niwot, CO: Roberts Rinehart, 1996. 237 pages. Illustrations, sources, index.

Goodstein, Phil. *Curtis Park, Five Points, the Heart of Historic East Denver and Beyond.* Denver: New Social Publications, 2014. 438 pages. Photos, bibliography, index.

Peters, Bette D. *Denver's City Park.* Rev. ed. Boulder: Johnson, 1986. 67 pages. Maps, illustrations, notes, index.

Raughton, Jim L. *Whittier Neighborhood and San Rafael Historic District.* Denver: Historic Denver, Inc., 2004. 96 pages. Maps, sources, index.

Snow, Shawn M. *Denver's City Park and Whittier Neighborhoods: Images of America.* Charleston, SC: Arcadia, 2009. 127 pages. Bibliography.

West, William A. *Curtis Park: A Denver Neighborhood.* Boulder: Colorado Associated University Press, 1980. 88 pages. Maps, photographs by Don Etter.

West, William Allen. *Curtis Park: Denver's Oldest Neighborhood.* Denver: Historic Denver, Inc., 2002. 96 pages. Maps, sources.

Northwest Denver Neighborhoods

Barnhouse, Mark A. *Northwest Denver.* Charleston, SC: Arcadia, 2012. 127 pages. Black-and-white photographs, map.

Goodstein, Phil. *North Side Story: Denver's Most Intriguing Neighborhood.* Denver: New Social Publications, 2011. 570 pages. Black-and-white photographs, bibliography, index, maps, notes.

Sagstetter, Beth, ed. *Side by Side: A History of Denver's Witter-Cofield Historic District.* Denver: C and M Press, 1995. 299 pages. Maps, illustrations, bibliography, index.

Wiberg, Ruth Eloise. *Rediscovering Northwest Denver: Its History, Its People, Its Landmarks.* Boulder: Pruett, 1976. 212 pages. Maps, index, bibliography, list of past and present street names.

Wilk, Diane. *The Potter-Highlands Historic District.* Denver: Historic Denver, Inc., 1997. 96 pages. Illustrations, maps, index.

Zelinger, Michael Jay. *West Side Story Relived.* Denver: West Side Reunion Committee, 1987. 288 pages. Illustrations.

South Denver Neighborhoods

Breck, Allen D. *From the Rockies to the World: The University of Denver, 1864–1989.* Denver: University of Denver, 1989. 228 pages. Illustrations, index.

Etter, Don D. *University Park: Four Walking Tours.* Denver: Graphic Impressions, 1974. 55 pages. Illustrations.

Fisher, Steve. *University Park and South Denver: Images of America.* Charleston, SC: Arcadia, 2009. 127 pages. Bibliography, photos, drawings, maps.

Goodstein, Phil. *South Denver Saga.* Denver: New Social Publications, 1991. 250 pages. Illustrations, bibliography, index.

Goodstein, Phil. *History of South Denver,* vol. 1: *The Spirits of South Broadway.* Denver: New Social Publications, 2008. 298 pages. Map, photos, endnotes, index.

McCarthy, Sarah O. *Denver's Washington Park.* Charleston, SC: Arcadia, 2014. 127 pages. Black-and-white photographs.

Van Wyke, Millie. *The Town of South Denver: Its People, Neighborhoods, and Events since 1858.* Boulder: Pruett, 1991. 150 pages. Maps, illustrations, bibliography, index.

Widmann, Nancy. *The Baker Historic District.* Denver: Historic Denver, Inc., 1999. 96 pages. Maps, sources.

Widmann, Nancy. *Washington Park.* Denver: Historic Denver, Inc., 2007. 96 pages. Maps, sources.

East Denver Neighborhoods

Bakemeier, Alice Millett. *Crestmoor Park Heritage: A History and Guide to a Denver Neighborhood.* Denver: Heritage, 2005. 120 pages. Index, bibliography, photos, maps.

Bakemeier, Alice Millett. *Hilltop Heritage: A History and Guide to a Denver Neighborhood.* Foreword by Thomas J. Noel. Denver: Cranmer Park and Hilltop Community Association, 1997. 155 pages. Index, bibliography, photos, maps.

Goodstein, Phil. *Park Hill Promise: The Search for an Idyllic Denver Neighborhood.* Denver: New Social Publications, 2011. 598 pages. Index, bibliography, black-and-white photographs, maps, notes.

Halaas, David F. *Fairmount and Historic Colorado.* Denver: Fairmount Cemetery Association, 1976. 104 pages. Illustrations.

Levy, Michael H., and Patrick M. Scanlan. *Pursuit of Excellence: A History of Lowry Air Force Base, 1937–1987.* Denver: Lowry Air Force Base History Office, 1988. 71 pages. Illustrations, chronology, index.

Noel, Thomas J. *Richthofen's Montclair: A Pioneer Denver Suburb: A Brief History, Illustrated Walking Tour, and Research Guide to Denver Houses and Neighborhood History.* Boulder: Pruett, 1976. 166 pages. Maps, illustrations, bibliography, index.

Noel, Thomas J., and William J. Hansen. *The Montclair Neighborhood.* Denver: Historic Denver, Inc., 1999. 112 pages. Maps, bibliography, index.

Noel, Thomas J., and William J. Hansen. *The Park Hill Neighborhood.* Denver: Historic Denver, Inc., 2002. 134 pages. Maps, sources, index.

Noel, Thomas J., and Chuck Woodward. *Lowry: Military Base to New Urban Community.* Denver: Historic Denver, Inc., 2002. 100 pages. Maps, sources, index.

Denver Mountain Parks

Noel, Thomas J. *Sacred Stones: Colorado's Red Rocks Park and Amphitheatre.* Denver: City and County of Denver, Arts and Venues, 2011. 136 pages. Color and black-and-white photographs, drawings, maps, appendixes, sources.

Rex-Atzet, Wendy, Sally L. White, and Erica D. Walker. *Denver's Mountain Parks: 100 Years of the Magnificent Dream.* Photography by John Fielder. Foreword by Thomas J. Noel. Afterword by W. Bart Berger. Silverthorne, CO: Denver Mountain Parks Foundation and John Fielder Publishing, 2013. 144 pages. Index, bibliography, color and black-and-white photos, drawings, maps.

About the Authors

Thomas Jacob Noel received a BA in history and an MA in library science from the University of Denver and an MA and a PhD in history from the University of Colorado at Boulder. He is a professor of history and director of public history and preservation at the University of Colorado at Denver and Director of the Center for Colorado Studies at the Denver Public Library. Tom is a columnist for *The Denver Post* and "Dr. Colorado" for Channel 9's *Colorado and Company*. Tom conducts walking tours of Denver neighborhoods, specializing in cemeteries, churches, libraries, saloons, and other prominent landmarks in Denver and Colorado. Tom is the author of forty-eight books, many dealing with Colorado landmarks. He served as a Denver Landmark commissioner, 1983–94, and as its chair; he also served as a National Register reviewer for Colorado. He and his wife, Vi, live in the historic Montclair neighborhood of East Denver. His books include *Richthofen's Montclair: A Pioneer Denver Suburb* (1976); *Denver: The City Beautiful and Its Architecture*, with Barbara S. Norgren (1987); *Denver: Mining Camp to Metropolis*, with Stephen J. Leonard (1990); *Colorado: The Highest State*, with Duane A. Smith (1995, 2011); *The City and the Saloon: Denver, 1858–1916* (1996); *Colorado: A Liquid History and Tavern Guide to the Highest State* (1999); *The Montclair Neighborhood*, with William J. Hansen (1999); *Buildings of Colorado* (2002); *Lowry: Military Base to New Urban Community*, with Chuck Woodward (2002); *The Park Hill Neighborhood*, with William J. Hansen (2002, 2012); *Guide to Colorado Historic Places* (2006); *Irish Denver*, with Dennis Gallagher and Jim Walsh (2012); *Colorado: A History of the Centennial State*, with Carl Abbott and Stephen J. Leonard (2013); and *Colorado: A Historical Atlas* (2015).

Nicholas J. Wharton received a BA in history and a BA in sociology from Colorado State University. He earned an MA in public history under the guidance of Thomas J. Noel and an MPA with a concentration in local government from the University of Colorado at Denver. In addition, he received a graduate certificate in historic preservation from the University of Colorado at Denver and garnered several awards, including the Ward Prize, Tryba Prize, and Coulter Scholarship. Nicholas has published multiple maps and book reviews and was an active member of Phi Alpha Theta History Society. He served as the 2011–14 King Fellow, one of the highest honored positions in the history department at the University of Colorado at Denver. In 2014 he received the Best & Brightest internship through the Department of Local Affairs and University of Colorado at Denver Public Affairs Department. Nicholas is now the Assistant Town Administrator for the Town of Severance. He and his wife, Christina Lee, live in Loveland, where they are immersed in history and enjoying the wonderful sites Colorado has to offer.

Index

1750 Gilpin Building, 80, 173

Aberdeen Quarry, 18
Abo, Ron, 93
Acacia Apartments, 82
Acacia Cemetery, 117
Accelerated Schools, 150
Adams, George H., 84
Adams, Noel, 48
Adams-Fitzell House, 84, 170
Aderente, Vincent, 21
Adrian, Brother, 47
Aeolian-Skinner, 57
African-American community, 103–8, 110, 142
Ainlay-Conley, Jacqui, xv
Aladdin Theater, 176
Alamo Placita Historic District, 66, 174
Alamo Placita Park, 66
Albany Hotel, 176
Albi, Chuck, xvi
Aldine Family Hotel, 74
Aldine-Grafton Apartments, 74, 75, 172
Allied Architects, 20
All Saints Episcopal Church-Chapel of Our Merciful
    Savior, 117, 170
Allyson, June, 128
Aloys, Sister Mary, xvi
Alvarez Morris Architects, 138
Amache Japanese Relocation Center, 78
Ambrusch, Julius P. 138
American Association of University Women, 91
American Institute of Architects, 8, 99
American Museum of Western Art, 24
American National Bank, 29, 172
American Woodman's Life Building, 108, 173
Amole, Gene, 25
Amter, Fred W., 158
Amter Residence, 153, 173
Amtrak, 43
Ancient Arabic Order of the Mystic Shrine, 57
Ancient Order of Hibernians, 118
Anderson, David, 123
Anderson, Monsignor John, xvi
Andrews, Jacques, and Rantoul, 28, 31

Andrews, Rantoul, and Jones, 95
Anfenger House, 100, 101, 171
Anfenger, Louis, 100
Anfenger, Milton, 100
Annunciation Catholic Church, 108, 109, 171
Anschutz, Philip, 23
Anthony, Emmett, 32, 102
Antioch College, 121
Apollo Hall, 176
Apollo Hall-Congdon Building, 36
Applebaum, Mark, xv
Arapahoe County, 4, 6
Arapahoe County Courthouse, 176
Arapahoe School, 176
Arbuthnot, Larry, 115
Arcanum Apartmens-Beldame Apartments, 58,
    173
Archdiocese of Denver, 102, 119
Archer Home-Denver Municipal Dispensary,
    176
Architectural Forum, 140, 168
Archuletta, Lena, 175
Argo Smelter, 87, 176
Armour Office Building, 12
Armstrong, Jasmine, xv
Arndt, Helen Millet, 175
Aromor Apartment Building, 56, 173
Arps, Louisa Ward, 94, 142
Arps House, 94
arson, 27, 42
Arthur House, 95
Art Deco style, 7, 10, 26, 27, 54, 60, 71, 79, 103,
    121, 137, 138, 141, 154, 160, 163
Art Moderne style, 54, 93
Arts and Crafts style, 134, 143
Art Students League of Denver, 139, 140, 172
Asbury, Francis, 116
Asbury Elementary School, 148, 172
Asbury Methodist Church, 9, 116, 169
Ashland School, 176
Ashley, Eli Melville, 160
Ashley Elementary School, 160, 171
Asset Investment Management, 44
Assistance League of Denver, 91

Assumption of Mary, 59
Atchison, Paul, 95
Atchison, Philip, 175
Atchison, Sandra Dallas *See* Dallas, Sandra
Atencio, Silvia, xvi
Athena, 72
Auraria (campus), 9, 38, 45, 46, 47, 49, 73
Auraria (town), 41, 45
Auraria Higher Education Center, 45, 48
Auraria Library, xv
Austin, Frank A., 91
Austin Apartments, 91, 172
Ave Maria Health Clinic, 47
Axtens, S. Arthur, 60, 154, 160

Baca, James, 109
Backus, Jason J., 46
Baerresen, Albert T., 57
Baerresen, Harold W., 43, 47, 57, 87, 107
Baerresen, Viggio, 43, 57, 107
Baerresen Brothers, 7, 57, 81, 87, 107, 108, 114, 115
Baerresen-Freeman House, 87, 170
Bailey, George M., Mansion, 73
Baker, Henry P., 60
Baker, James Hutchins, 137
Baker Junior High School, 137
Baker Neighborhood Historic District, 137, 174
Baker-Plested Cottage, 60, 170
Balcomb, Robert G., 73, 94, 139
Balcomb and Rice, 74, 114, 139
Balfour at Riverfront Park, 45
Ballpark Historic District, 102, 103, 174
Bancroft Block, 176
Baptist Home Missionary Society, 123
Barber, Michael, 30
Barber, Thomas T., 146
Bard House, 95
Barets, Sam, 115
Barlow, Kathleen, xv
Barnes, J.H., 114
Barney, Libeus, 36, 176
Barnhouse, Mark, xv, xvi
Barnum Building, 39, 171
Barrett, Marjorie, 25

Barrett, William, 25
Barrows, Stanley M., 132
Barry, Chips, xvi
Barry, Edward, S. J., 102
Barry, Joseph B., 175
Barth, M. Allen, 42
Barth Block, 176
Barth Hotel, 42, 171
Barton, Sister Eliza, 54
Basilica of St. Ambrogio, 144
Batschelet, Ralph, 93
Baur, Otto Paul, 33, 34
Baur's Confectionary Company, 33, 34, 173
Baxter Hotel, 103
Beatles, The, 168
Beaton, Gail, xv, xvi
Beatrice Creamery, 44
Beaux Arts, 7, 43, 72, 75, 83, 89, 93, 95, 124, 140, 143
Belcaro. *See* Phipps Mansion
Belcaro Realty and Investment Company, 146
Beldame Apartments, 58, 173
Bell, William A., 87, 113
Benedict, Jules Jacques Benoit, 7, 8, 27, 47, 60, 65, 66, 72, 83, 95, 105, 119, 125, 143, 154, 157, 158, 167, 176
Benedict, Mitchell, 68
Benjamin Moore Paint Company, 85, 102, 103, 173
Bennett, Edward H., 5, 17, 18
Bennett, Wagner, and Grody, 129
Bennett-Chappell House, 176
Benson, Lorenzo, 91
Benson-Orsborn House, 91, 92, 172
Benton, Frank, 78
Berger, Bart, xvi
Berkeley Lake Park, 126
Berkeley Neighborhood, 127, 128
Berkeley School, 127, 172
Bernard, The, 82
Bershof, James F. "Jim," xv, 175
Bessesen, Bill, xvi
Beth Eden Baptist Church, 129, 173
Bethel-Phipps House, 176
Bethesda Chapel and Gateway-Denver Academy, 12, 150, 173
Bettcher, George L., 65, 71, 72, 103, 161
Bewley, William W., 116
Bible, James A., 88
Bieluczyk, Sophie, xvi
Bingham, Hugh, xvi
Biscoe, Maurice, 7, 30, 54, 64, 83, 95, 110, 157, 158
Biscoe House, 95
Bishop, Tina, 18, 175
Black American West Museum, 9
Black Hawk, Colorado, 11, 54
Blake Street Bath and Racquet Club, 42, 171
Bliss, Gerald, 134
Bliss House, 134, 170
Blue Sky Studio, 21
Bluebird Theater, 93, 94, 171
Boal, Theodore, 7, 54, 63, 64, 176
Boal and Harnois, 137

Board of Capitol Managers, 19
Board of Trade, Denver, 38
Bockfinger-Flint Mercantile, 41, 170
Boettcher, Charles, 31, 62
Boettcher, Charles, House, 176
Boettcher, Charles II, Home, 176
Boettcher, Claude, 62
Boettcher Conservatory, 82, 83, 169
Boettcher Foundation, 62, 82
Boettcher School, 176
Bohm Mansion, 86
Bonfils, Belle, 92
Bonfils, Frederick G., 81, 92
Bonfils, Helen, 64, 92, 93
Bonfils Blood Bank, 64
Bonfils Memorial Theater-Lowenstein Theater-Tattered Cover Book Store, 92, 93, 173
Bonfils Theater (Denver Performing Arts Complex), 93
Bonnie Brae, 10
Borman, Rick, 103
Bosler, Ambrose, 126
Bosler-Yankee House, 126, 171
Boston Building, 9, 28, 31, 171
Boston Lofts, 31, 171
Bosworth, Joab, 91
Bosworth, Leora, 91
Bosworth House, 91, 170
Boulevard Congregational Church, 124
Bouvier-Lathrop House, 74
Bowman, William N., 19, 26, 56, 129, 134, 140, 141, 177
Boyer, John C., 115
Bradford-Robinson Printing Company, 68
Brantigan, Charles, xvi, 107, 108
Brantigan, Kathleen, 107, 108
Brettell, Richard, xvi, 7, 9, 19
Brewster, Albert, 74
Bridaham, Lester Burbank, 95
Bridaham House, 95
Briean, Josiah S., 80
Brierly, Justin W., 80
Briggs, Melissa, 105
Brind, J. Fritz, 60
Brind, Maria, 60
Brind-Axtens Mansion, 60, 171
Bringle, Carey, 116
Brinker Collegiate Institute, 23
Brinton Terrace, 176
British Primary School, 156, 157
Broadway Central, 137
Broadway School, 176
Broadway Theater, 177
Bromfield, Donald, 95
Broncho Buster, 18
Brown, Benjamin, 94
Brown, Benjamin, House, 94, 172
Brown, Carroll T., 65
Brown, Henry Cordes, 23, 53
Brown, John J., 69
Brown, John S., Mercantile-Wynkoop Brewing Company, 44
Brown, John Sidney, House, 176

Brown, Margaret "Molly", 67, 69, 70, 172
Brown, Molly, House, xvi, 67, 69, 70, 169
Brown-Garrey-Congdon House, 65, 171
Brown-Mackenzie-MacDougal House, 81
Brown Palace Hotel, 6, 9, 23, 42, 120, 171
Brown-Tabor Mansion, 176
Bryan, William Jennings, 33
Bryant-Webster Elementary School, 120, 121, 172
Buchan, Marion, 105
Buchanan, Brad, 175
Buchtel, Henry, 53, 61
Buckhorn Exchange Restaurant, 9, 48, 169
Buell, Temple H., xv, xvi, 8, 26, 33, 79, 95, 121, 144, 148, 164
Buena Vista Hotel, 68
Buffalo Bill Grave and Museum, 108, 167
Buffalo Bill's Wild West Show, 108
Bungalow style, 99
Burlington Hotel, 103, 171
Burnham, Daniel, 18
Burr, George Elbert, 59
Bust of a Girl, 72
Bust of a Youth, 72
Butterfly-Terrible Mining Company, 60
Butters, Alfred, 67
Butters House, 67, 170
Byers, William Newton, 4, 20, 21, 48, 49, 68, 137, 140
Byers Branch Library, 9, 48, 49, 171
Byers-Evans House, 20, 21, 148, 169
Byers Junior High School-Denver School of Science and Technology, 140, 144, 172
Byers-Porter House, 176

Cabrini, Mother Frances, 122
Cactus Club, 40, 176
Caesar, Sid, 128
California Building, 176
Calloway, Charles, 43
Calvary Baptist Church, 106
Cameron United Methodist Church, 146, 173
Campbell, Lafayette E., 61
Campbell, Margaret Patterson, 67
Campbell, Richard C., 67, 83
Campbell House, 61, 169
Campion, John F., House, 176
Canino, Joseph, 120
Canmann, Leo, 176
Cannon, Hugh Brown, 161
Capitol Hill, 4, 9, 10, 23, 52, 53, 56, 60, 61, 64, 67, 68, 74, 78, 84, 100, 113, 142
Capitol Hill Mansion Bed and Breakfast Inn, 68
Capitol Hill United Neighborhoods, 53, 84
Capitol Hydraulic Company, 142
Capitol Life Insurance Company, 60
Capuchin Poor Clares, 118
Capuchins (Franciscan Order of Friars Minor), 108
Cardenas Apartments, 61
Cardwell, The, 82
Carleton College, 148
Carnegie libraries, 20, 48, 126, 162
Carnegie Main Library-McNichols Building, 20

Carnegie Steel, 146
Carney, John, 27, 30
Carpenter Gothic Houses, 21, 173
Carpenter Gothic style, 21, 46
Carpenter, Dudley, 146
Carr, E.T., 55
Carr, Ralph L., 77, 78
Carr, Ralph L., Residence, 77, 78, 173
carriage blocks, 124
Carrigan, Joseph P., 118
Carrillo, Richard, xvi
Carroll, Jean Agnes, Memorial Chapel, 154
Casa Mayan Restaurant, 46
Casavant Fréres Limitée of St. Hycainth, 59
Casey, James V., 109
Cass, Emogene, 72
Cass, Oscar David, 72
Cass-Friedman House, 72, 171
Castle Apartments, 91
Castle Marne Bed and Breakfast, 84, 86, 87, 170
Castle Pines, 167
Catherwood, Jean, 175
Cato, Henry L., 125
Caulkins, Ellie, 33
Caulkins, Ellie, Opera House, 171
Causey Foster Securities Company, 64
Cazin, Alexander, 157, 158
Center for Colorado and the West, xv
Central Bank Building, 7, 8, 171, 176
Central Business District, 10, 22, 40, 104, 113
Central City, Colorado, 11, 61, 84
Central City Opera House Association, 80, 84
Central Park, 6
Central Presbyterian Church, 176
Century Building, 29
Cerrone's Grocery, 9, 120, 170
Certified Local Governments, 11
Chamber of Commerce Building, 176
Chamberlain, Humphrey B., 148
Chamberlain, William George, 36, 38
Chamberlain Observatory, 148, 149, 172
Chandler, Mary Voelz, xvi
Chapel of Our Merciful Savior, 9, 170
Chappell, Delos Allen, 86
Chappell House, 86, 170
Chariton, Owen, xv
Charity Organization Society, 72
Chase, Mary Coyle, 137, 138
Chase, Mary Coyle, House, 137, 138, 170
Chase, Robert, 137
Chateau/Chateauesque style, 9, 65, 67, 95, 159
Chaten, H., 91
Chavez, Edward, 49
Cheesman, Alice, 62
Cheesman, Gladys, 62
Cheesman, Walter Scott, 43, 62, 80
Cheesman Block, 176
Cheesman Esplanade, 80
Cheesman Park, 6, 80, 81, 83, 84
Cheesman Park Memorial Pavilion, 80, 169
Cherry Creek, 4, 40, 41, 45, 49, 113, 137, 142, 144, 153
Cherry Creek Shopping Center, 34

Cherry Creek State Park, 49
Chever Block, 176
Chicago style, 27, 29, 30, 39
Children's Hospital, 79
Childress, Cab, 42
Chinese community, 110
Christman, Abigail, 175
Christ Methodist Episcopal Church, 105
Chucovich, Vaso, 24
Church, John B., Residence, 176
Church, William, "Castle" Residence, 176
Church of the Ascension, 66, 173
Ciancio Park, 122
City and County Building, 17, 20
City Beautiful Movement, 5, 18, 20, 49, 72, 73, 90, 95, 124, 153, 167
City Beautiful Parkways Historic District, 153, 174
City Cemetery, 83
City Hall, 38, 177
City Park, 88, 89, 90, 124, 142, 159, 162
City Park Pavilion Historic District, 89, 174
Civic Center Conservancy, 18
Civic Center Historic District, 17, 18, 174
Civic Center Park, 5, 11, 17, 18, 19, 20
Civilian Conservation Corps, 167, 168
Civil War, U.S., 56, 130, 134, 139, 150
Clark, Gruber and Company Bank and Mint, 21, 176
Classical Revival style, 21, 162
Clayton, Charles M., 37
Clayton Building-Granite Hotel, 28, 37, 171
Clayton College Historic District, 110, 174
Clayton Early Learning Center, 110
Clayton School, 92
Clear Creek, 129
Clear Creek County, 6, 167
Clements, Alfred, Addition, 104
Clements Addition Historic District, 104, 174
Clements Rowhouse, 104, 170
Clemes, Cora, 66
Clemes, James H., 66
Clemes-Lipe-Sweeney House, 66, 170
Cleo Parker Robinson Dance, 105
Cleworth, Charles "Cal," xvi, 66, 78
Cleworth, Sheila, 66
Closing Era, The, 19
Club Building, 176
Coble, Norman, 105
Cody, Buffalo Bill, 48, 108
Cody House, 108, 171
Cofield, Joseph B., 131
Cold War, 163
Cole, David, 130
Cole, Linus C., 117
Cole-DeRose Apartment House, 117, 172
Cole Neighborhood, 108
Coleridge, Samuel Taylor, 155, 162
Colfax, Schuyler, 84
Collegiate Gothic style, 49, 126, 129, 134, 140, 148
Collins, John, 147
Collins, John, United Methodist Church, 147, 173

Colonial Revival style, 7, 9, 53, 58, 83, 86, 87, 140, 141
Colonnade, The, 78, 173
Colonnade of Civic Benefactors, 18
Colorado & Southern Railroad, 115
Colorado Association of Architects, 7
Colorado Bakery and Saloon, 40, 86
Colorado Board of Charities and Corrections, 147
Colorado Business Bank, 31, 170
Colorado Constitution, 42
Colorado Department of Education, 19
Colorado Federal Bank, 31
Colorado Gold Rush, 45
Colorado Historical Society, xv, 19, 21, 64, 68, 88
Colorado Legislature, 19
Colorado Milling and Elevator Company, 64
Colorado Mining and Marble Company, 56
Colorado Mortgage and Investment Company, 41
Colorado National Bank, 22, 28, 176
Colorado Outward Bound, 66, 67
Colorado Preservation, Inc., 4, 76, 161
Colorado Realty and Construction, 86
Colorado Rockies baseball team, 102
Colorado School for the Deaf and the Blind, 124
Colorado School of Mines, 123
Colorado State Capitol, xiii, 18, 19, 20, 53, 56, 77
Colorado State Library, 19
Colorado State Museum, 19
Colorado State University, 148
Colorado Supreme Court, 61, 68, 141
Colorado Telephone Company, 60
Colorado Territorial Court, 61
Colorado Woman's College, 159, 160
Columbia Hotel, 40, 41, 170
Comfort, Josh, 92
Community College of Denver, 45
Confederate Army, 56
Confluence Park, 49, 113
Congdon, Noel, 36, 65
Congdon, Tom, 36, 65
Congdon Building, 171
Congleton, Brian, 99
Congress Park, 80
Conine, John, 114
Conine, Marth, 114
Conine-Horan House, 114, 172
Conrad, Paul, 25
Constitution Hall, 42, 137, 169, 177
Contee, Jonathan R., 103
Continental Oil Building, 177
Convery, William J. "Bill," xv, xvi, 64
Cooper, Susan, 20
Cooperative Extension Service, 148
Cooper Building, 177
Coors Brewing Company, 129
Coors Field, 44, 102
Coquard, Leon, 58
Corbett, Kathleen, 175
Cornwall, The, 76, 77, 170
Cornwall, William T., 76
Coronado Building, 30

Coronado Club, 73
Corona School-Dora Moore Elementary School, 77, 170
Corson, Dan, xv, xvi
Cory, John Jerome, 144
Cory Elementary School, 144, 172
Cosmopolitan, 128
Cosmopolitan Hotel, 177
Cotopaxi Colony, 133
Country Club, 10, 84, 94, 95, 138, 140, 141
Country Club Gardens Historic District, 140, 141, 174
Country Club Historic District, 66, 95, 174
Country Club Place, 95
Cowe, William, 78
Cowell, David, House, 99
Cowie, Alexander Johnstone, 117
Cowie House, 117, 172
Cox, David, Sr., 128, 129
Cox "Gargoyle" House, 129, 169
Cox House, 129, 169
Craftsman style, 60, 67, 68, 84, 90, 123, 127, 131, 155, 161, 167
Craig, Alexander, 60
Craig House, 60
Cram, Ralph Adams, 104, 105
Cranmer, George, 154, 167
Cranmer, George, House, 154, 172
Cranmer, Jean Chappell, 154
Cranmer Park, 6, 154
Crash of 1893, 5, 53
Crawford, Dana, xvi, 36, 39, 43
Crawford, Jack, 36
Crawford Building, 9, 39, 171
Creede, Colorado, 61
Creede, Nicholas C., 61
Creekfront Park, 49
Crescent Hand Laundry Building, 116, 172
Creswell, Joseph, 56
Creswell House, 56, 170
Cripple Creek, Colorado, 11, 64, 78, 96
Cripple Creek and Victor Gold Mining Company, 18
Croke, Thomas B., 67
Croke-Patterson-Campbell Mansion-Patterson Inn, 9, 67, 169
Crook, John, House, 108
Crown Hill Cemetery, 124
Cruise Room, 10, 43
Cuerden, Glenn, xvi, 11, 30, 56, 75, 79, 89, 141
Culpin, Alan, xvi
Culpin, Marcy, xvi
Currigan, Tom, 36
Curry, James H., 24
Curry-Chucovich-Gerash House, 22, 24, 171
Curtis, Samuel S., 99
Curtis and Clarke Building, 177
Curtis Park "A" Historic District, 174
Curtis Park "B" Historic District, 174
Curtis Park "C" Historic District, 174
Curtis Park Community Center, 105
Curtis Park "D" Historic District, 174
Curtis Park "E" Historic District, 174

Curtis Park "F" Historic District, 174
Curtis Park "G" Historic District, 174
Curtis Park "H" Historic District, 174
Curtis Park Neighborhood, xvi, 4, 9, 99, 100, 101, 105
Cuthbert, Gertrude Hill Berger, 59
Cuthbert, Lucas Montrose, 59
Cuthbert-Dines House, 59, 85, 172
Cutshaw, Leonard, 178

Dallas, Sandra, xvi, 25, 61, 65, 69
Daly, Thomas F., 60
Daly House, 60, 170
Damascio, Frank, 9, 120
Damascio, Frank, House, 9, 120, 170
Daniels, Cicely, 167
Daniels, William Cooke, 35, 167
Daniels and Fisher Department Store, 34, 68, 167
Daniels and Fisher Tower, xvi, 34, 35, 169
Daniels Park, 167
d'Arbonne, Jessica, xvi
Daughters of America, 115
Daughters of Erin, 118
Davis, Herndon, 25
Davis, Rodney, xvi, 25, 160
Davis-Creswell Manufacturing Company, 56
Davis House, 46
DeBoer, Saco R., 5, 17, 20, 49, 62, 66, 89, 96, 126, 142, 147, 153
DeBoer Historic District, 147, 148, 174
Decker, Sarah Platt, 147
Decker, Sarah Platt, Branch Library, 146, 171
DeCunto, Frank, 70
Dedisse Park, 167, 168
Delgany School, 177
Democratic Club, 178
Democratic National Convention (1908), 33
demolition, 11, 34, 40, 86, 113
Dencla-Walker-White House, 81
Denham Theater, 177
Denver, James, 4
Denver, Salt Lake, and Pacific Railroad, 45, 87
Denver Academy, 143, 144, 150, 173
Denver & Rio Grande Railroad, 45, 87, 88, 100, 113, 125
Denver Art Museum, 20, 26
Denver Athletic Club, 25, 26, 131, 171
Denver Bears, 100
Denver Board of Health, 56
Denver Botanic Gardens, 80, 82, 83, 169
Denver Botanic Gardens House, 83, 169
Denver Center Theater Company, 35
Denver Chamber of Commerce, 160
Denver Charity Organization, 60
Denver City Cable Railway Building, 35, 169
Denver City Council, 56, 77, 134
Denver City Railway Company, 43
Denver City Railway Company-Sheridan Heritage Building-Streetcar Lofts, 43, 170
Denver Civic Theater, 93
Denver Club, 177
Denver Digs Trees, 147

Denver Dry Goods Building, 27, 28, 171
Denver Dry Goods Company, 28
Denver Dry Goods Tea Room, 28
Denver Evening Times, 131
Denver Fire Clay Company, 91
Denver Fire Department, 45
Denver Firefighters Museum, 24, 169
Denver Gas and Electric Building-Insurance Exchange Building, 32, 171
Denver General Hospital, 24, 45, 163
Denver High School, 177
Denver Homeopathic College, 72
Denver Horseshoers Union, 133
Denver International Airport, 161
Denver Landmark Preservation Commission, xiii, 4, 6, 10, 11, 22, 36, 45, 56, 77, 82, 126, 127, 175
Denver Machine Shop, 143
Denver Mountain Parks, xvi, 6, 108, 167, 168
Denver Municipal Auditorium-Ellie Caulkins Opera House, 33, 171
Denver Municipal Dispensary, 176
Denver Museum of Miniatures, Dolls, and Toys, 88
Denver Museum of Nature and Science, xvi, 66, 68, 89
Denver National Bank, 30, 31, 65, 170
Denver Orphans Home, 60
Denver Pacific Railroad, 100
Denver Performing Arts Complex, 64, 93
Denver Police Gang Unit, 90, 172
Denver Post, 34, 64, 79, 81, 92, 93
Denver Press Club, 25, 60, 171
Denver Public Library, 19, 20, 125, 142, 143, 147
Denver Public Library Western History & Genealogy Department, xv, 20
Denver Public Schools, 26, 66, 73, 124, 134, 139, 156
Denver Public Schools Administration Building, 26, 172
Denver School Board, 68, 122, 144, 160
Denver School District, 6
Denver School of Science and Technology, 140, 172
Denver School of the Arts, 140
"Denver Square" style, 9, 95, 99, 107
Denver Stockyards, 107
Denver Symphony Orchestra, 154
Denver Terra Cotta Company, 26, 138
Denver Times, 34, 60
Denver Tramway Company, 35, 118
Denver Tramway Company-Hotel Teatro, 35, 171
Denver Tramway Company Powerhouse-Forney Transportation Museum-Recreational Equipment, Inc., 113, 169
Denver Tribune, 142
Denver Turnverein, 9, 72, 73, 172
Denver Union Stockyards Exchange Building, 12
Denver Union Water Company, 62, 80
Denver Urban Renewal Authority, 28, 29, 36, 45
Denver US Mint, 21, 22
Denver Woman's College, 154
Denver Women's Press Club, 56, 60, 169

Denvue Apartments, 122
Dickinson, Emily, 147
Diego, Juan, 119
Diepenhorst, Jolie, xv
Dines, Isabel A., 59
Dines, Tyson M. 59
Dines House, 83
Dominick order, 124
Dominick, Peter H., Jr., xv, 40, 54, 93
Dominick, Philae, 93
Domoto, Wakako, 78
Dorman, Jesse B., 6, 7
Dorsett, Lyle, xvi
Dorset House Apartments, 60
Douglas County, 6, 167
Douglass, Frederick A., 103
Douglass Undertaking Building, 9, 103, 171
Dow, Charles L., 78
Downing, Sybil, 67
Downtown Denver Historic District, 223, 23, 174
Doyle, James, 78
Doyle-Benton House, 78, 173
Dozier, Henry, 108, 139
Driving Park Historic District, 94, 174
Dryden, David W., 7, 21, 77, 85, 122, 124, 141
Duckett-Emke, Andy, 175
Duff, James A., 41
Dugal Farmhouse, 154, 155, 173
Dugal, Louis, 155
Dunning, Walter, 68
Dunning-Benedict House, 68, 170
Dutch Colonial Revival style, 72, 88, 131, 137, 162
Dutch Mill Restaurant, 32
Dyce, Eric, xvi
Dyer, Elizabeth Casell, xvi

East High School, 90, 91, 124, 171
Eastman, George, 75
East Park Place Historic District, 110, 174
East Seventh Avenue Historic District, 10, 62, 174
Eberley, Frederick C., 7, 70, 42, 46, 47, 65, 99, 176
Ebert, Frederick J., 105
Ebert Elementary School, 105, 171
Ebert School, 177
EchoHawk, Dana, xv, xvi
École des Beaux-Arts, 7
Edbrooke, Frank, xvi, 6, 7, 10, 18, 19, 23, 24, 27, 28, 29, 32, 42, 56, 67, 71, 73, 74, 75, 92, 103, 123, 137, 149, 164, 176, 177, 178
Edbrooke, Frank, House, 74, 170
Edbrooke, Harry W. J., 29, 32, 75, 92, 93
Edbrooke, Willoughby, 6, 32, 178
Edbrooke Foursquares, 123
Edgecomb, Oscar L., 125
Edgewater, Colorado, 163
Edison, Thomas, 75
Edison Elementary School, 129, 172
Edwardian style, 137
Edwards, William Harry, 49, 126
Eggers, Henry, 65
Egyptian School of Embalming, 114

Eisenhower, Dwight D., 163
Eisenhower, Mamie, 163
Ekstrand, Peg, xv, xvi
Elbert, Josephine Evans, 148
El Centro Su Teatro, 109
Eleventh Street School, 177
Elfenbein, Sharon, xv, 175
Elitch, John, 127
Elitch, Mary, 128, 128
Elitch Gardens Amusement Park, 127
Elitch Theater, 127, 128, 172
El Jebel Temple-Rocky Mountain Consistory, 57, 107, 172
Ellie Caulkins Opera House. See Denver Municipal Auditorium-Ellie Caulkins Opera House
Ellis House, 95
Elyria, 109
Elyria Elementary School, 109, 110, 172
Emerson, Ralph Waldo, 85
Emerson Elementary School, 76, 77, 171
Emily Griffith Opportunity School, 144
Emmanuel Sherith Chapel-Student Art Gallery, 9, 46, 47, 169
Englewood, Colorado, 142
English Revival style, 7
Enos House, 72, 172
Enos, Charles W., 72
Epiphany Episcopal Church, 154, 173
Epworth Church/Community Center, 105, 173
Equitable Building, xvi, 9, 28, 29, 31, 84, 170
Equitable Life Assurance Society of New York, 28
Ernest and Cranmer Building, 177
Ervin, Raymond Harry, 29, 137
Espinoza, Carlota, 49, 102, 119
Essex Building, 177
Etter, Don, xvi
Evans, Anne, 84
Evans, Eugene F., 160
Evans, John, 4, 21, 35, 148
Evans, John, House, 177
Evans, John II, 62
Evans, John II, House, 177
Evans, William Gray, 21, 35
Evans and Brown, 39
Evans Memorial Chapel, 148, 169
Evans School, 21, 173
Evergreen Lake, 167, 168
Evergreen Lake Warming House, 167, 168, 172
Evergreen Nature Center, 168

Fager, Sarah J., 116
Fager Residence, 116, 172
Fairbanks, Douglas, Jr., 128
Fairmount Cemetery, xvi, 9, 41, 163, 164
Fairmount Cemetery Gate Lodge, 163, 170
Fairmount Cemetery Ivy Chapel, 9, 164, 170
Fairmount Mausoleum, 164, 173
Falkenberg, Ruth, xvi, 105, 175
Fallis, Montana, 31, 43, 62, 138, 178
Fay, Kathleen, 93
Fay, Nathaniel, 93
Federal Administration of Public Works, 155

Federal Housing Administration, 140
Fell, Jay, xvi
Fentress, Curt, xv, 32
Fentress and Associates, 23, 32
Fentress Architects, 26, 27, 78
Fentress Bradburn Architects, 29
Fenwick, Red, 25
Ferguson, John A., 29, 64
Ferguson, John A., Mansion, 177
Ferguson-Gano House, 64, 171
Ferril, Thomas Hornsby, 11, 19, 25, 107, 108, 175
Ferril, Thomas Hornsby, House, 107, 108, 169
Ferril Lake, 89, 142
Fetter, Rosemary, xv
Fieger, Henry, xvi, 161
Fieger, Jill, xvi, 161
Field, Eugene, 142
Field, Eugene, House, 142, 147, 169
Field, Kim, xvi
Field, Thomas, 148
Field, Thomas, House, 137, 148, 170
Field Officers Quarters, Fort Logan, 12
Fielder, John, xvi
Fifth Church of Christ Scientist, 92, 172
Fire House No. 15, 93, 171
Fire Station No. 1-Denver Firefighters Museum, 24, 169
Fire Station No. 3, 103, 104, 172
Fire Station No. 7, 122, 172
Fire Station No. 11, 138, 172
Fire Station No. 14, 155, 172
Fire Station No. 18-Denver Police Gang Unit, 12, 90, 172
First Avenue Hotel, 138, 171
First Baptist Church, 56, 57, 123, 169, 177
First Church of Christ Scientist, 59, 66, 169
First National Bank, 29, 42, 58
First National Bank-American National Bank-Magnolia Hotel, 29, 172
First Universalist Church, 85
Fisher, Alan B., 23, 30, 56, 175
Fisher, Arthur A., 7, 10, 17, 19, 22, 29, 30, 31, 35, 66, 72, 82, 83, 95, 140, 144, 145, 160, 177, 178
Fisher, Gladys Caldwell, 20, 30
Fisher, William E., 7, 10, 17, 19, 22, 29, 30, 31, 35, 66, 72, 82, 83, 89, 95, 140, 144, 145, 160, 177, 178
Fisher and Humphreys, 89
Fitzell, Grant R., 84
Fitzpatrick, Tabitha, xvi
Fitzroy Place-Warren-Iliff Mansion, 149, 150, 173
Five Points, 96, 99, 103
Five Points Historic Cultural District, 99, 103, 174
Fleming, James Alexander, 147
Fleming, James Alexander, House, 137, 147, 169
Fleming, Josiah, 68
Fleming Brothers, 138
Fleming-Hanington House, 68, 170
Fleming's Grove Methodist Church, 146
Fletcher, Donald K., Mansion, 177
Floating Bandstand, 89
Flores, Phil E., xv

Flores, Philip A., 175
Flower, John S., 73
Flower-Vaile House, 73, 74, 170
Ford, Barney, 9, 42
Ford, Barney, Building, 42, 171
Ford, Justina, 9, 99
Forney, J. Donovan, 113
Forney Transportation Museum, 113, 169
Forrest, Kenton, xvi
Fort Logan, 12, 61, 150
Fort Logan Field Officers Quarters, 150, 171
Fort Logan Mental Health Center, 171
Fort Logan National Cemetery, 150
Foster, Alexis C., 64
Foster, Ernest LeNeve, 108
Foster, Henri, 123, 124
Foster, Henri, House, 123, 124, 170
Foster, Jack, 25
Foster, Mark, xvi
Foster, Paul, xv, 42, 49, 175
Foster-Brantigan House, 108
Foster-McCauley-Symes-French Consulate House, 64, 169
Four Mile Historic Park, 153
Four Mile House, 153, 169
Four Seasons Hotel, 8
Foursquare style, 10, 60, 67, 94, 99, 110, 137, 140
Fowler, Gene, 25
Fox, David, 115
Fox, Edward L., 117, 118
Fox, Mary, 118
Fox-Schlatter House, 117, 118, 172
Fred Mueller Harness Shop, 39
Freeman, William R., 87
Fremont County, 66
French, Park M., 44
French Consulate, 64
French/French Revival style, 7, 9, 89
French Gothic/French Gothic Revival style, 9, 58
French Renaissance Revival style, 54
Frewan, Frank W., 105, 161, 164
Frey, James, 72
Friedman, William S., 72
Fries, Mike, xvi
Front Range Research Associates, xv
Froula, Barbara, xvi
Fryburger, Frank P., 114
Fuller, A. W., 177
Fuller, Kenneth R., xv, 76
Fuller, Mrs. (Frances Walker) Pierpont, 175
Fuller, Robert, 7, 20, 95, 129
Furney, Laura, xvi

Gahan, John, Jr. 38
Gahan, John, Sr., 38
Gahan's Saloon-Miller Building, 38, 171
Gale Abels and Associates, 46
Gallagher, Dennis, xvi, 122
Gallegos, Magdalena, xvi
Gallup, Avery, 38
Gallup-Stanbury Building, 38, 171
Gamer, Michael, xvi

Gano, George A., 104
Gano, George W., 64
Gano and Thomas Furniture, 104
Gano-Downs Clothing Store, 64
Gardens at St. Elizabeth's, 124
Gardner, John M., 160
Garrey, Anne Reynolds, 65
Garrey, George H. 65
Garrison, Robert, 17, 19, 144
Gates, Russell, 91
Gates House, 91, 170
Gates Mercantile Company, 91
Gebhard, Henry, 107
Gebhard/Smith House, 107, 170
Gebhart, David, xvi
Gehrig, Coi, xv
Gelertner, Mark, xvi
Genessee Park, 167
Gensler and Associates, 30, 34
Gentleman's Driving Association, 94
Georgian Revival style, 7, 9, 55, 57, 61, 62, 64, 81, 82, 84, 85, 124, 148
Gerash, Walter
German community, 9, 47, 72, 73
German House-Denver Turnverein, 72, 73, 172
German National Bank, 110
Gettysburg Cyclorama Building, 177
Ghost, Allen M., 131
Ghost, Allen M., Historic District, 174
Gibson, Barbara, xv, 175
Gilbertson, Alice, xv
Gill, Tim, 146
Gilpin School, 177
Girard College, 110
Glandon, Beth, xv
Glen Park School, 134
Globe Smelter, 134
Globeville, 134
Globeville School, 12, 134, 173
Golden, Colorado, 129
Golden Eagle Dry Goods, 177
Golden West, The, 49
Goldstein, Marcia, xv
Goldstein, Martin, 175
Gonzales, Caroline, 46
Gonzales, Ramon, 46
Goodhue, Bertram G., 105
Goodnow, Franklin, 41, 107
Goodridge, J.A., 75
Goodwill Industries, 105
Gordon, Tracy, and Swarthout, 21, 71, 95
Gothic/Gothic Revival styles, 9, 46, 53, 54, 59, 66, 71, 72, 105, 110, 117, 121, 124, 130, 134, 147, 148, 157, 164
Gottesleben, Peter, Residence, 177
Gould, Jay, 41
Gove, Aaron M., 7, 43, 44, 45, 58, 62, 83, 163, 176, 177
Gove and Walsh, 43, 44, 45, 58, 83
Governor's Award for Preservation, xiii
Governor's Mansion, 62, 169
Governor's Park, 62, 64
Grable and Weber, 61

Grace Methodist Episcopal Church, 148
Grafton, The, 74
Graham, Alexander J., 88
Graham-Bible House, 88, 172
Granada, Colorado, 78
Granada Apartments, 61
Grand Army of the Republic, 130
Grand County, 6, 167
Granite Hotel, 37, 171
Grant, James B., 63, 140
Grant, Mary, 140
Grant, Rich, xvi
Grant, Ulysses S., 84, 146
Grant, William W., 158
Grant Avenue Methodist Episcopal Church, 140
Grant House, 140, 172
Grant-Humphreys Mansion, 63, 64, 140, 170
Grant Middle School, 171
Grant Smelter Stack, 177
Grant Street Historic District, 140, 174
Grasmere Lake, 142
Graves, Michael, xv, 19, 20
Gray, John, 146
Great Depression, 54, 61, 93, 124
Great Fire of 1863, 8
Great Western Sugar Company, 83
Greek Revival style, 85
Greek Theater (Civic Center Park), 18
Greenblatt, Sarah, 175
Greenleaf, Lawrence N., 94
Greenleaf Masonic Lodge, 94, 171
Greeters of America, 160, 171
Grimes, Tammy, 128
Grinstead, Leigh A., xv
Grodavent, Frank J., 150
Groussman, Albert B., 46
Groussman Grocery, 46
Grover, Breck, xvi
Grover, Mary Lynn, xvi
Groves, Eugene G., 7, 150
Guaranty Bank and Trust Company, 30
Guaranty Bank Building, 29, 39, 171
Guerreri, Frank, 70
Guerreri-DeCunto House, 70
Guldman-Bonfils Mansion, 177
Gunnison County, 18
Gusterman's Silversmiths, 39

Haber, Francine, 76
Haish Manual Training School, 177
Hale, Fred A., 24
Half-Moon House, 131, 132, 170
Haller and Larson, 124
Hallet, Lucien, 61
Hallet, Moses, 61
Hallet House, 61, 169
Halprin, Lawrence, 178
Hamilton Apartment Building, 78, 79, 173
Hamman, James A., 116
Hammersmark, Eric, xv
Hampf, Ashleigh, xv
Hancock, Michael, 5

Hangar 61-Ideal Basic Cement Company Corporate Hangar, 160, 161, 173
Hanington, Charles, 68
Hannigan-Canino Terrace, 9, 119, 120, 171
Hansen, Samuel, 71
Hanson, Bruce, xv
Hanson, William J., xvi
Harman, Edwin Preston, 94
Harman, Louisa, 94
Harman, town of, 94
Harman Town Hall-Greenleaf Masonic Temple, 94, 171
Harnois, Frederick, 7, 54, 63, 64
Harper Humanities Gardens, University of Denver, 148
Harris, Julie, 128
Hart, Gerald T., 175
Hart, Martyn, 59
Hartman, James, xv
Harvard Gulch Golf Club, 148
Harvard Gulch Park, 148
Harvey, 137, 138
Harvey, George F., Jr., 78
Harvey Park, 142
Hatami, Marvin, 47
Hathaway, Anne, 146
hauntings, 56, 63, 67
Havekost, Daniel, xvi, 55, 64, 65
Havey, Jim, xvi
Hayden, Dickinson, and Feldhauser Building, 27, 172
Hayes Townhouses, 70, 173
Hearst, William Randolph, 128
Hegner, Frank, xvi
Heiser, Herman H., 130
Heiser, Herman H., House, 130, 169
Helene Apartments, 71, 172
Helmuth, Obata, and Kassabaum, 47
Hendrie, Edwin, 157
Hendrie, Gertrude, 158
Hendrie and Bolthoff, 43
Henson, Alley, 43
Hering, Elsie Ward, 117
Heronema, Ralph, 86
Hewitt, Henry H., 64, 83, 110
Hickenlooper, John, xiii, xvi, 5, 44, 62
Higgins, Brian, 67
Highland, 113, 126, 129
Highland Ditch, 129
Highland Park, 123, 124, 125
Highland Park Addition, 113
Highlands, 4, 9, 113, 123, 124
Highlands Chieftain, 115
Highlands Masonic Temple, 123
Highlands United Methodist Church, 130, 172
High Street Community Center, 105
Hill, Crawford, 9, 54
Hill, Crawford, Mansion, 9, 54, 171
Hill, Mrs. Crawford, 54, 81
Hill, Nathaniel, 59
Hill, Nathaniel, Residence, 177
Hill, Roscoe C., Middle School, 154
Hilltop, 153

Hinckley Express Company, 72
Hiraga, Eric, 175
Hispanic community, 9, 10, 49, 102, 103, 110, 113, 119, 120
Historic American Buildings Survey, 153
Historic Denver, Inc., xvi, 4, 26, 45, 67, 69, 70, 76, 99, 154
History Colorado, xv, 4, 11, 19, 21, 64
History Colorado Center, 19
Hitchings, Horace B., 40
Hitchings Block, 40, 41, 170
Hodgson, Edgar, 67, 68
Hodgson, Isaac, 67, 72, 177
Hoeft, Kathy, xvi, 99, 175
Hoehn Architects, 147
Holdorf, Ryan, 175
Holiday Chalet Victorian Hotel, 84, 86
Holladay, Ben, 40
Holland House, 150, 173
Holmes, Clarence, 9, 107
Holmes House, 9, 107, 172
Holtze, Eric, 29
Holtze, Steve, 29
Holy Ghost Catholic Church, 64
Holzman House, 177
Home Construction Company, 123
Hoover, Berg, Desmond, 121
Horan, Elizabeth, 114
Horan, William P., 114
Horan and McConaty Funeral Service, 114
Hornbein, Marjorie, xvi, 101, 175
Hornbein, Victor, xvi, 7, 30, 82, 144
Hornby, Barbara Sudler, 175
Hose Company No. 1, 45, 171
Hotel Hope, 38, 171
Hotel Teatro, 35, 171
Houck, Frank, 78
Houdy, W. P., 105
House of a Thousand Candles, 85
House of Mirrors, 41
House with the Round Window, 125, 172
Hover, William A., 35
Hover-Bromley Building, 35, 172
Howard, Colorado, 66
Hoyt, Burnham, 7, 8, 19, 20, 22, 25, 66, 72, 79, 95, 103, 132, 140, 141, 154, 162, 168, 176
Hoyt, Merrill, 7, 22, 25, 66, 72, 79, 103, 123, 132, 140, 141, 162
Hubbell, Walter L., 140
Huddart, John J., 7, 56, 71, 93, 100, 156, 176, 177
Huddart/Lydon House, 100, 171
Huddart Terrace, 71, 172
Huff House, 95
Huffman, Harry, 93
Hughes, Amos B., 123
Hughes, Amos B., House, 123, 173
Hughes, Arthur, 108
Hughes, Lafayette, Mansion, 177
Hughes Block, 30
Humboldt Island, 80, 81, 83
Humboldt Street Historic District, 80, 81, 174
Humboldt Street-Park Avenue Historic District, 79, 174

Humphreys, Albert E., 63, 140
Humphreys, Ira, 63
Humphreys, John J., 70, 84, 116
Humphreys, Ruth Boettcher, 81
Humphreys Aviation, 80
Humphries, Dennis, xvi, 175
Humphries Poli Architects, 19, 20, 21, 108, 124, 127
Hungarian Flour, 64
Hunt, Rebecca, xvi
Huntington, Daniel Riggs, 89
Huntington, Glen W., 7, 24, 58, 122, 123, 127
Hyde Park Elementary School, 109
Hyder, James B., 49
Hyperbolic Parabloid, 8, 177

Ice House Lofts, 44, 172
Ideal Building-Denver National Bank-Colorado Business Bank, 31, 170
Ideal Cement Company, 31, 82, 161, 173
Iliff, John Wesley, 149
Immaculate Conception Cathedral, 9, 55, 59, 59, 120, 169
Independence Hall, 90
Indian Concession House, Red Rocks Park, 168, 172
Indian Memories, 23
Insoloid Dynamite Fuse Company, 60
Inspiration Point, 6
Insurance Exchange Building, 32, 171
International Order of Odd Fellows, 32, 42, 117
International style, 95, 154
Interstate Trust Building, 10, 177
Ireland, Frederick W., Jr., 176
Irish community, 9, 102, 114, 118, 120
Iron Building, 177
Italian Renaissance Revival style, 66, 72, 91, 92, 95, 99, 125, 144, 154, 162
Italianate style, 7, 9, 38, 40, 41, 42, 43, 46, 67, 80, 100, 101, 104, 107, 143
Italian community, 9, 70, 102, 113, 117, 120
Iverson, Kristin, 70
Ivy Chapel, Fairmount Cemetery. *See* Fairmount Cemetery Ivy Chapel

Jackson, Frank H., 106, 159
Jackson, William Henry, 31, 158
Jacobean style, 64, 90, 145
Jacobs, John Joseph, 34
Jaka, G. Charles, 7, 43
James, Bill, 104
James, Kay, 104
Jameson, Savannah, xv
Janisch, Walter J., 139
Janisch, Wenzel, 115
Japanese Americans, 77, 78
Jefferson County, 6, 132, 167
Jespersen, Jesse, xvi
Jewish community, 9, 46, 47, 54, 70, 133
Ji, Maharaja, 85
John Paul II, Pope, 59
Johns Hopkins Medical School, 162
Johnson, Van, 128
Johnson and Wales University, 154, 160

Jordy, Charles, 175
Joshel House, 154, 172
Joslin, John Jay, 99
Judd, E. James, 35

Kahn, Hans, 154
Kansas Territory, 4
Kapper-Cannon-Fieger House, 161, 173
Kappler, Otto H., 161
Karagas, Jim, xvi
Karns, Robert, 49
Kaub, Babette 99
Kaub, Frank, 99, 100
Kaub House, 100, 172
Keating House-Capitol Hill Mansion Bed and
    Breakfast Inn, 68, 170
Keating, Jeffrey, 68
Keating, Mary, 68
Kelly, Grace, 128
Kenehan, Roady, 133, 134
Kenehan House, 133, 134, 170
Kennedy, John F., 30
Kent School for Girls, 33
Kerr, John G., 66
Kerr Gulch, 66
Kerr House, 66, 170
Kessler, George, 5, 6, 49, 89, 153
Ketchum, Rodney, 160
Kettle, George, 39
Kettle Building, 39, 171
Keys on the Green Clubhouse, 167, 168
Kidder, Franklin E., 57, 66, 84, 94, 105, 116
Kingston Row, 104
Kinneavy Terrace, 100, 172
Kipp, Jeff, 91
Kipp, Lisa, 91
Kirchner and Kirchner, 177
Kistler, William H., 72
Kistler Building, 31
Kistler-Rodriguez House, 72, 170
Kistler Stationery Company, 72
Kittredge, Charles, 26, 155
Kittredge, Charles, Mansion, 177
Kittredge Building, 9, 26
Klipp, Brian, 19, 20
Klipp Architecture, 22
Klipp Colussy Jens DuBois, 19
Knight, Stephen, 46
Knight House, 46
Knights of Pythias, 115
Kountze, Charles B., Home, 177
Kountze, Charles B., Mansion, 177
Kountze Heights, 131
Kreck, Dick, xvi
Kroenke Sports, 26
Kroll, Jim, xv
Krupa, Leslie Mohr, xv
Ku Klux Klan, 81, 105
Kylberg, Holly, xvi

Lady of the Lake with the Sword Excalibur, The,
    147
Lafayette (Maria Mitchell) School, 177

Lafayette Street Historic District, xvi, 108, 174
Laird, Pam, xvi
Lake Middle School, 132, 172
Lambert, Edmund L., 49
Lamm, Dick, xvi
Lang, William A., 6, 7, 12, 54, 67, 68, 69, 70, 74,
    86, 87, 108, 133, 134, 176
Lang and Pugh, 73, 133, 134
Lang townhouses, 74
La Paz Billiard Hall, 103
Laradon Hall, 134
Larimer, William H., Jr., 4, 36, 39, 113
Larimer Square, 9, 36, 37, 38, 39, 49
Larimer Square Associates, 36, 39
Larimer Square Historic District, 36, 174
Last Supper, The, 59
Laughing Latte Coffee Shop, 163
Layton, Solomon A., 114
Leadville, Colorado, 69
Leadville Democrat, 68
Leavitt, Craig W., xv
Lee, Charles Gordon, 124, 144
Lee, Charles Herbert, 127
Lee, Henry, 124
Lee, Henry, House, 124. 170
LEED Certification, 76
Leeman Auto Company, 137, 173
Leonard, Stephen J., xv, xvi, 175
Lepore, Mariano Felice, 120
Levinsky, Annie Robb, xvi
Lewis, R.H., 154
Liden, Rudolph, 127
Liebhardt, Gustavus C., 41
Liebhardt Brothers Commission Company, 41
Liebhardt-Lindner Building, 41, 170
Liggins, Wendell T., 106
Lighthouse Writers Workshop, 86
Lincoln, Abraham, 134
Lincoln Elementary School, 140, 172
Lincoln Hall, 39, 171
Lindberg, Jim, xvi
Lindner, Hodgson, and Wright, 25
Lindner, Roland L., 20
Lindner Packing and Provision Company, 41
Lipe, Walter E., 66
Lipe, William C., 66
Lipe Brothers Real Estate, 66
Little Israel, 9, 46, 133
Little Italy, 9, 113, 120
Little Sisters of the Poor, 130
Littleton, Colorado, 142, 147
Littleton Creamery-Beatrice Foods Cold
    Storage-Ice House Lofts, 44, 172
Litvak, Dianna, xvi
Litvak, John, xvi, 133
Livermore-Benton House, 83
Lobach, Eugene, 131
Lobach House, 131, 170
Logan, John A., 150
Loire Valley, 67
Long, Gary, xvi, 99
Long, Margaret, 162, 163
Long, Margaret, House, 162, 163, 173

Long, Thomas, 128
Longfellow School, 177
Long Hoeft Architects, 18, 20, 42
Lookout Mountain, 108, 167
Lort, Joe, 153
Louisiana Purchase Exposition, 6
Lowenstein, Henry, 92, 93
Lowenstein Theater, 92, 93, 173
Lower Downtown, 36, 40, 43, 45, 113
Lower Downtown Historic District, xiii, 4, 40,
    41, 174
Lowry, Francis B., 163
Lowry Air Force Base, 4, 153, 163
Lowry area, 157, 163
Lowry Beer Garden, 163
Lowry Chapel No. 1-Eisenhower Chapel, 163,
    170
Lowry Officers' Row Historic District, 163, 174
Lowry Technical Training Center, 163, 174
Loy, Myrna, 128
Lumber Baron Bed and Breakfast, 123
Lundt, Patti, xv
Lydon, Cole, 100
Lyons quarry, 27, 123

MacMonnies, Frederick, 5, 17
Madden, Eugene, 46
Madden-Schultz Duplex, 46
Madison Square Garden, 33
Maer House, 95
Magafan, Jenne, 49
Magnolia Hotel, 29, 172
Maider, Peter, 160
Maiz, Chris, 175
Majestic Building, 177
Malmborg, Harold A. 56
Malo, Oscar, 64
Malo Mansion, 64, 170
Mammoth Mining Company, 61
Maniatis, Dino, xv
Mann, Horace, 121
Mann, Horace, Middle School, 121, 122, 172
Manning, Harry James, 7, 64, 83, 96, 101, 118, 130,
    140, 143, 150, 161, 177
Mapelli's Meats, 41
Marean, Willis A., 7, 62, 68, 72, 80, 81, 95, 134,
    146
Marean and Norton, 178
Market Center, 40, 41
Market Street red light district, 40, 41
Markham Hotel, 177
Marlow, Joseph P., xvi, 154
Marne Apartments, 86
Marquis Block, 113
Marriott Renaissance Hotel, 23
Martin, Florence F., 167
Martin, Florence F., Ranch, 167, 174
Martinez, Ramon F. 122
Masonic Building, 9
Masonic Temple, 27, 171
Masons, 27, 57, 94, 105, 117
Matz, Nicholas C., 59
Mayan Theater, 138, 139, 171

May D&F, 28
Mayer, Frederick, xvi
Mayer, Jan, xvi
Mayo, Margery Reed, Day Nursery, 96, 101, 102, 172
Mazzula, Fred M., 175
McAllister, Henry, 88
MCB Architects, 144
McBird, Matthew John, 107
McBird-Whiteman House, 107, 171
McCarthy, Sarah, 175
McCauley, Vance, 64
McCloud, Burnis, 106
McClure, Louis C., 32, 67, 162
McConnell, Carla, 175
McCourt, Peter, 86
McCourt, Peter, House, 86, 171
McCoy, Earl, xvi
McCrary Building, 41, 170
McCrary, Napoleon Bonaparte, 41
McFarland House, 95
McFarlane, Ida Kruse, 84
McFarlane, William, 84
McGlone Senior Center, 76
McKay, Anne, 123
McKay, Hugh, 123
McKay House, 169
McKay, Hugh, House, 123
McKibben Building, 38, 39, 171
McKinley Mansion, 61, 169
McMurtrie-Good Mansion, 177
McNally, Jim, xv
McNamara, Michael J., 28
McNamara Dry Goods Company, 27, 28
McNeil, John L., 61
McNeil House, 61, 170
McNichols, Stephen L.R., 20, 150
McNulty, Elizabeth, 134
McPhee Block, 177
Mead, Jay, xvi
Mediterranean/Mediterranean Revival styles, 7, 60, 64, 65, 66, 73, 75, 76, 93, 95, 109, 110, 161
Meir, Golda, 9, 46
Meir, Golda, House, 9, 46, 172
Melrose, Frances, xvi, 25
Menchaca, Juan, 119
Merchant of Venice, 65
Merrill, Louise A., 144
Merrill Middle School, 144, 145, 172
Meryweather, Harry, 89
Mesa Verde National Park, 147
Mestizo-Curtis Park, 99
Metropole Hotel, 177
Metropolitan Building, 177
Metropolitan State University of Denver, 45
Mexican Consulate, 64
Midyette-Seieroe Architects, 138
Milheim, John, 86
Milheim, Mary, 86
Milheim House, 84, 86, 171
Miller, Arthur S., 104
Miller, Byron L., 110
Miller, Edwin, 115

Miller, J. E., 139
Miller, Kent, 82
Miller, Lyle, xvi
Miller Building, 38, 171
Miller House, 110, 169
Millet, Daniel, House, 83
Milmoe, Jim, 36, 37
Milstein, Philip, 171, 175
Milton House, 123
Milwaukee Brewery, 47
Miner's Court, The, 20
Mining Exchange Building, 177
Mission/Mission Revival styles, 10, 54, 60, 66, 78, 105, 109, 118, 119, 148, 163, 168
Mission of the Holy Comforter, 54
Mitchell, John Clark, 65
Mitchell-Schomp House, 65, 170
Miyagishima, Kara, xv
Modern Civic Art, or the City Made Beautiful, 5, 17
Modernism, 67, 153
Moffat, David H., 45, 58, 61, 87
Moffat House, 177
Moffat Mansion, 177
Moffat Road, 45
Moffat Station, 45, 171
Molkery/Montclair Civic Building, xvi, 158, 169
Molly Brown House. *See* Brown, Molly, House
Monday Literary Club, 91
Monfort/Swift Meat Company, 41
Monroe, John K., 92, 119
Montclair, 84, 153, 155, 156, 158
Montclair Historic District, 10, 155, 174
Montclair School, 156, 173
Montclair Town Hall, 155
Montelius, William, 125
Montezuma and the Animals, 20
Moore, Harold Willis, 85
Moorish style, 61, 62, 70, 107
Moorman, Edwin, 41, 81, 90
Mordecai Children's Garden, 83
Morey, Chester, 72
Morey Middle School, 72, 172
Morey-Guggenheim House, 177
Morgan, James C., 42, 175
Morgan, Samuel B. 83
Morgan's Addition Historic District, 83, 174
Morin, Marcie, xv
Morley, Judy, xv
Morris, Langdon E., Jr., 65, 81, 175
Morse, Stanley, 65
Morton, Tom, xvi
Moses, William E., 130
Moses, William E., House, 130, 170
Mouat House, 123
Mouat Lumber and Investment Company, 180
Mountain Electric Company, 60
Mountain Motors Company, 68
Mountain View Apartments, 115
Mount Auburn Cemetery, 164
Mount Calvary Catholic Cemetery, 80, 83
Mountjoy, Frederick E., 33, 44, 105, 161, 164
Mountjoy, French, and Rewe, 126

Mount Prospect Cemetery, 80
Mt. Evans, 6
Muchow, William, 42
Mullen, Catherine, Nurses' Home-Mullen Building, 79, 80, 173
Mullen, Catherine Smith, 79
Mullen, Edith, 64
Mullen, John K., 47, 64, 130
Mullen, John K., House, 178
Mullen Building, 79, 80, 173
Mullen Home for the Aged, 130
Mulligan, Ryan, xvi
Mulvihill-Gurtler family, 128
murals, 18, 20, 21, 23, 49
Murata Outland Associates, 105, 126
Murdoch, James, 73, 74, 107, 117, 157
Murillo, Bartolome, 59
Murphy, Jack A., xvi
Murphy Stevens, 116
Musick, G. Meredith, 33, 56, 120, 178
Musick, J. Roger, 120
My Brother's Bar, xvi
Myers, Elijah, 18, 19
Myrtle Hill School-Washington Park School Annex-Myrtle Hill Lofts, 144, 173

Nagel, Clara Kaub, 99
Nagel, Peter, 99
Nagel House, 99, 100, 172
Nash, Charles, 92
National Association for the Advancement of Colored People (NAACP), 107
National Federation of Club Women, 147
National Gallery of Art, 168
National Jewish Hospital, 100
National Park Service, xv
National Register of Historic Places, 11, 70, 82, 113, 123, 127, 137, 167, 168
National Trust for Historic Preservation, 76
National Western Stock Show, 12, 107
Navarre-American Museum of Western Art, 23, 24, 169
Neahr, Will C., 143
Neahr House, 143, 173
Neef, Frederick W., 131
Neef, Frederick W., House, 131, 170
Neef Brothers Brewing Company, 131
Neef family, 110
Nelson, Larry, xvi, 40, 105, 161
Neoclassicism, 6, 7, 9, 18, 19, 20, 21, 24, 30, 33, 34, 35, 43, 45, 53, 54, 56, 58, 59, 60, 63, 65, 67, 71, 75, 78, 83, 86, 87, 92, 103, 113, 117, 123, 124, 138, 141
Neusteter, Max, 30
Neusteter Building, 30, 171
Neusteter-Chenoweth House, 83
Neusteter's, 30
New Deal, 5, 138
New Height Group, 141
New Isis Theater, 178
New Orpheum Theater, 178
Newsteter, Meyer, 30
Newton, Quigg, xvi, 33

New York Times, 60
Nichols, William J., 176, 177
Nicholson, Meredith, 85
Nicoletti-Gulliver-Lynch House, 173
Ninth Street Historic Park, xvi, 9, 45, 46, 122, 175
Noel, Jim, xvi
Noel, Vi, xvi
Norgren, Barbara S., xv, 175
Norman, Cathleen, xv
Norman Apartments, 141, 173
Norris, John, 59
North Denver Bank, 126
North Denver Mercantile Company, 120
Northglenn, Colorado, 67
North High School, 122, 124, 172
Norton, Albert J., 7, 62, 68, 72, 80, 81, 95, 134, 146
Norwest Bank, 30
Nunnally, Sharon L., 175
Nursery Building, 148, 172

Oakes Home, 124
Observatory Park, 148, 149
Odd Fellows Hall, 32, 169
O'Dell, John, xv
Office of Archaeology and Historic Preservation, 11
Ogden Theater, 75, 172
Old Highland Historic Business District, 113, 174
Old Ladies Home, 60
Old Post Office, Customs House, and Federal Building, 178
Oliphant, Pat, 25, 34
Olmsted, Clarence H., House, 85, 86
Olmsted, Frederick Law, Jr., 5, 17, 95, 167
Olmsted Brothers, 89
Olson, Albert B. 54, 105
Olson, John, xvi
O'Neil, Mary Rozinski, xvi
On the War Trail, 18
Ordway, Katy, xv
Orient Hotel, 123
Original Mexican Café, 119
Orpheum Theater, 178
Orsborn, George E., 91
Orsborn, Jeannette B., 91
Orsborn and Orsborn, 91
Our Lady of Guadalupe Catholic Church, 9, 119, 172
Our Lady of Light Monastery, 118
Our Lady of Mount Carmel Catholic Church, 9, 120, 170
Oxford Hotel, 9, 10, 40, 42, 43, 65, 171
Oxford Hotel Annex, 43
Oz Architecture, 124, 127, 146

Paddington Station Preschool, 156, 157, 173
Paddock-Wolcott Residence, 178
Paglia, Michael, xvi
Pahl-Pahl-Pahl Architects, 19
Palace Arms, 23

Palace Theater, 178
Palazzo Medici-Riccardi, 21
Palladino, Elisa Damascio, 120
Palladino, Horace, 120
Palladio, Andrea, 74
Palmer, Mrs. John, 107
Palmer, William J., 113
Paramount Theater, 10, 26, 171
Park Avenue Historic District, 74, 174
Park Club Place, 95
Park Hill, 10, 84, 90, 159, 160, 161
Park Hill Branch Library, 162, 171
Park Hill Elementary School, 161, 172
Park Hill Golf Course, 110
Park People, The, 147
Paroth, Frederick W., 47, 108, 120
Pasado, Presente, Futuro, 49
Paton, Bruce, xvi
Patterson, Katherine Grafton, 74
Patterson, Thomas M., 67, 74
Patterson, Thomas M., Residence, 178
Patterson Block, 178
Patterson Inn, 67, 169
Peabody, James H., 56
Pearce, Harold V., 87, 88
Pearce Mansion-Democratic Club, 178
Pearce-McAllister Cottage, 87, 88, 169
Pearson, Michelle, xvi
Pei, I.M., 8, 177
Peiker, James "Jim," xvi, 86, 87
Peña, Federico, 5, 138
Pennsylvania Street Historic District, 67, 174
Pesman, M. Walter, 132, 141
Peterson, Heather King, xv
Petri, Gary, xvi
Petrikin, Eloise, 83
Petrikin, William, 83
Petrikin Estate, 83, 173
Pharris, Kevin, xvi
Phillips-Carter-Reister, 161
Philpott, Bill, xvi
Phipps Mansion (Belcaro) and Tennis Pavilion, 145, 146, 170
Phipps, Agnes C., Memorial Sanitarium, 163
Phipps, Lawrence C., 84, 145, 146, 163
Pied Piper of Hamlin, The, 146, 147
Pierce, Ada, 139
Pierce, Arthur E., 139
Pierce, Arthur E., House, 139, 172
Pillsbury, Charles Francis, 89, 103, 138, 155
Pineapple House, 84
Pioneer Building, 178
Pioneer Fountain (Civic Center), 17
Pioneer Seed Company, 124
Platt, Charles Adams, 145
Platt, Geoffrey, 145
Platt, William, 145
Platte Valley, 114
Platt Park, 146, 147
Plested, Dolores N., 60
Poets Row, 54
Poor Sisters of St. Francis, 124
Pope John Paul XXIII Catholic Seminary, 148

Pope-Thompson-Wasson House, 84, 169
Porter, Henry M., 54, 55, 64
Porter, Henry M., House, 54, 55, 171
Porter, John, 64
Porter, John, House, 64, 170
Porter Memorial Hospital, 55
Portland Mining Company, 78
Postmodernism, 7, 157
Potter, Walter M., 123
Potter Highlands Historic District, 123, 174
Potter Highlands Preservation Association, 116
Pouw, Stanley, xvi, 48, 77, 175
Pouw and Associates, 25, 48, 77
Powell, Jane, 128
Powers, Preston, 18
Prairie style, 7, 123, 143, 154, 155
Pratt, Dan, xvi
Pratt, Darrin, xvi
Price, Charles S., 81
Price, Vincent, 128
Prince Hall Masons, 105
Proctor, Alexander Phimster, 18
Proctor, Susan, 116
Progressive Era, 5, 6, 18, 34, 81
Prohibition, 23, 38, 43, 64, 74
Prosser, John M., xvi
Prout, John W., 123
Providence House, 62
"Pueblo Deco" style, 120
Pueblo Revival style, 168
Pugh, Marshall R., 54, 133, 176
Pulitzer Prize, 137, 138

Quality Hill Historic District, 60, 61, 174
Quayle, A., 176
Quayle, Charles, 78, 104, 138
Quayle, Edward, 104
Quayle, William, 104, 138, 176
Queen Anne style, 7, 9, 53, 55, 56, 60, 66, 68, 70, 71, 73, 74, 79, 80, 86, 88, 91, 94, 99, 100, 104, 108, 115, 123, 124, 125, 128, 130, 131, 134, 137, 139, 147, 149, 150, 155
Queen Theater, 138
Queree, John Joseph, 55, 124
Queree, Pearl, 124
Queree House, 124, 169
Quincy Block, 178
Quinn Evans Architects, 19

Rae, Mary, 61
Railroad Building, 178
Ralph L. Carr Colorado Judicial Center, 78
Ranch style, 10
Randall School, 150
Rapp, C. W., 26
Rapp, George L., 26
Raymond, Wilbur S., 86
Raymond House-Castle Marne, 86, 87, 170
Ready, Martha A. *See* Silks, Mattie
Reagan, Ronald, 48
Recreational Equipment, Inc., 113, 169
Redgrave, Lynn, 128
Red Rocks Amphitheatre, 8, 11, 167, 168, 169

Red Rocks Park, 6, 7, 128, 167, 168, 169
Reed, Mary (Mrs. Verner Z.), 81, 96, 101
Reed, Verner Z., 96
Reed Mansion, 96, 101
Regional Transportation District, xvi, 43
Regis University, 128
Reiche, Carter, and Smith, 68
Renaissance Revival style, 19, 28, 35, 44, 78, 81,
    83, 105, 121, 148
Reps, Bonnie, xvi
Republic Building, 178
Reynolds, Audley H., 91
Reynolds, Debbie, 128
Rhoads, Harry, 54
Rice, Eugene R., 73, 81, 94, 139
Rice, Walter, 61, 76, 77
Rich, Myra, xvi
Richardson, David, xv
Richardson, Henry Hobson, 91, 116
Richardsonian Romanesque style, 6, 7, 23, 26, 31,
    53, 56, 68, 86, 91, 106, 109, 114, 134, 137, 139,
    159, 163
Richlieu Hotel, 23
Richthofen, Louisa von, 155
Richthofen, Walter B. von, 155, 157
Richthofen Castle, xvi, 157, 158, 169
Ries, Jane Silverstein, 65
Rise, Jane Silverstein, House, 65, 171
Ritchie Events Center, University of Denver,
    148
Ritter, Jeannie, xvi
Riverside Cemetery, 124
Rivinius, George F., 106
Roberts, Candy, xvi
Roberts, John W., 27, 42, 177
Robinson, Charles Mulford, 5, 17, 20
Robinson, Cleo Parker, 105
Robinson, Mary Byers, 68
Robinson, T. D., 140
Robinson, William F., 68
Robinson House, 68, 171
Robinson Printing Company, 68
Rocky Mountain Bank, 61, 131
Rocky Mountain Lake, 126
Rocky Mountain National Park, 147
Rocky Mountain News, 4, 21, 48, 49, 67, 68, 137,
    140
Rodriguez, Rene Alvarez, 72
Roeschlaub, Robert S., 6, 7, 35, 53, 76, 77, 82, 109,
    137, 148, 176, 177, 178
Roeschlaub, Robert S., Residence, 178
Rogers, Ginger, 128
Rogers, Jennie, 41
Rogers, John, 175
Rogers, Platt, Residence, 178
Rogers-Nagel, 22
Rogers-Nagel-Langhart, 21
Romanesque/Romanesque Revival styles, 6, 9,
    26, 27, 35, 47, 60, 77, 91, 103, 105, 108, 114, 118,
    120, 133, 137, 140, 146, 148, 156
Romeo and Juliet, 64
Romeo Block, 115, 171
Ronnebeck, Arnold, 31, 71, 72

Ronnebeck, Louise, 72
Rood, Hugh, 81
Rooney, Mickey, 128
Roosevelt, Hilbourne, 53
Roosevelt, Theodore, 48, 53
Root, Robert, xvi, 175
Rosche, Wilbert R., 168
Rose, Barry, xvi
Rose, Frances, 78
Rose Acre Farms, 41
Rosenman, Seth, 175
Rosenzweig House, 78, 170
Rosenzweig, Leopold, 78
Ross, Albert Randolph, 20
Ross, Frederick, 95
Ross-Lewin, George E., 58
Ross-Lewin Double, 57, 58, 172
Rossonian Hotel, 103
Royal Academy, Potsdam, 164
Rubin, Vicki, xv
Ruby Hill Park, 6
Rucker, Kevin, xv
Ruhoff, Ron, xvi
Runyan, Damon, 25
Ruskin, John, 105
Russell, Joseph, 45
Russell, Levi, 45
Russell, William Greeneberry, 45
Rustic style, 167

SaBell, Rich, xv
Sabin, Florence, 162
Sacred Heart Catholic Church, 102, 169
Sacred Heart School, 102
Sagstetter, Beth, xvi
Sagstetter, Bill, xvi
St. Andrews Memorial Episcopal Chapel, 104,
    105, 170
St. Cajetan's Catholic Church, 9, 47, 169
St. Charles Town Company, 93
St. Dominic's Catholic Church, 124, 172
St. Elizabeth's Catholic Church, 9, 47, 169
St. Elizabeth's Retreat Chapel, 124, 125, 170
St. Francis Conference Center, 47
Saint-Gaudens, Augustus, 117
St. George's Chapel, 105
St. John's Episcopal Cathedral, 9, 58, 59, 71, 72,
    95, 169
St. John's in the Wilderness Episcopal Church,
    40, 71
St. Joseph Hospital, 55, 79, 80
St. Leo's Church, 178
St. Luke's Episcopal Church, 9, 157, 170
St. Luke's Hospital, 66
St. Mark's Cathedral, 34
St. Mark's Episcopal Church, 9, 54, 169
St. Martin's Chapel, 71, 72
St. Patrick's Catholic Church, 9, 118, 119, 170
St. Patrick's Day Parade, 9, 118
St. Paul's Methodist Church, 73
St. Peter and St. Mary Episcopal Church, 137
St. Thomas Episcopal Church, 161, 162, 170
Salida, Colorado, 66

Salzman, Emanuel, 45
Salzman, Joanne, 45
Sanctuary Church, 116
Sanctuary Lofts, 106, 169
Sandberg, Carl, xvi, 128
Sand Creek Massacre, 62
Sands House Sanitarium, 163
San Rafael National Register District, 107
Santa Fe Railroad, 45
Saslow, William, 42
Savage Candy Company, 103, 172
Sayre, Elizabeth, 62
Sayre, Hal, 61, 62
Sayre-Brodie House, 123
Sayre's Alhambra, 61, 62, 172
Schaefer Tent and Awning Company, 36
Schlatter, Francis, 117, 118
Schlicting, Darcy Cooper, xv
Schlosser, Julie, xv
Schneider, Roslyn Yamashita, 175
Schomp, Kay, 65
Schradsky, Max, 133
Schuetze, Reinhard, 19, 80, 89, 142, 153, 164
Schulz, R. Ernst, 110
Schulz-Neef House, 110, 173
Scientific American, 23
Scott, Isaiah B., 105
Scottish Rite Masonic Temple, 56, 171
Scottish Village, 113, 123
Scott Methodist Church-Sanctuary Lofts, 9, 105,
    106, 169
Seawell, Don, xvi
Second Empire style, 7, 9, 39, 42, 43, 46, 99, 107
Secrest, Clark, xvi
Security-Midland Bank, 178
Seeber, Louise Combes, 58
Semple Brown Design, 92
Semple Brown Roberts, 33, 36, 38, 39
Senior Housing Options, Inc., 42
Seracuse, Lawler, and Partners, 53
Serafini, David, 70
Seventh Avenue Congregational Church, 134,
    173
Shafroth, Frank, xvi
Shalkey, Edward, 175
Shaw, Leonard, 33
Sheedy, Dennis, 54, 55
Sheedy Mansion, 54, 55, 169
Sheridan Heritage Building, 43, 170
Sheridan, Philip H., 150
Sherman, Ron, xv
Sherman, William T., 139
Sherman Elementary School-Art Students
    League of Denver, 139, 140, 172
Sherman-Grant Historic District, 54, 174
Shingle style, 61, 84, 88, 128, 133, 134, 140, 150
Ship Tavern, 23
Shorter A.M.E. Church, 9, 105, 172
Shorthorn Building, 178
Shriners, 57
Sigman Meats, 41
Silks, Mattie, 41
Silks, Mattie, House, 41, 170

Silver Circuit, 86
Simmons, Joe, 44
Simmons, Laurie, xv
Simmons, Thomas H., xv, xvi, 104, 115, 122, 123, 125, 127, 129, 144
Simon, Walter, 56, 154
Singer Sewing Machines, 149
Sinsheimer House, 95
Sisters of Charity of Cincinnati, 101, 102
Skid Row, 36, 42, 103
Skinner, Elizabeth Hope, 126
Skinner Middle School, 126, 171
Skyline Park, 128
Skyline Urban Renewal Project, 22, 34
SlaterPaull Architects, 47, 76
Sloan's Lake, 132
Sloan's Lake Depot, 178
Sloan's Lake Park, 124
Slockett Block, 113
SLP Architects, 41
Smedley, William, 46, 122
Smedley Elementary School, 122, 171
Smedley House-Casa Mayan Restaurant, 46
Smiley, William H., 126
Smiley Branch Library, 126, 127, 171
Smith College, 162
Smith Lake, 142, 143
Smith, Frank L., 9, 89
Smith, Frank L., Mansion, 9, 89, 169
Smith, Frank W., 133
Smith, Frank W., House, 133, 170
Smith, John W., 142
Smith, Milo A., House, 155, 172
Smith, Robert E., 67
Smith's Ditch-City Ditch Historic District, 142, 174
Smoky Hill Trail, 153
Snell, Frank S., 86, 94, 110
Snell House, 94
Snell's Subdivision Historic District, 94, 110, 174
Snow, Shawn, xvi
Sobriety House, 103
Society of Architectural Historians, 11
Solnhofen Quarries, 20
Sopris Duplex, 178
South Broadway Christian Church, 139, 169
South Denver (town), 137, 147
South High School, 124, 144, 146, 148, 171
South Lincoln Street Historic District, 12
South Platte River, 45, 49, 99, 113, 134, 137, 142
South Platte River Valley, 4, 167
Spangler House, 133, 170
Spangler, Jane, 133
Spangler, Mike, 133
Spanish Colonial Revival style, 10, 60, 61, 64, 95, 103, 109, 141, 161
Speer, Kate, 20, 95
Speer, Robert W., 5, 8, 17, 20, 24, 33, 34, 49, 73, 74, 95, 114, 153, 167
Speer Boulevard Historic District, 49, 174
Speer House, 95
Spice and Commission Warehouse, 45, 171
Spider Man case, 49

Stadium Arena, National Western Stock Show Complex, 12
Stanbury, Andrew, 38
Standard Meat Company, 80
Standart, Frederick W., 66
Standart-Cleworth House, 66
Stanley, Henry M., 156
Stanley School-Montclair School-Paddington Station Preschool, 156, 157, 173
Stapleton, Benjamin, 167
Stapleton International Airport, 160, 161
Starkey, Mary Louise, 59
Starkey Institute for Household Management, 59, 85
State Historical Fund, 11, 29, 102, 116
State historic preservation income tax credit, 11, 93
State Home for Dependent and Neglected Children, 148
State Office Building, 19
State Register of Historic Places, 11
State Theater, 178
Stearns House, 60, 170
Stearns, Joel W., 60
Stearns, Robert L., 175
Steck, Amos, 154
Steck Elementary School, 154, 173
Steele, Robert Wilbur, Sr., 141
Steele Elementary School, 141, 172
Stein, John J., 31
Sternberg, Eugene, xvi, 7
Sterner, Frederick J., 7, 25, 34, 59, 60, 61, 64, 66, 78, 81, 84, 85, 88, 91, 95, 124, 148, 176, 177, 178
Stevens, Eugene C., 92
Stevens Elementary School, 77, 92, 171
Stewart, Jimmy, 137
Stewart, John, xv
Stewart, Paul, xvi
Stick style, 128
Stobie, Charles Stewart, 38
Stockyards National Bank, 107
Stoiber, Edward G., 81
Stoiber, Lena, 81
Stoiberhof, 81
Stoiber-Reed-Humphreys Mansion, 81
Stoneman's Row, 114
Stores Restaurant Equipment Company, 42
Strand-State Theater, 178
Streamline Moderne style, 7, 10, 43, 60, 71, 108, 122, 140
Streetcar Lofts, 43, 170
Strong, Charles D., 54
Stuckert, A. Morris, 26
Student, Annette, xvi
Sudler, James, 25, 29, 95, 175
Sugar Building, 83
Sullivan, Kevin, 126
Sullivan House, 83
Sunken Gardens Park, 49
Sunnyside Nursery, 129
Sussex Building, 39, 171
Su Teatro, 109, 110
Svinarich, Beth, xvi

Swallow, George Ransom, 73
Swallow Hill Historic District, 73, 174
Swank, Christopher C., 94
Sweeney, Gerri, xvi
Sweeney, Robert, xvi, 66
Sweet, Joyeuse, 82
Sweet, William E., 81, 82
Sweet-Miller House, 81, 82, 171
Swett, B. Storey, 175
Sykes, Richard E., 85
Sykes-Nicholson-Moore House, 85, 170
Symes, J. Foster, 64

Tabor, Elizabeth "Baby Doe" McCourt, 86
Tabor, Horace, 6, 86
Tabor Block, 178
Tabor Grand Opera House, 6, 86, 178
Tabor Mansion, 178
Tall Bull Memorial Grounds, 167
Tallmadge, Charles E., 115
Tallmadge and Boyer Terrace, 115, 172
Tambien Saloon, 38
Tammen, Agnes Reid, 79
Tammen, Henry Heye, 79, 81
Tammen Hall, 79, 173
Tattered Cover Book Store, 92, 93, 173
Taylor, Frank M., 66
Taylor, James Knox, 21
Taylor, Lee Casey, 25
Taylor, William E., 43
Taylor House, 66, 67, 170
Teapot Dome scandal, 63
Tears, Daniel W., 84
Tears-McFarlane House, 84, 169
Ted's Montana Grill, 38, 171
Teikyo-Loretto Heights College, 137
Temple Emanuel, 9, 72
Temple Emanuel Event Center, 70, 171
Temple Hoyne Buell Theater, 33
Ten-Winkle, Herman, 21
Ten-Winkle Apartments, 21, 173
Tesky, Jonathan, xv
Theatines, 119
There is No Frigate Like a Book, 147
Thomas, Charles S., House, 178
Thomas, Harlan, 155
Thomas, Harry, xv
Thomas, Hugh H., 104
Thomas House, 104
Thompson Theater, 93
Thompson, Fred A., 61
Thompson, John, 75, 147
Thompson, John E., 94
Thompson, Lisa Werdel, xv
Thompson-Henry House, 81
Thornton, Guy, 29
Thorwald, Heather, xv
Tihen Tower, 148
Tilden, John H., 126
Times Building, 178
Tirsway, Dennis, 155
Titanic, 69, 81
Tivoli Brewery, 9, 45, 48, 73

Tivoli Terrace Night Club, 122
Tivoli Union Brewery-Student Union, 47, 48, 169
Toll, Henry, xvi
Torrey, Mabel Landrum, 142
Tower on the Park, 58
Town Club, 54
Tracy, Swartwout, and Litchfield, 30
Trading Post, Red Rocks Park, 168
Travels of Marco Polo the Venetian, The, 91
Treat, Jay Porter, 159
Treat Hall-Centennial Hall, 159, 160, 170
Trinidad Chronicle, 60
Trinity Church (Boston), 116
Trinity Church (New York), 42
Trinity United Methodist Church, 9, 53, 54, 57, 169
Tri-State Buddhist Temple, 41
True, Allen Tupper, 17, 18, 19, 20, 23, 146
Tryba, David Owen, xvi, 34, 35, 43, 59, 83, 125, 126, 146, 156, 162
Tryba Architects, 19, 34, 35, 43
tuberculosis, 10, 53, 84, 115, 124, 126, 148, 150, 155, 158, 159, 162, 163
Tudor style, 7, 9, 60, 64, 66, 83, 95, 96, 129, 131, 132, 134, 138, 146, 147, 158
Turn Halle, 73
Turner, Steve, xvi
Turnhalle Opera Hall, 9
Tutt, Marne, xvi
Tuxedo Place, 178
Twentieth Street Bathhouse/Gym, 34, 171
Twenty-Fourth Street School, 178
Twitty, Eric, xv

U-2, 168
Underground Railroad, 42
Union Block, 178
Union Foundry, 39
Union Hotel, 42
Union Ice Company, 126
Union Pacific Railroad, 45, 117
Union Station, 4, 43, 44, 45, 80, 118, 173
Union Wholesale Liquor, 42
United Banks, 30
United States Air Force Academy, 163
United Way, 60, 72
Unity Temple, 178
Unity Temple of Practical Christianity, 86
University of Colorado, 30, 78
University of Colorado Denver, xiii, xv, xvi, 35, 45, 100
University of Denver, 21, 53, 61, 84, 86, 137, 146, 148, 160
University Park, 148
University Press of Colorado, xvi
Unsinkable Molly Brown, The, 69
Upshaw, Mark, xvi
Urban Design Group, 19, 27, 43
Urban renewal, 10, 22
US District Court of Colorado, 61, 64
US Mint, 169
US National Bank, 30
US Postal Service, 30

US Post Office and Federal Building-Byron White Federal Courthouse, 30, 170
US Supreme Court, 30
Usonian style, 144, 153
Ute Indians, 38

Vaile, Charlotte, 74
Vaile, Joel F., 74
Vaille, Frederick J., 78
Valdez, Bernie, Hispanic Heritage Center, 49
Van Brunt and Howe, 43
Varian, Ernest P., 7, 25, 48, 49, 59, 61, 64, 85, 91, 148, 176, 177, 178
Varian, Lester E., 7, 48, 49, 59, 64, 66, 147, 148
Varian and Sterner, 73
Varone, John, 118
Vatican, 59
Vehr, Urban J., 64
Vetter, Joseph, 131
Victorian style, 38, 123
Vigil, Lance, 175
Villa Park, 134
Volunteers for Outdoor Colorado, 142
Voorhees, Mrs. Ralph, 133
Voorhees, Ralph, 133
Voorhees House, 133, 170
Voorhies, John H. P., 18
Voorhies Memorial, 17, 18

Wagner, Frances C., 118
Waite, Cheryl, xv
Waldman, David M., 82
Waldman, The, 82, 173
Waldron, Evelyn, xv
Walker, Bolivar, 128
Walker, Don, xv
Walker, John Brisben, 128
Walker, John Brisben, House, 128, 169
Wallace, Mary Kent, 78
Walsh, Thomas F., 7, 43, 44, 45, 58, 83, 163, 176, 177
Walter, Douglas, 175
Walter, John, 80
Walter-Bierly House, 80, 170
Walstrom, David, xvi
Ward, Judy, xvi
Ward, Mrs. Thomas, 66
Ward, Tom, xvi
Waring, James J., 83
Waring, Ruth Porter, 83
Warren, Elizabeth Iliff, 149
Warren, Henry White, 149
Warren-Iliff Mansion, 173
Washington Park, 141, 142, 143, 144, 147
Washington Park Bathhouse, 142, 172
Washington Park Boathouse and Pavilion, 143, 172
Washington Park Elementary School, 143, 173
Waters Building, 41, 170
Waters, Thomas, 41
Waterton Canyon, 142
Watkins Stained Glass, 66, 86, 146
Watkins, Frank, 146

Watson House, 85, 170
Watson, George H., Jr., 85
Webb, Wellington, xvi, 5
Webster, Ross, xv
Weckbaugh, Ella Mullen, 79
Weil, Steve, xvi
Weil, Wendy, xvi
Weiner, Louis M., 115
Weiner, Romeo S., 115
Welcome Arch, 178
Weller, Hugh, 91
Weller, John G., 126
Wells, Harry, 130
Wells Fargo, 30, 40
Wells Fargo Building, 40, 170
Wellsville, Colorado, 66, 145
Wendell, Harry T.E., 60, 81, 84, 163, 164, 178
Wenk, Bill, 49
West, William A., xvi, 110
West Court Hotel, 178
Western Architect and Building News, 6, 7, 24
Western Chemical Company, 160
Western Federation of Miners, 56
West High School, 49, 124, 171
Westside Courthouse, 49, 172
West Twenty-Eighth Avenue-Stoneman's Row Historic District, 114, 174
Wetzel, David, xvi, 76
Whalley, John J., 39
Wharton, Christina Lee, xvi
Wheaton, Rodd, xvi
Wheeler, Charles A., 114, 115
Wheeler Block, 114, 115, 170
Whitacre, Christine, xv
Whitacre, Roger, xvi, 4, 24, 26, 29, 30, 31, 40, 63, 75, 85, 100, 101, 104, 133
White, Byron, 30
White, Edward D., Jr., xv, xvi, 24, 30, 62, 65, 82, 150, 153, 175
White, Gordon D., 108, 146
White, Sally, xvi
White, W.A., 118
Whitehead, William R., 56
Whitehead-Peabody House, 56, 171
Whitehouse, James, 23
Whiteside, Jim, xvi
Whittier neighborhood, 110
Whittier School, 178
Widmann, Nancy, xv, 62
Wieger, Thielman Robert, 66, 70
Wilk, Diane, xvi
Williamson, George H., 34, 60, 64, 81, 90, 95
Willis Case Golf Course, 57
Willison, Robert, 33, 34, 43, 47, 124, 178
Wilmott and Stoddard, 103
Wilson, Arthur S., 130
Wilson, Luther, xvi
Wilson, Robert A., 113
Wilson and Wilson, 109
Windsor Farm Dairy, 161
Windsor Hotel, 42, 178
Windsor Stables and Storefront-Blake Street Bath and Racquet Club, 42, 171

Wings Over the Rockies Museum, 163
Winter Park Ski Area, 6, 146, 167
Wirth, Timothy, 132
Wirth, Wren, 132
Witte House, 46
Witter, Daniel, 131
Witter-Cofield Historic District, 131, 174
Witting, Ruth Drumm, 73
Wolcott School Apartments, 78, 170
Wolcott School for Girls, 78
Wolcott, Anna Louise, 78
Wolcott, Henry R., 78
Wolf House, 107, 173
Wolf, Jacob L., 107
Wolfe Hall, 178
Wolff, Hiram G., 129, 130
Wolff Place Historic District, 129, 130, 174
Wood, Guilford, 64
Wood, Louis M., 114
Woodbury, Frank E., 131
Woodbury, Frank E., House, 131, 170
Woodbury, Grace Lobach, 131

Woodbury, Roger W., 125, 131
Woodbury, Roger, Mansion, 178
Woodbury Branch Library, 125, 126, 171
Wood-Morris-Bonfils House, 64, 171
Woodsen, Mary, 178
Woodson, Marie L., 147
Woodward, B. F., Residence, 178
Woodward, Chuck, xv
Wootton, Richens L. "Uncle Dick," 178
Works Progress Administration, 49, 138
World War I, 73, 148
World War II, 5, 10, 59, 73, 78, 109, 134, 147, 163
World's Columbian Exposition, 5, 17, 18, 19
Woulter, Matthew, 130
Wray, Diane, xvi
Wren, Christopher, 124
Wright, Frank Lloyd, 144, 153, 154
Wurlitzer pipe organs, 26
Wyatt, George W., 109
Wyatt-Edison Charter School, 109
Wyatt Elementary School, 77, 109, 171
Wyman Elementary School, 178

Wyman Historic District, xvi, 84, 87, 174
Wyman, John H., 84
Wynken, Blynken, and Nod, 142
Wynkoop, Edward, 45
Wynkoop, Edward, Building, 171
Wynkoop Brewing Company, 144

Yamsaki, Minoru, 22, 23
Yankee, William H., 126
Yokota, Kariann, xvi

Zancanella, Frank, 45
Zang, Adolph, 65, 74
Zang, Adolph, Mansion, 65, 170
Zang Brewery, 65, 74, 178
Zang Townhouse, 74, 170
Zetter Royal Bavarian Art Institute, 59, 109
Zietz, Henry H., 48
Zimmer, Amy, xv, xvi, 175
Zion Baptist Church, 9, 106, 169
Zoning, 11